Gender and Technology at Work

This book brings together the vast research literature about gender and technology to help designers understand what a gender perspective and a focus on intersectionality can contribute to designing information technology systems and artifacts, and to assist organizations as they work to develop work cultures that are supportive of women and marginalized genders and people. Drawing on empirical and analytical studies of women's work and technology in many parts of the world, the book addresses how to make invisible aspects of work visible; how to recognize women's skills without falling into the trap of gender stereotyping; how to engage in improving working conditions; and how to defend care of life situations and needs against a managerial logic. It addresses challenges for design, including many overlooked and undervalued aspects, such as the complexities involved in human–machine interactions, as well as the need to create safe spaces for research subjects.

ELLEN BALKA is a professor in the School of Communication at Simon Fraser University, British Columbia. She has published in the fields of gender and technology, health informatics, health and medicine, and community academic research partnerships. She received a YWCA Women of Distinction Award for Workplace Innovation, a career achievement award from British Columbia Faculty Associations, and a Michael Smith Senior Scholar's Award, and she has held international research fellowships in Austria and Norway. She served as the Principal Investigator of Action for Health and contributions she and her team made received the Artful Integrators Award for Participatory Design.

INA WAGNER is affiliated to the University of Siegen, Germany after retiring as professor at the Vienna University of Technology, Vienna. A leader in the field of work and technology, her research focusses on work practices and the design of supporting technologies. She has published on computers in hospitals and in architectural planning, feminist perspectives in science and technology, and ethical and political aspects of ICT. She recently coauthored the books *Future-proofing: Making practice-based IT design sustainable* and *L'urbanism informel. Au-delà du droit à la ville,* and received the Woman's Prize of the City of Vienna and Gabriele Possanner Staatspreis.

ANNE WEIBERT is a research associate at the Institute for Information Systems and New Media at the University of Siegen. She has conducted participatory design projects in socially and culturally diverse settings, working with children and adults, and vulnerable populations including refugees. Her research is focussed on computer-based collaborative project work and inherent processes of technology appropriation and media literacy, intercultural learning, and community-building. She is a coauthor of *Future-proofing: Making practice-based IT design sustainable.* Anne Weibert has been awarded the Förderpreis des Augsburger Wissenschaftspreises für Interkulturelle Studien and the Rolf H. Brunswig-Promotionspreis at the University of Siegen.

VOLKER WULF is a professor at the Institute for Information Systems and New Media at the University of Siegen. His research interests lie primarily in the areas of socio-informatics, computer-supported cooperative work, participatory design, and human–computer interaction. He has published more than 400 academic papers and edited fifteen books, including *Expertise sharing: Beyond knowledge management*; *Social capital and information technology*; *End-user development*; and *Socio-informatics: A practice-based perspective on the design and use of IT artefacts*. He has been appointed to the CHI-Academy and the Leibniz Sozietät der Wissenschaften, Berlin.

Gender and Technology at Work
From Workplace Studies to Social Justice in Design

ELLEN BALKA
Simon Fraser University

INA WAGNER
University of Siegen

ANNE WEIBERT
University of Siegen

VOLKER WULF
University of Siegen

CAMBRIDGE
UNIVERSITY PRESS

Shaftesbury Road, Cambridge CB2 8EA, United Kingdom

One Liberty Plaza, 20th Floor, New York, NY 10006, USA

477 Williamstown Road, Port Melbourne, VIC 3207, Australia

314–321, 3rd Floor, Plot 3, Splendor Forum, Jasola District Centre,
New Delhi – 110025, India

103 Penang Road, #05-06/07, Visioncrest Commercial, Singapore 238467

Cambridge University Press is part of Cambridge University Press & Assessment,
a department of the University of Cambridge.

We share the University's mission to contribute to society through the pursuit of
education, learning and research at the highest international levels of excellence.

www.cambridge.org
Information on this title: www.cambridge.org/9781009243711

DOI: 10.1017/9781009243728

First published 2024

A catalogue record for this publication is available from the British Library

Library of Congress Cataloging-in-Publication Data
Names: Balka, Ellen, author. I Wagner, Ina, 1946– author. I Weibert, Anne, 1978– author. I
Wulf, Volker, 1962– auth–or.
Title: Gender and technology at work : from workplace studies to social justice in design /
Ellen Balka, Ina Wagner, Anne Weibert, Volker Wulf.
Description: Cambridge : Cambridge University Press, 2024. I Includes bibliographical
references and index.
Identifiers: LCCN 2023042148 (print) I LCCN 2023042149 (ebook) I ISBN 9781009243711
(hardback) I ISBN 9781009243698 (paperback) I ISBN 9781009243728 (epub)
Subjects: LCSH: Women in technology. I Technology and women. I Technology–Social
aspects. I Information technology–Social aspects. I Diversity in the workplace.
Classification: LCC T36 .B35 2024 (print) I LCC T36 (ebook) I
DDC 331.4/256–dc23/eng/20231213
LC record available at https://lccn.loc.gov/2023042148
LC ebook record available at https://lccn.loc.gov/2023042149

ISBN 978-1-009-24371-1 Hardback
ISBN 978-1-009-24369-8 Paperback

Contents

Preface

This book grew out of a strong interest in understanding women's work from a feminist and intersectional perspective and designing better IT-based systems and artifacts. It started with two of us – Ellen Balka and Ina Wagner, who had together written a series of computer-supported cooperative work (CSCW) conference papers on health-care informatics, ethical issues related to IT in health care, and configuration work – deciding, whilst skiing together, to work on a paper that provides a historical view of women's work. Our aim was to demonstrate how fieldwork-based studies which have focussed on women's work have attempted to locate it in a larger context that addresses its visibility and value. It resulted in a large collection of studies of women's work from the end of the nineteenth century to the 1990s, and a paper published in the *Journal of Computer Supported Cooperative Work* (Balka and Wagner 2021).

For this book project Ina Wagner activated her long-standing relationship with Volker Wulf's research group on socio-informatics, with Volker and Anne Weibert joining us as coauthors. What connects us is that we are all part of the CSCW and participatory design (PD) communities, with a focus on understanding work practices, and an interest in and commitment to designing IT-based systems and artifacts in collaboration with their users. We are all committed to making these systems and artifacts sustainable in the future. We also share a commitment to social justice and design justice, based on care, reciprocity, agency, and empowerment. That also means that we are critical of the ways software is produced when it does not leave much space for taking care of the views, life situations, and needs of marginalized groups. We think of a feminist/intersectional perspective as a chance to reconceptualize how we think about design and what it is, and we see it as a means of creating seeds of alternative ways of designing at the fringes of the mainstream world of IT.

We come to our shared interests from a variety of countries and social locations. Collectively, we bring many disciplinary backgrounds to this project. We also bring diverse past experiences with us – we currently live in three countries (and have lived in some more), and span in age nearly forty years. We are aware that one's social location can serve as an important resource in design. It can also serve to reinforce the status quo. Given the value we place on context and situating ourselves as designers as a strategy for increasing transparency about how values come to bear on design (what Lucy Suchman calls 'located accountability'), we begin by situating ourselves.

Ellen Balka: I came of age in the USA during the Vietnam War. My not-at-all religious Jewish parents sent me to Quaker school, reflecting the value they placed on education, civic engagement, and social justice. My parents were actively engaged in desegregation, and the school community was extremely engaged with the anti-war movement and environmental issues, which were part of everyday life.

I developed an interest in alternative energy (no doubt influenced by the US energy crisis of the 1970s). I moved to Seattle, took up rock climbing and mountaineering, and took classes in social aspects of technology and a class on women and work in women's studies. I spent a summer climbing with two feminists, one of whom was a lesbian, and developed a feminist analysis and familiarity with lesbian culture.

I came out as a lesbian in my third year of university, into a world where the dominant lesbian uniform was blue jeans, plaid flannel shirts, and short hair. It was a time when the lesbian community still socialized largely in women-only bars, coffee houses, and bookstores, and mothers who came out were at risk of losing their kids. My first real job – in a hippie engineering firm where I was hired to do technical work and where I was the only woman – together with what I learned from my climbing friends, turned me into a rabid feminist and sowed the seeds for my academic focus on women and technology.

I moved to Canada to attend graduate school in the mid-1980s and earned the first graduate degree in women's studies awarded in Canada. I've lived in Vancouver (twice), Toronto, and St. John's Newfoundland, where I met my partner of thirty years, at meetings to organize feminist events.

I think about gender a lot: throughout my life I have been mistaken for a man (including by two of my three young grandchildren) regularly, but not consistently. I prefer to be referred to as a lesbian rather than queer. I am proud of my two now adult (step)sons and hope my granddaughter will live in a world where she doesn't face the same injustices related to her sex and gender as I have. I am an avid skier and cyclist.

Ina Wagner: I grew up in several places – Vienna, the Tiyrol, Germany – to return to Vienna for most of my adult life. My mother had trained as a company lawyer, which was quite unusual for a woman born in 1909; my father was a mechanical engineer. They were both traumatized from World War II (WWII), which my father – son of a Jewish mother – had survived as a highly gifted engineer. He was a socialist and political discussions became part of my life as soon as I was old enough to participate. My parents travelled a lot, and they loved the fine arts (I remember being dragged to old churches and museums early on), literature, and music.

I spent most of my childhood in the Tyrolian mountains, where in elementary school needlework (compulsory for girls only) alternated with skiing (I was one of the few girls who skied). My father had a small bicycle factory at that time and sponsored a racing team. The factory where workers assembled the bicycles left a strong impression. When we moved to Germany where my father constructed large presses for the automotive industry, he sometimes took me with him on business trips. I remember walking alone high up along the assembly hall at Volkswagen when I was about fifteen, watching the assembly of the 'Käfer'. My parents later moved to Brazil.

My interest in gender and feminist theory was formed when I experienced being treated differently (and several times rather badly) during my studies of physics – I was one of just a few women doing a doctorate. I was a politically active student and visible as a critic of teaching methods and of some of the professors' reactionary views. I started reading what are now classics about the feminist critique of science and technology and developed my academic focus on work, technology, and gender.

Although the centre of my personal life is in Austria, I always felt European/ cosmopolitan. I spend a lot of time with my grandchildren, a boy and a girl (Austrian/Colombian) who live in the USA; and a girl (Austrian/Australian) who lives in Vienna. Although they are still young, I am continuing the family tradition of talking politics, skiing, and hiking.

Anne Weibert: I grew up in the Ruhr area in Germany. My father was a teacher of German, history, and religion; my mother studied law and engaged in international charity work. During my childhood, I remember how my parents' house always had open doors for people from various countries, who stayed as visitors and returned – and keep returning to this day – as friends. I remember joint explorations of the changing character of places in the Ruhr area, endless (from a child's perspective) discussions about life and politics and culture in a mixture of languages, and early attempts to participate therein and ask questions myself.

Asking questions became my first profession when I graduated in journalism and American studies at the University of Dortmund, and then worked as a journalist for different media in the Ruhr area.

I did not actively study gender and technology at first; it's rather that the topic kept occurring to me in various contexts. I came to work as a research associate in socio-informatics, and to also complete my PhD in this domain at the University of Siegen. I followed my interest in answers to questions of media diversity and the accessibility of digital and media learning across cultures, languages, and age boundaries.

I keep focussing on the topic of (digital) learning and its accessibility. I work as a teacher now, teaching informatics, English, and German classes at a large comprehensive high school in the Ruhr area.

Volker Wulf: I grew up in a small village in the Sauerland, the geographical centre of former West Germany. My family had farming roots. Starting from renting a small farm, my father worked in a variety of jobs in post-WWII Germany. My mother, a teacher, was the first academic in her family. So, I had little academic orientation and few role models when I finished high school. I was not so sure what to do, what to study. At that time in the early 1980s, job centres suggested that computer science would be a field with a sound future. Following that advice, I was quite excited to leave the narrow valleys of the Sauerland.

However, I quickly became rather disappointed by the focus of computer science on formal methods and a lack of concern about societal implications. I was on my way to giving up on my studies and I started to travel extensively, first in South-East Asia; then I spent half a year in Paris. I finally decided to return to university and to finish my studies. At a time and in a country in which tuition fees were almost unknown, I had the privilege of an extensive period as a student. Karl Georg Zinn, a left-wing Keynesian economist, attracted my attention as well as Britta Schinzel, a theoretical computer scientist who had just started to build research activities in the field of women in computing.

Even after finishing my studies, I continued travelling in the Global South on a shoestring. The cultural, political, and geographical diversity fascinated me and trained my ethnographic sensibilities. However, I was always appalled and saddened by the vast social differences between North and South but also in many of the societies of the Global South. I somehow felt committed to challenging conditions of injustice. It took me quite some time to find a research style which fitted with my normative ambitions. I am not a traditional gender researcher, rather an ally in their epistemological and normative positioning. For me it was always important to explore the potential of IT design in practice to support diversity and social justice towards a 'better world'.

Our diverse research experiences and our political commitments helped us to develop a shared account of women's work in different fields, a shared ethical-political perspective on design, and a shared understanding of how feminist/intersectional approaches to design support us in addressing challenges. Our experiences have helped us in figuring out how to contextualize women's work from a design perspective and aided us in forming views about how to build pathways to gender equality in design. One of the challenges we faced has been how to explicate the key concepts and theories leading our work: feminist theory, queer theory, and intersectionality; but also, what we mean by 'women', how we refer to other genders, to 'race' and ethnicity.

We were greatly helped in these efforts by eleven colleagues we interviewed about the topics of this book: Pernille Bjørn, Luigina Ciolfi, Ingrid Erickson, Joan Greenbaum, Maria Menendez Blanco, Toni Robertson, Angelika Strohmayer, Lucy Suchman, Marja Vehviläinen, Judy Wajcman, and Marisol Wong-Villacres. We are grateful for the inspiring conversations we had with them and their contributions that helped us manoeuvre through the myriad of questions that kept demanding our attention.

0

Introduction

In a world where the pace of technological change moves fast and it seems that things change quickly, some things appear to remain little changed with time. One of those things is women's relationships to technology. Although it is true that many of us know women who work in technological fields feeling comfortable with working in what society once considered (and arguably still does) the male domains of computing and engineering, and that many girls and women feel they can enter those fields, women's low representation in computing and engineering persists.

This book revisits the vast research literature about gender and technology with the aim of helping designers understand what a gender perspective and a focus on intersectionality can contribute to designing information technology (IT) systems and artifacts and assisting organizations as they work to develop work cultures that are supportive of women and marginalized genders/people. The book will also be of interest to a range of readers interested in gender and technology at work, including those interested in the sociology of work, gender and occupational health, gender studies, and technology studies. We argue that the design of information and communication technology (ICT) systems that promote gender equality has to be anchored in the particular context that the design of those systems addresses. This requires designers to deeply engage with this context. This is a complex endeavor. This chapter takes a first step toward this aim by introducing the key concepts that will be used and further developed throughout the book: gender, gender subtext / the genderedness of organizations, technology, work practice, working conditions, skill, intersectionality, feminist theory, queer theory, race/racism.

1

Framing the Book

In the last forty or fifty years we have seen ebbs and flows in scholarship concerned with varied aspects of women and technological change – many of which we will address in the pages that follow. Much has been written across multiple disciplines and areas of study (e.g., labour history; sociology of work; women's occupational health; women's and gender studies; science, technology, and society studies), which has informed debates about women and technological change at work. Both historic and contemporary studies concerned with women and technological change at work have yielded important insights about how technological change is implicated in ongoing power struggles women and men experience at work. However, little has been written about how to design technological systems in general, and information technologies in particular that support more than just workplace experiences for women and other disadvantaged groups. With this book we seek to address this gap.

Areas such as computer-supported cooperative work (CSCW) and human–computer interaction (HCI) increasingly grapple with what it means to employ a design-justice framework (Costanza-Chok 2018) and design for the overlooked (e.g., Schorch et al. 2016). While we are excited to see new generations of scholars and practitioners address these issues, we are also aware that considerable work related to these areas has been undertaken in the past. As much of the early work was completed prior to the widespread digitization of scholarly sources we now take for granted, one of our interests and aims is to bring some of this historic work to contemporary audiences. Recounting some of the historic work concerned with women and technological change yields insights about the links between varied epistemological traditions that contemporary HCI and CSCW practitioners increasingly draw on. It also allows us to foreground the many ways that exploring the broad contexts in which women's work occurs has yielded insights about how the interplay between technological and gendering processes occurs.

There is much to be gained by focussing on the rich insights past work has produced as we seek to move beyond what were arguably simplistic views of gender in the past, towards approaches that reflect today's sensitivities towards gender as well as intersectionality. Taking a historical and intersectional approach allows us to outline what a gendered perspective can contribute to the design of technologies in general, and in particular the designing of IT systems and artifacts. It also provides a starting point for probing how research concerned with intersectionality can enrich design practices and emergent work concerned with design justice.

In this book we explore these issues in several steps. We go back to the rich debates about gender, science, and technology that emerged in the 1960s and 1970s, and in particular the ethical and political issues feminists raised. A large part of the book deals with work in different domains – from factories to hospitals and the gig economy – from a gender perspective. Our goal is to highlight the importance of considering context in a design-justice framework, and through a review of past work about women and technological change to identify some key aspects of context that have yielded significant insights about the gendering of technological change.

The material here will be of interest to those in computing (and especially those working in CSCW and HCI), design, social sciences, occupational health, and organizational studies. As new generations of scholars across areas such as gender studies, labour studies, sociology, and design seek to understand the interplay between technological and gendering processes in order to influence change, historical work offers a foundation while more recent work in HCI, CSCW, and design justice yields insights of interest to those in the social sciences concerned with work, technology, and gender.

There is much to be learned from looking back at theoretical work. However, we seek here also to move beyond a recounting of how varied disciplines have informed theoretical debates and the insights they have yielded. In the final chapters of the book, we revisit the contributions that feminist debates have made to the ethical political perspective towards design. We also discuss the challenges of contextualizing women's work and focus on steps we can take in taking gender and intersectional approaches forwards in thinking about gender and technology and gender and work.

Such a project needs to be informed by many voices. Towards that end, we have interviewed pioneers as well as researchers who are earlier in their career: women who have influenced feminist scholarship concerned with design or who currently work in CSCW, HCI, and adjacent areas (such as science, technology, and society studies), addressing gender issues. We have attempted to include women from varied parts of the world (Australia, Canada, Denmark, Finland, Ireland, Italy, Ecuador, the UK, and the USA). This allowed us to broaden the voices and perspectives upon which we have drawn. We have included materials from these interviews throughout the text. Among the interesting points that emerged in conducting these interviews is the different pathways that members of our team and those we interviewed travelled to arrive at their interest and focus on gender issues.

The Focus on Women

Why write a book about the gendering of women's work, not including men? Why not be more inclusive of other marginalized groups, such as gender minorities and people of color? In her book *Shaping women's work: Gender, employment and information technology* (1996), Juliet Webster argued,

> Many feminist thinkers, particularly those working in a post-structuralist or post-modernist tradition, might argue for a wider focus on 'gender' as opposed to one simply on 'women', in order to introduce an understanding of the shaping of people's (men's and women's) gender identities experiences and subjectivities into the analysis. . . . By focusing on 'women' as opposed to 'gender' in the broad sense of the concept, I am choosing not to focus on men and masculinity. I am less interested in the gender relations of work and technology and their implications for men and masculinity than I am in the gender relations of women's work.
>
> (Webster 1996, p. 2)

The last sentence in this quote also presents our position – we are mainly interested in the *gender relations of women's work* and how an understanding of those can help achieve more gender equality in IT/technology design. We are, of course, aware that as gender norms are changing, the concerns of gender minorities need proper attention.

We use 'woman' here as a category that stands for an enormous diversity of people from different cultures, ethnic and social backgrounds, and sexual identities that, historically, have been called women without considering and respecting their diversity. Of course, we are aware that the category 'women' is tremendously diverse and includes (for example) heterosexual, lesbian and bisexual women (who may be CIS-gendered or trans),[1] as well as those who identify as queer.[2]

Writing about women without recuperating the male/female binary is challenging. In the words of Lucy Suchman, the rise of queer theory and queer studies has 'not only destabilised the idea of gender as binary' but

---

[1] CIS-gender (an antonym of transgender) refers to persons whose gender identity corresponds with the sex registered for them at birth; not transgender. It does not say anything about a person's sexual orientation though. 'Cisgender has its origin in the Latin-derived prefix cis-, meaning "on this side of", which is the opposite of trans-, meaning "across from" or "on the other side of"' (https://en.wikipedia.org/wiki/Cisgender, viewed 06/02/2023).

[2] 'An umbrella term for people who are not heterosexual or are not cisgender' (https://en.wikipedia.org/wiki/Queer, viewed 06/02/2023).

called attention to the multiplicity of relations between experienced and enacted ... So if anything, I would say that gender has been exploded' (Lucy Suchman, interview 04/22/2022).

We try to navigate through the 'gender labyrinth' of the multiplicities of identities and relations that the rise of queer theory has opened. Queer theory, sometimes referred to as a 'postmodern critical theory that grew out of the women's, gay, and queer studies' movements of the 1990s' (Goodrich et al. 2016, p. 612), is often traced back to the work of Teresa De Lauretis (1991), Judith Butler (1990), and others (e.g., Pullen et al. 2016). It scrutinizes normativity in general and heteronormativity in particular, and challenges essentialist constructions and categories of gender and sexuality. Queer theory raises important questions about the status of gender/sexuality categories and highlights the relational constitution of identities (Watson 2005) – all of which are important and have implications for how as a culture we understand gender.

But we retain a focus on women's work because

> ... historically work is operating with the category of women. And it needs to recognize that within that category there has been far greater heterogeneity than that category does justice to. ... [T]hat category has historically been a very salient one, it's had huge consequences for distributions of labor and value and reward and so on. ... [I]t's been an incredibly consequential category.
>
> (Lucy Suchman, interview 04/22/2022)

Suchman adds that studies of women's work look at 'the work of those living in that category' and 'you can assume that, within that category, there is tremendous heterogeneity' (Lucy Suchman, interview 04/22/2022). We are certainly aware of the heterogeneity and diversity (which also includes women who are ethnically diverse, live in different parts of the world, and come from varied class backgrounds), and we ask our readers to read our use of the term 'women' as expansive and inclusive rather than as naive.

We have tried to strike a delicate balance between acknowledging several areas of study such as queer theory and critical race theory (see below) and the differences they highlight and contributions they make, while retaining our focus on insights derived from empirically grounded research about women. We have cast our net widely, wherever possible referring to countries beyond the borders of North America and Europe, and within those regions, addressing (for example) ethnic, class, and other differences in women's workplace experiences with technologies.

We are certainly cognizant of the different experiences that women have at work in relation to technology, which are mediated in complex ways by ethnic and class backgrounds as well as issues of sexuality (whether one is straight or gay, or bi) and gender – whether a person is CIS-gendered, trans, or gender queer. And we also know that we don't yet have good data that would allow us to more fully understand how (for example) the interplay of gender and technology differs for a butch lesbian and a CIS-gendered heterosexual woman. These are interesting questions we hope will be taken up by others in the future. We have included material about the experiences of lesbian, gay, bi-sexual, trans, and queer (LGBTQ+) people whenever possible. We recognize there is tremendous diversity within this grouping as well, and that the terminology used to signal these differences varies across national contexts (for example, in Canada, LGBTQ2S+ is often used as an acronym that stands for lesbian, gay, bisexual, transgender, queer or questioning, and two-spirit, in recognition of the unique experiences of indigenous community members). When referring to the work of others we have retained the terminology used in the original, and otherwise use LGBTQ+ to signal an inclusiveness that varies cross-nationally.

We have discussed ethnicity when data are available and highlighted the need for the collection of data (particularly about non-binary genders), which will help us develop more nuanced views of the experiences of gender queer and trans workers in relation to technology. Yet we also acknowledge that this may be problematic. As Zooey Sophia Pook (2020) points out in relation to the collection of data about personal pronoun preferences, 'these practices have unintended consequences as they contribute to the ever-expanding economies of data collection' (p. 6). Pook cautions us that 'the internet is the new locus of economy and power ... [I]t is important to think about identity and data practices in line with these emerging technologies and in consideration of larger flows of information and capital' (p. 10). She suggests that struggles for autonomy and control have shifted in important ways to the Internet, which, in the age of neoliberal capitalism, presents challenges with respect to queer autonomy.

We remain aware that our coverage of these and other topics (such as feminist theories, theoretical developments in science, technology and society studies), which have contributed to how we understand gender and technology at work, is limited. These shortcomings represent just a few of the many directions warranting greater attention than we have been able to grant them here. Indeed, the topic of gender and technology at work has both drawn on insights from many areas and contributed to insights in numerous adjacent areas of inquiry. Given that in many cases (e.g., feminist theory and queer theory) entire subfields of study have emerged within disciplines – the entirety of which is too great to address here – readers will almost certainly feel at times that there are intellectual roads not taken. This is true. We have limited our scope here to a focus on insights gained from empirically grounded studies of women's experiences with workplace technology, and how that corpus of material has broadened our understanding of both gender and workplace technologies. 'Gender', Raewyn Connell (2009) has written, 'is the structure of social relations that centres on the reproductive arena, and the set of practices that bring reproductive distinctions between bodies into social processes' (p. 11). Feminists have taken this insight as a starting point for analyzing gender inequality, recognizing that women's location in the world and their experience is not only different but also unequal to those of men, also considering how systems of power and oppression interact. Some feminists also have studied both hegemonic and subordinated masculinities; and queer theory has extended feminist work on sexuality by 'expanding the range of visible, plausible, and livable sexualities', hence also 'the meanings of woman and man' (Marcus 2005, p. 200). The book will take up some of this work on men and masculinities in discussion of the genderedness of organizations and technologies.

There is growing empirical evidence of gender minorities (and people of color) experiencing social injustice in the form of bias, social exclusion, and harassment and that they are not represented in how technologies are designed nor adequately supported in their work or other activities. For example, a growing corpus of literature within HCI deals with how to make the voices of queer, trans-, as well as gender diverse individuals heard (e.g., Ladwig 2020; Burtscher and Spiel 2020). Research documents the obstacles experienced by women of color in computing (e.g., De Oliveira Lobo et al. 2019; Rankin and Thomas 2020; Erete et al. 2020). In spite of this work, current research that addresses gender minorities and design only covers a few areas of work, notably computing, and 'numbers' are often too small to support doing a comparative analysis of working conditions and technology relations from a fully intersectional perspective. Hence, our project is incomplete, as our understanding of gender has evolved more quickly than our data collection infrastructures – a point we return to in our discussions of design in the several parts of the book. And although we lack data that would allow us to more fully examine gender and technology from an intersectional perspective, this growing corpus of research provides valuable insights into how to account for multiple experiences and perspectives in design, and these insights remain salient even as our understanding of gender changes over time. We hope our work will contribute to future discussions about strategies and methods that can be used to explore the interplay between gender and technology for those who are gender queer and non-binary.

Feminist scholars in what is called 'the Global South',[3] which is immensely diverse in itself, question the dominance of Western feminist theorizing, critiquing the dominant Western frames of computing cultures and bringing forward accounts of stories about women with other histories with technologies (as for example in rural Mali; Twagira 2020). Feminist scholars that advocate decolonizing approaches also emphasize the complexity of identity concerns given the realities women have to face, as for example expressed by Maffía (2007), who thinks that Western feminist positions

> can result in a seductive trap from the intellectual point of view, immobilizing in a region where women can barely perceive the gender oppression among so many overlapping oppressions. Feminist criticism of science is a problem of academics when ancestral knowledge (of women also, but not only of women) is ignored by a relationship between center and periphery that is as sharp as patriarchal domination.
>
> (Maffía 2007, p. 92)

This book addresses these 'other' perspectives by including studies of the gender relations of women's work by postcolonial feminists (and others) that help us to understand the particular and diverse experiences of women working in export-oriented factories, in the computing industry and/or doing data work in the gig economy. 'Feminist and postcolonial projects will always be multiple and distinctively local if they are to serve those escaping local male-supremacist and Western-supremacist histories' (Harding 2009, p. 415). Apart from making these diversities visible, a postcolonial perspective also enriches thinking about how to do computing otherwise. Some material from our interviews sheds light on the challenges and complexities of adopting a postcolonial perspective.

A Historic Perspective

We anchor our inquiries in a review of historic debates about women's work. One reason for returning to work previously undertaken is that it offers valuable insights that we can make use of for advocating the approaches we present in the final section of the book. Also, as argued in Balka and Wagner (2021), we seek 'to bring the different lenses through which women's work

---

[3] The term 'Global South', inspired by Antonio Gramsci's idea of the 'South' (of Italy), marks a shift from a focus on development or cultural difference towards an emphasis on geopolitical power relations. It 'functions as more than a metaphor for underdevelopment. It references an entire history of colonialism, neo-imperialism, and differential economic and social change through which large inequalities in living standards, life expectancy, and access to resources are maintained' (Dados and Connell 2012, pp. 12–13).

has been viewed historically into clearer focus, in order to set out new conditions of possibility' (p. 253); what Kate Soper (1993) has described as potentially allowing access to hitherto 'subjugated knowledges'.

Studies of women's work reach back to the beginning of the twentieth century. Among the particular 'treasures' of research from this time are Elizabeth Beardsley Butler's survey of the working conditions of women in nearly 400 companies (as part of the so-called Pittsburgh Survey, 1909); Marie Bernay's study of the 'selection and adaption among the workers in large, self-contained industrial enterprises, based on conditions in the Gladbach spinning and weaving company in Mönchen-Gladbach' (1908); and Frances Donovan's books, among them *The woman who waits* (1920). In France, Marcelle Capy, a journalist and political militant, wrote 'Avec les travailleuses de France' (With the women workers in France; with Aline Valette) (1937), which was based on work in factories as an incognito, arguing that this is the only way to get to know the work situation.

The specific interest in women's work was continued after WWII. While some of this research may be well known to an Anglo-American readership, influential research was also carried out in other traditions (most of which has not been translated into English), notably German industrial sociology and Francophone ergonomics, with numerous studies of the work of telephone operators, nurses, or women assembly workers in the electronics industry. While most of these studies were carried out by social scientists, the rise of feminism in the mid- to late 1960s brought women's work into the focus of attention also of labour historians who started looking at women's situations in different parts of the world. Examples are Heidi Tinsman's study of women agricultural workers in rural Chile; and Mirta Lobato's (2001) study of the meatpacking industry in Buenos Aires (for an overview of these studies of women's work see Balka and Wagner 2021).

Characteristic of feminist studies of work was from the very beginning, and still is, the attention they paid to the larger context of work – policymaking, organization, power relations, gender relations, relations of paid work and work done in the home. Much of the early work was driven by labour questions, namely working conditions and women's health, and a commitment to improving women's professional education in order to advance their chances in the labour market. With the rise of feminism, the relationships between paid work and the family, as well as the relation between the public and the private, or the political and the personal, moved to the foreground. From the 1980s onward, feminist scholars debated the nature of technology and started discussing issues related to 'women, work and computerization' with a focus on design.

This book provides access to key studies of women's work, past and more recent. It follows a path that leads from early studies of factory work, office work, data processing, nursing, and women working as IT professionals and how technologies were used to define gender relations of work and technology, to studies of contemporary workplaces dominated by artificial intelligence (AI), robotics, and the platform economy. This is done with a view towards what can be learned from these trajectories – from early office automation, the first nursing information systems, as well as the role of traditional machines in cementing labour market segregation and a gendered work organization – for the design of new technologies.

Finally, we take a historical perspective because our motivation in writing this book lies in part in our observation that at times design methods are used without reference to the epistemological stances that have given rise to methodological approaches. When this happens the potential strength of these methods to inform a design-justice framework is diluted.

Disciplinary Orientations

Our discussion draws on scholarship and empirical work in a number of disciplines including feminist theory, science, technology, and society studies (STS), sociology of work, political economy, organizational studies, labour history, as well as CSCW, HCI, and participatory design. We bring the insights of these cognate areas together to highlight the benefits and necessity of working across disciplines in order to understand the contexts in which designing for equity and justice must take place.

The *historical focus* of the book highlights the importance of the broad contexts in which work is carried out to technology design, while at the same time foregrounding key points and debates that, we argue, should be addressed in designing technology to support women at work. Several large debates that shaped the studies of women's work were driven by what came to be women's studies, with researchers coming from the sociology of work, labour history, organizational studies, and occupational health bringing gender issues into the focus of attention. Using mainly qualitative research methods in an interpretative tradition, including ethnographic fieldwork, they studied labour market segregation and its roots in gendered notions of skill, working conditions, and women's health, as well as gender relations/power relations and the ways these play out in the work lives of women (and men). They contributed to an understanding of skills as not only technically constructed but also as socially determined. Many of these studies sought to make the invisible, undervalued aspects of women's work visible; and they understood the confinement of women to certain types of work as deeply connected with their responsibilities in the home. Some research focussed specifically on how skill and gender intersected in paid and unpaid work.

Another highly influential strand of thinking that feminists, namely Dorothy Smith (1987 and 1990) and Joan Acker (1990 and 1992), brought into the debate is the genderedness of organizations, as expressed in the gendering of jobs and other manifest gender inequalities and the hidden 'gender subtext' that produces and maintains gender distinctions in organizations. Numerous empirical studies point to the persistence of a masculine culture and images of masculinity in many areas of work, in particular but not only engineering, where the ideal worker is male. These studies often highlighted the 'undoing' of gender.

Feminist theory – the different discourses seeking to understand gender inequalities (extended and enriched by queer theory and the notion of inter-sectionality) – has influenced many disciplines. Key to our book are the views about the nature of technology that evolved in parallel with the emergence of science, technology, and STS. They focus on gender technology relations, asking 'Do artifacts have gender?' Another relevant strand of thought to this debate is feminist ethics, which aims to understand and criticize how gender operates within our moral beliefs and practices. It has contributed to the concept of care as fundamental to human activities and to achieving social justice. It includes all forms of (professional or informal) care work but also caretaking in relation to data and technologies. The idea of design justice is anchored in these theories. More recently, gender-technology scholars have sought to theorize the Western cultural association between technology and masculinity. The increasing use of the term 'gender studies' (as opposed to feminist critique) of technology signals a more serious effort to study gender as a cultural construction implicating both women and men (as opposed to studying only women). Contemporary studies that problematize the gender–technology relation, however, remain informed by largely feminist, or pro-woman, liberatory goals.

Finally, we make use of design-oriented traditions. Foremost of these is participatory design, which at its beginning was deeply political, seeking to support workplace democracy. Although not focussing on gender, its mandate has always been to have multiple voices not only heard but also included in decision-making. The notion of skill and women's invisible skills plays a large role in technology and work (re)design (Balka and Wagner 2021). The parts of CSCW and HCI that focus on technology design have worked in close connection with ideas of participatory design. There are other traditions we can learn from with respect to design, namely German industrial sociology and Francophone ergonomics. Both focus less on the design of new technological artifacts than on workplace (re)design with a perspective on working conditions and workers' health. They have much to offer to technology design, which focusses on equity and justice.

Several themes come up repeatedly as we review scholarship across areas of work and disciplines. These include the genderedness of skill, invisible work, the genderedness of organizations, ideas of 'undoing' gender, the concept of care, and how we can understand each of these concepts in relation to intersectionality. In addressing these topics, we come up against issues of responsibility, power, agency, and control, which we argue should be understood in a design-justice framework in relation to intersectional concerns.

Conceptualizing (Gender) Equality

Sex/Gender

Key to discussing gender equality is the distinction between sex and gender that has been widely taken up by researchers and institutions alike:

> Sex refers to biological differences between men and women such as chromosomes (XX or XY), internal and external sex organs (ovaries, testes) and hormonal profiles (of estrogens and androgens). Biological sex differences are often viewed as dichotomous, either male or female, although biological variability is substantial.

> Gender refers to the socially constructed roles and relations, personality traits, attitudes and behaviours and values that are ascribed to the two sexes in a differential manner. While sex is a biological fact that is the same in all cultures, the meaning of sex in terms of gender roles can be quite different across cultures.
>
> (Klinge 2010, p. 18)

Although in recent years the notion that sex is rooted in biology has been the subject of debate and 'the use of binary sex as a meaningful category explaining human biological variation across contexts' is being challenged (DuBois and Shattuck-Heidorn 2021, p. 13), in general, the term sex is reserved for discussions of anatomy at birth. Gender is the more inclusive term when talking about differences between men and women and a much more complex concept than sex:

> Gendered behavior arises out of a dauntingly complex, reciprocally influencing interaction of multi-level factors, including structural-level factors (e.g., prevailing cultural gender norms, policies and inequalities), social-level factors (e.g., social status, role, social context, interpersonal dynamics) as well as individual-level

factors such as biological characteristics . . . , gender identity, gendered traits, attitudes, self-concepts, experiences, and skills.

(Rippon et al. 2014, p. 3)

Sex and gender are not mutually exclusive – 'cultural expectations for women and men (gender) are not separable from observations about women's and men's physical bodies (sex)' (Lips 2017, p. 6) and we often don't know whether particular differences between men and women are due to biology or culture. Examining Western notions of sex/gender Oyěwùmí (1997) states, 'the distinction between sex and gender is a red herring. In Western conceptualization, gender cannot exist without sex since the body sits squarely at the base of both categories' (p. 9). Judith Butler (1990) pointed to the interconnectedness of sex and gender:

> It would make no sense, then, to define gender as the cultural interpretation of sex, if sex itself is a gendered category. Gender ought not to be conceived merely as a cultural inscription of meaning on a pregiven surface (a juridical conception); gender must also designate the very apparatus of production whereby the sexes themselves are established. As a result, gender is not to culture as sex is to nature; gender is also the discursive/cultural means by which 'sexed nature' or 'a natural sex' is produced.
>
> (Butler, 1990, p. 11)

Gender is used as a label for the system of expectations held by societies with respect to feminine and masculine roles. Michel Foucault's notion of 'normalization' addresses the power of these expectations that create an enormous pressure to conform to certain ways of behaving and presenting oneself (Foucault 1979). Foucault has described this pressure in particular with respect to the ways the body and sexuality are defined and experienced (Foucault 1973).

Harding distinguished between three aspects of gender: (i) gender structure, or the sexual division of labour (men and women are situated in sex typed ways); (ii) gender identity or individual gender; and (iii) gender symbolism, a fundamental category within which meaning and value are assigned to everything in the world (Harding 1986, p. 57). In its meaning here, gender structure is articulated in relation to hierarchical structures of class and race (and, it can be argued, other forms of difference). Gender identity or individual gender has two meanings or aspects. Gender identity is projected (potential, actual, or desired identity as others perceive or portray them) and/or subjective (the gendered sense of self – the identity created and experienced by an individual). Gender symbolism involves representations and meanings, held by individuals as well as the larger society in which gendered individuals exist. Although Harding's articulation of gender predated the emergence of queer theory, the two concepts remain intellectually compatible. Although no doubt some contemporary theorists deny the existence of biological sex, with the exception of Harding's use of the word sex her articulation of how gender works remains salient.

Thus, we could say that technologies are part of the gender symbolism system (big machines such as earthmovers are seen as male). In using technologies, individual gender is created through the simultaneous activities of projecting a gender identity (where the ways our projection is understood are partly determined by wider social norms), and our own subjective understandings of our interactions with technology are part of bigger gender systems.

Intersectionality

In addition to highlighting the connections between issues and key concepts and components of gender, as we move through topical areas in the chapters in Part II, we will also highlight the relevance of the topics we discuss to intersectionality. Many researchers today argue that addressing gender equity/equality requires examining the complex relationships between biological and social dimensions. They also have extended their thinking to embrace *intersectionality*, an approach that builds on the insight that important social identities such as gender, ethnicity, and social class 'mutually constitute, reinforce, and naturalize one another' (Crenshaw 1991, p. 302). Crenshaw saw intersectionality as a 'provisional concept' that helps explore the interlinkages of gender and race that in politics (and often also in academia) are treated as separate.

Feminist writing about intersectionality builds on a 'long history of black feminist theorizing about interlocking systems of power and oppression, arguing that intersectionality is not an account of personal identity but one of power' (Cooper 2016, p. 1) (see also Chapter 1). With respect to computing research, Keyes et al. (2021) argue that 'Our understanding of intersectionality, then, is of a way of thinking about identity that is deeply attentive to questions of power, history and context – and one fundamentally grounded in the possibility and desire for change' (p. 12). Costanza-Chok (2018), in proposing the notion of design justice, emphasizes intersectionality, asking how to 'escape from the matrix of domination', a concept that Black feminist scholar Patricia Hill Collins 1990 developed to refer to race, class, and gender as 'interlocking systems of oppression, rather than each operating on their own' (p. 4).

The Problematic Notion of Race

Writing a book about women's work calls for respect for how the category 'women' is used in relation to other genders and how it intersects with other categories connected with the marginalization of particular groups of people. From a European (Anne, Ina, and Volker) and Canadian (Ellen) perspective, we feel uneasy with another category: the notion of race. The idea of 'race' and its transference to human history dates to the eighteenth and nineteenth centuries, when pseudo-biological studies that used phenotypic features to categorize people became popular:

> 'Race theorists' interpreted history as a 'racial struggle' within which only the fittest 'races' would have the right to survive. They employed the political catchword with its vague semantic contours almost synonymously with the words 'nation' and 'Volk' for purposes of their biologistic, political population programs of 'racial cleansing', eugenics and birth control.
>
> (Reisigl and Wodak 2001, p. 4)

After 1945, the idea of race became deeply discredited. In Germany and Austria, it is strictly taboo for academics, politicians, the media, and the public to refer to 'race' and German law prohibits statistical material that refers to ethnic groups, races, or skin colour. In 2013 a draft law for the suppression of the word 'race' from the French legislation was adopted. In the same year, two influential anthropologists and authors of *L'errore della razza* (2011), Gianfranco Biondi and Olga Rickards, appealed to the Italian government to eliminate the word 'razza' from all legislation (Scacchi 2016). Even in the medical field in these countries the category race is avoided and often replaced by country of origin to be able to account for the genetics of different populations. In the USA, the term race is used for classifying people in the decennial census and

> the US federal government now structures the remedial allocation of certain goods such as social services, jobs, and political representation according to race, thus ensuring that race is continually reinscribed into American politics from above as well as from below.
>
> (Kim 2004, p. 340)

What does this resistance against a discredited term mean? Certainly not (or not necessarily) an insensitivity to racial discrimination but a clear rejection of a notion that characterizes persons

> as communities of descent and to whom are attributed specific collective, naturalised or biologically labelled traits that are considered to be almost invariable. These traits are primarily related to biological features, appearance, cultural practices, customs, traditions, language, or socially stigmatised ancestors.
>
> (Reisigl and Wodak 2002, p. 10)

'Races do not exist, but racism does' – the position of UNESCO reflects the work of Critical Race Theory (CRT) that holds that 'race and races are products of social thought and relations. Not objective, inherent, or fixed, they correspond to no biological or genetic reality; rather, races are categories that society invents, manipulates, or retires when convenient' (Stefancic and Delgado 2010, p. 3).

Referring to Foucault, Goldberg (1993) defines racialization as a process that establishes 'forms of power/knowledge relationship which focus on the body and processes of subjection' (p. 54). Historically, the racialization of the world has come out of Europe to define the inferiority of other cultures and negate them. Barot and Bird (2001) refer to Frantz Fanon and his book *The wretched of the earth* (1963/1968) where he described the deep-seatedness of racialization that 'has something to tell us about oppressors and oppressed and about the physical and psychic damage done by racism' (Baron and Bird 2001, p. 613).

We propose to have the history of race as a concept and its use as well as the different standpoints that have been put forward with respect to how we understand the racialization of the world in mind when thinking about gendered racialism. We also emphasize the need for research about racism to consider differences in language usage and their roots in different historical realities. Given our own histories, we often use the term ethnicity, and reserve use of the term 'race' for contexts where it is in common use (e.g., critical race theory) or it has appeared in a piece we are citing.

The Design Perspective

The third focus of the book is on technologies themselves, their 'making', the role of women engineers in their development, women's agency, and the multiple ways technologies influence women's lives. Here the book moves from more traditional technologies used in different industries and workplaces to early ICT-based tools and contemporary and future technologies. Finally, the book embraces a global perspective, seeking to assemble studies and viewpoints from different parts of the world.

A Word about Technologies

Technology is, as Leo Marx (1997) remarks, a 'hazardous concept'. Historically, as Kjeld Schmidt (2018) has shown, there is a strong connection between practices and the techniques that practitioners of a particular art or trade have developed. He quotes Johannes Beckmann, a German scholar of the eighteenth century, who defines technology as follows:

Technology is the science of the transformation of materials or the knowledge of handicrafts. Instead of merely instructing workers to follow the master worker's prescriptions and habits in order to fabricate a product, technology provides systematically ordered fundamental directives; how one for exactly these ends can find the means on the basis of true principles and reliable experiences, and how one can explain and exploit the phenomena occurring in the process of fabrication.

(Beckmann 1777, p. 19, quoted in Schmidt 2018, p. 91).

Technical knowledge changes 'when scientific knowledge or science-based techniques (or "technology") are somehow incorporated in the techniques of a given practice' (Schmidt 2018, p. 107).

Despite its origins in the systematic study of practices, most famously in Diderot's *Encyclopédie, ou dictionnaire raisonné des sciences, des arts et des métiers* (1751–1766), the concept of technology is often narrowly conceived as standing for the technical artifact, its material aspect, such as a particular machine or device. Leo Marx (1997) points out,

Although in common parlance nowadays this material aspect often is what the concept of technology tacitly refers to, such a limited meaning . . . is ambiguous and misleading. It is ambiguous because, for one thing, the artifactual component only constitutes a part of the whole system, yet the rest is so inclusive, so various, and its boundaries so vague, that it resists being clearly designated.

(Marx 1997, p. 979)

This holds true in particular for modern technologies that comprise a whole system of ancillary equipment, specialized forms of technical knowledge (and the associated techniques and work practices), a specialized workforce, as well as the 'complex social and institutional matrix' in which they are embedded. Pipek and Wulf (2009) have tried to frame this complex phenomenon as 'infrastructuring'.

Bush's (1981) definition of technology – now somewhat dated – captures many elements of technology that have been important to contemporary STS scholars:

. . . technology is a form of human cultural activity that applies the principles of science and mechanics to the solution of problems. It includes the resources, tools, processes, personnel, and systems developed to perform tasks and create immediate particular, and personal and/or competitive advantages in a given ecological, economic and social context.

(Bush 1981, p. 1)

Central to this definition of technology – and much contemporary STS research – is a focus on the social nature of technological development: new technologies don't simply pop out of the sky, but rather result from the coordination of vast networks of people, machines, processes, materials, and so on – what Callon (1979) and Latour (2007) called actor networks. Noble (1979) similarly suggested that technology bears the 'social imprint' of its authors. The technologies we live with in our lives seldom represent the only technological solution possible (just as a finished piece of art does not represent the only possible outcome of working with the constellation of materials an artist had at hand). Rather, the technologies in our lives represent the outcome of a complex series of negotiations that occur between a web of actors – both human and non-human (e.g., the installed base of a computer system). Technology development and use are both social processes, whose outcomes depend upon social and technical factors.

The particularity of computer-based technologies (and the various associated fields of research and development) is that, as Schmidt (2018) among others observes, they are highly malleable. He refers to Mahoney's observation that

> there was a time, a rather long time, 'when the question "What is a computer, or what should it be?", had no clear-cut answer', and the computer and computing thus only acquired 'their modern shape' in the course of an open-ended process that has lasted decades (Mahoney 1992, p. 349). And there is no reason why one should assume that the concept of 'computing' has stabilized and solidified: the jury is still out, as the immense malleability of 'the computer' or 'computing' is being explored in all directions. In other words, it is confused to conceive of 'the computer' as a distinct technology.
>
> (Schmidt 2018, p. 67)

Analyses of the gendered nature of technology have to keep this enormous variety (and malleability) in mind. They also have to contextualize technologies, paying heed to the learning, skills, practices, and social and institutional arrangements enabling their development, implementation, and use.

Supporting Work Practices

To achieve design justice, it will be important to move beyond understanding women's work and how technologies, and in particular ICT-based artifacts and systems, shape the gender relations of women's work, to a focus on design, and how to – from the point of view of design justice – strengthen practices of 'user-sensitive inclusive design' (Stumpf et al. 2020) that benefit women and other people at the margins of technology production. This ideally includes taking action to counter existing inequalities (of access to skills, jobs, careers, and a 'good life') and reflecting on how to best serve democratic ideals.

In writing about gender as an important issue to address in computing it is important to recognize that in the 1980s and 1990s there was a strong positivist community in both HCI and CSCW in the USA, which lately has been strengthened again by research on AI and machine learning. However, overall, the Computers and Human Interaction (CHI)/HCI conferences have become open to a diversity of approaches, including participatory approaches, ubiquitous computing, as well as work practice studies. There is an increasing amount of literature that addresses how to engage people in digital (and other) projects that seek to contribute to more socially just worlds. Examples include Strohmayer's (2021) work on participatory e-textiles; advocacy and initiatives aimed at including Black women (e.g., Erete et al. 2020), and trans- or nonbinary experiences (e.g., Keyes et al. 2021) within the CSCW and HCI communities, and, more generally, *Advancing Diversity*, the focus of the third Gender IT conference (2015).

While acknowledging these important research initiatives, we want to foreground the European tradition in CSCW research that emphasizes the critical role of (ethnographic) workplace studies for designing supporting technologies, arguing that design criteria cannot be separated from the context of the work setting. As Wulf et al. (2011) have pointed out, 'CSCW was the first research community in applied computer science which stressed the importance of an in-depth understanding of practices when designing ICT artefacts. From our point of view, this is the key achievement of the research field' (p. 505).

The practice-based, mostly European, tradition of CSCW research bridges between ethnographic studies of work practices and the design of IT-based artifacts and systems. One of the influential scholars in this tradition was John Hughes, who argued that 'the relevant properties of the social organization of work do not appear as "readily packaged" within work domains but need to be brought out by an analysis of the ethnographic materials' (Hughes et al. 1994, p. 130). The emphasis on understanding the embeddedness of (work) practices in a particular organizational, political, and cultural context also strengthens the attention to gender and feminist theory in design.

Another research alliance of designers who work to benefit women and other people at the margins of technology production is Participatory Design (PD), which has developed methods and techniques for involving future users in design, by not just giving them 'a voice' but having them participate in decision-making in design. What Hayes (2011) formulates for Action Research (AR), also holds for PD: 'the credibility and validity of AR knowledge is measured to a large degree by the "workability" of solutions – that is, their ability to address real problems in the lives of the participants' (p. 158) and to contribute to changes wanted by the participants. 'Giving voice', Bratteteig and Wagner (2014) argue, goes beyond listening to the future users of an IT artifact; it is about sharing power with them by involving them in design decisions. They provide examples of how users can contribute to 'creating (design) choices, selecting a choice, concretizing choices, and seeing/evaluating a choice' (p. 4). In this spirit, Wilson et al. (2020) emphasize the need 'to broaden the inclusion and support of communities who have different communication needs' (p. 1). With respect to how young people with disabilities 'consume, create and circulate media', Alper (2017) has argued that 'technologies largely thought to universally empower the "voiceless" are still subject to disempowering structural inequalities' (p. 3).

Taking these positions seriously means that the design of IT-based artifacts and systems that promote gender equality (as a whole, for everyone, women, men, and other genders) has to be anchored in the particular context the design addresses, requiring designers to deeply engage with this context. The chapters on women's work in different domains in this book provide designers who plan such an engagement with insights from research that points out the working conditions to be found in these domains or fields of work (in terms of work organization, (gendered) culture, skill requirements, stress and other forms of hardship, specific barriers/opportunities for women, etc.), which design oriented toward social justice must engage with if it is to succeed in transcending design solutions that reproduce existing gender–technology relations.

The Ethical-Political Dimension of Design

One aim of this book is to promote a view of engineers/designers making ethical-political choices, by arguing that taking account of gender issues (or not doing so) is a part of such choices.

Ethical issues in engineering have increasingly drawn attention in recent years, including discussions about the extent to which engineers/designers are to be held morally responsible for the dangers, risks, and possible misuses of their technological products. One of the philosophers who emphasized the moral dimension of technologies was Hans Jonas. He argued for the ethical importance of finding ways to better predict the effects of new technologies as a way to strengthen and improve our decision-making about their design and use – a topic that also gave rise to formalized technology assessment processes beginning in the late 1960s. Because of the magnitude of the implications a technology may have, Jonas contends, 'nothing is more natural than the passage from the objects to the ethics of technology, from the things made to the duties of their makers and users' (Jonas 1979, p. 41).

The 2005 Universal Declaration on Bioethics and Human Rights advocates that the moral dimension of science and technology not only concerns the individual, as the human rights perspective traditionally assumes, but also insists this perspective has to be complemented by a focus on socially excluded groups and the dimension of collective action. It highlights

> the importance of developing 'new approaches to social responsibility to ensure that progress in science and technology contributes to justice, equity and to the interest of humanity' (Preamble); of taking into account 'the special needs of developing countries, indigenous communities and vulnerable populations' (idem); of promoting 'solidarity and cooperation' (Article 13); and of fostering the sharing of benefits resulting from scientific research within each society and between societies (Article 15).
>
> (Andorno 2014, p. 56)

Recognizing the moral dimension of technologies is consonant with a feminist ethics that understands moral agency in terms of power, asking who is recognized as a moral agent, and how agency is constrained or facilitated by power relations. Feminist ethics, although by no means homogeneous, tends to prioritize

> the moral contexts in which differently situated and differently gendered agents operate, the testimony and perspectives of the situated agent, the power relationships and political relationships manifest in moral encounters, the vulnerabilities of embodied actors that yield a plurality of approaches to ethical situations, and the degrees of agency or capacity that are shaped by experiences with oppression and misogyny.
>
> (Norlock 2019, p. 3)

Overcoming the historical invisibility of women (and other genders) in the ways most technologies have been made is a question of 'doing justice' to women's lives and experiences (Riley 2013) – and results in part from what Messing (2014) has identified as an empathy gap. Costanza-Chok (2018) articulates this concern with respect to design as 'design justice', which she defines as aiming 'to ensure a more equitable distribution of design's benefits and burdens; fair and meaningful participation in design decisions; and recognition of community-based design traditions, knowledge, and practices' (p. 5).

Overview of the Book

We organized the complex web of issues we plan to address in an arc leading from concepts to case studies of women's work in different domains to 'designing better futures'.

Part I provides an introduction to feminist thinking about gender and technology as well as about the ethical-political dimension of design. After looking back at the contributions of early work undertaken in an effort to understand the ways in which women and technology mutually constitute one another through gendering processes at work (Chapter 1), we move on to outlining the ethical political perspective of technology (Chapter 2), which developed out of a feminist critique of traditional ethical theorizing. Here we highlight some key feminist debates, which have implications for design. In Chapter 3 we introduce the women we interviewed for this book (whose insights we quote throughout subsequent chapters), using their accounts to demonstrate that there is no singular pathway or route that leads to a focus on gender and technology at work. We decided to include our own pathways in this reflection about which moments and contexts gave rise to a focus on gender as our paths too have been quite varied.

The second section of the book consists of chapters dedicated to women's work in different domains: machine work in the factory (Chapter 4), office automation and work (re)design (Chapter 5), data work and the platform economy (Chapter 6), AI-based technologies (Chapter 7), the computerization of care work (Chapter 8), and the gendering of computer work (Chapter 9). As we move through these areas, we provide a more in-depth discussion of key concepts, such as skill, invisible work, and the genderedness of organizations. Throughout these chapters we highlight how gendering processes have worked, returning to Harding's (1986) articulation of the various aspects of gender. In each of these chapters we move from early examples of workplaces and technologies to more contemporary ones, asking how technological changes brought about new issues and challenges. Each chapter ends with insights into how to address these issues in design, from both an intersectional and a design-justice perspective.

This sets the stage for Part III of the book ('Gender and Design'), about how to use feminist/queer theory as well as an intersectional perspective in designing ICT systems that support social/design justice (Chapter 10) and how to contextualize women's work in design (Chapter 11). The final chapter (12) reflects on designing better futures, highlighting a set of paths to follow.

PART I

Gender and Technology

A Research Trajectory

1

Gender and Technology

A Historical Perspective

The gendering of science and technology as a research topic originates in the 1980s with the work of Sandra Harding, Donna Haraway, Lynda Birke, Evelyn Fox Keller, Cynthia Cockburn, and others giving the emergent field a strong profile.[1] Since then, an impressive corpus of literature has evolved. Feminist scholars have explored a great variety of technologies, from classic machines to robots and AI-based technologies, practising what Judy Wajcman has termed *technofeminism*. While early feminist studies of ICTs focussed on office automation, computers in nursing, and the gendering of professional IT work, there is a plethora of new work about women's (and other genders') access to and use of social media and the Internet, feminist hackathons, as well as all kinds of technology-supported practices of 'making'. These studies describe instances of creative appropriation and empowerment, while at the same time stressing the continuation of patterns of (male) power and dominance, which seem often to persist even when prior work practices are significantly altered.

Key Approaches and Concepts: An Overview

The aim of this chapter is to demonstrate how the feminist critique of science and technology stimulated thinking about 'how the inclusion of women would change how scientists think about nature and the kinds of machines engineers build' (Balka and Wagner 2021). We first revisit some of the most salient feminist work that developed insights and concepts that were to shape the subsequent debates about the gendering of technology. As part of this debate Sandra Harding and Dorothy Smith developed feminist standpoint theory,

---

[1] Two anthologies about women, science, and technology were also published in 1983: Rothschild's *Machina ex Dea* and Zimmerman's *The technological woman*.

which emphasized the need to take women's experiences as a starting point for any process of inquiry. Feminist scholars demonstrated that women's knowledge was excluded from the sciences based on an understanding of scientific objectivity as linked to autonomy and masculinity. We then draw a line from Cynthia Cockburn's seminal work about how technologies and gender mutually define each other, using the example of work in the factory, to the growing body of research on the gendering of technologies in everyday life and ICT-based workplace technologies, many of which still seem to be designed for a 'genderless user' (Bardzell 2010). The final part of this chapter looks into engineering practices from a feminist and postcolonial perspective, examining Wendy Faulkner's (2007) argument that 'heterogeneous engineering requires heterogeneous genders' (p. 351), an argument that opens up to the key question of this book – how a gender perspective and a focus on intersectionality can contribute to designing IT systems and artifacts.

A second strand of feminist research concerns technologies of the body – reprogenetics, reproductive, and other technological interventions in the body – that are based on the philosophical work on the body, subjectivity, and sex/gender by leading feminist theorists, including Judith Butler and Rosi Braidotti. What is often also called *cyberfeminism* has been stimulated by the work of Donna Haraway, in particular by the cyborg metaphor she introduced into feminist theorizing. Wajcman (2006) has stressed the liberating influence of the cyborg metaphor – 'the collapse of these oppressive binaries – nature/culture, animal/man, human/machine, subject/object – is liberating. The cyborg creature, a human–machine amalgam, fundamentally redefines what it is to be human and thus can potentially exist in a world without gender categories' (p. 13). The cyborg has become a sort of cipher for 'otherness' (of gender, culture, geographical position); and it evidences novel configurations of humans and machines. In discussion of this extensive body of work – philosophical/theoretical and empirical – about the gendering of science and technology, Sandra Harding's (1986) triad for analyzing gender relations (see the Introduction) is helpful. We will use this framework throughout the book.

The Feminist Critique of Science

Views about science and the nature of technology evolved in parallel with the emergence of science, technology, and society studies. Feminist scholars, such as Sandra Harding, Evelyn Fox Keller, Donna Haraway, and others, reflected on the gendered nature of science and engineering and influenced a whole generation of women. The early critiques of the dominant model of practising science articulated some points that are still of relevance. In *Reflections on gender and science* (1985) Evelyn Fox Keller formulated an insight that was formative for many feminist scholars in the 1980s:

> In a science constructed around the naming of object (nature) as female and the parallel naming of subject (mind) as male, any scientist who happens to be a woman is confronted with an a priori contradiction in terms. This poses a critical problem of identity: any scientist who is not a man walks a path bounded on one side by inauthenticity and on the other by subversion.
>
> (Keller 1985, p. 174)

Scholars from different scientific disciplines started almost in parallel to reflect on what Harding (1986) called a masculine bias in the sciences, delineating the consequences of such a bias and also musing about how the sciences could be changed from inside by women (and 'people of color and gays and lesbians and working-class people and people of various ethnicities'; Hirsh et al. 1995, p. 194). They identified some of the major problems of the sciences at this time. Pioneering biologists such as Lynda Birke and Anne Fausto-Sterling started academic critiques of biomedicine (Birke and Vines 1987; Fausto-Sterling 1985). They argued that processes of gender have an influence on the production of biomedical knowledge. They (and others) demonstrated how gender norms determine how women's (and men's) health problems are interpreted and treated, often exposing the predominance of the 'male' norm in research and treatment (Klinge and Bosch 2005).

Fausto-Sterling, from the very beginning, tried to understand 'the "minority experience" as endured by minority men, minority women, and white women' (1985, p. 30). She, like Keller, disputed 'the claim that science operates solely and successfully by separating the subjective and objective aspects of our experience' (Fausto-Sterling 1985, p. 31), anchoring its theories and its methodology in a mind/body dualism. She saw this dualism as connected to her personal experience that her work *about* science was much less visible and recognized among her male colleagues than her work *in* science. Birke and Vines (1987) criticized biological determinism in how gender development was conceptualized following a nature/nurture dualism that fails to recognize that gender development involves complex and variegated processes. They argued that this is mainly due to the fact that science proceeds 'by using a kind of methodological reductionism, by means of which factors are isolated and controlled' (p. 565), asking, 'But if development involves complex, multifarious processes, how and why does uniformity (such as a definably female or male gender identity) arise at all?' (p. 565). Hence, already in the 1980s Birke and Vines' work referred to the possibility of multiple gender identities.

The debate about gender issues in biomedicine continues, alongside efforts to attain gender equity. From the point of view of research, an important initiative was to develop tools for carrying out gender analysis in biomedical research (see e.g., Schiebinger 2012). For example, the position paper of the European Commission's Horizon 2020 Advisory Group for Gender (December 2016) emphasizes that

> addressing the gender dimension in research and innovation entails accounting for sex and gender in the whole research process, when developing concepts and theories, formulating research questions, collecting and analysing data, and using the analytical tools that are specific to each scientific area.

The Canadian Institutes for Health Research (CIHR)

> is a signatory on the Government of Canada's Health Portfolio Sex- and Gender-Based Analysis Policy, as well as the Tri-Council Policy Statement on Ethical Conduct for Research Involving Humans. Both policies underscore the importance of integrating sex and gender into health research when appropriate. As such, CIHR expects that all research applicants will integrate sex and gender into their research design and practices when appropriate.
> (https://cihr-irsc.gc.ca/e/50833.html, last accessed 12/19/2022)

In her widely influential book *The science question in feminism* (1986) Sandra Harding addressed the issue of women/gender in science from the point of view of the philosophy of science. She used feminist standpoint theory to categorize epistemologies that emphasize women's knowledge. Feminist sociologist Dorothy Smith (1987), who is often credited as the founder of feminist standpoint theory, reflected insights which were also being raised in the social sciences, concerning the need to take women's experiences as a starting point. Another significant contribution to this debate was Belenky et al.'s (1986) *Women's ways of knowing: The development of self, voice, and mind*, in which they proposed a new model of education that accounts for women's experiences.

With respect to the sciences, Harding's (1986) key argument was that the only way to increase the objectivity of scientific findings is by starting from the lived experiences of people who have been traditionally excluded from the production of scientific knowledge. Already Donna Haraway (1988) had stated, 'Feminist objectivity means quite simply situated knowledges' (p. 581). Harding took up this notion, asking, 'Now, what does it mean to have socially situated knowledge, to use the place from which we speak as a resource, a part of the method, a part of the instruments of inquiry?' (Hirsh et al. 1995, p. 206). In a conversation with Elizabeth Hirsh and Gary A. Olson in 1995, Harding restated the other key concept of feminist standpoint theory – 'strong objectivity' (Harding 1992) – as something scientists should strive for: 'Strong objectivity requires that the subject of knowledge be placed on the same critical, causal plane as the objects of knowledge. Thus, strong objectivity requires what we can think of as "strong reflexivity"' (p. 458). Harding also made clear that the 'masculine bias' that entrenches scientific practices and results 'lies in the selection of problems for inquiry and in the definition of what is problematic about them' (Harding 1996, p. 652). Similar concerns were raised by Kathryn Addelson, a philosopher of science, in her piece 'Man of professional wisdom' (1983). She also pointed to the necessity of focussing on the activities of science and how those contributed to bias.

Other feminist writers, such as Evelyn Fox Keller, who is a scientist herself, have used gender as an analytical tool for elaborating and concretizing the idea of difference and dissent within the sciences. Built into science and technology, Keller argued, is a dualistic worldview which excludes otherness and difference as non-scientific while claiming the universality, objectivity, and value-neutrality of its own cognitive structures and methods. Science has defined its way of knowing in a gender-based language. The focus on gender, Keller wrote, 'enables us to see the values that have been excluded from the norms of universality because they were identified with women' (Keller 1987, p. 45). Keller put forward strong arguments for 'the inclusion of difference – in experience, perceptions, and values – as intrinsically valuable to the production of science' (p. 40).

One of Keller's examples is Barbara McClintock, whose biography, *A feeling for the organism*, she had published in 1993, a decade after McClintock was awarded the Nobel Prize in Physiology and Medicine. McClintock was a geneticist, who as a young scientist achieved a level of recognition that few women could then imagine. She then retreated into obscurity. Her extraordinary findings – she invented the concept of 'transposition' of genetic elements – clashed with what her scientist fellows were prepared to understand. They thought her bizarre and difficult, yet after years of obscurity she later became famous again and connected with the revolution in biological thinking. When Evelyn Fox Keller came to talk to her, she did not see how her life could be of possible interest to the world:

> On this she was adamant; she was too different, too anomalous, too much of a 'maverick' to be of any conceivable use to other women. She had never married, she had not, as an adult or as a child, ever pursued any of the goals that were conventional for women ... Barbara McClintock has lived most of her life alone – physically, emotionally, and intellectually. But no one who has met her could doubt that this has been a full and satisfying life. ... Where has this extraordinary 'capacity to be alone' come from?
>
> (Keller 1993, p. 17)

McClintock had learned very early in her life to, as she says, 'handle her difference', and gives many accounts in her biography about her unusual behavior others did not understand and often did not appreciate at all. She worked with maize, planting the young seedlings, watching them grow. She told how she became apt at recognizing structural alterations in chromosomal composition by simply looking at the plants. She never made a mistake!

In reflecting on McClintock's story, Keller asks, 'What then do we make of the fact that so much of what is distinctive about that vision and practice – its emphasis on intuition, feeling, connectedness, and relatedness – conform[s] so well to our most familiar stereotypes of women? And are, in fact, so rare among male scientists?' (1987, p. 42). Keller sees this as a consequence of science being named as masculine, while intuition (one of McClintock's resources) is named as feminine and repudiated. The 'difficulty so many of us have in thinking about difference in any other terms than – either duality or universality' she argues, is 'rooted not in biology but in politics: not a conse-quence of any limitations in the way in which our brains are constructed, but rather the consequence of an implicit contest for power' (p. 44). This insight, that 'the ideological ingredients of particular concern to feminists are found where objectivity is linked with autonomy and masculinity, and in turn, the goals of science with power and domination' (Keller 1982, p. 594), is an ongoing theme in feminist discourse about science and technology.

These key insights about how the gendering of science rests on the exclu-sion of women's knowledge (and the knowledge of other genders) prepared the philosophical and methodological grounds for the feminist critique of technology. Many of the feminist scholars who got involved in research on the gendered nature of different technologies – from machines in the factory to ICTs – read and debated the work of women who had pioneered feminist science studies. Many of the concepts which emerged in discussions about the gendering of science (including the importance of standpoint and context) have played a significant role in related areas, such as queer theory and critical race theory.

Technology as Material of Male Power

While the debate about the gendered nature of technology evolved alongside the feminist criticism of science, there are some differences. These are to do with the fact that technologies are not only produced with particular purposes in mind, but they will be used in different contexts, and how users appropriate a technological artifact, integrating it into their practices, is a question that has to be investigated empirically. Suchman and Wynn (1984) argued that the design of technology is only fully completed in its use; hence we need to focus on processes of appropriation that have to be observed. They used two methods – ethnographic studies and interaction analysis – in their research. Judith Wajcman (2006) uses the term *technofeminism* to express the need to combine feminist thinking with observational studies of technology use: 'My own perspective, technofeminism, fuses the insights of new streams of gender theory with a thoroughgoing materialist approach to the social studies of technology' (p. 15). She also stands for combining a historical perspective on how feminist thinking about technology developed with an interest in understanding new and future technologies. Referring to Donna Haraway's famous take on the figure of 'cyborg' – 'a cybernetic organism, a hybrid of machine and organism, a creature of social reality as well as a creature of fiction' (Haraway 1990, p. 190) – she argues,

> The most influential feminist commentator writing in this vein is Haraway . . . . She too argues that we should embrace the positive potential of technoscience, and is sharply critical of those who reject technology. Famously, she prefers to be a 'cyborg' – a hybrid of organism and machine parts – rather than an ecofeminist 'goddess'. She notes the great power of science and technology to create new meanings and new entities, to make new worlds. She positively revels in the very difficulty of predicting what technology's effects will be and warns against any purist rejection of the 'unnatural', hybrid, entities produced by biotechnology. Genetic engineering, reproductive technology, and the advent of virtual reality are all seen as fundamentally challenging traditional notions of gender identity.
>
> (Wajcman 2006, p. 13)

Early feminist thinking about technology at times had a tendency towards being dichotomous. It either reflected the liberating potential of technology (e.g., Shulamith Firestone's *The dialectic of sex: The case for feminist revolution* [1970] where she posited the possibility of reproduction without men) or its destructive tendencies – reflected in many ecofeminist views, which built on the notion that women are closer to nature than men.

Taking up a historical perspective inevitably leads to the work of Cynthia Cockburn, who had an enormous influence on feminist thinking about the gendering of technologies, which she combined with her socialist engagement. She pointed out that most research into the workplace prior to the 1980s could be characterized by its focus on men: it was about men, gave pre-eminence to men's experiences, and assumed that the relations between capital and labour were relations between bosses and men. Additionally, she pointed out that prior to the 1980s most workplace studies focussed on labour and wage relations but neglected gender relations. After *Brothers: Male dominance and technological change* (1983a), which was based on observational work in the printing industry, she went on to study the use of three technologies: computerization of pattern and cutting processes in the clothing industry; computerization of goods handling and merchandizing processes in mail order warehouses; and computer tomography (CT) scanning in radiology departments. In her next book, *Machinery of dominance: Women, men and technical know-how* (1985), she looked at computerization as a process by which men asserted their power through the control of technology.

Cockburn argued that neither an ideological nor an economic explanation could provide 'an adequate account of male supremacy or female subordination' (Cockburn 1985b, p. 138). She emphasized the need to look at the material conditions of women's work, 'narrating also the concrete practices through which women are disadvantaged' (p. 137). She used her fieldwork material to demonstrate how technologies become gendered and are at the same time used to define gender relations. She did this first by looking at the introduction of computerized photocomposition in printing. She described how this technology threatened the power of the highly skilled and well-organized compositors – most of them male – as the technology 'wipes out many of the aspects of the work which have served as criteria by which "hot metal" composition for printing has been defined as a manual skill and a man's craft' (Cockburn 1985a, p. 136). Cockburn saw the technology in this case as producing both class and gender relations. While before the new technology was introduced, unskilled or semi-skilled labourers had not been allowed to enter the composing room, the craft workers now formed an alliance with the union of unskilled workers, in order to fend off women. Cockburn identified a combination of physical power and technical effectivity ('relative familiarity with and control over machinery and tools') as sources of male power at the workplace, arguing that it is important

> to study the way in which a small physical difference in size, strength and reproductive function is developed into an increasing relative physical advantage to men and vastly multiplied by differential access to technology. The process, as I will show, involves several converging practices: accumulation of bodily capabilities, the definition of tasks to match them and the selective design of tools and machines. The male physical advantage of course interacts with male economic and socio-political advantage in mutual enhancement. *The appropriation of muscle, capability, tools and machinery by men is an important source of women's subordination, indeed it is part of the process by which females are constituted as women.*
>
> (Cockburn 1985b, p. 140)

Cockburn's analysis identifies two steps in the process of constituting gender: the mutual definition of men and women through their relation to the same technology; and the distinction between skilled and unskilled workers. Looking back at her fieldwork in clothing manufacture, warehousing, and the hospital X-ray service, she observed,

> The significance of the role we've found women playing in the three new technologies is simple: they are operators. They press the buttons or the keys. They are the ones who do with the machine what it is made for: they produce on it . . . Their role is output, not input. What women cannot be seen doing in any of these three kinds of workplace is managing technology, developing its use or maintaining and servicing it.
>
> (Cockburn 1993, p. 113)

Cockburn's focus was on how technologies at the workplace were used to define men's work versus women's work based on a gendered definition of technical competence, thereby ensuring men's power position relative to women. Her next study, with Susan Ormrod, was *Gender and technology in the making* (1993), 'a gender analysis of the life cycle of a microwave oven, from design through production to sales, marketing, and consumer use, to see how gender relations shape technology while technology relations shape gender' (p. 271). The Science, Technology and Society (STS) approach Cockburn and Ormrod assume in this study was highly influential among feminists studying technologies, their production and use. For example, Judy Wajcman's work on gender and technology has been shaped by STS, as is the case with Lucy Suchman, who has brought attention to STS and feminist theory to the field of computing, clarifying the relationship between them:

> I take it that a virtue of STS is its aspiration to work across disciplines in constructing detailed and critical understandings of the sociality of science and technology, both historically and as contemporary projects. Feminist scholarship, similarly, is organized around core interests and problems rather than disciplinary canons, and comprises an open-ended and heterodox body of work. The aspects of feminist STS [that I trace out in this chapter] define a relationship to technoscience that combines critical examination of relevant discourses with a respecification of material practices. The aim is to clear the ground in order to plant the seeds for other ways of configuring technology futures.
>
> (Suchman 2008, p. 140)

The Case of Computer-Based Technologies

It took some time until the rich discourse on the gendering of technologies initiated by feminist theory and STS came to the attention of computer scientists, although issues around women and ICT had already gained prominence in the 1980s, with the advance of office automation (OA) (Marschall and Gregory 1983) and with emergent computer networks. The contributions in Cheris Kramarae's edited book *Technology and women's voices: Keeping in touch* (1988) put forward a nuanced view of computer technologies and their (potential) uses.

While in the 1980s many feminist scholars saw ICTs as perpetuating masculine images and privileges, some such as Margaret Benston (1988, 1989) began exploring the relationship between the design of ICTs and women's options and agency. By the 1990s there was some optimism about the possibilities of ICTs to empower women and change gender relations. Feminist writers such as Sadie Plant (1997) perceived digital technologies that are 'based on brain rather than brawn, on networks rather than hierarchy' as a chance to revalue 'the feminine, bringing woman's radical alterity, her difference, into being' (Wajcman 2007, p. 291).

The important series of 'Women, work and computerization' conferences that were organized as part of IFIP (International Federation of Information Processing), the first of which took place in Riva del Sole, Italy, in 1985, offered women (and men) a forum for presenting and discussing mostly empirical work about how computers were used in different areas of work and the challenges and opportunities they brought with them. The emergent paradigm of participatory design made researchers think about how to design ICT systems in ways that they could be easily adapted to the needs of users in a particular context.

ICT-based systems and artifacts are indeed different from traditional machines. A specific characteristic of systems and artifacts that have been developed in a context-aware and participative way is their technical tailorability and malleability. Carla Simone (2018) defines malleability as a prerequisite of a system that can be appropriated by users in a particular context and made useful:

> ... the overall socio-technical system needs to be continuously re-designed to cope with different requirements and constraints, and must then be malleable at both the community and organizational levels. According to any good engineering approach, to make continuous re-design of (Socio-Technical ST) systems effective we have to take design for malleability at any level as a basic and unavoidable principle for the construction of (ST) systems.
>
> (Simone 2018, p. 3)

Hence, in principle computer-based artifacts and systems can be made to include the experiences and specific needs of women (and other genders and marginalized groups); with some limitations. Margaret Benston (1988) argued that technology itself can be seen as a 'language' for action and self-expression with consequent gender differences in ability to use this 'language'. . . . [M]en's control over technology and their adherence to a technological world view have consequences for language and verbal communication and create a situation where women are 'silenced'.

(Benston 1988, p. 12)

The challenge was in providing women with a vocabulary for action. Benston (1988) – who taught computer science – contended that with computers 'new styles, embodying more of the things women value, may in fact be possible' (p. 18).

From the point of view of the design disciplines HCI, CSCW, and PD, the question 'Is there a gendering of computer technology?' is intimately related to the question of methodology: whether women's voices (and those of other genders) are included in generating design ideas and whether they participate in the shaping of technological artifacts. Fundamental to PD is the inclusion of future users through having them participate in the conception, design, and evaluation of an artifact or system that supports their practices. However, in the early days of PD gender was not an issue and very few projects at that time actually engaged in systems design in support of women's work. Only one of the early participatory design projects, the *Florence* project (Bjerknes and Bratteteig 1986, 1988), had women – nurses – as its main user group. Marja Vehviläinen developed the study circle method, which she used with women office workers in defining their requirements for a computer system that would be useful for them (1991). Eileen Greene, Jenny Owen, and Den Pain (1993) used the study circle method with women library assistants, pointing to important changes:

For the first time, large numbers of women library assistants took part in detailed discussions and assessments of IT possibilities, both through the study circles and through the subsequent systems demonstrations. Their views were formally expressed through study circle reports, evaluation questionnaires and contributions to the systems specification.

(Greene et al. 1983, p. 141)

There are several possible reasons for the absence of women from early PD projects: women's work frequently remained unrecognized and invisible; it was often considered simple, routine and 'of too little consequence to warrant the attention of system designers' (Balka 1997, p. 101); and women had difficulties finding time to participate in a design project and to have their voices heard, given their family responsibilities (Hales and O'Hara 1993). An additional reason also may be that most designers were men with a tendency to focus on areas of work that they considered interesting to contribute to. The trade unions, the key cooperation partners in PD projects in the

Nordic countries, had an interest in strengthening workplace democracy in the industrial sector. The situation in Germany was similar, where industrial sociologists mainly studied workplaces in manufacturing, the metal and automotive industry, mining, and shipbuilding, with typical areas of women's work not entering their field of vision (Balka and Wagner 2021). This is confirmed in a paper by Clement and Van den Besselaar (1993), in which they take stock of PD projects in the 1970s and 1980s:

> The list of projects shows a shift from PD in manufacturing industry in the 1970s and early 1980s to PD in offices and service industries in the late 1980s. In the earlier projects, the emphasis was on male-dominated crafts in unionized environments. This stands in sharp contrast to the later projects, which focus on settings in which women workers and traditionally female occupations dominate. As a consequence, in the later PD projects, more attention is paid to gender issues than to union issues.
>
> (Clement and Van den Besselaar 1993, p. 32)

The absence of women also has deeper methodological and epistemological roots, Lucy Suchman (2002) argued. She brought her engagement in feminist STS and the sciences of the artificial to PD by taking up Haraway's notion of partial translations, proposing

> a shift from a view of objective knowledge as a single, asituated, master perspective that bases its claims to objectivity in the closure of controversy, to multiple, located, partial perspectives that find their objective character through ongoing processes of debate.
>
> (Suchman 2002, p. 92)

Suchman suggested that we need to 'locate' design, by identifying the participation of all the implicated actors in the production and use of a technology so as to make their contributions and responsibilities visible – to make clear that a design presents a 'view from somewhere'. But what if this 'somewhere' excludes women and, as Shaowen Bardzell (2010) critically points out, design activities work with the assumption of a 'genderless user' or practitioner?

From an HCI perspective, Bardzell (2018) proposes to strengthen the connection of PD with feminist/queer theory by developing 'a cooperative engagement between feminist utopianism and PD at the levels of theory, methodology, and on-the-ground practice' (p. 1). The HCI research community has come a long way, with feminist and queer theory being currently strongly present in research and design committed to social justice, as numerous recent projects show; such as the work of Dombrovsky et al. (2016) on social justice-oriented interaction design; Bennet and Rosner's (2019) critical examination of empathy as a concept leading design work with people with disabilities; as well as Strohmayer and others' work with charities that provide services to women who are sex workers or have experienced sexual exploitation (2017, 2020).

The fact that women's voices are often not included in the design of ICT-based artifacts and systems has also been debated by feminist scholars in Germany (see e.g., Schmitz and Schinzel 2004; Draude and Maaß 2018). Corinna Bath (2009) describes several mechanisms that contribute to the gendering of computational artifacts: the assumption that technology is basically neutral; gendered structures, symbols and stereotypes that are inscribed in IT systems and artifacts – the ways 'the human' is represented – in them; as well as 'decontextualization and disputable epistemological and ontological assumptions' (p. 1). While not explicitly referring to Sandra Harding's triad for analyzing gender relations, Bath's approach has some similarities with this framework. Bath also uses the notion of 'gendered scripts', a term that goes back to Madeleine Akrich (1992), meaning that 'like a film script, technical objects define a framework of action together with the actors and the space in which they are supposed to act' (p. 208). Technological objects may thus reinforce existing 'geographies of responsibilities' (pp. 207–208) but also transform them or create new ones. This argument echoes Margaret Benston's (1988) view that technologies provide a means of expression, in that the constraints of technologies could limit alternate ways of doing things.

Gender has also been largely absent from CSCW research, for a variety of reasons. Central to the practice-based tradition of (mostly European) CSCW is the understanding of work practices with a view towards designing better systems. However, historically the focus of many fieldwork studies carried out in this tradition was (and still is) on work practices 'as they occur' and unfold situationally. This does not categorically exclude but also not oblige researchers to pay heed to the larger context of work, including working conditions and the gender subtext in organizations. This wider context also comprises 'the wider engagements that people have', for example, their family responsibilities, as well as 'the politics of work, the gender politics of work' (Suchman, interview 04/22/22). We think that the tradition of 'ethnomethodologically informed ethnography' in the context of European CSCW makes it difficult to identify or see most aspects of gender articulated by Harding (1986): gender structures – which often operate at a macro level – can easily elude detection with a focus on practices. Similarly, gender identity and gender symbolism may both come to bear on work practices, but when focussing on these practices can easily recede from view.

However, ethnomethodologically informed workplace studies in the European CSCW tradition have indirectly contributed to understanding gender issues at work because they make the often-invisible skills in work visible. In 1999, *JCSCW* (*Journal of Computer-Supported Cooperative Work*) published a special issue with papers that were to become highly influential, among them Leigh Star and Anselm Strauss' 'Layers of silence, arenas of voice: The ecology of visible and invisible work' and Yrjö Engeström's 'Expansive visibilization of work: An activity-theoretical perspective' that presented different frameworks for analyzing invisible work in CSCW systems. The main motivation behind this special issue was that 'understanding the nature and structure of invisible work is crucial to designing and managing organizations' (Nardi and Engeström 1999, p. 1), hence also to the design of computational artifacts.

Balka suggested that

> there are at least three different kinds of invisible work. Work can be invisible because it is non-standard, because of the political consequences of acknowledging it, or because the configuration of technologies used to complete a constellation of tasks was unable to capture all aspects of the work, requiring that a worker complete either articulation work[2] or a workaround in order to accomplish a set of tasks.
>
> (Ellen Balka 1997, p. 166)

Dave Randall (2022, p. 556) argued that 'work cannot be either invisible or visible in and of itself, but will be so in virtue of certain interests, for certain purposes'. This leads back to women's work and the invisibility and undervaluation of skills, one of the major concerns of feminist scholars with considerable implications for the design of computational artifacts. One of the scholars who brought this issue to the attention of CSCW research early on is Toni Robertson, who proposed to use the notion of 'language as embodied skill' within CSCW:

> The aim is to use this feminist work categorising women's language skills as key workplace skills to emphasise the centrality of these skills to core workplace activities – particularly the successful use of CSCW technology. This can then provide a valuable resource to those technology designers seeking to build technology that enhances the capacities of those who use it to control their own work practices. At the same time feminist theory gains an opportunity to be applied within technology design practice.
>
> (Robertson 2000, p. 214)

Although deeply interested in a feminist perspective on technology design, Robertson is skeptical of the idea of designing for any specific group of people, which poses the risk of essentializing differences. She emphasizes the

---

[2] Articulation work, a term that goes back to Anselm Strauss (1988), is work needed in the orderly accomplishment of cooperative work. It involves activities such as to distribute work, align contributions, clarify issues, provide instructions, and point out errors.

importance of designing for 'flexible use' – 'it seemed to me if you were designing for people who worked in different ways, then you ... you just designed the technology differently, and people could appropriate it as normal' (Robertson, interview 05/18/22). This is an important stance, we think, that points to the practice of PD, which, starting out from a deep understanding of a specific workplace and practice and the context in which it is embedded, joins forces with the practitioners in the field in developing computational artifacts. It also emphasizes the significance of aiming at tailorability and malleability with a view to 'flexible use'.

The Configuring of Technology and Gender in Everyday Life

While there are numerous empirical studies about the role of technologies in different workplaces, they do not necessarily take a design perspective, showing how work-related computational artifacts are gendered and how they shape women's work. A number of recent cultural studies focus on the gendering of technologies that are designed for use in everyday life: heat pumps and solar stations, radio tinkering, electronic music-making, and, more generally, 'making' have been objects of both STS and cultural studies. While feminist scholars working within an STS framework are interested in understanding how technologies and gender mutually define each other, following technical artifacts from their conception to their uses in different contexts, cultural studies look into how on a symbolic level, gender is

> attached to actions, things, and people. In addition to being part of individual identities and institutional structures, gender functions symbolically and metaphorically: to say that a particular technological activity is symbolically 'gendered female', for example, does not mean that male people never participate in it.
>
> (Lerman et al. 1997, p. 2)

Cultural studies of technology, which address how technologies and gender mutually define one another, can help us understand what Harding (1986) has identified as gender symbolism. Some of these studies fail to address the making of technological artifacts but explore gender in situations of technology use. De Wilde (2021) looked at gender relations in maintenance and repair work, carrying out ethnographic fieldwork about interactions between households, technologies, and technicians around heat pumps and solar power stations. Her observations were led by the analytical lens of care – taking care of and caring about technologies. De Wilde saw 'technicians creating settings that encouraged conversations about main components, specialized high-tech features, and the technical rationale for renewable energy technologies' (p. 1269). But they also

> actively engaged female users, as they held women responsible for and knowledgeable about the domestic routines that affect a heat pump's performance, such as securing thermal comfort, creating a pleasant living environment, or cleaning its parts. Just as gendering in engineering practices is not as binary as it may appear, technician–user relationships are likewise multifaceted.
>
> (De Wilde 2021, p. 1280)

This study points out the co-existence of hegemonic and heterogeneous gender–technology relations – technicians pay heed to the needs of both men and women with their traditionally different roles in the home.

Another interesting case is prestigious technical objects, such as the electric guitar, which have been defined by male rock stars, and became physically as well as symbolically gendered:

> Through body positioning and flamboyant physical displays, players like Jimi Hendrix fortified male dominance over the electric guitar with a large dose of phallic symbolism. Male electric guitarists often handle their instruments in ways that recall sexual acts or emphasize the phallic symbolism of their guitars.
>
> (Bourdage 2010, p. 3)

Of course, women can play the electric guitar and there are female rock bands, but the barriers they face when trying to get onto the stage are enormous. Bourdage contends that many people consider 'low-slung guitars as the only positioning that looks right. Therefore, even on women, the instrument appears as an extension of the male body, reinforcing the idea that the electric guitar should be left to male hands' (p. 3).

That gendered notions of technology are persistent and make it difficult for women to move to some fields of activity that are attractive to them is also demonstrated by recent studies of radio tinkering and, more generally, 'making'. A fascinating study by Dunbar-Hester (2008) depicts radio tinkering as a site of masculine identity construction. She engaged in participant observation in the so-called 'Geek Group', a small US-based 'radical pedagogical activity, which constitutes an aspect of activism surrounding citizen access to low-power FM radio' (p. 201). Although the group was conceived as a place for both women and men to learn technical skills, Dunbar-Hester found a division of labour 'about which the participants were uneasy, and which specifically hinged on technical skill' (p. 201). While the women were radio activists, few of them attended the group meetings and possessed the technical skills related to the hardware. On the other hand,

Women who do have technical skills related to FM or more 'hardcore' electronics tinkering claim to feel empowered by these skills, and some women who do not have them have expressed regret, or to some extent resentment. Janet said how exciting it was for her to 'demystify' FM production technology by learning to use it, and stated that the next step in the process of 'demystification', which she would find interesting if she had more time, would be something akin to learning 'to look under the hood'.

(Dunbar-Hester 2008, p. 221)

Even men that were open to feminist ideas were not averse to displaying masculine identities when tinkering. This is consonant with an earlier study by Susan Douglas (1999) of amateur operators' work with radio. She observed that for men,

radio colonized and reinforced new and old territories of masculinity. Tinkering with machines was nothing new for men. but radio brought such tinkering into the safety and comfort of the domestic sphere and of leisure time. It made being a nerd almost glamorous.

(Douglas 1999, p. 99)

Men's practices of radio tinkering led to a reinterpretation of masculinity. This observation indicates a tendency of men to appropriate new technologies that would on principle also be open to women associating them with ideas about masculinity, as is the case with for example the digitization of parts of mining (see Chapter 4).

Hence, although in particular young women have started appropriating technical artifacts, for example in electronic music-making (e.g., Abtan 2016, Parsley 2022), and are increasingly participating in male-identified maker cultures or starting their own maker projects, they continue to be confronted with masculine symbolisms as well as the fact that full participation in these activities requires hard-core technical skills that many of them did not have the opportunity to develop. This gender messaging is often reinforced by an absence of appropriate tools (e.g., safety gear) required to participate fully. Moreover, some kinds of technologies are valued over others, with those that are involved in feminist making, such as 'zine making, meme propagation, hashtags, and textile crafting' (Rentschler 2019) assigned lower cultural value.

In FabLabs and hacker- and makerspaces these topics become manifest and have increasingly attracted the attention of researchers in HCI, CSCW, and related communities. Studies exploring the reasons for the low diversity in such spaces (Lewis 2015; Davies 2017; Smit and Fuchsberger 2020; Campreguer et al. 2021) find them along social and material lines. Smit and Fuchsberger (2020) describe the social fabric of the makerspace community to be a strong factor that is making the place uninviting to a more diverse audience:

... communities, and their implicit rules and social norms can be 'wicked ways of closing a system', turning a makerspace into an impenetrable fort. If we want to design (interventions in) makerspaces to make them more inclusive and welcoming, we might relate the norms and rules of communities of practices that already exist, to how women* (are unable to) enter these communities. By understanding the communities, we can then co-create, evolve, design and build makerspaces to be inviting to anyone who considers or would like to consider themselves a maker.

(Smit and Fuchsberger 2020, p. 8)

The way maker identity has developed over time is rather constricted. Quoting Dunbar-Hester (2014), Cid Cipolla emphasizes

that the maker movement's appeal to universality only appeals to those who feel universal to begin with – those whose identities are unmarked and that activists should both consider the fact that making technology 'has long been associated with white masculinity' and remember that it is not enough to simply express an embrace of egalitarianism'.

(Dunbar-Hester 2014, quoted in Cipolla 2019, p. 267)

Cipolla stresses that such a view is not easy to overcome, as it also touches upon factors that may reside well outside of the makerspace itself.

Efforts to achieve more diversity and inclusivity are varied. They are seeking to challenge dominant categorizations of what making is, arguing for an inclusion of crafting (Kafai and Peppler 2014) and tinkering (Cipolla 2019), bricolage, fixing, and maintenance (Jackson et al. 2012). Along material and technology lines, a range of technologies and tools are developed to further challenge established notions of 'hard and soft engagements with technology' (Cipolla 2019), creating links with traditional crafts like sewing (Weibert et al. 2014; Strohmayer 2021) or origami (Qi et al. 2018).

Gender and the 'Pleasures of Engineering'

In an article with a question in the title – 'The power and the pleasure?' (2000) – Wendy Faulkner discusses studies of engineers and the links between modern technology and hegemonic masculinity. Starting out from what Harding (1986) has proposed as the triad for analyzing gender relations, she argues that while technologies are a source of male power, men also have an expressive relationship with technologies. While this is not a new insight, Faulkner uses it to develop the notion of heterogeneous engineering.

Well-known early studies of engineering are Samuel Florman's *The exist-ential pleasures of engineering* (1976), Sally Hacker's *Pleasure, power and technology* (1989), and Gideon Kunda's *The culture of engineering: Control and commitment* (1992), each taking a different stance. Florman described the rewarding experiences of being able to solve difficult problems, mastering formidable obstacles, as well as the intimate contact with technical artifacts engineering affords. Although the book was criticized as directed against the anti-technologist movements of his time (and hence as being basically apologetic of engineering work), Florman made an important point, as Ina Wagner (1994) argues:

> Science and technology provide actors with an environment (a lab, a mathematical theory, a computer screen) in which they can act out without being held back by concerns that provide guidelines in real life. Samuel Florman (1976) defines this distance as a central source of the pleasure of engineering.
>
> (Wagner 1994, p. 260)

Wagner interprets this distance as a source of social irresponsibility, as it encourages engineers to blend out social issues (of use) and suspend social norms.

In an entirely different spirit, Sally Hacker (1989) described engineering as an archetypal masculine culture and the pleasure and power men derived from it, stating, 'It is as though an intricately controlled erotic expression finds its most creative outlet today in the design of technology' (pp. 45–46). Among the pleasures that the engineering students she interviewed mentioned were

> 'The best hard science is flawless with simple systems [so large] you can deal with them by statistical methods'; 'The mathematical symbology seems to me very pretty ... can represent to many different things and subtle connections; it's very hard to remember enough to put order into nature. You have to have some structure for it always, and that structure is beautiful': 'reducing to rationality although it is right on the border, just barely rationalizable'; ... 'Some degree of elegance, aesthetically and technically': 'The beauty of finding that single equation that sums up everything, that explains everything'.
>
> (Hacker 1981, pp. 345–346)

Hacker asked how it can be that the pleasures of engineering got gendered and how it was possible that making things work had turned into a process of domination. She tied the feminist discussion of 'eroticism, domination, and the subordination of women to the development of a technology that is a central aspect of core institutions, the economy and the military' (Acker 1996, p. 441).

Wendy Faulkner proposes a 'shift' to men/masculinity and technology wondering why masculinity studies have not looked at engineering practices. She points to Bob Connell's notion of hegemonic masculinity 'as the pattern of practice (i.e., things done, not just a set of role expectations or an identity) that allowed men's dominance over women to continue' (Connell and Messerschmidt 2005, p. 832). It emphasizes a particular version of masculinity that is connected with (white) men who are in power, while acknowledging 'the plurality of masculinities and the complexities of gender construction for men' (p. 832). Faulkner argues that while the masculinity–technology connection had contributed to the exclusion of women, a closer look at engineering practices points to 'contradictory constructions of masculinity in the detail of engineering knowledge and practice' (p. 92). She suggests that we examine cultural images of technology and the dualisms inherent in these images from the point of view of masculinity studies; and also that we look at the mismatches between images of masculinity and actual practices of engineering.

One of the core dualisms, in addition to the mind–body dualism, is that of 'hard' and 'soft' technologies. While the former ones are considered the real powerful ones, 'soft' technologies are 'smaller scale, like kitchen appliances, or more organic, like drugs' (Faulkner 2000, p. 73). The hard/soft distinction, while quite pervasive in engineering, has been defined in various ways. Soft technologies are thought of being those that embody 'psychological, social and cultural factors' (Jin 2005, p. 51), while 'hard technologies are based on natural science knowledge aiming at 'changing and control the nature and substance of materials' (p. 52). In the field of computing the hard–soft dualism is still quite dominant, with areas such as software engineering, HCI, and CSCW being contrasted with the highly mathematical and engineering-based areas of research.

The hard–soft dualism is not only problematic because it reduces the heterogeneities that characterize different fields of engineering (which differ with respect to the required mathematical rigor, the importance of hands-on 'tinkering' work, as well as the distance from the complexities that arise with the uses of a technology in different contexts). Ashcraft (2022) has argued that the 'hard–soft' split is a *gender binary*. So too are notions of hard and soft, which are associated with a different style of thinking, juxtaposing a hard male style with a soft female style. Holth's (2014) interview study with male and female engineers discards dualisms such as these. She found 'passionate men' and 'rational women', challenging essentializing assumptions of gender and technology. Women may choose engineering as a profession for the same reasons as men and experience the same kinds of pleasure that solving difficult problems and making things that work offer.

However, for some time the notion of gendered styles in engineering had been quite popular in the early days of gender and computing studies. It had been taken up by Turkle and Papert (1990) who identified two ideal-type programming styles: the style of the bricoleur who works in an associative mode, negotiating and rearranging his/her way through a program; and the structured programmer who thinks in an analytic and rule-oriented way. These different styles became associated with men and women respectively, based on characterizations of femininity and masculinity that were often 'not read as symbolic constructs or as power-stabilizing ideologemes, but as sets of empirically identifiable properties in a binary social code' (Wagner 1994, p. 258).

While problematic in the ways it has been associated with stereotypical images of masculinity and femininity, the recognition of a diversity in learning styles had an important liberating effect on teaching practices. It led to a refocussing of a discourse that had started out with the acknowledgment of coding skills as central in a world that has become increasingly digital. Jeannette Wing has famously conceptualized the skill set needed as *computational thinking*. She is taking a broader view that is also concerned with concepts and analytical thinking, as a complement to mathematical and technical logics (Wing 2006, 2008) – as a means 'for everyone', inside and outside of computing. This universal approach entails a focus in STEM education on learners instead of contents to be learned, asking how access to skills could be ensured for a spectrum of learning styles. Subsequently, the acquisition of computing and programming skills is seen as closely related to matters of the self and as embedded in social context and community, thus motivating learning as 'computational participation' fostered by 'wider social networks and a DIY culture of digital making' (Kafai and Burke 2014):

> Participation in computing is more than just having access; it also involves the quality of what a child actually does with the computer. This issue extends beyond gender, race and socioeconomic equity. Even many schools in high-income communities remain entirely on the receiving end of computer screens and are unacquainted with how programming allows users to become multimedia creators themselves.
>
> (Kafai and Burke 2014, pp. 11–12).

This approach has been linked to craftsmanship and questions of aesthetics (e.g., Buechley et al. 2008), marking a turn from STEM to STEAM, explicitly including the Arts (Boy 2013). Rode et al. (2015) have argued for an inclusion of aesthetics, creativity, constructing, visualizing multiple representations, and understanding materials as physical skills, allowing to embrace more learner styles (such as creative, hands-on, less linear) in computing. Faulkner's (2000) argument that the distinction between styles can be pursued without falling into the trap of essentialism is highly relevant in this context:

> But it seems to me that both the potential for pluralism in technological design and the actual suppression of some styles and voices are extremely interesting politically. It would be very useful to explore further which 'styles' get suppressed and whether this is gendered at all.
>
> (Faulkner 2000, p. 103)

She contends that 'many dualistic epistemologies found in engineering prac-tice are gendered in contradictory ways and that many fractured masculinities within engineering are sustained simultaneously – among engineers as a group and, to varying degrees, by individuals: they coexist in tension' (p. 98).

Scholarship about technology and gender undertaken from a cultural studies perspective points to the ways that gender and technology are constituted at a symbolic level. Work by Faulkner (2000) and others that addresses gender and engineering, however, helps us to see and understand that while these dichoto-mies exist and are predominant, engineering practices are gendered in contra-dictory ways. This insight is important both because it signals on the one hand the existence of broader role possibilities for women than dichotomous views imply, and on the other hand, it points to the ways that gendering is manifest at an ideological level. Acknowledging and understanding these contradictions is an important aspect of understanding how gender works in relation to Harding's (1996) articulation of individual gender and symbolic gender.

Sources of Heterogeneity: Postcolonial Gender and Technology Studies

Postcolonial gender and technology studies have helped to take the acknow-ledgement of heterogeneous engineering a step further. The masculinization of technology, Ruth Oldenziel (1999) argued, is largely a product reflective of racial, gender, and international relations in the twentieth century. Increasingly, researchers from the non-Western world voice criticism of some of the main arguments about science and technology developed by feminist scholars. They sketch a much more nuanced picture of technology and women's participation in its production and use.

For example, Ong (1987) describes how the gendering of microchip pro-duction jobs in Malaysia is less indicative of male privilege than of profit maximization and labour control. The 'electronics' women working in high-tech factories 'were stamped with a negative "electronics" image implying low-grade labour and cheap female sexuality. For working-class men, the new technology was also tainted by its manual and female associations. Men instead aspired to white-collar employment in the government bureaucracy' (p. 622). Ong sees the fact that office jobs, whether performed by men or women, have high status in Malaysia as defying the assumption that simply 'working on machines' rather than developing, configuring, and maintaining them 'invalidates universalizing feminist logic about the links between gender, technology, and meaning' (p. 622).

While men and women may relate differently to different technologies (e.g., Benston 1988; Livingstone 1992), this is not necessarily culturally universal. In many Asian countries, neither computing nor engineering are considered masculine areas of work (see Chapter 9), as witnessed by the predominance of Indian women programmers in the IT industry and the effort of companies to make the work attractive to them, including free transportation to work and generous maternity leave: 'This is understood by women and men alike who perceive working in IT as a highly desirable career, regardless of gender' (Corneliussen et al. 2018, p. 5). The Philippine's ICT industry as well has 'female spaces', in particular in areas that are characterized by disciplinary hybridity, requiring a mix of ICT skills with non-technical skills. Saloma-Akpedonu (2005) argues that this is in part also due to the fact that 'women's epistemic privilege and standpoint' (p. 102) are recognized by industry.

Other studies suggest that this is not a new phenomenon but that women in traditional non-Western societies, even though not necessarily enjoying gender equality, regularly and competently have been using and still use different kinds of technologies. For example, Twagira's (2020) historical examination of technology use in grain mills in rural Mali shows 'not only women's concern for labour-saving technologies, but also women's ability to shape the infrastructure of their work. In so doing, they gender their tools as women's things and assert control over the meanings of their own work and status' (p. 77).

Studies such as these point to the need to explore the 'huge spectrum of variations in gender subjectivities in relation to artefacts and technology' (Mellström 2009, p. 888). They advocate more context-sensitivity and focus on the different meanings gender–technology relations may have assumed in different cultures. It is precisely this type of context-sensitivity when focussed on gender–technology relations that has yielded important insights about the nature of women's work and technology, which in turn have had significant impact on CSCW and PD in particular. Research concerned with queer gender identities (in Harding's (1986) terms, both projected and subjective gender identity) and how queer gender identities may both be influenced by technology and influence our views of technologies is in its infancy, and warrants further examination. Recent years have seen the formation of a queer special interest group in the HCI community. However, papers addressing gender and queer issues remain limited, and largely focussed on areas other than paid employment. These topics also remain on the outskirts of CSCW and PD (for an exception see Rizvi et al. 2022).

Summary

In this chapter we went back to the feminist discourse on science/technology and gender, which started in the 1960s and 1970s and was led by women scientists as well as scholars of STS and cultural studies. Very early on, feminists criticized the gender binary and other dualisms and brought forward an understanding of 'scientific objectivity' as being rooted in the multiplicity of experiences. Feminist criticism of science and technology was later enriched by queer theory and a focus on intersectionality. It serves as a reminder that our gender expressions are not dichotomous, can change over time, and take myriad forms of expression, which has implications for how we both think about gender and think about technology. Of particular influence on a feminist approach to science and technology were feminist standpoint theory and, connected with it, Donna Haraway's notion of 'situated knowledge' – that we use the place from which we speak as a resource – that juxtaposed prevalent connotations of science and technology with hegemonic masculinity that is associated with domination and control.

Cynthia Cockburn, in an STS tradition, analyzed the gendering of technologies – or the mutual shaping of gender and technology – using a wide range of examples, from computerized photocomposition in printing to the microwave oven. Judy Wajcman (2006) coined the term 'technofeminism', insisting on a 'thoroughgoing materialist approach to the social studies of technology'. While researchers in the field of cultural studies have followed the STS tradition with empirical studies of how gender plays out in activities such as radio tinkering or in makerspaces, this tradition has not been taken up with respect to computational artifacts in support of work. Although there is a large body of literature on women's work and technology, what is missing are analyses of the processes underlying the gendering of these technologies. Thinking about how to better understand these processes from the perspective of intersectionality is one of the challenges the book seeks to meet.

We touched on the challenges that practice-based research poses in relation to seeing gender relations, and highlighted the contributions that practice-based research has made to understanding the invisibility of women's work.

One of the important insights on this way to a gender/intersectional perspective on design is Faulkner's work on engineers and her understanding that the gendering that occurs in engineering practices is complex and heterogeneous. She emphasizes the importance of promoting heterogeneous images of engineering which, to be more inclusive, must also challenge the gendering of 'the social' as feminine and 'the technical' as masculine – and thus promote new 'co-constructions' of gender and engineering simultaneously ... *heterogeneous engineering requires heterogeneous genders* – in the sense that it requires various mixes of stereotypically masculine and feminine strengths.

(Faulkner 2007, p. 351)

Part III of this book will look into this notion of heterogenous engineering done by those of heterogenous gender with a view to the design of workplace technologies.

We now turn to the ethical-political perspective, outlining the contributions it has made to developing insights about the gender–work–technology nexus.

2

The Ethical-Political Perspective

The aim of this chapter is to promote a view of engineers/designers making ethical-political choices, by arguing that taking account of gender issues (or not doing so) is a part of such choices. In the previous two chapters, we sketched the broad foundations upon which our inquiry here rests. We provided an overview of how we think about technology and how we think about gender and outlined some of the key issues and debates that have been central to the evolution of scholarship concerned with gender, technology, and women's work, and linked these to our understanding of how information and communication technologies, artifacts, and systems shape the gender relations of women's work. We also introduced the concept of design justice and the notion of strengthening practices of user-sensitive inclusive design and made an argument for taking a historical perspective as it offers valuable insights about why we advocate for the approaches we present in the final section of the book.

In this chapter we introduce key concepts that feminist scholars contributed to our understanding of ethics and politics, concerning the relationships between equality, difference, and social justice, as well as the ethics of care. The material we present here offers context for our position that designers should assume an ethical-political perspective (which we will revisit when addressing ethical-political perspectives in technology design in Chapter 10) and situates the ethical-political perspective in feminist theories and in the broader debates about the philosophy of technology. The space we dedicate to introducing these concepts reflects our belief that they are essential elements of a feminist/intersectional approach to design.

While the ethical and the political are connected, there are differences between politics and ethics. Politics have to do with the exercise of power through varied means, whereas ethics debates the morality of choices that may be enacted through politics, and whether they are just and/or equitable.

An example that helps delineate these differences in the context of the design of ICT-based systems is from Blomberg et al.'s (1996) work on designing computer support for litigation work in a large US-based law firm, where they describe in great detail their encounter with organizational politics. Litigation work is about the defence of corporate clients against suits brought by other large companies. It may involve hundreds of thousands of documents that have to be examined and classified. The design team in this study first heard about the work of document coding from a senior attorney, who made a distinction between two types of coding: 'what he termed subjective, or issues coding done by attorneys, and objective coding which he described as follows':

> You have, you know, 300 cartons of documents and you tear through them and say, I'm going to put Post-Its on the ones we have to turn over to the other side. And then, ideally, you hire chimpanzees to type in From, To, Date. And then, ideally, you then have lawyers go through it again and read each document, with their brain turned on.

> (Blomberg et al. 1996, p. 252)

Politics in this case refers to the strategies of the firm's management to make the skills in the work of document coding invisible and to limit the allocation of resources to this work in order to ultimately pay less to document workers than their skills would require. This example is about the politics of invisible work in a company, emphasizing the importance of making this work visible for the design of computational artifacts.

Politics means taking sides; it is partisan (Mansfield 1995) and driven by the interests of groups that have access to political systems. Politics is, in essence, power: the ability to achieve a desired outcome. In democratic societies politics is about resolving conflict: that is, by compromise, conciliation, and negotiation, rather than through force and naked power.

The ethical perspective focuses on the moral dimension of these management practices: that management trivializes the work of document workers and does not pay them the acknowledgement and respect they deserve; that it refuses to engage in looking at the ways this work is carried out in practice. Ethical principles that may be referred to in this case include responsibility, harm, and justice. Ethical debates in this case might address terms of what may be considered 'good' – responsible, beneficent, and just.

Ethical Theories and the Influence of Feminist Ethics

The subject matter of ethics or moral philosophy has to do with questions relating to how we should live a good life (what is a good life?), what kind of society we should have (how to distribute goods and burdens?), and how we should treat others.

Much of traditional ethical theorizing deals with the logic of moral reasoning: valid moral reasoning and sources of our duties have for a long time been seen as resting either on single principles such as the greatest happiness principle proposed by the utilitarian philosopher John Stuart Mill or the categorical imperative (in its different versions) formulated by the German thinker Immanuel Kant. Mill and Kant's views on the rightness or wrongness of an act depend either on the consequences of the act (Mill) or on its correspondence with a duty (Kant). Kant proposed a very strict view: he believed that an act is morally praiseworthy only if it is done neither for self-interested reasons nor because of natural disposition. Moral praise is reserved only for acts done out of respect for moral duty. Virtue theory, a third type of approach to ethics, places value on the cultivation of the character of a person. Plato and Aristotle, for example, conceived of ethics in terms of virtues instead of rights and obligations.

The so-called common morality pluralist view on ethics presents the possibility of many principles. It was and still is a particularly popular approach in the field of health-care ethics. Among the key ethical principles that have been defined are autonomy, justice, privacy or confidentiality, beneficence, nonmaleficence (avoidance of harm), responsibility, and care. These are complex concepts that philosophers have discussed for centuries.

In the 1980s, feminist philosophers began to change the discourse about ethics, science, and human rights. Feminist ethics aims 'to understand, criticize, and correct' (Lindemann 2019, p. x) how gender operates within our moral beliefs and practices. More specifically, Norlock (2019) states in the *Stanford encyclopedia of philosophy* that feminist ethics is concerned with

> (1) the binary view of gender, (2) the privilege historically available to men, and/or (3) the ways that views about gender maintain oppressive social orders or practices that harm others, especially girls and women who historically have been subordinated, along gendered dimensions including sexuality and gender-identity.
>
> (Norlock 2019, p. 1)

Norlock also emphasizes a commitment of feminist ethics to arrive at a better understanding of the experiences of 'persons oppressed in gendered ways'. Methodologically, this means that it seeks to include empirical material in its arguments.

Among the main contributions of feminist ethics are the ongoing debate about whether to put the emphasis on equality or on 'difference' and the implications for the notion of social justice; the concept of relational autonomy; and the introduction of a care-based approach to ethics and politics.

Equality versus Difference

Equality as a human right is the principle that recognizes that the same rights apply to all citizens. An important distinction has been made between gender equality and gender equity:

> Gender equality, equality between men and women ... does not mean that women and men have to become the same, but that their rights, responsibilities and opportunities will not depend on whether they were born male or female. Gender equity means fairness of treatment for men and women according to their respective needs. This may include equal treatment or treatment that is different but which is considered equivalent in terms of rights, benefits, obligations, and opportunities.
>
> (ABC of Women Worker's Rights and Gender Equality 2000, p. 48)

While many issues concerning gender are to do with fairness and social justice (equity), it is important to maintain the perspective on equality as a human right, acknowledging that throughout history women have always struggled to gain equality, respect, and the same rights as men. This perspective may get lost, when neoliberal politics take over, reducing 'the agenda of the feminist movement to a narrow set of policy options', argues Schild (2000, p. 25) in view of the situation of women in many Latin American countries. She stresses that, 'for these working class and activist women, gender justice is intricately linked to social justice' (p. 28).

A special role in this debate about equality and social justice is filled by the work of philosopher Martha Nussbaum, who took up Amartya Sen's (1993) notion of 'capabilities' – what people are actually able to do and to be. She proposed an open-ended list of such capabilities, arguing that in order for citizens to be able to actively participate in society, they have to be able/ enabled to think, imagine, voice their opinion and interests, and negotiate issues that are of concern for them. Nussbaum sees the concept of capabilities as closely related to human rights, as it looks at a woman in terms of 'What is she actually able to do and to be?' (Nussbaum 1999, p. 233). It is a basic human – moral – right of each individual to have these capabilities developed so as to be able to exercise their rights (as equal to men):

> Women all over the world have lacked support for central human functions, and that lack of support is to some extent caused by their being women. But women, unlike rocks and trees, have the potential to become capable of these human functions, given sufficient nutrition, education and other support. That is why their unequal failure in capability is a problem of justice. It is up to all human beings to solve this problem. A cross-cultural conception of human capabilities gives us good guidance as we pursue this difficult task.
>
> (Nussbaum 1999, p. 243)

Critics of Nussbaum contest the very assumption underlying her approach, that is 'making the idea of human choice and freedom central' (p. 238). They refer to the work of Carol Pateman who (amongst others) has pointed out that the concept of equality has been constructed as a relation between individuals that are essentially the same. In her books *The sexual contract* (1988) and *The disorder of women?* (1989) Pateman developed a critique of liberal contractarianism, arguing that the social contract 'concluded between separate and autonomous men and was premised on a prior sexual contract that delivered them control of the women' (Phillips 2001, p. 253). 'Pateman's deeper point' is, according to Phillips, 'that liberalism has drawn on notions of self-ownership for its understanding of freedom and choice, and that in doing so, it reflects a misleadingly masculine model of human interaction' (p. 253).

Underlying these concerns is a feminist debate that reaches back to the 1990s about whether to emphasize equality or difference. In her analysis of this debate, Gisela Bock, a German historian who has pioneered a feminist critique of the sciences, formulates as its key question whether or not women want to be 'equal with men'. Italian feminists wrote about

> *il pensiero de la differenza sessuale*: thinking and acting in terms of sexual difference, affirming a female subjectivity which refuses to be assimilated ('homologised') to male versions of subjectivity such as the values and rights to compete, to possess, to dominate.
>
> (Bock 1991, p. 11)

One of them, Adriana Cavarero (1987) claimed that 'different and equal is possible'; and African American feminist Margaret Wright wrote,

> In black women's liberation we don't want to be equal with men, just like in black liberation we're not fighting to be equal with the white man. We're fighting for the right to be different and not be punished for it.
>
> (Wright 1972, p. 608)

Bock points to the principle of tolerance as a way of embracing both equality and difference, as it 'emphasised, at least in its early and radical formulations, liberty, justice and mutual respect' (p. 14).

Feminist scholars have applied the critique of liberal individualism to the concept of autonomy that plays such a large role in the human rights debate. In what has become a classical text in bioethics, Beauchamp and Childress (2001) have provided a definition of personal autonomy as 'at a minimum, self-rule that is free from both controlling interference by others and from limitations, such as inadequate understanding, that prevent meaningful choice' (p. 58). Feminist philosophy has responded to an understanding of autonomy that places the freedom of individual decisions in the forefront, suggesting the notion of relational autonomy (Mackenzie and Stoljar 2000). Relational autonomy assumes that the interests of human beings cannot be addressed without also considering the context of their social bonds and their social environment, and that these factors shape, characterize, and influence the moral decisions of all actors:

> The term 'relational' here may serve simply to deny that autonomy requires self-sufficiency. If relationships of care and interdependence are valuable and morally significant (cf. Mackenzie & Stoljar 2000b, 8–10), then any theory of autonomy must be 'relational' in the sense that it must acknowledge that autonomy is compatible with the agent standing in and valuing significant family and other social relationships. 'Relational' may also deny the metaphysical notion of atomistic personhood, emphasizing instead that persons are socially and historically embedded, not metaphysically isolated, and shaped by factors such as race and class.
> (Stoljar 2022, p. 1)

The 'undercurrent of rage against anything liberal', as Jennifer Nedelsky (1989, p. 9) notes, is present in many feminist writings. Women are more likely than men to recognize the centrality of relationships in constituting the self; they know this through experience, 'but the experience has been an oppressive one' (p. 9).

These understandings – the criticism of the notion of autonomy that results from a libertarian view of the social contract as one between individuals, and the insight into the social and historical embeddedness of persons – have become strongly anchored in feminist thinking. The centrality of relationships for women's thinking leads to another cornerstone of feminine ethics: the ethics of care and responsibility.

An Ethics of Care and Responsibility

The ethics of care originally emerged as a feminist critique of traditional ethical theorizing that goes back to the pioneering work of Carol Gilligan (1982). While it first focussed on personal relationships and on character traits that are valued in them, it later was reformulated as an ethics of responsibility. It has not only influenced the way the caretaking professions define their work but, more widely, shaped the approach to ethics and politics in general.

Joan Tronto's book *Moral boundaries* (1993) in particular influenced (and continues to influence) the debate about care ethics. The opening question in this book reads,

> What would it mean in late twentieth century American society to take seriously, as part of our definition of a good society, the values of caring – attentiveness,

responsibility, nurturance, compassion, meeting others' needs – traditionally associated with women and traditionally excluded from public consideration?

(Tronto 1993, pp. 2–3)

Care is not only about the actual work of care but about how it is done and about the distribution of resources. Hence, it is not just a private issue, adequate for personal relationships, but as well a social and political one. This is already reflected in a 1990 article 'Toward a feminist theory of caring', where Berenice Fisher and Joan Tronto defined care as 'a species of activity that includes everything we do to maintain, continue, and repair our "world" so that we can live in it as well as possible. That world includes our bodies, ourselves, and our environment' (Fisher and Tronto 1990, p. 40). Care can be used as an instrument of critical analysis, helping to understand which qualities citizens would need to live together well in a pluralist society.

Consequentially, Tronto saw an ethics of care as strongly interrelated with social justice – the concept of 'justice without a notion of care is incomplete' (1993, p. 167); as the ways care is performed and institutionalized are deeply entangled with issues of power and inequality. As part of a review symposium that was held on occasion of the 25th birthday of *Moral boundaries* (2018), Tronto stresses that 'any model of justice as a distributive system is fatally flawed . . . . The necessity of human care, and the ways it is organized in our society, are central dimensions in creating a more just society' (p. 22). She identified several causes of injustice: paternalism, when those who care pretend to know best what others need; parochialism, which is about caring only for those who feel closest and important to yourself; and 'privileged irresponsibility', which alludes to the fact that those who can afford to ignore domination 'have shaped a world in which care has been devalued' (p. 22). Also, Nancy Hirschman (2018) emphasizes the need to understand care as a political concept, pointing to capitalism as 'an important source of care's distortion, its assignment to women and to men of color, and its devaluation and poor remuneration in the market' (p. 5).

An important argument concerns potentially essentializing notions of care as corresponding to women's values and a female culture:

> It is philosophically stultifying because, if feminists think of the ethic of care as categorized by gender difference, they are likely to become trapped trying to defend women's morality rather than looking critically at the philosophical promises and problems of an ethic of care.
>
> (Tronto 1987, p. 647)

Her point is that considered 'women's morality' is not in fact about women: 'we need to stop talking about "women's morality" and start talking about a care ethic that includes the values traditionally associated with women' (1987, p. 646). Care is not a gender issue, she argues, but one of power and inequality; hence, it is not accidental that most care work is performed by women.

Many feminist scholars refer to Tronto's writings, also in critical ways. One of the main arguments comes from research on intersectionality. Although Tronto treats care as both a moral and a political concept, Hankyvsky (2014) asks if the concept of care as she defined it adequately attends to power. She suggests that we enhance care ethics with intersectionality, which

> . . . rejects the a priori analytic prioritization of any one category of difference, which in turn challenges assumptions that gender is always the most significant structure of difference in configurations of social inequality and by extension care work, care practices, and/or care discourses.
>
> (Hankyvsky 2014, p. 256)

Hankyvsky proposes to move beyond 'gendered manifestations of power' and look at how power operates through the intersections of different structures, relations and institutions and how this works against practicing an ethics of care.

Many feminist scholars have integrated the notion of care as well as an understanding of the 'politics of care' into their thinking, further elaborating on what a care-based approach actually means in practice. For example, Wickson et al. (2017) summarize the characteristics of a care-based approach as including

> 1) a relational worldview, 2) an emphasis on the importance of context, 3) a recognition of the significance of dependence, 4) an analysis of power, including a particular concern for those most vulnerable, 5) a granting of weight to the significance of affect, and 6) an acknowledgment of an important role for narrative.
>
> (Wickson et al. 2017, p. 195)

They also emphasize that a care-based ethics and politics must pay specific attention to the distribution of power, and particularly any abuses, inequalities, or imbalances that may exist.

In the Scandinavian context, feminist sociologists have emphasized the rationality of caring. This is an interesting move that, with respect to design, has been used to avoid essentializing notions about gender and technology (see e.g., Holth's (2014) juxtaposition of 'passionate men' and 'rational women', as well as Faulkner's (2000) notion of heterogeneous engineering). Hildur Ve (1994) used the notion of 'responsible rationality', a term that had been introduced by Björg Aase Sørensen (1982). Norwegian feminists brought it into the debate as a way of reinforcing 'the standpoint of women's dignity and abandon[ing] the tendency to explain women's behaviour as inferior or lacking in comparison with men's (e.g., fear of success, fear of conflict, being irrational, no understanding of labour unions, etc.)' (p. 329). Using the example of mothers taking care of a child, Kari Waerness (1996) insisted on the 'rationality of caring' (as opposed to scientific rationality), conceptualizing care as both 'labour' and 'love'. In caretaking 'one has to understand from the position of an insider', she argued, 'and the kind of generalized scientific knowledge one may have at best seems very insufficient in guiding one's practices' (p. 242). Care (including professional, institutional forms of caretaking) in this view is about the need of experience, relationship-building, and attentiveness/adaptability to the needs of those we take care of on top of practical skills and codified knowledge. This is an insight that we will come back to when discussing the computerization of care (Chapter 8).

There is a connection between caretaking and the many forms of invisible work that socialist feminists claimed women do to maintain the paid labour force and their domestic labours that ensure social reproduction. This has been emphasized by Maria Puig de le Bellacasa (2011): 'Understanding caring as something we do extends a vision of care as an ethically and politically charged practice, one that has been at the forefront of feminist concern with devalued labours' (p. 90). She also proposes that we 'treat matters of fact and sociotechnical assemblages as "matters of care"' and she argues 'that engaging with care requires speculative commitment to neglected things' (p. 86). With reference to debates about 'the futures predicted by software agent and smart machine enthusiasts', Lucy Suchman (2007) insists that 'the prior and more immediate question of what kinds of social relations are assumed to be desirable in these scenarios, whose interests are represented, and whose labors are erased' (p. 224) have been neglected. Hence, we may want to link to notions of social reproduction and reproduction of the paid labour force as work women have done, which historically has remained hidden from view, and debates that these 'feminized' tasks do not constitute skill by virtue of being linked to femininity, and hence are often neglected in design.

From 'the Personal Is Political' to the 'Matrix of Domination': Feminist Politics

Feminism and feminist theory are deeply political. Among the main issues of feminist politics are: How do we counteract the devaluation of women's reproductive work and, consequently, the devaluation of women? How do we in particular, bridge the private and the public spheres? And how do we make use of an intersectional perspective in addressing power relations and the inequalities they produce and reproduce? Although feminist politics may appear peripheral to the practice of design, we think it offers important perspectives on how to analyze the context in which technologies will be embedded and how to open up dialogue between different positions that should be included in design.

Ever since feminist scholars and activists coined the slogan 'The personal is political', the analysis of power relations and the structures that maintain them has been at the core of feminist theorizing. It is instructive to look back at this debate. In the 1970s many women that belonged to the early women's movement proclaimed that the private domestic sphere be made public. They

> based their demand for equal political citizenship precisely on this vision of the 'separate sphere', understood not as a dichotomy of mutually exclusive and hierarchical terms, but as a source of equal rights and responsibilities of the female sex in respect to civil society. On this basis, they did not so much challenge the sexual division of labour, as the sexual division of power.
>
> (Bock 1991, p. 5)

In particular women activists in Italy connected their demands to a radical critique of Marxism, pointing to 'the umbilical connection between the devaluation of reproductive work and the devaluation of women's social position' (Federici 1975/2014, p. 5). Silvia Federici wrote that

> ... once housework was totally naturalised and sexualised, once it became a feminine attribute, all of us as females are characterised by it. If it is natural to do certain things, then all women are expected to do them and even like doing them – even those women who, due to their social position, could escape some of that work or most of it .... We might not serve one man, but we are all in a servant relation with respect to the whole male world. This is why to be called a female is such a putdown, such a degrading thing.
>
> (Federici 1975/2014, p. 4)

Maria Mies used the term 'housewifization' to describe the naturalization and sexualization of housework, which she thought of as key to understanding women's subordination. She connected it to the development of capitalism under conditions of patriarchy, which made it possible to '"externalize and exterritorialize" costs to women, colonies, and nature' (Prügl 1996, p. 115).

'The personal is political' is often referred back to Hanna Arendt who, in the *Human Condition* (1958), had outlined a conceptual distinction between public and private that is based on a separation of spaces. Although Arendt was criticized by feminists (see e.g., O'Brien 1981), Françoise Collin, a Belgian philosopher, took up her thinking, arguing that

... women, recognized as *animal laborans*, slowly admitted into the stage of *homo faber*, are still excluded from the *activity* that is constitutive of the *polis*. ... They haven't been able to access this type of existence except by constituting their own *polis*, their own political life, among them.

(Collin 1985, p. 82)

Collin thought the separatism underlying this strategy insufficient and 'illusory'. She, in 1973, founded *Les Cahiers du Grif* (Grif stands for Groupe de recherche et d'information féministes), the first Francophone magazine of 'second wave' feminism. It provided women with a forum for debate and the possibility 'to jump out into the public sphere'. The 'dialogical structure of the magazine materialized a practice which was in itself political, for it consisted of women speaking and listening, committing and acting, thus introducing a plurality of new voices and practices into the common world' (Hoogeveen 2021, p. 168).

The private/public distinction and 'the personal is political' is like a red thread through accounts of labour-market segregation and working conditions in so-called areas of women's work. It is present in the restrictive practices of companies of allocating the work – women being thought of as easy to find and cheap, also easy to lay off and send back home (Lappe 1981); as well as in the lack of support of working women with family responsibilities. It is also evident in women's difficulties of getting a voice in the trade union movement or in the absence of gender issues from design projects. As Lamoureux (2010) pointed out, one key problem is that 'it is the public sphere that decides what is private and what is public, as well as the rules of access into the public' (pp. 151–152).

In terms of politics and policy-making the *matrix of domination* points to the need to understand how inequalities may be constituted on different levels and through different relations, among them, but not always dominantly, gender relations; and that the latter may not always be the most important in terms of politics and policy-making. The concept has been proposed by Patricia Hill Collins, who in 'Black feminist thought in the matrix of domination' (1990) elaborated the notion of intersectionality from the perspective of Afrocentric feminist thought. In what was to become highly influential in how feminists think about power she proposed a shift of thinking from additive to interlocking systems of oppression, distinguishing between four interrelated domains that organize power in societies: the structural domain – interlocking large-scale social institutions; the disciplinary domain of norms, rules, and, for example, surveillance technologies, that manage oppression and can only be overcome by resistance; the cultural domain that produces hegemonic ideologies that need unpacking to be overcome; and the interpersonal domain that 'encompasses the myriad experiences that individuals have within intersecting oppressions' (Collins 2017, p. 26). Collins emphasized the links between intersectionality and participative democracy, reflecting on what is needed for women and marginalized groups to be able to take this jump into the public sphere. Her conclusion is that this important step can only be done through developing 'roots within existing communities of inquiry and praxis as well as build[ing] new coalitional communities' (2017, p. 37).

Other feminist scholars have contributed to feminist political thinking. 'Transversal politics', a term introduced by Nora Yuval-Davis (1999, 2006) is based on the belief that 'the only way to approach "the truth" is by a dialogue between people of differential positionings, and the wider the better' (2006, p. 281). The notion of feminist solidarity understands participatory democracy as 'a form of organizing, which envisages a shared responsibility for the lives of others, working with care and intimacy, and toward social transformations that are made possible through "democratic engagement"' (Segal, 2017, p. 228).

We will take up these concepts and approaches to thinking about gender/ intersectionality in the design of computational artifacts in the last chapters of the book. There is the field of engineering ethics with its own tradition that needs consideration, looking at arguments brought forward most prominently by Hans Jonas but also at what feminist scholars contributed to the debate.

Engineering Ethics

Even before ethics became a common concern in engineering studies, scholars reflected on the political nature of technology; foremost among these was Herbert Marcuse who argued in *The one-dimensional man* (1968) that technology is not neutral as the values and interests of the ruling classes have been inscribed in it. 'The principles of modern science were *a priori* structured in such a way that they could serve as conceptual instruments for the universe of self-propelling productive control', he wrote. 'Today, domination perpetuates and extends itself not only through technology but *as* technology, and the latter provides the great legitimation of the expanding political power, which absorbs all spheres of culture' (p. 62).

Today we would avoid the technological determinism that Marcuse's thinking may suggest, knowing that technologies are socially shaped and that they are appropriated in use. The important argument Marcuse has made is that technologies have a political dimension. His example also suggests that the power that has been inscribed in technologies and organizations is somehow hidden in the routines people follow, and hence may be difficult to identify and criticize. Langdon Winner (1980) built a similar argument using the development of the tomato harvester, the functioning of which required the breeding of harder but less tasty tomatoes, as an example. The tomato harvester is the result of 'an ongoing social process in which scientific knowledge, technological invention, and corporate profit reinforce each other in deeply entrenched patterns that bear the unmistakable stamp of political and economic power' (p. 126). It is a technology that is 'thoroughly biased', in the sense that the different stakeholders involved in its development and use take totally different views on it.

Activities of making and doing have escaped scrutiny of moral and ethical questions in part because cultural discourses about technology have ascribed the characteristics of inevitability and neutrality to technological change, and in doing so have effectively taken debates about morality and ethics out of public scrutiny. One of the philosophers who emphasized the moral dimension of technologies was Hans Jonas. He argued for the ethical importance of finding ways to better predict the effects of new technologies as a way to strengthen and improve our decision-making about their design and use. He emphasized that the ethical significance of technology originates in the fact that

> the indefinite future, rather than the contemporary context of the action, constitutes the relevant horizon of responsibility. This requires imperatives of a new sort. If the realm of making has invaded the space of essential action, then morality must invade the realm of making, from which it had formerly stayed aloof.
>
> (Jonas 1984, p. 9)

Jonas pleaded for acting responsibly as a designer; however, he thought more of evaluating the design result after it was completed. Bush (1981) also sought to emphasize responsibility in design in arguing for a feminist technology assessment. However, like Jonas, her focus was on evaluating design results. Verbeek (2006) takes a stronger and more contemporary position, claiming that technologies are 'inherently moral entities', with the consequence that 'designers are doing "ethics by other means": they materialize morality. Usually, this "doing ethics" happens in an implicit way' (p. 369). Engineers have the functionalities of a design in mind and not necessarily the context of use. Verbeek's proposal to designers is to give the things they design 'a desirable form'. He concludes: 'Morality then, in a sense, becomes part of the functionality of the product' (p. 369).

This resonates with the core principle of participatory design that Robertson and Wagner (2012) define as 'that people have a basic right to make decisions about how they do their work and indeed any other activities where they might use technology' (p. 65). In their view this is

> the most contested aspect of Participatory Design, its most directly stated ethical commitment and its main point of difference to more mainstream user- or human-centred design approaches. It is why, for example, Participatory Design has important political agendas expressed by its close collaboration with identifiable political movements that are informed and underpinned by ethical discourses around human rights and a robust civil society.
>
> (Robertson and Wagner 2012, p. 65)

Recognizing the moral dimension of technologies is consonant with a feminist ethics that understands moral agency in terms of power, asking who is recognized as a moral agent, and how agency is constrained or facilitated by power relations.

Feminist scholars have proposed various approaches to engineering ethics. Under the influence of Tronto's work they took up care ethics early on as a possible source of change in the practices of engineering. Care is a notion that not only applies to human relationships. In her study of women and men shop-floor workers in the mechanical industries (*Daring to be equal*), Swedish work–life researcher Ewa Gunnarson (1994) suggested that we transfer the notion of caretaking to jobs in industry. She took up the notion of responsible rationality arguing that

> women develop an adjusted form of responsible rationality in this technical industrial work situation expressed in three care dimensions: Care for interpersonal relations at work, care for the human being in the man–machine relation and care in relation to the machine, the product and the workplace.
>
> (Gunnarson 1994, n.p.)

Gunnarsson expressed that for engineers to act in an ethically responsible way goes beyond addressing the social issues that have to do with the workplace and the relationships between workers. It also involves thinking about the relationship between people and the machines they operate, as for example the potential for development and empowerment this relationship may offer or take away from them; and it includes taking care of the machine, in terms of careful handling, maintenance, and repair.

Gunnarsson's work focuses on care as a key aspect of the contexts and situations in which technologies are put to use. It connects well with the notion of 'situated ethics' that Balka et al. (2007) use as an approach to understanding the ethical implications of situated everyday conflicts around the use of technologies. The idea behind this approach is that ethical questions do not only concern 'big' problems and dilemmas. They pose themselves with respect to the numerous small questions that people deal with in their daily life, at work or in their private lives. This insight applies to situations of technology use as well.

Pantazidou and Nair (1999) have applied the values of caring (Tronto 1993) to engineering design:

> Thus, attentiveness (caring about) ought to be present in what is conventionally thought of as need identification; Responsibility (taking care of another's needs) is required in problem conceptualization; competence (caregiving, meeting needs through action) maps to feasibility analysis, as one ensures the design meets intended needs; and responsiveness (care-receiving), is identified in the production process and iterative improvement.
>
> (Pantazidou and Nair 1999, p. 28)

They refer to Hans Jonas' claim that an ethics of engineering needs to be aspirational (rather than merely preventive), because of the obligations brought about by the power and pervasiveness of technology, and its potential to affect the global future (Nair and Bulleit 2020, pp. 71–72). Donna Riley (2009, 2013) taking up their work on care ethics in engineering, proposes to use it as an approach to educating engineering students. She asks a series of useful questions, such as

> who counts morally in engineering? Who is served, who benefits, and who pays the cost? What communities do engineers claim to represent, and who is actually represented? What modes of communication facilitate interactions in engineering, and who has access to these? How does professionalization 'deform the abilities of all concerned to hear and be heard'? Who decides what is ethical? Who holds whom accountable and how?
>
> (Riley 2013, p. 203)

While some of these questions require an analysis that reaches beyond individual design projects, some could and should be addressed by participants in such a project.

Overcoming the historical invisibility of women (and other genders) in the ways most technologies have been made is a question of 'doing justice' to their lives and experiences (Riley 2013) – and results in part from what Messing (2014) has identified as an empathy gap. In 2015, a group of designers, artists, technologists, and community organizers convened to discuss and develop the notion of 'design justice' (see Lee 2016), which builds on the idea of intersectionality and the matrix of domination. Sasha Costanza-Chok (2018) defines 'design justice' as aiming 'to ensure a more equitable distribution of design's benefits and burdens; fair and meaningful participation in design decisions; and recognition of community-based design traditions, knowledge, and practices' (p. 5). Design justice is not only concerned with the impacts technologies may have on people's everyday lives and work situations that correspond to the classic notion of technology use, it also applies to the institutional level, asking us

> to consider the ways that various design institutions reproduce and/or challenge the matrix of domination in their practices. This might include large companies (Google, Apple, IDEO), venture capitalists, standards-setting bodies (ISO, W3C, NIST), laws (such as the Americans with Disabilities Act), and universities and educational institutions that train designers.
>
> (Costanza-Chock 2018, p. 5)

Although for many these ideas are new, it is important to recognize that for over half a century – since the late 1960s – many cultures have recognized that technological change more often than not results in the unequal distribution of benefits. Indeed, it was concern for equity and the need to distribute the benefits of technological change fairly that fostered the growth of technology assessment practices in the late 1960s. As cultural understandings of technological change evolved, important developments in feminist ethics as well as philosophy of technology have contributed to the evolution of design justice, which expands our ethical focus beyond the activities of use to the making of technology.

Summary

In this chapter we have introduced readers to the ethical-political perspective on design. It serves to situate design as an ethical and political undertaking and locate our concern for gender relations as a key site for design justice, which we will return to in the final section of the book. We have shown how key concepts from feminist scholars have enhanced our understanding of ethics and politics and have added to our understanding of ethics and politics through consideration of equality, difference, social justice, and care. We have also suggested that accounting for gender issues in design – or failing to do so – are ethical and political choices with real-world consequences.

We have highlighted some key feminist debates that have implications for design, including whether in efforts to bring about a more just society we should emphasize equality or difference. The material we have touched on here led us to a discussion about relationality and context, and the ethics of care, all of which have been central to feminist discussions about care-based approaches to ethics and politics, which have implications for technology design and have contributed significantly to the ethical-political perspective. This also applies to intersectionality and the 'matrix of domination', concepts that help us understand how power as a source of inequalities is organized on different levels and what to do to enable marginalized groups to 'jump into the public sphere', become visible, and have a voice.

3

Pathways to a Gendered and Intersectional Perspective

The interviews we conducted with women who pioneered research on women's work and technology as well as with researchers who are earlier in their career and continue this tradition with their own ideas about gender and design show that the ways that people come to focus on gender are varied: they come from different disciplinary backgrounds, developed their approach in different contexts seizing different research opportunities, and forged their own pathways in making a career in women/gender studies and technology development. This chapter takes up these personal biographies, highlighting the different starting points, research interests, and struggles. The women's personal accounts go beyond official biographies and are not in any way complete. We – Anne, Ellen, Ina, and Volker – included our own pathways in this chapter.

Transitions from Computer Science

Among the women we interviewed for this book, Marja Vehviläinen, Luigina Ciolfi, Pernille Bjørn, Maria Menendez Blanco, and Marisol Wong-Villacres have a background in computer science and/or HCI and most of them have done technical work. Each of them at some point in their career got interested in gender and this interest evolved in different ways.

Marja Vehviläinen, who studied computer science and mathematics, did a master thesis in human–computer interaction, a topic that she pioneered in Finland. A report about women's careers in universities and research institutions opened her eyes to gender issues and that she was not the only one feeling that there was no place for her. But she was accepted to do a PhD in information systems at Tampere University, where she continued to study social sciences and women's studies and worked with Liisa Rantalaiho:

67

> She had a project on office automation and on office work. And that was very
> influential for me because, like, it seems that office automation, it was introduced
> into workplaces strongly in the 80s.

Marja also discovered the Nordic conferences on gender, science, and technology in the 1980s and 'those Nordic networks, they have been very important for me all the time'. She did her PhD thesis, for which she received much recognition in the PD community, on setting up and collaborating with a female office workers study circle, in which the women studied and evaluated information systems and analyzed their own work offering proposals about how IT systems can support it. While doing her research with office workers, Marja started studying social sciences, connected with women studies, and also learned how to do qualitative research that helped her with doing biographical interviews with the women in her study.

Marja continued her studies in the sociology program at the University of Toronto, where she learned about

> the situated knowledges from Donna Haraway, as it is still very important, and
> institutional ethnography how to study practices, like mapping out gendered race
> relations that are organizing everyday life or practices. That is one method of
> Dorothy Smith, and it works very well still.

Her conclusion from these first years of research are:

> I was first profiling out[1] after my master's thesis and my second time I was profiling
> out after my doctoral thesis. I was profiling out from information systems. I felt that
> I wasn't needed anymore. I then moved to work research.

At her postdoctoral stage, she continued her work on women and technology in collaboration with various centres and women's groups, seeking to understand 'how they were doing information technology for themselves, but this time it was not in the work context, but it was a sort of everyday context'. But later she ran out of funding and gradually technology received less attention in her work.

When returning from Toronto, Marja joined a group of women that discussed gendered practices and working life. They 'gathered together for five years, every month, and we were commenting each other's papers. And this group, we actually still meet each other, although it's already thirty-two years'. What she appreciates most is the experience of 'working communally'.

---

[1] Marja uses the term 'profiling out' to express that she did not fit into any academic job profile at that time.

Marja followed the path she had started with her interdisciplinary PhD against many odds, and she found multiple opportunities to continue her work on gender equality. Having been 'profiled out' from information systems, she pursued her interests in social science and gender studies, while keeping her focus on women and technology.

> However, it has not been a perfect match to be in gender studies either, because it is a sort of wrong kind of interest – being interested in technologies or nature-cultures, which I have been doing also. It should be more about gender and gender studies. But I have been sort of tolerated in there, and as I have a very broad interest.

She held a teaching position in gender studies and supervised a good number of doctoral theses in Finland and Sweden, a few of them in gender and technology or science and technology.

The first part of Marja's professional career is a story of making a transition from computer science to social sciences and women's studies, a period that involved an enormous amount of studying and learning. While she did her first academic work at a time when the first women's studies as well research on gender and technology were established as fields of work, Pernille, Luigina, Maria, and Marisol made a quite different transition from computer science to a gender and intersectional perspective.

Pernille Bjørn was the first woman who got a full professor position at the computer science department at Copenhagen University since it was started in 1970. She was not thinking to work on gender and IT at that time but was shocked when seeing the statistics and, as a full professor, she felt free to 'maybe relax more and kind of do other things that might not necessarily result in papers right away'. The *FemTech.dk* project was created as an action research project – to understand the situation of women students, create interventions, and collect data about it. It was very important for Pernille that it was not a recruitment project but a research project with publications. Over the years, Pernille worked with multiple people in *FemTech.dk* – however, most importantly she worked with Maria Menendez-Blanco and Valeria Borsotti and they have co-authored several papers. In the beginning *FemTech.dk* was about bringing more women students and faculty to computer science at the University of Copenhagen, to 'challenge the dominating narrative about gender and computing' and propose alternatives in a traditional computer science department of around seventy people. At the core of this project were workshops with high school students

> where we wanted to give them an idea about how to program microcontrollers ... [Y]ou can encrypt messages on Facebook and decrypt them. And the way you interact with it is through movement, and then different colour strings ... It also tells

a story about how interaction is not about keyboard or touchscreens, but it's about movement, the material, it doesn't look like a computer in any way.

While Pernille together with Maria Menendez-Blanco developed the concept of the *FemTech* workshops and taught the first two editions, since 2018 other people in the department have been conducting the workshops, building new design artifacts while following the principles that had been created initially. This continuation of the work (without Pernille's direct involvement) took the form of an online variant of the workshop during the pandemic where up to 100 participants could join from Denmark, Greenland, and the Faroe Islands. Another important initiative was to 'make the workshops mainstream', ensuring that the workshops would continue with someone else doing them.

A Fulbright scholarship at the University of Washington in 2019 provided Pernille with the opportunity to deepen her interest in gender and IT. Here she, in collaboration with Daniela Rosner, got interested in the women that developed computer games in the 1970s and 1980s. She managed to find fifteen of the so-called Atari women, interviewed these women, and took steps to make them visible:

> I want to celebrate what they did. Because the thing is that it's been forgotten, or nobody remembers this. And they're not part of the official archive . . . I made sure that all the Atari women . . . have Wikipedia pages in different languages and we have all the official sources linked to that, which are published on the university website, and then papers like academic papers. . . . I started to collect on Craigslist all the games made by the women. So it's just like the old cards, I just bought them on Craigslist. And then I got the women to sign up just like you know their names. And then we made these frames that kind of makes them into art pieces.

When Pernille returned to Denmark she brought all her 'Atari women artifacts' with her and 'it got a lot of attention!' The *FemTech* project and *AtariWomen. org* have received much attention in the media and Pernille has been invited to talk with journalists and participate in podcasts. The *AtariWomen* artifacts have been displayed at Emerald City ComicCon, Seattle Retro Gaming, The Living Computer Museum, and the Danish National Art Gallery (SMK). In the fall of 2022, Pernille together with Maria Menendez-Blanco and Valeria Borsotti published an open-access book about the *FemTech* research called *Diversity in computer science: Design artefact for equity and inclusion*, which has been downloaded thirteen thousand times as of February 2023.

Luigina Ciolfi studied communication sciences at the University of Siena (Italy), specializing in human–computer interaction. She holds a PhD from the University of Limerick (Ireland). She defines herself as an HCI and CSCW researcher and scholar. Ten years ago, Luigina started research on mobile workers – people who don't have an office and work from many places – together with a colleague from sociology, Dr Breda Gray, who is an expert in women studies and who

> started teasing out all kinds of gender dimensions of that, which obviously to me, it was like a revelation. So obviously, I knew that it was an issue, but it never occurred to me to kind of build it into my own research ... And from there it has become a kind of a recurrent theme in all the work that I have done on the subject of flexible work and mobile work.

Notably, the gender dimension of mobile work is one of the core themes in a monograph that Breda and Luigina co-authored (together with Fabiano Pinatti) and published in 2020. Through her work on a series of projects and on a book on these topics, she has become more and more influenced by research by feminist scholars such as Arlie Russell Hochschild, Judy Wajcman, Lisa Adkins, Christena Nippert-Eng, and Rosalind Gill.

Another connection to gender and feminist theory for Luigina was when she, towards the end of her PhD, was looking into the experience of place and how technology affects it. She came across the writings of Doreen Massey:

> the whole idea of place, not just as a location, but as a process as something that is emergent and co-constructed, and how she talks about gendered experiences of it. And the whole idea that the flow of places and merging is linked to all kinds of agencies and gender agencies and for example, women's place
> experiences are different.

Throughout her career she collaborated with cultural heritage institutions in various design activities. This is still one of her main areas of interest, and she points to the need to think of the relationship between heritage institutions and communities from a gender point of view. Cultural heritage also has a strong connection with refugee and migrant communities, requiring an intersectional approach when developing technology design. One of the collaborations she built up was with

> the People's History Museum in Manchester, which is an activist Museum, focussing on labor history, and social movements and workers' rights. And they were looking at communities of refugees who are LGBTQ and are refugee because they are LGBTQ, because in their country, they can't live their lives, or else they get arrested or worse. And their relationship to culture is really interesting. Because, you know, back in their country of origin, culture is encoded in a way that has certain values and they feel it doesn't belong to them. Whereas when they found themselves in that museum with, for example, the history of gay rights in the UK, and all the material that is archived there, in terms of all the victories of social justice that were achieved, they feel like that's a place for them in the discourse around heritage.

Luigina also became involved in initiatives to do with gender diversity in STEM academic careers while still working as a professor in the Department of Computing at Sheffield Hallam University, such as mentoring early career women and identifying the barriers women and girls face in STEM education, including HCI education:

> as a human–computer interaction researcher, obviously, the relationship between people and technology has always been there in ways that is problematic, as much as in ways that maybe is productive to improve people's lives. And, when I was a student, gender wasn't one of the explicit dimensions of the type of research that we do.

The focus on gender opened new research aspects for her within projects, past and current, such as for example the notion of emotional labour and gender differences in engaging with it, as a mobile worker working from home but also in workplaces – 'it is emotion, maintenance, relationship maintenance, and this is highly gendered'.

Luigina has spent most of her professional life as

> a woman in a predominantly male-dominated subject, which is computer science, I've always been very keenly aware of gender issues to do with the perception of women in technology and the perception of gender in relation to technical innovation.

This changed in 2020 when she became full professor at the School of Applied Psychology at University College Cork, Ireland, 'where the majority of our students are women, and the majority of academics are women, and I'm the one who talks about technology'. This has given her opportunities to further reflect on gendered aspects of teaching and doing research.

Maria Menendez-Blanco, who joined the *FemTech* project as a postdoc had already participated on a European project with the aim to examine the 'leaky pipeline' argument as member of a multidisciplinary group at the Information Engineering and Computer Science department of the University of Trento led by Antonella de Angeli and Vincenzo D'Andrea. After having engaged in research on the institutional aspects of gender, she felt frustrated about the fact that in universities the focus is mostly on recruiting women, 'and they were coming, and they couldn't find a nice environment'. One of her concerns is the physical spaces women enter when they decide to study computer science. She has a folder in her phone,

> which is called sexism in everyday life. I take pictures of all kinds of sexist images, that I see ... the toilet in the department, which is pure porn ... or the student-run cafeteria that still is extremely misogynistic as a space.

Maria encountered feminist literature only after she already had begun writing about the experiences of *FemTech*. This was an occasion for her to start a reading program: 'Feminist HCI' by Shaowen Bardzell, works by Sarah Fox, Jennifer Rode, Daniela Rosner, Katta Spiel, Sarah Ahmed, and many others.

Marisol Wong-Villacres graduated as a computer engineer in Ecuador and worked for a while in industry as a developer before going 'totally into academia'. She did a masters in HCI at the University of Bloomington – her advisor was Shaowen Bardzell:

> And the program in Indiana University was all about the humanities, and nothing about development of technologies necessarily. And so that changed everything for me. And gradually, I started working more and more like participatory design, more and more with more vulnerable groups in my country, when I came back. So, the idea was, in my mind, these feminist ideas are out there, but I don't fully understand how they go together with technology. And then in getting involved in academia allowed me to see how different scholars were using this framework that Shaowen Bardzell had already proposed.

When doing her PhD at Georgia Tech, she got excited about the notion of care and intersectionality, seeking to understand 'how these theories, ideas from other people could enrich our understanding of technologies, especially in developing countries ... and how we can use it to unpack complexity'. For example, before doing her PhD she had collected data in Ecuador after an earthquake about people's initiatives after the event.

> So, there were so many activities that people were doing that had to do more with this human side of a need to repair and care ... And that was something that the literature in HCI was also looking at. So, we decided to engage a little bit with this idea of care and wrote a paper on that.

Marisol made a lot of effort to introduce an intersectional perspective and the notion of care into the contexts in which she was working. However, her encounters with feminist theory were complicated. These concepts, she feels, are tightly connected to discourses that she finds difficult to relate to 'in the right way'. She expresses her concerns with reference to Chandra Mohanty's 'Under Western Eyes'. Marisol observes,

> ... it's interesting, academically, the way HCI works, where we are like, there's HCI, and there's ICT4D (information and communication technology for development), ICT4D is for the poor people, and HCI is for the world ... the whole of like keeping things in silos not being able to actually show solidarity naturally, directly to each other.

Being from Ecuador and working in the USA was a strong incentive for her to focus more and more on issues of culture. In her work with Latino immigrants in Atlanta she observed that the educational technologies used in schools

... were not necessarily being helpful to Latino immigrant parents, not only because of the language, there were a lot of things that these technologies were assuming culturally, and in general, about parents, that Latino immigrant parents didn't, weren't working in the way the technologies were expecting.

She decided to look at problems

more from a cultural base, like, what are the strengths that people have? And also, what are the cultural roots of those strengths? What are the systemic ... roots of those strengths? And also the way systems are preventing those strengths to be mobilized to actually produce the impact that communities want to produce or have?

After having completed her PhD, Marisol went back to Ecuador. She had come to the USA with her husband and their kids, because this 'was the future'. She had coped with the pressure to be successful, she had tried to 'sound respect-ful' and not to appear 'superficial':

But for me, it was like, there might be things that we get excited about, because they seem so promising for our own agendas. But maybe we don't understand them fully. And it's harmful to move forward.

Marisol teaches at the School of Electricity and Computer Engineering, and she continues her work with immigrants with the Venezuelan diaspora in Ecuador.

Growing into an 'Ally' of a Feminist/Intersectional Approach to Design

Volker Wulf does not define himself as 'a classical gender researcher'. However, his pathway from studying computer science in the 1980s at RWTH (Rheinisch-Westfälische Technische Hochschule) Aachen, Germany, to his present position at Siegen University where he built a strong research group in socio-informatics made him an 'ally' of those pursuing gender and technology studies. As a student, Volker engaged in activities that had a political and partly activist impetus. These included organizing students around the topics of technology assessment as well as in solidarity with the Global South and trying to establish and institutionalize 'Computers & Society' teaching in the RWTH's computer science curriculum (though with-out success). At the end of his interdisciplinary studies, he was hired on an early groupware design project at the University of Bonn. Over time, he and his group strengthened the ECSCW (European CSCW) research program by intensifying the interconnectedness of ethnographic work, the design of innovative IT artifacts, and the development of social practices. They suggested that an empirical understanding of the relevant social practices ought to become an integral part of IT design in which empirical and participatory design elements would interweave over a longer period of time.

Having established a design paradigm in traditional work settings, Volker was eager to explore the emancipatory effects of digitalization in other domains. He started to develop a network of computer clubs in disadvantaged neighbourhoods, at first tackling the problem of integration in German neighbourhoods in which a high percentage of migrants were living. Later on, he and his colleagues transferred their approach to computer clubs to other cultures, such as Palestinian refugee camps and disadvantaged regions in Morocco. During the last decade, Volker and his colleagues expanded their research agenda investigating IT design in countries such as Tunisia, Syria, Madagascar, Botswana, Saudi Arabia, and Iran, working preferably with those who were political engaged, disadvantaged, suppressed, marginalized, or overlooked. From the beginning of the Arab Spring, the group expanded its research activities into understanding the role of IT, specifically social media, in supporting political activists and opposing authoritarian regimes. This research program has as its long-term aim improving the quality of life in the Global South.

Volker's normative position and research style is oriented towards social justice. Epistemologically, Volker emphasizes the influence Lucy Suchman's work had on him. He thinks of her as having had a crucial role in establishing ethnographic methods, thinking, and worldviews while framing a participatory design agenda in CSCW and PD.

Following an agenda of societal relevance and social justice, gender issues became a more explicit part of his research activities. During his time at RWTH Aachen, Britta Schinzel had made him aware of gender dimensions in computing. Christiane Floyd became a role model of an outstanding academic following a societally engaged agenda in PD. In Siegen, gender issues were immanent at the traditional workplaces, in computer clubs, as well as in school settings. He explored the gendered appropriation of programming tools in computer clubs together with Anne Weibert and Jennifer Rode. Specifically, they became interested in smart textiles as a means to engage girls (and boys) in computational thinking.

Based on these experiences, Volker and Anne have worked on gender-sensitive design of computer curricula in German middle schools. They elaborated a curriculum that would engage students from the beginning in designing and programming IT applications: namely by avoiding an early focus on mathematical concepts of computability, emphasizing instead creativity and practice orientation. They believe that such a curriculum would not only engage female students but also a wider variety of students with a design orientation.

Politics, Feminist Activism, and the Influence of the Women's Movement

Joan Greenbaum started out with computing, moved on to get a PhD in economics, and later became a professor at the City University of New York, doing research on work, gender, and engaging with PD. As a young single mother, she needed a job that paid well and started work as a programmer at IBM at the time of the big mainframe computers. As she relates,

> I very quickly realized that my interest was in systems development because all of the issues that were coming to us, the tricky ones were handed to me. Because they involved people. And no one else seemed able to involve people. So, I liked going out and talking to people and trying to figure out what it was that they really wanted or were trying to say, and this is in 1967.

So she 'got into technology literally through a back door into IBM'. Around 1968 she joined Computer People for Peace and became active organizing tech workers. She edited the newsletter *Interrupt*, which 'was a signal – you could program an interrupt to the mainframe. We meant it in a political way' (*Logic (s) Magazine* 6 (2019) https://logicmag.io/play/joan-greenbaum-on-the-early-days-of-tech-worker-organizing/). She also realized that she was really interested in work and started studying the computer industry, observing

> that it was work that was being changed by management, something that I had seen at IBM and also experienced at a startup company. We saw that management had a way of reorganizing work – so that of course, it went to the lowest paid people. And what I was experiencing in the US was, women were getting those jobs, because they were accepting lower pay. By the mid 1970s commercial programming was almost 50 percent women.

While doing research and teaching Joan continued doing political work, such as participating in the unionization of her university, and she still is doing work with the union, like for example training staff in health and safety issues during the pandemic. Feminist studies have always been about trying to give voice and make things visible that are not, she argues, and it is important to make the struggles that are needed visible. For example, when thinking about STEM and opening the doors for women, women need to ask, 'What happens when you get in? What support is there? What are the alternatives? Who are you going to align with for strategy to get … being paid well, and have interesting work?'

Toni Robertson's undergraduate degree was in art history and philosophy. She worked for many years as a printmaker and poster-maker. Some of her political posters are exhibited in the National Gallery of Australia in Canberra and other museums. Toni became involved in feminism in the early 1970s and was a key member of the Sydney Women's Art Movement. She had to give up doing artwork as a result of health concerns from chemical exposure and retrained as a computer scientist with a graduate degree in data processing. She then spent a few years 'as a systems lackey in industry' and after that enrolled in a masters degree in cognitive science. She was already familiar with the work of Foucault, Freud, Merleau-Ponty, and Deleuze, as well as the work of feminist philosophers 'of the body' including Luz Grosz and Moira Gatens. She revisited these works as she wanted to further develop her understanding of 'power, basically, and how it's embedded in infrastructure'. While studying cognitive science she enjoyed arguing with 'the philosophers who were absolutely in the cognitivist mind–brain dichotomy, brain in a jar – artificial intelligence will be able to do anything we can do in ten years, you know, that stage, and totally missing the body'. Toni points out an interesting difference between the philosophers and researchers at the medical faculty for whom the interior of the brain was still hard to study. They had an

> enormous vocabulary ... for expressing doubt. Whereas the philosophers who were just making stuff up, were absolutely sure of the mind, body, spirit. .... And in the meantime, the people who were actually working with the bodies and working with the physical system that enabled us to live in the world, were tentatively taking these little steps.

Toni then encountered ideas about situated, embodied cognition, which led her to Lucy Suchman's work and from there to feminist perspectives on technology design and most importantly to PD. She also learned about the women, work, and computerization conferences and thought 'I have to find these women'. She sent Lucy the catalogue from her last poster exhibition and, having arrived in Palo Alto, she said, 'I found that all of that work, I thought that I can see a path in computer science'.

Toni continued her political work as a full professor at the University of Sydney (UTS), for example setting up the Indigenous Participation in IT program at UTS. She and her team interviewed educators and Indigenous people with the idea to develop 'a non-heroic program' that simply focussed on supporting Indigenous students through the particular challenges of IT. She told the dean at some point, 'These people do not want to be made into public figures; they want to be supported in their studies. And that's a different way of doing it'. She also supported the election campaigns of independent candidates in various ways, including organizing and working on polling booths and scrutineering for her candidate during the vote count after the elections.

Ellen Balka took a different path from an early interest in alternative or green technology, a geography major and environmental studies minor, and courses in technology assessment to participating in the first graduate degree program in women's study in Canada where she went to work with Maggie Benston. For her PhD she did the first study that fully explored the use of computer networks for feminist social change (1991). She was fortunate in that she was also working with a national women's group in Canada that was trying to use computer networks in their work, and they became a site of participatory engagement for her. Working with them – they flew her to various places to give workshops or talk to board members about computer networking – yielded a lot of insights about the challenges of implementing computer networks in small nonprofits.

An important conference for her was where she

> met Judy Smith and Corky Bush. Judy had written a piece about gender and alternative technology that argued that women were disproportionately disadvantaged by the 'back to the land' movement, and that women were getting the short end of the stick with alternative technology. Corky had written a really brilliant piece about doing technology assessment from a feminist perspective. I immediately connected with both of them, and they became really important influences for me going forward.

Like Joan, Ellen learned programming in the early 1980s, when taking a job in a hippie engineering firm that did work on alternative energy research and solar homes. She was the only woman when she started and

> got to do all of the really cool technical work. After a while, they hired a junior guy and all of a sudden, I had to struggle to be given the work I had previously done. I was learning in the workforce about gender politics.

After having moved to Vancouver, she got a job at the Brotherhood of Railway and Airline Clerks Airline division, to do a study looking at how technological change was influencing work. About 75 percent of the Brotherhood's Airline Division was made of women.

Ellen was always politically engaged. For example, in Newfoundland she organized two workshops called 'the university in the community', which brought women's organizations and social change organizations together with members of the university community to talk about how to work together. Another important collaboration for her was with a feminist collective in Vancouver called Women's Skills. They ended up getting grants to study women work and technology, and there was also a city-wide group of academics, working with trade unions that met regularly in the late 1980s to talk about research. Women's Skills micro-technology working group produced two books based on case studies. A lot of the work focussed on the skills and simultaneous upskilling of certain jobs, and the lack of homogeneity of changes. It also highlighted how often when women's jobs became more skilled, the pay did not go up. Ellen also got interested in Francophone ergonomics in the mid-1990s, which combined qualitative and quantitative methods.

IT in health care became Ellen's main field of work. She put together a large SSHRC grant that addressed computerization of women's work and health care. It had three foci: the role of women and issues they faced in searching for online health information; work practice studies that focussed on varied aspects of health sector work; and issues related to data, indicators, technology, and women's work. An affiliation with Vancouver General Hospital provided the opportunity of doing embedded ethnography, where researchers are embedded in work contexts for long periods of time. She engaged in several small projects within the hospital attempting to solve problems for the organization while at the same time collecting ethnographic data to inform her academic research. For the last decade she has focussed on engaging with design of a single system, ActionADE, the adverse drug event reporting system.

> I continue to focus on gender. However, I can also say that in the last project in some ways, it was the toughest focus on gender, although my co-investigator was also a woman. That project (and others before it) got me thinking about how professional affiliations can soften the blow of one's gender – until they don't.

Ellen considers herself in many ways fortunate as she found and later created contexts that allowed her to develop her research – 'I was able to craft a career which focussed largely on gender and technology from the start'. All these opportunities are a result of Ellen's activist and action-oriented approach to research and her ability to develop relationship with women's groups, trade unions, or hospital administrations. She sees herself as having had a 'male career'. She did not take time out of the paid labour force and she was willing to travel and accept visiting positions abroad: 'And some people would even say, some of my behaviors are male, but I still got treated like shit and did not get paid like a guy and didn't progress like a guy would'.

Angelika Strohmayer embarked on a long transition from doing an undergraduate degree in primary school education in Linz, Austria, to working on a master's degree in international development and education in Newcastle in England, where she started 'getting really interested in technologies and what they can bring' to her present position at Northumbria University School of Design, where she is one of the co-leads and founding members of the Design Feminist Research Group. Her master's thesis was based on research with people experiencing homelessness in Romania, where she had previously lived, working in a computer science research lab where 'technologies just kept coming up, even though I wasn't necessarily prompting it, and they came up in really interesting ways'.

Angelika has built long-standing collaborations with Changing Lives, which is a national charity in the North East of England, where she for the last six-to-seven years has been working primarily with its women's and children's services to explore the inclusion of trauma-informed, craft, and technology-related support structures for the people the organization supports and their staff.

Working on her PhD at that time, she first focussed on designing technologies and integrating technologies into service delivery; later she collaborated with sex-work support services, all of it deeply political work. She also moved for a short while to a criminology department. In the Design School she is doing 'lots of things around topics of safety and technologies, as well as kind of craft, feminism, and social justice'.

Angelika remembers that 'I wasn't calling my work feminist when I started. I didn't really have that language. Looking back, I know that I was doing a lot of very feminist things'. Her first big conference was CHI in 2015 – 'and I felt so incredibly out of place'. She and others in her research group had the feeling that 'topics related to women were just sidelined or openly made fun of in some instances'. Out of their regular meetings grew the *fempower.tech* network, 'which ended up becoming a new international network of HCI, researchers, practitioners, other technologists coming together around the topic of thinking and understanding what feminism is or could be'. At the next CHI conference, she was carrying around 'a cross stitch with lots of different threads and needles, and just encourag[ing] people to come have a chat and do some cross stitch'. Angelika developed a political orientation 'to inclusion, to respect, to responsibility and kindness', engaging in 'labour organizing, feminist organizing', with an emphasis on community, collaboration, participation, and collective action.

Science, Technology, and Society Studies and Its Relationship with Gender and Work

Lucy Suchman and Judy Wajcman have been and still are highly influential for all who do research on feminist/queer theory, technology, and work. We focus on parts of their stories that are of relevance for this book. Both are strongly connected to science, technology, and society studies (STS) but their pathways to a gendered and intersectional perspective are quite different.

Lucy Suchman started to work at Xerox Palo Alto Research Center (PARC) in the 1970s where she led a small interdisciplinary research program concerned with the ethnographically based design of digital technologies. Her first engagement with gender was when she and Brigitte Jordan decided to write a paper together for the 1988 Women, Work and Computerization Conference (Suchman and Jordan 1988):

> We had this crazy idea of drawing together the work that Gitti had done on midwives in the Yucatan and birth and technology more generally, and my work on office automation, particularly women office workers and procedural office work. The through line there, the thing that joined these two completely different and unrelated kinds of work, was the erasure of women's knowledge.

With respect to childbirth the argument was built upon Gitti's observation that 'when you have fetal monitors then you no longer have to listen to the woman giving birth or look at her', because you have this technology 'that's telling you what's really going on'. With respect to office automation, Lucy drew from her critique of the assumption that the knowledge of women office workers was 'fully captured by the procedural representations of their work'. She became deeply interested in developments in feminist theory, including Donna Haraway's notion of situated knowledges and 'the idea of moving from a universalized figure of the knower'. This inspired her well-known notion of located accountability and her writings about feminist STS and the sciences of the artificial (Suchman 2002, 2007). However, Lucy sees her work as having been less specifically focussed on gender than having been informed and inspired by feminist research that also shaped her attention to 'small "p" politics of the valuations of invisible labor' (Suchman 1995).

'Each of us comes to feminism in different ways', Lucy remarks, characterizing her own trajectory:

> ... my identification with feminism came relatively late. And it was almost more a discovery that I was a feminist than an aspiration to be one. It was recognizing that all of the things that I thought and cared about, the people whose ideas are most generative and powerful for my thinking, are feminists.

In hindsight, however, she acknowledges that in some of her ethnographic work, such as a project with the California Department of Transportation (Caltrans), she left the gender implications 'somewhat more implicit'. A key figure in that project about civil engineers designing the alignment of a bridge was an 'incredibly eloquent and thoughtful' woman, who Lucy interviewed on her practices at her CAD workstation (Suchman 2000). Lucy saw her as an example of a person with a 'much fuller embodied understanding of the fate of the object that she was working on, than the rendering of it on her workstation'. In retrospect, Lucy sees important connections between this engineer's appreciation for the value of situated knowledges and her experience as a woman in engineering.

Judy Wajcman's background is in sociology. Her main transition was from studying work as a 'labour process' person to STS, where she initiated gender and technology studies: 'I was a sociologist of work and employment, and came into this through work, through knowing about factories and assembly lines, and I think that is a different origin story, a bit separate from the typical STS one'. Judy has not been as close to the practice of IT design as Lucy was during her time at Xerox PARC. Her initial interest was in how both women and men combined working and family, given the domestic division of labour. It was the beginning of the women's movement, when one of the key topics was looking at different types of work (both paid and unpaid), how they are differentially evaluated in terms of wages, what skills they required, and 'how much of that has to do with femininity and masculinity'. 'In terms of my origins', Judy remarks,

> I think of those things, really, the sociology and history of science, domestic technology and studies of work and the intersection between them are, I think, some of the things that really were part of my formation.

In 1985 Judy, together with Donald MacKenzie, published an influential anthology on the social shaping of technology and, in 1991, *Feminism confronts technology*, which was one of the first major studies that analyzed the genderedness of technologies and their influence on women's lives – work that later developed into the notion of 'gendered technoscience' or technofeminism, as her book was titled. Reflecting on early work on science, technology, and gender, she emphasizes the need to pay attention to where feminist theories of science and technology come from, the key concepts that were shaped back in the 1970s and 1980s. For example, 'the radical thing' to talk about then was the technical as socio-technical, about science and technology as a culture, and 'all of that fantastic feminist literature on science, biology, the body ... That was very important for me, and it stayed with me always, you know, those deconstructions'. She also reminds us of

> all of the technologies that we analyzed, and the examples we used, in the 80s and 90s, and how to try and bring those intellectual tools to look at what seems more abstract, such as artificial intelligence and the automation of various decisions, and the ways in which similar issues are coming up.

Judy is continuing her work on gender and technology in her role as a fellow at the Alan Turing Institute in London, where she directs the project Women in Data Science and AI.

Coming from the Margins and Even Further Out

Being relegated 'to the margins' is a common experience of all those who do not fit into the academic mainstream. Marja has been quite explicit about being 'profiled out' as she calls it, and maybe some others we interviewed would see being at the margins as one of the characteristics of their careers. For *Ina Wagner* this experience has been formative of a large part of her professional life. She studied physics, graduating with a PhD in nuclear physics to then embark on a long trajectory, which started with her strong interest in historical and social aspects of physics, a topic that attracted many left-wing physicists at that time. As an assistant professor in the Physics Department of the University of Vienna in the 1970s, she attempted to develop a socio-historical and project-oriented approach to physics education in schools, which was not received well, and the few high school teachers with whom she collaborated were discouraged by the school authorities to carry these ideas into their teaching.

Ina was aware that she needed to qualify herself to be able to work on the topics she was interested in and worked her way through an enormous amount of literature – from the more classic social science disciplines, psychology, psychoanalysis (and Marxism), (social) history of science and technology, to the writings of the Frankfurt School. She turned into an 'autodidact' and never acquired a formal social science degree. At that time, she also worked on a book *Die neue Ordnung der Welt. Zur Sozialgeschichte der Naturwissenschaften 1500–1700* (The new ordering of the world: A social history of the sciences 1500–1700), which was published in 1984. Her readings brought her to the feminist critique of science and technology, and she wrote her first papers on women and science; the first one for an invitational seminar 'Grenzprobleme der Naturwissenschaften' (Problems at the 'borders' of science) (1983) at ETH (Eidgenössische Technische Hochschule) Zürich in honor of Paul Feyerabend (who was not a friend of feminist theory and quite dismissive of her talk). About the same time, she was invited to a small seminar in Athens organized by Helga Nowotny and Karin Hausen, which resulted in an edited book, *Wie männlich ist die Wissenschaft?* (How male are the sciences?).

A project on young women in non-traditional occupations (carpentry, auto mechanics, electricians, etc.) that the women's section of the Austrian Ministry of Social Affairs asked her to do, brought her closer to work issues and

German industrial sociology, which had a strong section of women's studies, to which she felt attracted. A second study for the Ministry on office automation in five large organizations in the public and private sector laid the grounds for her being appointed Professor of Informatics at TU (Technische Universität) Wien. By that time, she had already published widely using the empirical material from her projects and she embarked on yet another transition to CSCW research and PD. Although the specific research fields she engaged with on this journey were different, Ina sees gender, technology, and work as forming a strong 'red thread' through them.

Ina feels to have been a person at the margins and as having experienced both, being excluded/isolated, and that marginality can be a powerful experience. The 'normalization' of her career started when she first travelled to and became active in international women's conferences, such as GASAT (Gender and Science and Technology) and later the IFIP (International Federation for Information Processing) Women, Work and Computerization conferences, where she met many of the women with whom she is still in contact today – among them Joan, Marja, and later Ellen. Then came the first COST Action (international research networks funded by the EU) that helped her forge connections with colleagues from CSCW and PD with whom she also worked on European projects. But this great experience of being embedded in a research community did not translate to the institutional level at her university, where Ina was for a long time perceived as 'other' and became only gradually accepted – as one of the older faculty members remarked, 'We must acknowledge that she has a PhD in physics!'

Ingrid Erickson was trained in work studies at the Center for Work, Technology and Organization at Stanford University, but she also has a history with CSCW, including a strong interest in the European approach. She remarks feeling 'slightly out of both communities and inside both communities at the same time'. Ingrid did her undergraduate and first master's degree in religion. She moved towards technology, when she, in 1999–2000, did her second master's degree at the University of Michigan School of Information, where 'Gary and Judy Olson were really influential to me'.

Her interest in religion was 'always very gender-oriented' and it spurred her interest in norms:

> Social systems, and now I look at socio technical systems: why and how are those social systems organized the way that they are? What are the values that motivate them? What are the norms that those values put into place? You know, how are they materialized into certain designs, into certain practices?

Some of Ingrid's commitments – 'creating structures for equity . . . so everyone has a voice' and to working collectively, because this makes everyone's work better' – date back to the 1980s and 1990s.

One of her formative experiences was when she was in junior college and spent a year as a student in Nepal, at a time of political trouble with a lot of Tibetan refugees. This was when she got interested in how religion was practiced 'in these interstitial places'. She realized that Buddhism 'is a very inclusive set of ideas, but it's practiced, very gendered'. She did her thesis on Buddhism in the USA wondering 'about how the culture of the United States was shifting or shaping the practice of women who are participating in Buddhism'. She then went on to study religion at the University of Chicago Divinity School continuing the theme of culture and religion. She became a book editor, using her role to 'focus a little bit' on gender. She also did Asian studies with a focus on gender and found herself 'just wrestling and talking to people'. This deep interest in people and cultures was 'moved by people and stories . . . people's ideas'. Today, Ingrid considers herself a scholar of work and technology, with an interest in gender and in the future of work. She describes how feminism has influenced her approach to teaching:

> I see women realize their own power and/or voice or that perspective, and how that perspective actually then can be applied toward decisions that they make about their own career, their own path . . . there's this kind of voice meets voice meets voice sort of idea . . . I consider that to be a very
> feminist, pedagogical maneuver.

Anne Weibert is a journalist by training. She completed her diploma degree at Dortmund University. During her studies she was part of a research project that was looking into mechanisms of journalism reporting and news coverage in the USA, Canada, and in Germany, and by comparing the structures in the three countries was aiming to figure out how these mechanisms support or discourage diversity. Gender was neither actively addressed in this research nor was technology explicitly in focus. However, looking back, this is where her interest in the topic has a root.

> Because a take-away from this research work for me was the insight how powerful small changes in the organization of [journalism] work can be, such as
> implementing rules about newsroom diversity, e.g. in regard to who gets to report what, giving journalists a visible face in [newspaper] reporting, so it becomes apparent to readers, if there is a migrant, a woman, a man, a young person, an old person . . . doing the reporting. Also, how much effort and patience is needed, until changes are implemented and have an impact. And how very much the topic of diversity in the media is also connected to learning opportunity.

When she started as a research associate in socio-informatics at the University of Siegen, Anne worked on a project that initiated computer clubs as spaces for an open and low threshold acquisition of computer and media skills at the local neighbourhood level. She came to value the principles of PD and action research, because

> there is 'built in' a continuous reminder to reflect on how and with whom to approach finding an answer, developing a solution or building a piece of technology or implementing a socio-technical initiative. To be mindful about the inaccessibility that [design] research can bring along, and to make an effort to minimize these barriers and think about how to invite and include the perspectives that people can bring to the table. Have them realize they have a place there.

In the computer club projects Anne learned to appreciate constructionist approaches to appropriating technologies – to have people connect a learning topic with materials, things, relations, experiences from their individual every-day life. With Jennifer Rode she used e-textiles in working with young girls and boys

> and it was the open atmosphere of the computer club, I think, which helped with having those two positions move towards each other, so that a spectrum of learners felt comfortable. A liking for coding and electronics helped with curiosity for sewing, and a fondness with sewing fostered a learning interest for coding and electronics.

Anne mentions that she was still a child in the early days of gender and technology studies. She notes, however, a shift, or a broadening of attention – to not only look at how to enable access

> but more broadly and more fundamentally look at how to create conditions that let girls, let women, let a diverse range of people want to stay and to participate . . . creating welcoming conditions.

Anne has engaged in other gender-related research in Siegen, but her main focus is on learning. From 'everything that's evolving around chatGPT at the moment' and the danger that AI-based technologies perpetuate biases and discrimination, she concludes that it is important to

> make an effort for more low-cost, open-access materials and activity. So many so very cool tools and technologies were developed around that recognition that there is a broad diversity of learners to speak to and engage with regarding computing and programming skills. But much of this is just so expensive.

In one of the computer club projects, Anne and her team devised an activity that combined origami with basic electronics and programming and this was great, because the children could 'take it home': paper as a material is everywhere, LEDs and coin cell batteries are available for cents, so we could see the learning take off, to the playground, to children's homes ... and come back to the computer club unexpectedly weeks later, when we had already considered the topic closed and had moved on to another activity.

Marginalization and Its Consequences

Women who are doing research on gender and technology from a feminist/ queer and intersectional perspective often experience marginalization or straightforward discrimination. Be it that they find out that they earn less than their male colleagues, even those who have published considerably less; be it that they have difficulties acquiring funding or getting their papers accepted or that they are overlooked when it comes to promotion; be it that their research turns out not to be helpful for their professional career. Judy remembers

> Cynthia Cockburn saying to me, and we're going back like thirty years or so. When she had done her work on the microwave oven, which is just such a classic book, right? It is such a brilliant book. It's completely under-cited, undervalued, and I was thinking of doing a project, I can't remember if it was on sewing machines or on another domestic technology. And she just said to me: Judy, don't choose a domestic technology. It's just kind of career damaging.

Maria and Pernille encountered many obstacles when trying to publish their work in *FemTech*. While the project was highly visible in Denmark, academic recognition came rather late. 'I have never had rejected so many papers in my entire life', Maria states. She counted six rejects, one of them a desk reject, with various arguments:

> They say: important topic; very nice; this is about STEM education; doesn't belong to CHI ... an expert in feminist studies said that it wasn't feminist enough. And of course, it wasn't feminist enough ... because I had no idea about feminism ...
> It was also like we didn't mention inclusivity, we didn't have a good measure of how we included people. They didn't know what was the relevance ... [I]t was always the problem that it was not grounded enough in feminism and intersectionality ... because we were only looking at women.

We think this number of rejects is extraordinary. While there may have been legitimate arguments that have to do with the scientific quality of the papers, they also reflect that papers on gender issues still have difficulties finding a place in IT-related conferences and that reviewers have strong ideas about how to present and use feminist concepts. Maria got the impression that

I'm really like, kind of, I don't know … like shooting myself in the foot. Not publishing! I mean, I like this topic, it is very interesting but by working on this topic I have the feeling I'm actually ruining my own career.

She in the meantime also worked on papers about civic participation that got accepted – 'so, it's not that we were doing bad research, or that we are not able to do research'. Maria also mentions several encounters (for example, after having given a keynote) where she felt rejected and humiliated by professors who had valued her technical work. Academic recognition for *FemTech* came with a book publication *Diversity in computer science: Design artefacts for equity and inclusion* (2022).

In Marisol's story, problems with getting her papers with an intersectional perspective published are intermeshed with feeling 'constantly dismissed' when she came to do her PhD at Georgia Tech in Atlanta. This had to do on the one hand with being from Ecuador:

> People don't know whether we're Western or not, starting from there. Because we are Latin Americans … So it was like, OK, we're not Western, but definitely not as exotic as Indians or like South Africans or Chinese. We're not as exotic. So, what are we? And so, what's coming from that understanding?

Another alienating experience was that in the USA Marisol found herself being considered a woman of colour:

> In Ecuador I'm not a woman of colour. Of course, I have some colour on my skin, but I'm just a woman. If you are not Black or Indigenous, people don't even tell you, you're a person of colour. … In my case, I'm Mestiza. And I don't go around saying I'm Mestiza, it's so obvious, it doesn't make part of my identity at all. Once you move to the US, you have to undertake a new identity.

Marisol's experiences have both a deeply personal but also a theoretical dimension, which has been addressed by feminist scholars from other cultures in their fight against the hegemony of Western thinking as visible in the growing body of literature on postcolonialism.

Discrimination at the workplace is something that predominantly affects those that are perceived as 'other' – women and other genders or simply people that are thought of being different in a variety of ways. There are a lot of data about the obstacles women encounter in academia and the professional careers we describe in this chapter provide examples. Joan's experiences are typical of a women's career in the 1970s and 1980s (and later). She worked as a lecturer at LaGuardia Community College, which is part of City University of New York – 'it was a very, very exciting job and one that I really wanted. And I was in what was then called the data processing department. And of course, I was the first woman. And this was in 73'. After ten years she did not get promoted to assistant professor.

> The department didn't see any reason why I should be despite the fact that I was publishing way more than the rest of the department. I also focussed on cooperative education, which LaGuardia was dedicated to, and adult education, which is what were the pillars of what the college was founded on. I was looking at education and women. And they didn't think that had anything to do with technology, from their perspective, which was mathematics. So, I wasn't promoted. I then got promoted because the union had just been formed. . . . Called the professional staff union, and they'd won a labour case on gender.

She was in the same situation fifteen years later when she was eligible to be promoted to full professor. Joan had published three books and was also teaching and mentoring PhD students.

> When the head of the department said, well, I am putting Bob up for promotion to full professor. I said, Well, why? And he said: Well, he has a family to support. The kids *are* used as an example – on the wrong side of the equation. I was a single mother with three children, but that didn't count! So, I wasn't put up as the first priority of my department, which meant that I wouldn't get it. But there was a rule that you could present yourself to the entire college, what's called Personnel and Budget Committee. And I did. And I was awarded a professorship.

Joan got into a position of power, despite all the obstacles she met, and she used it very well in many ways, including all the union work she did. When Ina arrived at Vienna University of Technology, even demeaning and patronizing remarks did not affect her knowing that once you are a full professor not much can happen to you, and you have (almost) all the space to do what seems right to you. While she was met with open hostility at her university, she stuck to her vision regarding research and teaching and the promotion of young women. A first provocation for the old professors in informatics was that she took the freedom to offer master's thesis and PhD topics in CSCW, PD, and, in response to her students' interest, in computer support for art and design – all topics that were not considered worthy of an engineering degree (the faculty changed completely when younger professors, also women, were hired a decade later). She also supported a colleague from the trade unions who had for a long time been active in IFIP Working Group 'Computers and Work' in his habilitation – that was considered outrageous. Having contributed to establish the Equal Opportunities Committee at her university and having co-authored the first legislation in support of the advancement of women in Austrian universities were not well received either.

Being marginalized and being denied professional recognition and their consequences may be hard to cope with. However, it is important to realize for young women in academia that these experiences can also provide the strength to pursue research and other aims against the 'mainstream' and find allies on the way.

Driving Forces

Despite all the difficulties women still have in the academic world, Judy argues, it is important to see and acknowledge the enormous achievements of the women's movement. One of the 'incredibly positive things', she says, is that, when 'you look at the papers that have been given there (the American Sociological Association) over the last thirty years, you know, the gender section is now one of the biggest sections'. Also, if you look at

> who are active and running centres, and writing about AI, and gender and race, it is predominantly women, ... all of the fantastic centres, you know, the *AI Now* Institute, *Data & Society*, DAIR ... there are a whole other generation of fantastic women doing this work.

Also on the level of government there has been visible progress. The EU, she points out, has done 'fantastic reports on socially responsible innovation'; and

> Biden has appointed some incredibly radical people onto the science committee in the US, not only Alondra Nelson, but lots of anti-trust lawyers and ... imagine that STS people are now in government science offices in the States!

What made this possible are the enormous intellectual and political resources women were able to build over decades of outstanding academic scholarship, political struggles, and building alliances.

Influences and Connections

The women's stories refer to numerous people that were important to them, as well as books that motivated them and made them curious to move forward. Of course, there are generational differences. The senior researchers among us refer to what are now considered 'the classics', for example Evelyn Fox Keller (whose work seems to have been forgotten), Cynthia Cockburn, and Maggie Benston whom many have known personally. Maggie Benston had trained as a theoretical chemist, been exposed to computing, and ended up with a joint appointment in computer science and women's studies. Ellen, for example, refers to Maggie Benston (so does Marja) and Elaine Bernard (who went on to become the head of the labour studies program at Harvard). They both legitimated my interest in and focus on working with women and unions, . . . [and] in the early days as a young professor Karen Messing certainly had a big impact on me and still does. . . . Then there were a lot of key collections from the early days, Joan Rothchild's *Machina ex Dea*, particularly the article by Feldberg and Glenn, which I still think is a terrific article, and Bush's article on feminist technology assessment, David Noble's work about social bias in machine design, the work coming out of Scandinavia that I got a hold of through conference proceedings. And later all the work on social construction. Eileen Green's edited collection *Gendered by design* was really important. And in Canada, Heather Menzies' work, *Women and the chip*, which came out around 1981.

The younger generation emphasizes the work of more contemporary feminist scholars as having been influential. Shaowen Bardzell and her paper 'Feminist HCI' is mentioned by many as having provided a strong incentive to think about gender and feminist theory. Donna Haraway is a common reference point, also for the younger scholars. Angelika's selection is quite representative. It also shows the growing interest in queer theory and an intersectional perspective:

Madeline Balaam is an absolutely phenomenal woman. . . . Mariam Asad, Jill Dimond, Katta Spiel . . . Reading wise I was really inspired by Joan Haran's work on hope as praxis, and Maria Puig de la Bellacasa's notions of care. Mariam Asad's work has been really powerful. . . . Alex Ahmed's work on trans technologies and Oliver Haimson's work on trans technologies has been really, really inspirational. I think Reem Talhouk's work is super, super amazing. And Ebtisam Alabdulqader's work on Arab HCI. And especially like, all of the work around what communities [are] doing – Shaimaa Lazem, just so many people!

Anne's selection of influential literature is more design-oriented:

The works around the US computer clubhouses have been important for me: Mitchel Resnick, the works from the Lifelong Kindergarten Group, Seymour Papert; Yasmin Kafai's work around children's participation in STEM learning, and how gender stereotypes are perpetuated there . . . *Beyond Barbie and Mortal Combat, Connected code*, etc. . . . Leah Buechley's Lilypad for e-textiles, or the chibitronics for paper circuitry, which are the result from Jie Qi's research at the MIT media lab.

Another path to an interest in gender and technology is politics. Most of the women that pioneered feminist studies of technology were in one way or the other connected with the women's movement, which was an enormous source of strength and confidence but also of controversies and oppositions. Without the women's movement and women's fights for equality and access to resources, 'crafting a career' with a focus on feminist approaches to design would have been even more difficult. Connections to the trade unions was another important resource. Angelika's academic and political engagements demonstrate that doing feminist research today is also often connected to an activist approach, as issues of gender and other forms of injustices still prevail in many areas of life and work. We would identify not only being an activist but also action-oriented in their approach as a common characteristic of many feminist scholars.

In some cases, personal experiences, in particular the situation of being the only woman in a male-dominated field and the resulting feeling of marginality and aloneness led to an interest in gender issues. For Marja and Ina an attention to gender and the feminist critique of science and technology also had such a personal dimension, as it brought their being different to a point and helped transform this experience in productive ways.

Educating Yourself

The path from computer science and other disciplines to a perspective on gender and technology requires to step over disciplinary boundaries and engage with a highly developed field of thoughts, which are not easy to use and develop further. This transition was in all cases only possible by engaging intensely in education and learning; far beyond what is a necessary part of academic life.

Marja has been pioneering studies of gender and IT in Finland. The way there was long; it led her through social science studies, in particular qualitative methods, and women's studies. Ellen moved from methods of technology assessment and quantitative methods to learning about interviewing and participant observation as well as discourse analysis. Dorothy Smith and her notion of embedded ethnography was highly influential for this generation of feminist scholars. For Ellen, Dorothy Smith's work was also helpful in that it allowed her to see how text was used in people's lives to affect change, and how it was an important aspect of institutional relations of ruling. Ina read her way through several disciplines until she arrived at a point where she was able to do research on participatory IT design, workplace studies, and gender. Some of it turned out to be completely useless. But other venues proved extremely important as they helped her acquire a sound epistemological grounding for her research, based on reading Jürgen Habermas ('The logic of the social sciences'), Alfred Schütz, Max Weber, among others, and major works on the philosophy and history of science. Coming from physics, the feminist critique of the sciences was particularly important for her – gender and technology as a topic came later with a project on women and office automation.

These learning processes depended much on where you came from and how easy or difficult it was to bridge the different disciplines of relevance for a feminist perspective on gender, technology, and work. For Luigina, the support of an experienced academic collaborator was instrumental to this. The younger scholars found an already established field of research that, however, is not easily accessible due to the complexity of the topic and the many partially overlapping, partially diverging streams of thought. Marisol and Maria's stories are examples of this. Marisol describes the difficulties that women from other cultures may encounter when trying to work with feminist theories that have been shaped in an Anglo-American and European context. This problem is raised in the numerous publications that insist on the need for a decolonizing approach to understanding issues of gender and technology. However, there is also a wider concern about what is accepted (for example, by reviewers) as a feminist/queer/intersectional analysis. There is the danger of an 'orthodoxy' that goes beyond insisting on conceptual clarity, and some knowledge where a specific concept comes from. This may make it difficult for younger scholars to get their papers accepted and make it difficult to take concepts using them in other cultural contexts. The book will return to these issues.

The Value of a Historical Perspective

Not surprisingly, the senior researchers among us emphasize the value of a historical perspective. Joan thinks that it is important to make 'our struggles' visible. She refers to the abortion struggle in the USA – 'none of it came naturally, all of it required struggle, it required resistance, and it required strategy'. She also points to work about labour struggles and women, much of which has been done by labour historians that 'cannot go back to the actual workplace, but they work with documents, they collect oral histories'. Judy refers to recent examples of new technologies, such as the rise of big data and AI. She sees them as prompting us 'to bring our feminist perspectives that we had on, for example, the pill, and work' to the analysis to these new phenomena. She thinks young researchers may benefit from knowing the history of feminist thought and the women's movement – the work they build upon. Referring to the current debate on intersectionality and the fact that the category of woman is not homogeneous, she observes,

> While this emphasis is welcome, some writers imply that the women's movement never noticed this, you know, as if we treated all women the same. . . . [W]hereas my memory is that, from the beginning, we were deconstructing the simple binary between masculinity and femininity.

Summary

Ellen points to 'the disappearance of women' as one of the big things that has changed. In a relatively short period of time we moved from an era where the only way to focus on women was to organize separate events focussed on women (the era of women's bookstores), to a mainstreaming of sorts about women (where you could write articles about women and publish them someplace other than special issues or anthologies about women); the era of sections first on women and later on gender studies in mainstream bookstores; to an era where it is not considered appropriate in many circles to speak about women because doing so is seen as reifying dichotomous views of gender in a world that increasingly rejects women as a meaningful category of analysis.

This is a huge change. We have moved from an environment where it was considered legitimate to talk about women and women's lives, and how in a general sense, those lives are different from those of men, to an environment, where on the one hand (quite reasonably), we've been trying to think about gender differently, and gendered as a woman as being only one of many potentially marginalizing factors influencing one's life experiences. As a result, the emphasis on social construction of gender and gender as a continuum threatens to erase the concept of women. This is not to say that it is not important to study the experiences of queer people or gender diverse people as well as the experiences of women (CIS-gendered, queer, and lesbian), but we will lose a lot of significant history (which we are possibly doomed to see reinvent itself) if we don't continue to acknowledge the significance of women as an analytic category, particularly historically.

In Part II, 'Gender and Technology at the Workplace', we discuss some of the key insights which emerged from early as well as more current research on women's work and technology in different domains and parts of the world, which has been undertaken in an effort to understand the different contexts in which women (and other marginalized groups) work and the challenges they meet. We do this with a focus on gender issues and a commitment to design justice.

PART II

Gender and Technology at the Workplace

The six chapters that focus on women's work are organized along several aspects: the key concepts guiding studies of women's work; the historical pathways highlighting developments over time; and the desire to include empirical work and nuanced analyses from different parts of the world.

The *gendered definition of skills* that prevent women from accessing better-paid jobs, the invisibility and undervaluation of skills that women need in their work, are phenomena that can be observed in all areas of work; hence they will be addressed in all chapters. However, we felt that a 'natural' place for dealing more extensively with the *notion of skill* and women's work is the debate on office automation in the 1990s (Chapter 5). This debate promoted the idea of skills as socially constructed, with studies demonstrating the professional nature of office work and how gender stereotypes were used to discriminate against women in the labour market.

The *genderedness of organizations* is the second cross-cutting concept. We decided to introduce the theoretical work addressing the institutional nature of gendered notions of skill and performance – the gender subtext in organizations and its 'omnirelevance' – in the chapter on women's factory work (Chapter 6). Factory work was and still is strongly connected with images of masculinity and the ideal worker being a man, while women were mostly relegated to 'easy' tasks such as assembly work. Studies of women in non-traditional occupations and workplaces demonstrate the persistence of a masculine work culture and the consequences this has for women who try to enter these fields of work.

A third key concept, the *notion of care*, is discussed extensively in connection with the chapter about the computerization of care (Chapter 8). Main themes in this chapter are the nature of care and how to balance caregiving with the exigencies of a managerial logic. Also, the research on AI in real-life/ works contexts highlights a diversity of practices of care, in the form of care for datasets or repair work (Chapter 8). Hence, practices of care are also a point of concern with respect to technologies.

Automation/digitalization, its impact on workplaces and organizations and its limitations, is another cut-crossing theme. It is closely connected to the gendered redefinition of skills, the genderedness of the organization, and, in general, the space it leaves for human action. It raises more specific questions for each field of work: for example, what to automate; how to make space for judgment based on experience and intuition; how to avoid or countervail bias, build trust in algorithms; how to strengthen human–algorithm collaboration.

As concerns the historical perspective, we followed different pathways. 'Women and Machines in the Factory' (Chapter 4) starts from early studies of women's work in the factory in different industries – assembly work in the electronics industry, meatpacking, and work in the automotive sector – to then focus on male-dominated industries and the diversity and persistence of masculinities; with the question what it means for women when the ideal worker is a man and in how far advanced forms of digitalization can help 'undo gender'. The chapter also describes the ambiguous role of trade unions with respect to women's work, emphasizing the importance of feminist trade unionism.

'Office Automation and the Redesign of Work' (Chapter 5) introduces the research and debates about office automation, which ended in the late 1990s. At the core of these debates were reflections on the nature of clerical work in connection with findings about management strategies to centralize and deskill or upgrade the work of secretaries and typists. Office automation gave rise to initiatives exploring practical ways of supporting office workers in appropriating new office equipment and redesigning their work. The chapter offers orientations for studying modern forms of data work.

'Beyond the Office: From Data Work to the Platform Economy' (Chapter 6) discusses data work (data processing in the early days of computing) as a specific but increasingly important part of the modern workplace. Like clerical work and the work of secretaries before, much of data work is skilled but undervalued, while other parts of data work are highly standardized and repetitive, organized via platforms, and encouraging working from home.

In discussing women's platform work, we show how themes that emerged in earlier research about automation of the office remain salient when discussing contemporary platform-based work. The chapter highlights the importance of labour issues connected to modern workplaces – the invisibility of the workers, the precarity of their work situation, the lack of opportunities for learning, and so forth – their continuity but also the new forms they take with technological change.

'AI-Based Technologies: New Forms of Invisibility and the "Ironies of Automation"' (Chapter 7) follows the debate of data work, without which AI-based technologies would not exist. The chapter presents critical studies of the construction of big datasets and algorithms and the biases built into many of them. It looks at AI-based technologies in work contexts, and at how feminist ethics can contribute to thinking about how to make use of big data and ML in ways that support human actors rather than replace them.

'The Computerization of Care Work' (Chapter 8) focuses on the work of nurses and a feminist care ethics. It follows a path from early nursing information systems to modern decision-support systems (nursing protocols and care plans) and to care robots. These technologies stimulate a debate about care and its nature. They also raise design-related issues concerning the limits of automation with respect to standardization and modelling and the possibilities of delegating care to a robot.

'The Gendering of Computer Work' (Chapter 9) starts with the invisibility of women in the early days of computer science and their substantial contributions to the field. An important part of this chapter is studies demonstrating the differences in women's participation in the computing field in different countries and their cultural origins. Power issues continue to determine women's opportunities to enter a career in the computing field. The chapter describes women's work experiences in IT professions, the male-dominated working culture, and forms of gendered racism in IT companies.

A thread that runs through these chapters is the globalization of work and its implications for the work of women in countries of the so-called Global South, each with their different histories and cultures. Among the examples we discuss are women working in the textile mills in Ahmedabad and Bombay, steel workshops in contemporary Delhi, and female assembly workers in Sri Lanka; 'off-shore pink-collar work' in Barbados; a micro-tasking platform that is designed for low-income, digitally novice communities in India; outsourced ML data work in Latin America (Venezuela and

Argentina) and Bulgaria; and the situation of women IT professionals in
India, Bangladesh, Malaysia, and the Philippines. The aim is with these
examples to draw attention to the different contexts in which women work
and the specific feminist discourses about women's work that developed in
different parts of the world.

4

Women and Machines in the Factory

Many early studies of women's work were carried out in factories. One of their aims was to make the skills in women's work visible as part of a global discourse about how gender relations impact what counts as skilled work and to understand the role that technological change played not only in relation to skill, but also changing demographics of the paid labour force.

A key aspect of mechanization/automation of factory work was not necessarily deskilling but a tendency to keep women out of the new skilled technical jobs (e.g., Oldenziel 1999; Webster 1996). Some of the studies, notably those that were performed in the tradition of Francophone ergonomics, also looked into ergonomic issues – workloads as well as the stresses and strains that women experienced – and the consequences for women's health. Other studies documented women's participation and their roles in organized labour struggles. From the very beginning in the late nineteenth and early twentieth century, the studies connected women's work with their work in the home, examining the interrelations between those two spheres (e.g., Scott and Tilly 1975; Dublin 1979). Apart from pointing out the gendered division of labour and deplorable working conditions, researchers also investigated how women and men, their employers and legislators, deal with sexuality, job sociality, and flirting (French and James 1997). These studies were remarkable in that they paid attention to the larger context of work (Balka and Wagner, 2021).

Typically, in industrial settings women, many of them immigrants and/or of colour, were predominantly confined to low-paid manual work, with only few gaining access to skilled job categories. Hence, factories are highly gendered organizations. The strong division of labour to be found in most industrial companies has historical roots and it seems particularly illogical, since in WWII many factory jobs were performed by women (such as working in munitions factories, shipyards, etc.), where they were perfectly capable of doing the hard work that previously only men were thought of as fit to do. With the end of the war there were huge campaigns aimed at moving women, who had filled wartime jobs that, prior to the war, were held by men, out of the paid labour force and into the home. The campaigns also contributed significantly to the ideal of the 1950s hyper-feminine housewife. For many of the well-paid jobs in industry the 'ideal worker' was and still is a man, and types of work that require physical strength and/or the skill to handle particular tools, such as a knife, and complex machineries are connected with images of masculinity that proved persistent through (technological) change.

Images of masculinity are particularly dominant in male-dominated industrial companies – in construction, mining, oil and gas, and the automotive sector – which continue resisting acceptance of women workers and women engineers, although new technologies have reduced the physical strains of the work together with a shift of skills requirements. There is a distinctive gender subtext that runs through these organizations, reflecting commonly held beliefs that strength is an important factor for the allocation of jobs to men, which Messing and Stevenson (1996) have thoughtfully demonstrated is considerably overstated. Gender stereotypes of strength required for what we think of as traditionally men's jobs and the invisibility of strength requirements of what we typically think of as women's jobs leads to poor health outcomes for both groups of workers. They base their argument on the finding that 'average differences between the two sexes cannot be presumed to apply to individuals' and proposed 'that standards be set for job requirements, such that all manual handling jobs become physically accessible to at least 75% of all workers'. Messing et al. (1998) conclude from this and other studies that 'task assignment by sex may appear to be a solution to excessive job demands which would be better addressed by job re-design' (p. 451).

For systems designers entering this field who hope to contribute to improving working conditions and realize a commitment to gender equality, it becomes crucial to understand the perseverance of a division of labour based on historic understandings of biological sex (similar to Harding's gender structures), which feminists have attributed to opposition to women. Perhaps more than in other types of organizations, designing technologies to be used in factory work requires addressing the wider issues of labour market segregation and gendered work organizations, which, as much of the research we cite suggests, have been impacted by what Harding (1986) would refer to as gender symbolism.

After 'setting the scene' with some selected studies of women's factory work, this chapter discusses key concepts – the gendering of organizations, images of masculinity as one of the main barriers to 'undoing gender' in modern industrial settings, as well as the need for organizational change in order to achieve gender equality. Case studies from East Asian countries stand for the 'feminization of global manufacturing' (Caraway 2007): to what extent do the experiences of women workers in these countries differ from those in the highly developed parts of the world? The chapter concludes with a discussion of the implications of advanced forms of digitalization on women's work in industrial settings. It outlines strategies as well as possible venues for technology designers to consider when engaging with industrial companies.

Women Factory Workers: A Historical View

The early examples of women studying women's wage labour are not feminist in the way we understand feminism today, but they were all motivated by a commitment to improving women's professional education in order to advance their chances in the paid labour market. Among the influential studies were Beatrice Webb's (1898) *Diary of an investigator* about women's work in sweat shops in the UK, Marie Bernay's (1908) study of work in a German spinning and weaving factory, as well as Elizabeth Beardsley Butler's (1909) survey of the working conditions of women in over 400 companies as part of the so-called Pittsburgh Survey (Balka and Wagner 2021; Salembier and Wagner 2021).

After WWII numerous studies of women's factory work and technology were carried out. Following an ergonomic approach, French researchers studied the work of women operating hydraulic (and other types of) presses (Duraffourg et al. 1976) or women doing assembly work in the electronics industry (Teiger et al. 2006). In Germany, Lothar Lappe (1991) conducted a large study of women's work within the electronics, mechanical (optical), clothing, and food industries that sought to capture the organizational environment, the technologies in place, the organization of the work itself, and the (hidden) human resource strategies of the companies. In the UK, Ruth Glucksmann's (aka Cavendish) (1982) *Women on the line*, which reflects her experiences as a participant observer of women on the assembly line of a large motor components factory in London (1977–1978), and Anna Pollert's (1981) *Girls, wives, factory lives* stand out.

We have selected studies covering three areas of work – assembly work in the French electronics industry, meatpacking in the USA, Canada, and Argentina, and women's work in the automotive industry. These studies highlight some of the key issues of women's factory lives.

Women's Assembly Work in the Electronics Industry

Assembly work in the electronics industry was (and still is) mostly carried out by women. In her seminal paper 'Female factory labor and industrial structure: Control and conflict over "woman's place" in auto and electrical manufacturing' (1983), Ruth Milkman demonstrated that the main purpose of job segregation in these industries was to keep women in low-paying jobs, hence enforce their dependence on men, preserving their status as main breadwinners. Milkman dismantled the justifications that were brought forward – the 'light' character of women's work, their natural aptness for tasks 'requiring manual dexterity, attention to detail, and ability to tolerate monotony' – as ideological, without an empirical basis. Not only did the companies' assessments of what was to be considered 'light' or 'heavy' work vary considerably: 'The idiom focused not only on the lesser physical strength of women, but also elevated more dubious presumptions about the mechanical capacities of men and women to the level of organizational principles' (p. 170). Milkman also offered a detailed analysis of the situation of women workers during the war (when they were badly needed) and after it, concluding:

> Management frequently claimed that women were physically unfit for available jobs, or deliberately assigned them to the most difficult jobs and then harassed them in an unrelenting effort to induce them to quit. Under these circumstances, only locals where women workers were strongly organized were able to resist these tactics effectively, since male unionists' support was so ambivalent.
>
> (Milkman 1983, pp. 191–192)

A study carried out in the tradition of Francophone ergonomics of women's work in the electronics industry 1963–1973 foregrounds women's skills. It was published in 1972 under the title 'Conséquences du travail répétitif sous cadence sur la santé des travailleurs et les accidents' (Consequences of repetitive piece work for workers' health and work accidents) (Laville et al. 1972). The study was undertaken upon request of the trade unions (Confédération française démocratique du travail CFDT) and the director of the company with the intention of clarifying the complaints brought forward by women workers and their health problems with respect to the characteristics of the work: the assembly of television sets. Teiger et al. (2006) provide a detailed account of the research, and highlight a remark by Alain Wisner, then director of CNAM (Conservatoire National des Arts et Métiers) and initiator of the project:

> The question concerning women workers in the electronics industry had been asked by the electronics branch of the CFDT perfectly illustrating the masculine power at that period. The question had been formulated as follows: we are in charge of the electronics branch, all of us men, and our members, all of them women, find the

work really hard. They even have nervous breakdowns and we want to know if all this is to be taken seriously ... I hardly exaggerate!

(Teiger 2006, p. 82)

The fieldwork that took place from 1969–1973 combined participatory observation with electro-physiological measurements, as well as individual and group interviews. It produced a series of 'unexpected results'. Considered repetitive, monotonous, and only requiring a limited set of skills, seemingly justifying the low pay, close observation of the work brought forward a whole array of previously unrecognized features. The work *was* repetitive (piece work, most of it carried out on a belt, with a cycle of 90 sec.) and monotonous, but it was highly variable, due to frequent incidents (about one third of all operations); hence, the way the 'real' work unfolded was in most cases not identical with the prescribed sequence of activities. Although this caused stress and provoked anxieties, the women showed ingenuity in how they coped with the difficulties caused by cycles of varying length, in how they managed to gain time and keep their level of attention and morale high – 'an intense mental activity of regulation and recovery' (p. 21). They in fact made numerous micro-decisions, which allowed them to accommodate and make up for incidents. The researchers also highlighted the precision of gestures performed at high speed, all of which caused considerable muscular pain.

This is one side of the story; it points to the importance of researchers acquiring a deep understanding of the work with a high level of detail, making the skills workers develop visible. Exploring the differences between predefined tasks and real activity (as expressed by the subject) is one of the cornerstones of Francophone ergonomics. Although the focus of research is often focussed on the cognitive dimension of an activity, the approach reflects Lucy Suchman's (1987/2007) notion of planned and situation actions. Suchman observed that how work is planned often differs significantly from how it is carried out in real-world work environments, and we must understand the situated actions worker's carry out in order to support their work through design. This concept – together with the related issue of the invisibility of some kinds of work (e.g., the micro-decisions that allowed the micro-electronics workers to deal with the frequent incidents on the assembly line) have been central to the development of computer-supported cooperative work.

The other side of the story is the engagement for change that the researchers brought into the project, which is part of the research tradition of Francophone ergonomics. The project was carried out in a participatory way, with researchers discussing the objectives with the supervising 'Comité d'Entreprise' as well as the women workers. They, together with the women whose work they had studied, explained the methods and communicated the results to union representatives as well as organizational and technical management. Teiger et al. resume:

> The progress of the research does not immobilize the combativeness of the workers. The fieldwork observations have to be interrupted several times due to strikes. A number of specific actions are produced (production stoppages, etc. . . .) and the content of the grievances changes, not so much as concerns the basis of the problems – speed of production and work organization, discriminating disciplinary measures, women's work, union rights – but the lines of argumentation that have been developed and the instruments to regulate problems.
>
> (Teiger et al. 2006, p. 16)

Hence, there have been small changes; however, not the more radical ones some of those involved in the project had hoped for. However, the study confirmed the 'manifest combativity' of the women workers and completely debunked the common idea that women 'seem to adapt easier than men to the monotony of certain jobs'. 'Wisner will publicly declare that "women too have brains!"', Teiger et al. (2006, p. 21) concluded.

Recent data about women in the electronics industry are hard to come by, but nothing seems to have changed. Most electronic products today are assembled in the Global South. An article in Business Today (03/10/2023) proudly reports, 'recruiters say the demand for women in the assembly of mobile phones, consumer durables and even electric mobility is increasing. Several of these new factories are specifically asking to hire women'. According to Maja van der Velden in an article about women's health (2019), 'in Vietnam alone, 80% of workers in the electronics industry are women. The vast majority work at assembly lines'. Also factories in Brazil, Thailand, Malaysia, and China preferably hire young women for assembly jobs in the electronics industry. In particular in chip production, these women are exposed to highly toxic materials and the associated health risks.

This electronics case is an example of how what Harding (1986) called gender structures (similar to what is more commonly referred to as a division of labour based on sex) have a political dimension. Here, assumptions about the nature of work (that it requires attention to detail and manual dexterity, historically viewed as inherently female skills) interact with gender identity specifically, perceptions about gender (that the work must be unskilled if it is done by women) to justify low pay. However, when observational methods are used to further explore women's work, often a more complex story emerges that demonstrates that the work is skilled – and arguably rendered unskilled for political reasons. This suggests that the assertion that the work is low-skilled and that low pay is justifiable is politically motivated rather than based in reality.

The Hardships of Meatpacking

Our second example is meatpacking, inspired by Mirta Zaida Lobato's (2001) book about life in 'las catedrales del corned beef' in Buenos Aires that documents the technological changes that took place from 1904 to 1970 and how these affected the work of women (and men). It brings forward the power of images of masculinity in keeping women away from the better-paying jobs while threatening their integrity. 'I think that all the women who ended up working in the frigorifico felt the same', recalled a former worker, 'because it is a place, well it's like a monster when you go in there, in that darkness, that dampness, in that situation of lines of men with knives in their hands, I don't think that was very nice, you felt bad, but necessity made you get used to it' (French and James 1997, p. 11). It was hard and strenuous work, dirty and dangerous; safety standards were low. Jobs were allocated following a division of labour based on sex, with skill in the use of a knife being defined as an exclusively male domain, with consequences for women's pay cheque:

> Even where women did work with a knife, as in the *depostada* (deboning) section where meat was separated from the bone and cut into chunks, the men received higher pay for separating the meat from bone than the equally skilled women who cut the meat up.
>
> (Lobato 1997, p. 62)

Also Paulson (2017) in a study of the industry in British Columbia, Canada, emphasizes the exclusion of women from meat-cutting (and of men from final-stage processing of the meat). Horowitz's (1997) study of the meatpacking industry in the USA – 'Where men will not work' – confirms these findings. He describes the array of tasks performed by women packinghouse workers: 'Their jobs ranged from the brutal toil in offal and casings, to the skilled knife jobs in the frigid "ice hell" of the pork trim, to the simple, repetitive operations in the immaculate sliced bacon department' asking, 'How did such different settings all become places dominated by women workers?' (p. 187). Gender was encoded in the physical structure of the packinghouse – 'a seemingly intrinsic element of the production process reflected in the places where men and women worked, and the way meat flowed through the plant' (p. 189). Observations about the encoding of gender in the physical structure of factory workplaces echoed those observed a century earlier about the organization of space in New England textile plants (Dublin 1979).

Despite the difficulties women experienced abandoning their home and adapting to the tough regime of large-scale meatpacking plants, working there was valued as a source of paid employment. One of the key problems Lobato found, was that factory life for many implied a loss of their feminine body identity (1997, p. 60):

> Strength was a positive sign of masculinity and for many reasons the frigoríficos were considered a male space ('de machos'). In contrast, the women experienced a permanent devaluation which was above all associated with their bodies. The work may imply the loss of feminine body identity: it was a clothing that disfigured your presence as a woman and even provoked men's rejection. Ay ... pobrecita, when she came out of the frigorífico she smelled badly for 24 (hours), a worker mentioned with respect to his wife and the marks that were left on her after a day of work.
>
> (Lobato 2001, p. 79)

Here we see again how what Harding referred to as gender structures (the division of labour based on sex) working together with the gendering of things (frigoríficos were considered a male space) and projected gender identity (the perception that women's bodies were devalued through the clothing required by their jobs and the smell that was hard to wash away) work together to maintain the status quo of men in the higher-paid jobs. Lobato also points to deeply gendered notions of skill: 'Physical strength and skill are masculine, manual dexterity feminine. A woman worker remembers: the "triperia" seems a dirty and ugly thing but it is rather important and very delicate, and it requires a women's hands handling it' (Lobato 2001, p. 79).

The automation/mechanization of some of the work brought some changes to the gendered organization of work. Sausage production in the USA became routinized when stuffing machines were introduced. Packing firms started hiring women, often recent immigrants, to fill these new jobs, a move that the skilled male workers objected to. Men still controlled the machine-supported stuffing of sausages while the women 'linked' them 'by flipping the meat-filled intestines so as to twist the casings at regular intervals' (Horowitz 1997, p. 204), at an incredible speed and to the detriment to their health. Also in Argentina more than half of workers in meatpacking plants were immigrant women, from abroad as well as from the countryside outside of Buenos Aires (Lobato 1997).

In the meatpacking plants in British Columbia, Canada, only women worked in the machine-automated processing departments 'and they bore the consequences of this in their paycheques and on their bodies' (Paulson 2017, p. 116). In contrast to the USA, new technologies resulted in a considerable upskilling of women with employers starting to look for 'skilled girls' to operate the machines, while the distinction between craft-based (male) skills and machine-processing (which could be done by women) was reinforced. Paulson adds, 'Perhaps this tenuous – but meaningful – element of skill in mechanized processing rested on the ongoing whiteness of the job' (p. 142).

He refers to a study by Cynthia Loch-Drake (2007) that shows how immigration that brought in people of colour led to a 'racialized-gendered' understanding of job categories. Men working in meatpacking thought of themselves as 'a special breed' – rough and hardened men – seeking to distinguish themselves from new immigrants, many of them women of colour.

> Rough male behaviours, particularly packinghouse language, physical aggression, verbal abuse, and harassment, were vehicles for asserting this control. Many women workers who turned down jobs that involved working with 'blood and guts', saying they preferred 'clean' jobs, were undoubtedly influenced by the stigma of promiscuity or unfemininity attached to women who accepted 'male' work once it was made available in the 1970s.
>
> (Loch-Drake 2007, pp. 139–140)

This attitude was linked with notions of whiteness and racial prejudices. The male-dominated unions at a time of rising labour tensions by 'subordinating women and reinforcing ethnic divisions ... limited women's activism and weakened working-class solidarity' (p. 143).

Automation has progressed in the primary and secondary processing of meat, making jobs potentially cleaner and safer (e.g., Barbut 2020), although the work has become even more dangerous. In many large-scale plants working conditions are deplorable, a fact that received much media attention when plants became hotspots of corona transmission (e.g., Dempsey et al. 2022). Immigrants, many of them women, form a large part of the labour force, in the USA as well as Germany and other rich countries, often working for less than minimum wages. However, gender issues are conspicuously absent from the current debate about meatpacking, making women working in the industry invisible.

The Automotive Industry: A Mixture of Paternalism and Masculinity

While women workers historically made up a large part of the workforce in the electronics and meatpacking industry, they remained a minority in the automotive industry. In a study of teamwork and how it helped restructure gender imbalance at the Volvo truck company, Wallace (1999) observed:

> In 1988, at Volvo's car assembly plant in Canada, a female worker brought a case of sexual discrimination against the company which resulted in the company agreeing to employ 15% women. By mid-1994, however, there were still no women assembly operators in the plant .... There are no women operators in the Belgian car plant ... or in Volvo's truck and bus plant in the UK.
>
> (Wallace 1999, p. 21)

Statistics about female participation in production in the large automotive companies are hard to come by (as we'll see, a lack of data influences our ability to better understand not only women's lives, but the experiences of gender and racial diversity as well). 'The German automotive industry is a male bastion. Women's income is approximately 9% to 14% lower than men's income' (Utzeri 2019, p. 41). According to a study by IG Metall (the German metal workers' union), in 2011 only 7.5 percent of those at Mercedes-Benz working in production were women; at VW Volkswagen 15 percent of those employed in assembly and only 6 percent of the foremen were women. In Canada in 2022, 23 percent of the jobs in assembly and 11 percent of those in parts production were occupied by women (www.catalyst.org/research/women-in-the-automotive-industry/).

Historically, women's access to the automotive industry has always been limited (apart from the period of WWII), although due to mechanization most of the jobs did not require particular physical strength, as Ruth Milkman pointed out:

> 'The rank and file of men come to us unskilled' wrote Henry Ford in 1922. 'They do not have to be able-bodied men. We have jobs that require great physical strength – although they are rapidly lessening; we have other jobs that require no strength whatsoever-jobs which, as far as strength is concerned, might be attended to by a child of three'.
>
> (Milkman 1983, p. 169)

These were well-paying jobs made possible by the Fordist revolution – 'the predominant policy of the major auto firms was to pay high wages in exchange for subordination to the machine-paced organization of production' (p. 174).

One of the key findings of early studies of work in the automotive industry is expressed by Fine (1993) who looked at a small company in Michigan, USA – Reo Motor Car Co. – in the 1930s that employed men only, most of them semi-skilled operators or assemblers. She observed,

> The management appealed to the workers by providing an environment that supported the family wage, a 'man to man' personnel philosophy, job security with the promise of promotion, and organized leisure and various services for the worker and his family, while preserving prevailing notions about the proper racial and political make-up of the working class.
>
> (Fine 1993, p. 277)

Where women managed to enter the industry, they found themselves discriminated against by male co-workers, management, and the union, Lucier (2001) reports from a study of working conditions at Chrysler's minivan plant in Windsor, Ontario. She focussed on the lack of seniority equality in the plant, which negatively affected women's transfer to other jobs and their lay-off rights, all in the name of the male breadwinning ideology. When in 1976, upon pressure exerted by the government, seventy-five women (out of 1,000) were hired to fill the second shift at a neighbouring Chrysler plant, particularly discriminating criteria were applied. The women not only met

> with a hesitant male workforce but also with a corporate policy that had them changing their bodies to fit Chrysler regulations. The women who passed the two-week training period were required to weigh 140 pounds and be at least five-feet, five inches in height to enter what Windsor Star reporter C.A. Patch called a 'man's world'.
>
> (Lucier 2001, p. 60)

The women's integration in the plant was not so simple, Lucier states, with the women themselves tending to accept that they would not be suited to all types of heavy work. Their being hidden and 'shipped around' 'from department to department not only protected the male workers' jobs but also tested the strength and endurance of the female workers' (p. 61). The consequence was that 'despite their fight for equality, the majority of women are still found in many of the auto industry's cut and sew departments, shipping departments, and inspection departments while only a minority work "in the metal shop welding"' (p. 62).

This combination of 'masculinity and paternalism' continues to dominate the industry, as Belinda Leach's work with unionized women workers in rural Ontario (Canada) demonstrates. Her research

> contributes to debates on rural gender identities by treating rural masculinities and femininities as classed constructions. The question is what happens to entrenched gender identities when relatively well-paid jobs in the automotive industry are available. The clashes that arise as these identities are pushed and pulled in different ways are the focus of my attention here.
>
> (Leach 2016, p. 129)

Women workers were largely unwelcome, she found, and their work lives were made extremely difficult by rotating shifts and mandatory overtime. Their presence threatened the link between operating heavy machinery and masculinity and male workers often 'failed to provide women with assistance in handling unwieldy jobs, when typically, more than one man would perform the task' (p. 140). This is a case of 'paternalistic cross-class relationships' supported by the unions that are typical of rural areas (Leach 2016). However, experiences with the unions as concerns gender equality vary. For example, Woodhall and Leach (2010) emphasize the positive role of the Canadian Auto Workers' (CAW) Union with its unique women's advocacy program. They emphasize that this program 'is innovative and beneficial in maintaining women's employment as they attend to personal problems' (p. 44).

Given that in the automotive sector the unions that were typically dominated by men played an ambiguous role, trade union feminism was and continues to be of great importance. A case study by Bracke (2019) of the labour struggles at Fiat, Turin, Italy in the 1970s and early 1980s demonstrates the power women workers can exert. She describes the situation at that time: 'dramatic changes in gender relations since the 1960s, ongoing industrial unrest since 1968 and the introduction of new gender-equality legislation, fatefully coinciding with the onset of de-industrialisation and the rise of unemployment in manufacturing' (p. 484). In 1978, Fiat announced that it would hire 250 unskilled workers, indicating that it wanted men, considering women 'physically unsuited' to do the work, 'much of which was welding and sanding' (p. 494). The union, FML-Turin, tried to convince Fiat to accept women workers:

> A key reason why trade union feminism's agenda resonated with the FLM's post-1968 radical culture was that the former aimed to move beyond women's needs, more widely rethinking the quality of work conditions (conveyer belt speed, health issues), self-determination and decision-making in the workplace, and what today we call the work-life balance. The FLM appreciated the feminist focus on health in the workplace – traditionally an area of neglect in the Italian labour movement, although it had emerged among the radical demands of 1969. Adopting an ICD campaign,[1] FLM-Turin now called for rigorous workplace health checks, acknowledging the feminist origins of such demands and arguing that 'women are less willing [than men] to accept the commodification of health risks'.
>
> (Bracke 2019, p. 496)

This seems an exceptional case that reflects the fact that Italy in the 1960s–1970s experienced intense social conflicts also expressed in workplace radicalism. Italian feminists played a large role in these conflicts.

There are some positive examples of automotive companies seeking to improve gender equality. In his research in the Volvo truck company in the Swedish Uddevalla plant, Wallace (1999) investigated the company's teamwork experiments. These were carried out with the intent to have 40 percent women in production, with the idea that as 'people are different and that they have different positive and negative qualities' (Ellegård 1995, p. 55) it would be sensible to make use of this diversity. Wallace describes these experiments as successfully demonstrating that assembly work in teams offers the possibility to restructure gender imbalances in blue-collar work. However, he also

---

[1] ICD is the Turin-based women-only trade union Intercategoriale donne.

points to the persistence of stereotypes on the shopfloor. Women were thought of as being more careful with the expensive equipment, not necessarily believing that they could fix a machine on their own – 'and that is one of the reasons we have women around more expensive machinery' (p. 24). The general conclusion of the study was that indeed

> the gender balance of blue-collar work teams can reduce stress levels, alter the behaviour of team members and reduce the demand for first line supervision, and, in so doing, reduce labour costs and, more contentiously, to take advantage of what are seen as stereotypical feminine traits.
>
> (Wallace 1999, p. 28)

Hence, the perceived benefits of including women in assembly team-work reflect gender stereotypes that attribute specific social skills – 'such as conflict resolution, humane decision making, the ability to build a pleasant and relaxed atmosphere' (p. 29) – to women blue-collar workers, a phenomenon which has historically been referred to as having an essentialist basis. This might have an excluding effect on women who do not seem to have these desirable characteristics (Eveline 1994), and also reinforces the idea that women and men are born with certain attributes that make them well- or ill-suited to particular jobs. In Harding's (1986) terms, gender identity (perceptions about women being more careful and having better social skills) work with the gendering of things (the expensive equipment) to justify a breakdown in gender structures (all male teams). What is notable about this case is that when there is political will to challenge the division of labour it can be achieved. However, the case also shows how breaking down gender structures may not lead to changes in gender identity – how men and women view themselves in relation to gender, or how others perceive their gender (or for that matter, the gendering of things).

Pervasive Masculinities: The Gendered Organization

The findings from studies of gender in three industries – electronics, meat-packing, and automotive – point to theories of the gendered organization as well as the diversity and persistence of masculinities as important sources for understanding the possibilities of action from a gender perspective.

Gender Subtexts and How to Change Them

One of the most important feminist scholars, Dorothy Smith, proposed that we think about 'a sociology that addresses society and social relations from the

standpoint of women situated *outside* rather than within the relations of ruling'
(p. 46). Her main argument was as follows:

> The making and dissemination of the forms of thought we make use of to think
> about ourselves and our society are part of the relations of ruling and hence originate
> in positions of power. These positions of power are occupied by men almost
> exclusively, which means that our forms of thought put together a view of the world
> from a place women do not occupy. The means women have had available to them
> to think, image, and make actionable their experience have been made for us and not
> by us.
>
> (Smith 1987, p. 19)

This and other texts by Dorothy Smith have greatly influenced how we think
about organizations and (male) power. Smith located the problematic in the
everyday world and how it is socially organized, suggesting we write a
sociology from people's standpoint. She advocated and developed an approach
known as 'institutional ethnography' as a mode of inquiring about or interrogating everyday life (2005). Smith contended that also the working class is
excluded from the 'ruling apparatuses', as are 'the many voices of women and
men of color, of native peoples, and of homosexual women and men' (p. 107);
stressing, however, the distinctiveness of the standpoint of women. It is
important here to place Smith's work in historical context. She was writing
in the 1980s prior to the emergence of contemporary views about gender
diversity. For the time, work focussing on women – and particularly the
standpoint of women – was groundbreaking.

In her work on the gendered organization Joan Acker (1990) refers to
Dorothy Smith's thinking, in particular to her claim that researchers and
organizational theorists are part of the relations of ruling. Following the line
of thought Smith developed in *The conceptual practices of power* (1990),
Acker argues, 'that break between a gendered reality and gender-neutral
thought is maintained, I believe, through the impersonal, objectifying practices
of organizing, managing, and controlling large organizations' (p. 256).

Acker introduced the term gendered processes, by which she meant that
'advantage and disadvantage, exploitation and control, action and emotion,
meaning and identity, are patterned through and in terms of a distinction
between male and female, masculine and feminine' (Acker 1990, p. 146).
She distinguished four sets of such processes: the production of gender
divisions, visible in the gendering of jobs, in organizational hierarchies, and
wage structures; the 'creation of symbols, images, and forms of consciousness
that explicate, justify, and, more rarely, oppose gender divisions' (1992,
p. 253); the interactions between individuals and how they cement patterns
of dominance and subordination; and the 'internal-mental work of individuals

as they consciously construct their understandings of the organization's gendered structure of work and opportunity and the demands for gender-
appropriate behaviors and attitudes' (p. 253). The notion of gendered processes
is similar to what Harding (1986) called the triad for analyzing gender
relations (Chapter 1).

Acker's work was widely received and continued, garnering some criticism
(e.g., that Acker was rather late (2006) in incorporating class and race in her
analysis), but, above all, offered further conceptual work and new insights.
Already Acker had criticized the notion of the abstract, disembodied ideal
worker – flexible, available full-time, work-focussed – and its presentation as
gender-neutral. Benschop and Doorewar (1998a) take up this notion as being
at 'variance with women's work realities' (p. 9). They observe

> that both the persistency of gender inequality and the perception of equality emerge
> from a so-called gender subtext: the set of often concealed, power-based gendering
> processes, i.e. organizational and individual arrangements (objectives, measures,
> habits), systematically (re)producing gender distinctions.
>
> (Benschop and Doorewar 1998b, p. 787)

Also the term 'gender subtext' goes back to Dorothy Smith's writings, indicating that while organizational discourse may appear gender-neutral, the underlying subtext reproduces gender distinctions (Bendl 2008). While Acker
(1992) took job evaluations as an example of assumed gender-neutrality,
Fenech et al. (2021) in a study from 2021 examined performance appraisals
in the financial industry in Malta, showing how women's contributions are
undervalued on the basis of a seemingly gender-neutral set of criteria:

> Women's perceived invisibility at social events, and their real difficulties attending,
> were used to justify their lower behavioral, and thus overall performance, and this
> was considered an acceptable outcome of mothers' (in particular) inferior status . . . .
> Women misrecognized that performance is a 'game' defined by socializing in the
> behavioral criteria. They express frustration at not scoring highly despite working
> hard and achieving on 'objective' measures.
>
> (Fenech et al. 2021, p. 438)

The study confirms the institutional nature of gendered notions of skill and
performance, their persistence; but also what West and Zimmerman (1987)
pointed out, that 'the interactional validation of gendered distinctions leads to
their naturalness and thus invisibility' (Fenech et al. 2021, p. 428).

In their study of three organizational settings in the Dutch banking sector,
Benschop and Dooreward (1998b) identified three gendering processes and the
underlying gender subtexts. Women in this sector were identified (and identified themselves) as '*show pieces* (the token position of the few women in top

functions) or as being on *the mommy track* (the sidetrack many women with young children are shunted to)' (p. 792). The third gendered process Benschop and Dooreward describe concerns career-making and '*the importance of being asked*' (p. 792). They observed women tending to comply with these charac-terizations, with the consequence that

> implicitly the female show pieces consent to the depreciation of femininity, because they confirm the association of femininity and incapacity. To consent to the perception that part-time work is only possible in low qualified jobs implies acceptance of the practice of the mommy track, including the acceptance of the quality loss for the organization and of the end of the career for the employee.
>
> (Benschop and Dooreward 1998b, p. 802)

Other studies of gender in organizations have confirmed these (and other) mechanisms of gendering. The key question then is how social change can be brought about, given the 'hegemonic character of the gender subtext' (p. 801). With the question of change in mind, Britton (2000) voices uneasiness with any a priori assumption that organizations are 'gendered drastically', observing,

> Under these conditions, it becomes impossible to imagine what an 'ungendered' bureaucratic organization would look like or how 'ungendered' work could be carried out. Presumably, this is something for which we might all hope, or if not an ungendered organization, at least an environment in which hegemonically defined gendered characteristics are not presumed and reproduced – in which men neither 'do domination' nor women enact subordination.
>
> (Britton 2000, p. 422)

How is it possible to bring about change, given the 'omnirelevance' of gender in how people and the activities they carry out are perceived and performed? In their influential paper, West and Zimmerman (1987) had not only made the point that doing gender 'involves a complex of socially guided perceptual, interactional, and micropolitical activities' (p. 126), they emphasized the inescapability of gender attributions:

> virtually any activity can be assessed as to its womanly or manly nature. And note, to 'do' gender is not always to live up to normative conceptions of femininity or masculinity; it is to engage in behavior *at the risk of gender assessment.*
>
> (West and Zimmerman 1987, p. 136)

Hence, it is possible to behave in ways that question gendered expectations, but this always involves the risk of being judged. Reflecting on this omnirelevance, Deutsch (2007) used the term 'undoing gender' that had been introduced by Judith Butler (2004). Butler referred to it as a subversive activity that aims at destabilizing (binary) codes: 'undoing gender for her meant doing gender in another irritating way, undermining and confirming it' (Hirschauer 2016, p. 117). Deutsch asked if the pressure to conform with gendered expectations is so strong that it survives any kind of structural change. She suggests that we study on an interactional level

> (1) when and how social interactions become less gendered, not just differently gendered; (2) the conditions under which gender is irrelevant in social interactions; (3) whether all gendered interactions reinforce inequality; (4) how the structural (institutional) and interactional levels might work together to produce change; and (5) interaction as the site of change.
>
> (Deutsch 2007, p. 114)

Most of the studies that have looked into evidence of women and/or men 'undoing gender' have focussed on non-traditional occupations and work-places. Examples of men constructing a different kind of masculinity in particular work contexts include Cross and Bagilhole (2002) who studied British men doing different kinds of 'women's work'; or Henson and Krasa Rogers (2001) who addressed masculinity among male temporary clerical workers. Ely and Meyerson (2010) in an observational study of men working on offshore oil platforms argued that these can be important sites for 'undoing gender' provided they engage in organizational change. The men they studied

> readily acknowledged their physical limitations, publicly admitted their mistakes, and openly attended to their own and others' feelings. Importantly, platform workers did not replace a conventional image of masculinity with an unconventional one and then set out to prove the new image – revealing mistakes strategically, for example, or competing in displays of sensitivity.
>
> (Ely and Meyerson 2010, p. 3)

The researchers identified three characteristics of the organizations they studied as key to bringing about change that results in an environment that is less gender-stereotyped: 'collectivistic goals, the alignment of definitions of competence with *bona fide* task requirements rather than with idealized images of masculinity, and a learning orientation toward work' (p. 27).

As concerns women in non-traditional roles and/or occupations, it is well known that they need to fill the masculine script if they, for example, want to be acknowledged as managers (e.g., Wajcman 1998). Johansson et al. (2020) in their excellent study of women (and men) in the digitized metal industry point to the barriers against undoing gender, even in an environment where most of the work is no longer physically heavy but takes place in front of computers:

> Despite working alongside their male peers and maintaining the same pace and patterning in various processes, many female operators feel the need to constantly

prove themselves as capable steelworkers. They describe, with certain discomfort, the need to conform to a masculine way of behaving.

(Johannson et al. 2020, p. 1333)

They also observed how women in this environment enacted their femininity, considering it important and 'potentially agentic' – 'they use it as a source of pleasure, agency and enhancement of their self-worth parodying and contesting the masculine norm' (p. 1337). So, while confronted with persistent forms of masculinity, these women resist the pressure to undo their own gender. Saifuddin et al. (2018) in their study of women professionals in high-tech careers in Bangladesh observed both: women demonstrating agency and resilience at the workplace, while still conforming to norms of femininity and respectability:

> By simultaneous expressions of doing and undoing gender, these women dealt with hierarchies and inequalities, navigated masculinized industry and empowered themselves within a patriarchal culture. The strategies effectively allowed them to demonstrate agency and persist in tech occupations.
>
> (Saifuddin et al. 2018, p. 673)

All these studies point to the persistence of a masculine culture and images of masculinity in industry as one of the main problems women have to face when entering non-traditional workplaces or working along men in gender-segregated environments.

Masculinities at Work

We know that women and men are not homogeneous; that there are 'many strands of femininities and masculinities which cut across class, race, ethnicity, sexuality, and other factors' (Sappleton and Takruri-Rizk 2008, p. 310); that not all men hold power and men may also experience marginalization (albeit in a different way); and that 'power within and between men and women in organizations is complex, fluid and ever-changing' (p. 310). However, it is important to understand how men enact masculinity and how this helps them hold on to their power.

In her paper 'Caught in the wheels: The high cost of being a female cog in the male machinery of engineering' (1983), Cynthia Cockburn wrote,

> Engineering represents everything that is defined as manly – the propensity to control and manipulate nature; the celebration of muscle and machine in action upon raw materials; the tolerance, even pleasure in, dirt viz, grease, swarf and metal shavings ... Technical work involves the acceptance of physical risk – exposure to frequent accidents, cuts, contusions. It affords free movement round and about its

object, in contrast to the physical confinement of much women's work. It implies control – designing solutions to physical problems, making energy work for you. The all-male workshop fosters and develops masculine patterns of relationships, it is the home of camaraderie based on the exchange of anecdote and slander concerning women.

(Cockburn 1983, p. 57)

In the context of factory work, masculinity was (and partially still is) connoted with physical strength, particular craft skills, such as being able to handle a knife and manipulate heavy tools, and exposure to dangerous working conditions (as if women working in meatpacking or assembling computer chips were not equally exposed). This seemingly entitles them to 'rough male behaviours, particularly packinghouse language, physical aggression, verbal abuse, and harassment' (Loch-Drake 2007). In his book *The limits to masculinity* (1977), Andrew Tolson made a distinction between middle-class and working-class types of masculinity; the latter of which he saw as most obviously paradoxical:

Because of the often brutal and unpredictable nature of the work, the worker is directly dependent on 'masculine' compensation, and in some situations, patriarchal aspects of working-class culture may even be potentially subversive. A male chauvinism of the shop-floor is a way of asserting collective control, and, sometimes, sabotaging the production process itself.

(Tolson 1977, pp. 58–59)

Fine's (1993) study of the Reo Motor Car Co. found that management explicitly sought to change the image of working-class masculinity. They stressed that their male workers who were doing machine work were not machines themselves, foregrounding a service attitude as well as family values:

The working class man at the Reo was loyal to company and country, sober and straightforward; he demonstrated his masculinity by his service to his two families – his public family, the company, and his private family, the wife and children he supported at home. He expressed this masculinity, not through manly independence on the shop floor but through his cooperation on the line and on the baseball field . . .

(Fine 1993, p. 281)

While images of masculinity change with the nature of the work itself, the surrounding organization as well as institutional arrangements, it is astonishing how persistent they are in their being flexibly adapted to new working conditions. A study by Abrahamsson and Johansson (2020) in the Swedish mining industry confirms this. They state,

Even when technology has contributed to improving the work environment, the aura of very dangerous, heavy, and dirty work has continued to surround mining.

> The current local hegemonic mine worker masculinity is still to a great extent constructed around the mystery of the rock and old tales about mining; as one of the interviewed men stated: 'As a miner, you must learn how to cope with and appreciate the secrets of the mine. The environment in the mine is unique and the mine itself is mysterious, it's important to keep it that way!'
>
> (Abrahamsson and Johansson 2020, p. 4)

It seems that the fact that in many parts of the world, women have worked and continue to work in mining has been largely forgotten. Historically, in the preindustrial world women made up a large part of workers in mining. This dramatically changed during the period of industrialization, to slowly change again after the 1980s. Currently, about 15 percent of the mining population in Sweden, Canada, and India, where much of the large-scale mining takes place, are women. Despite this (varying) presence over time, 'the old mining narratives of both trade unions and the mining industry have made women invisible, positioned as different and their mining work devalued' (Abrahamsson and Johansson 2020, p. 4). There are many reasons why images of masculinity survive in a place such as large-scale mining. One is 'to provide barriers against other men, lower-ranked masculinities and, especially, unmanliness'; and, more generally, 'women, office staff, management; and people from other parts of Sweden, other countries, and subcontracting companies. This controls and reinforces the similarities between workers' (p. 5). However, also new forms of masculinity emerge, with some men acknowledging how automation changes the work and the importance of having more women as co-workers.

The Ideal Worker Being a Man: What It May Mean for Women

Most of the studies of women in male-dominated workplaces agree that what women need most to survive is resilience. A survey of women working onsite in construction in Australia (Turner 2021) found that

> resilience is considered as a mandatory capability by women working onsite to manage gendered workplace hazards and attain career success. The findings indicate that these women had high levels of resilience despite little to no support from their workplace.
>
> (Turner 2021, p. 839)

Other international studies have confirmed this finding. For example, women working in the oil and gas industry in Canada have experienced the need 'to have a tough skin' on top of being self-determined and 'agentic' (Murphy et al. 2021). Wang (2021) points to the insight of several studies of women in the construction industry that 'focusing on the job and the pleasure of work, rather than gendered issues, help emancipate women from gender norms, becoming an empowering characteristic from within, for women's success in the industry' (p. 18).

This is certainly not easy to achieve without support, given that workplace marginalization, often combined with sexual and other forms of harassment, is difficult to cope with even for an 'agentic' woman. Exploring the experiences of women in male-dominated workplaces, Hall and Gettings (2020) identified several marginalizing communication strategies: '(a) isolating communication, (b) being silenced, (c) facing consequences for breaking gender norms, (d) markers of disrespect, (e) violence or sexual harassment, and (f) lack of tolerance for physical needs/body' (p. 490). The women participating in this study shared stories of micro- as well as macro-aggression that made them feel different, unwelcome, and uncomfortable. The authors deem markers of disrespect, some of them subtle and not easy to pin down, as particularly problematic, 'because they can erode participants' beliefs about their own abilities to successfully accomplish work, create workplace climates that support (or at least do not discourage) gender-based marginalization, and may ultimately hamper women's abilities to progress in their careers' (p. 16).

A strong example of what being marginalized and harassed may mean to women is the analysis of a diary written by a woman engineer working in the British construction industry (Bagilhole et al. 2002). This woman experienced 'serious sexual discrimination and harassment' (p. 422) without receiving any support by her employer against the 'pack-like mentality' (p. 426) that had developed around her. Sadly, but not surprisingly, her diary showed 'evidence of denial, endurance, detachment and a significant amount of self-blame for the actions of her colleagues' (p. 427). Sappleton and Takruri-Rizk (2008) interpret this diary experience as typical of 'tokenism' (Kanter 1977), adding, 'Thus, in the engineering or technology firm, the masculine hegemony *accommodates* equal opportunities but does not have the comprehension, commitment or capability to effectively *implement* them' (p. 306).

The historical studies of women's life in the meatpacking history pointed to the threats that a masculine culture at work poses to women's femininity. This experience had to do with traditional notions of women's decency and with the roughness, the heat, dirt, and smells women were exposed to in the factory. These threats to women's femininity are partially to do with questions of equipment and clothing that may make their 'gendered difference and embodiment more marked and visible' (p. 48), Ainsworth et al. (2013) argue. Their study of women volunteer firefighters describes their exposure to problematic male practices but also their identification with a construction of 'preferred femininity': 'For example, the repudiation and parodying of emotion considered "feminine" by men was reframed by these women as a strength that helped them as firefighters' (p. 49).

An Australian study of women in the skilled trades (Wulff et al. 2021), makes a similar point, diverting the perspective from a notion of women as victims to a much more agential view:

> Utilising masculine gender capital through their identification as 'tomboys' and socialisation with brothers and male friends in preference to socialisation with other women, tradeswomen identify with the masculine attributes of strength, toughness and competencies that are important to prove in the workplace.
>
> (Wulkff et al. 2021, p. 3)

On the other hand, these women also made use of their perceived feminine capital in 'how they approached their work (attitudes and desire to learn), what they brought to the workplace (skills) and how they can use their bodies' (p. 12). This observation has also been made by Ibáñez (2017) who studied women in construction work in Spain. She found that, for example in the case of self-employed women painters, 'gender stereotypes favour women (cleanliness, attention to detail, good taste for decoration), and once they have obtained a portfolio of clients, the visibility effect becomes positive' (p. 41). Examining 'the relationships between structural constraints and women's agency' in a study of women in the building trades, Denissen (2020) identified a whole range of strategies

> in their response to normative constructions of gender. Rather than being forced into choosing between a stereotypically 'masculine' or 'feminine' role, tradeswomen manipulate gender rules by engaging in reflexive gender displays that emphasize the most advantageous identity for each situation.
>
> (Denissen 2020, p. 1051)

All these studies emphasize the fact that the women they interviewed constructed 'multiple versions of masculinity and femininity in complex configurations' (Ainsworth et al. 2013, p. 51), a point that is consistent with social constructivist views of gender, and Harding's (1986) two aspects of gender identity (subjective gender – how an individual views their own gender – and projected gender – how your gender is perceived by others).

Lewis and Simpson (2010) link these experiences to the wider issue of (in) visibility. As tokens, they argue, women 'symbolize their category and experience material consequences of over-exposure and the marking of their bodies as gendered' and find themselves exposed to the 'male gaze' (p. 8). They address the multiple varying aspects of (in) visibility: the fact that 'as tokens women are both conspicuous, as "physical spectacle" and invisible in terms of authority required for the job'; being made visible within an organization's 'emotional as well as aesthetic regimes'; being highly visible when pregnant, 'their bodies marked as disturbing and potentially disruptive to organizational routines'; and, finally, as mothers with children 'different from the norm of the fast track, high commitment career' (p. 8).

In a study of women and men in so-called *maquiladoras* (or *maquilas*) – export processing factories owned by foreign (mostly US) capital in Mexico – Salzinger (2001) came to the conclusion that the gendering of jobs can be part of explicit management strategies. She observed a diversity of 'femininities' and 'masculinities' depending on the plant's management in the different *maquilas*. In one plant where women assemble television sets, 'behavior, attitude, demeanor – typically in highly gendered form – is evaluated here. Skill, speed and quality rarely come up' (p. 17); whereas in an auto parts assembly plant management 'dismissed the notion that their rural women workers were merely "traditional Mexican women" and organized them into teamwork and leadership training' (p. 15). Salzinger proposes that

> productive femininity is a paradigm through which managers view, and therefore structure, assembly work and through which they imagine, describe and define job applicants and workers. The people we think of as classic 'women workers' are formed within these ways of thinking and being. Thus, it is a mistake to think that their presence in the factory makes global production possible. To the contrary, they are global production's finished product.
>
> (Salzinger 2001, p. 14)

The study demonstrates different strategies of management of manipulating gendered notions of skills and capabilities to the advantage of the company. The examples she provides suggest that these strategies of defining workers are driven by a mixture of ideological position and productivity concerns.

An important point concerns the question of whether or not the women working under male-dominated leads are exposed to the 'devaluation' of their skills and their suitability for particular tasks. This is a complex question that cannot be answered on the basis of qualitative evidence alone. We think of this question more in terms of how women experience their own performance and how they are valued by supervisors and male colleagues. An action-research project with young women apprentices in non-traditional occupations in Austria (Wagner 1986) observed that

> the jobs of skilled women workers are in many subtle or less subtle ways compared to what women in industry 'normally' do. This becomes the main criterion against which their abilities and aptitudes are measured. As a consequence, they find themselves in an in-between position between the less qualified women workers and those whose work they actually share: skilled male colleagues.
>
> (Wagner 1986, p. 325)

Although these women had grown into highly motivated and competent craft workers, this in-between position affected their self-confidence and also, in several cases, showed on their pay slips. They felt they had to prove their competences again and again, sought to avoid risks and often felt 'too insecure to urge their superiors to provide better work' (p. 325). A much more recent study by Andrew (2009) of women in the engineering construction industry partially confirms these observations. She looked into notions of 'employability' finding that

> 'fitting in' and gaining legitimacy were continuing issues for women progressing through their apprenticeships and beyond, as well as for those who left for reasons including difficulties in obtaining work post-qualification and perceived incompatibility of the work with domestic commitments.
>
> (Andrew 2009, p. 345)

Andrew emphasized that women's interpretations and strategies varied, depending on the setting and the specific circumstances. One of the main problems she identified is that the women's employability was often seen as a matter of individual attributes, hence their individual responsibility to improve, 'underplay(ing) the significance of social practices and power dynamics in interaction with individual agency' (p. 356).

Women's Factory Work and Globalization

Much of women's industrial work has moved to East Asia, with women flowing primarily into low-paid jobs in a few mostly export-oriented industries (see, e.g., Caraway 2007). Well known are recent studies of young Chinese women from rural areas undertaking physically exhausting work in urban factories, mostly in the electronics industry (e.g., Ngai 2005). The work experiences of women factory workers in East Asia are not so different from those of women in more developed countries, as concerns low pay, physical hardships, and unacknowledged skills. However, the level of exploitation is much higher, protection from dangerous working conditions often non-existent, and surveillance and control in many cases harsher. What makes these women and their lives different is the dominating role of the family, namely the women's responsibilities for the larger family and their dependency on men. We think that 'acknowledging feminist research on gender dynamics of globalization of production and household relations in "making available" women's labour to the global capital' (Dutta 2019, p. 888) is an important part of reflecting on design issues with respect to women's work.

Barua (2021) explores these particular conditions women face, between 'feminine domesticity' and work lives in the textile mills in Ahmedabad and Bombay and steel workshops in contemporary Delhi. She describes a situation where 'bodily discomfort, pain and exhaustion emerge as crucial ways of relating to the work process, work tools and the spatial environment' (p. 16). However, there are also other, positive, emotions connected with work outside the home 'in terms of skill, mastery and pride'; and although machine work can be dangerous, as one of her informants described, it provides the opportunity to display her strength and skills:

> Pinky works a cutting machine, which flattens steel circles into bowls and plates. This kind of work is imprinted on the body, as Pinky shows me the scars on her forearms and feet: 'This is very risky work, but ladies do it. The kind of work that ladies do, many men can't even do. We run cutter machines, press machine, but it's back breaking. My arms and legs are sore after standing at my machine the whole day. I am covered in dirt and dust. And I can't lose my focus for a second. I have to keep up with the machine. If my body stumbles, there will be splinters of steel flying all over'.
>
> (Barua 2021, pp. 17–18)

Barua argues that women's ambivalent feelings towards work outside the home and work in the home originate in 'the ideologies and practices of domesticity' (p. 17). She suggests that

> the implications of sexual impropriety and the persistent threats of being labeled unchaste were underlying concerns that governed women's work in the factory. Daily spatial maneuvering is expected in the workplace to avoid a reputation of being 'loose'. Women in the Bombay textile mills ate their lunch on the shop floor, while the machines were being cleaned, trying to protect their food from the flying dust, only so that they could avoid the much cleaner canteen, where they 'would get no respect' and their presence would be seen as an invitation for harassment
>
> (Barua 2021, p. 17).

Barua's analysis reflects the findings of many other studies of women's factory work in developing countries, namely in East Asia: the centrality of the family and feminine domesticity in the women's lives while performing hard work under poor working conditions; however, they also stress women's actions as 'tactical agents' in their immediate environment and their political activism. Kim (1996) described the low-paying jobs women had in the South Korean export industry – they were defined as 'industrial soldiers and dutiful daughters'. In some factories work was organized in three shifts, which was extremely hard to adapt to. In the words of a garment worker,

> The shop floor felt almost like being in the army. It was very hard for me to adjust to factory life. . . . I had to work three shifts – starting at six o'clock in the morning, two

o'clock in the afternoon, and ten o'clock at night – my living schedule changed completely according to which shift I was on. In my village, we went to sleep when night came and got up when dawn came, but we don't even know what the weather is outside the factory, we are slaves of time.

(Kim 1996, p. 41)

Overtime work was expected on a regular basis. Some of the work was extremely dangerous and the women that worked there received a special compensation. 'Accidents were common; some women got lead poisoning, and the skin of their fingers turned black. Workers were rotated to lessen the chances of poisoning, but lead poisoning could cause permanent damage that did not become apparent until much later' (p. 45). Kim did her ethnographic study as a 'disguised' participant observer. She also witnessed a labour conflict in the late 1980s, in which women workers actively participated – a risky move, as particularly the married women had to fear the loss of their jobs and much needed income. Warouw (2008) adds work about women in manufacturing in post-1997 Indonesia, describing the factories he visited as 'total institutions' that have built a system of rules and tough controls that compels women, most of them from small villages, 'to industrial discipline and the work rhythm of the factory' (p. 105).

Many of the young women looking for work in the factories that form part of the electronics special zone in Tamil Nadu, India, want to be independent. One of Dutta's (2019) informants found work in an auto factory assembling and visually inspecting auto parts. She told her,

It was a very hard job. My hands would bleed. The materials would be so sharp, it would cut my hands. We were all such young kids and our hands were soft. The materials would be heavy and very difficult to lift. This was no salary for how much we struggled at work, but we did it anyway because there was nothing else at that time.

(Dutta 2019, p. 896)

The women's main motivation to work in a factory was the expectation of gaining independence from the men in the family; many of them lived in abusive relationships. Dutta depicts them as agentic subjects 'who under different conditions define/re-define work relations which can both "liberate" them and at the same time tie them down with more responsibilities and roles' (p. 898). With their decision to work in the factory they challenge the traditional gender script. For these women, Dutta contends,

'becoming' worker is much more than just about entering waged work, it is part of a process of becoming conscious of the labour process and making tactical decisions. The cycle of escape and responsibility is part of their everyday negotiations of relations that they perceive to be exploitative and precarious.

(Dutta 2019, p. 900)

Exploring the working lives of female assembly workers in Sri Lanka, most of them from rural areas, Hewammane (2018) emphasizes that accepting harsh working conditions is a way for the women to achieve some social mobility and also gain voice and agency. The women, most of them young, unmarried, and rather well educated, work as machine operators for minimal wages under exploitative conditions. Having moved from the village to an urban area and

> living with other young women in an urban area causes these women to undergo social, cultural, emotional and cognitive changes. For instance, they start to value relative freedom of movement and new lifestyles; they acquire global knowledge flows; and the intense socialisation process in factories and boarding houses encourages them to dress, behave, think and desire in new ways. Moreover, their salaries allow them increased decision-making powers within their parental households.
>
> (Hewammane 2018, p. 2174)

Hence, despite low salaries and difficult working conditions, the women Hewammane interviewed manage 'to "develop" themselves to a better social position than their parents', even when they return to their village and get married, with their savings (based on a special financial arrangement) eventually helping them, in combination with micro-credits, to pursue an entrepreneurial activity.

Studies also stress the women workers' readiness to engage in labour struggles. Examples of women's labour activism have been described by Chi and van den Broek (2020):

> The first case indicates how female workers in a Japanese-owned electronics firm in Hanoi developed collaborations with higher-ranked (male) engineers and office clerks to change and influence the union leadership to explicitly represent the rank-and-file workers' issues. The second case explores how female workers in a Korean-owned garment factory in Ho Chi Minh City managed to improve conditions regarding strictly controlled rest breaks and the safety of pregnant women working in the factory. This was achieved by leveraging supply chain actors and issues regarding brand reputation.
>
> (Chi and van den Broek 2020, p. 1146)

They point to the informality of women's industrial activism, given their marginalization in trade unions, which pushed them to develop their own strategies for action. Based on his experience of 'worker movements in Tangerang in the mid 1990s', Warouw (2008) argues that 'female workers' superior skills of persuasion and communication, as well as their patience in labour organizing work, often placed them in leadership positions in industrial actions' (p. 111). Research on the role of women in grassroot neighborhood and community-based groups confirms these findings: it demonstrates the strength of poor, disadvantaged women, and their will to organize and pursue their goals (Terrin and Wagner, 2023).

Digitalization and the Gendered Work Organization

Joan Greenbaum began working in the computer industry in the 1960s. She

> realized that it was work that was being changed by management, something that I had seen at IBM. . . . So that of course, it went to the lowest paid people. And what I was experiencing in the US was, women were getting those jobs, because they were lower pay. So, it became . . . for a period in the 70s a female occupation at a lower wage. . . . [W]omen in England and Europe were fighting to get into these jobs. And here I was writing, how do we get out of the jobs and get to something that will really pay?
>
> (Joan Greenbaum, interview 05/05/2022).

In many ways, this comment points to one of the key concerns of early debates about digitalization and gendered work organizations.

In the 1970s the sociology of work was dominated by the so-called 'automation debate', which referred to how automation of work would change workplaces and the organization of work. Feminist scholars, such as Cynthia Cockburn, contributed to the automation debate with nuanced analyses of the impact of technology on workers' skills, arguing that skill has a class and gender dimension. A key aspect of automation was not necessarily deskilling but a tendency to keep women out of the new skilled technical jobs, as numerous studies corroborated (e.g., Westwood 1984; Acero 1995). Lothar Lappe (1988) who had studied women's work in several areas of industry with a high percentage of female workers, argued,

> It is generally agreed that the various strands of development in the capitalist work process need elaboration so that questions about downgrading and de-skilling can be answered for specific, definable, empirical areas and manageable time periods rather than continuously being treated in a general fashion. . . . Only when specific production areas are taken into consideration can one really understand and interpret the forms of human labour linked to the varied technological levels of the production process.
>
> (Lappe 1988, p. 234)

Similarly, Feldberg and Glenn (1983) argued that in making sense of the impact of technological change (in their case office automation), women's work required looking at it across a multiplicity of contexts: the work practices, the organizational structure, and the occupational structure. Speaking about prospects for women in manufacturing, Joan Greenbaum commented that 'it would be great [if] there wasn't a closed door, and that [manufacturing jobs were] made more readily available – that they could get in. But once in – what's going to happen to those kinds of engineering jobs?' (Joan Greenbaum, interview 05/05/2022).

'It is striking', Alemann et al. (2020) contend, 'that the current debate on digitalisation in the world of work and its consequences is dominated by gender-blind perspectives, especially in economics, labour research, computer science, and technology research' (p. 4). Indeed, few studies examine issues of digitalization in modern industrial workplaces and their consequences for women workers, as a literature study by Koller (2021) confirms. She saw some indications that 'digitalisation was, in fact, already able to improve working conditions and promoted the integration of women and older employees in a few selected areas, especially through reducing physical demands of labour by implementing assistive digital technologies' (p. 2). But it is far from clear how digitalization will affect women's employment in industry in the near future.

As concerns work in production, automation is expected to make assembly lines shorter without fully replacing them any time soon. In low-income countries where women produce excellent quality at low cost, there may be no perceived need for automation, in particular when women with highly developed manual skills are readily available. While it might be relatively easy to purchase imported machinery, it might be hard to find workers that can operate and fix them. Automation will require more skilled workers for machine programming and maintenance. Having less access to upskilling programs that would qualify them to operate complex machines, women are generally more vulnerable than men to being made redundant.

Among the research on women's factory work and the effects of automation, Brumley's paper on the gendered ideal worker stands out. Based on qualitative interview with workers and management at a Mexican-owned multinational manufacturing cooperative, she found that with automation, management reassessed skills with the result that 'Automation and teamwork are recast as men's work; women are sent home' (Brumley 2018, p. 406). The company had always seen women's work as temporary, having defined a 'marriage/pregnancy bar' for women. But women could always be replaced by women. This changed and presumed gender traits played a strong role in this process, with skills being redefined in a gendered way – 'manual physical jobs remained the domain of men, but technical, high-skill jobs replaced women's unskilled, manual jobs' (p. 413).

> The dearth of women was not simply their retirement or marriage, or that women's work ended. Rather, it was the result of management redefining jobs to correspond

to presumed masculine attributes. Automation and teamwork justified the entrenchment of the breadwinner–caregiver model, reserving increasingly limited factory jobs for men. Consequently, women's exit was not about the nature of the work but about how the required skills fit with presumed gendered, management manipulated gender ideology to fit a specific division of labor. Men were trainable to become knowledgeable and responsible leaders rather than 'needing guidance', but women were not.

(Brumley 2018, p. 414)

In the Swedish mining and metal industry, a shift of the notion of the ideal worker is taking place with digitalization. But the story is more complicated. A study of women in Sweden participating in digitalized metal workplaces – while pointing to ambivalences – stresses that women metal workers 'through the construction of their sense of self as competent digital steelworkers, take on a vital role in re-formulating the gender script of the digitalized metal industry' (Johansson et al. 2020, p. 1321); and that the 'influx of women and new ways of organizing tasks upon the implementation of digital technology lead to diversified performances in metal workplaces' (p. 1337). At the same time, the researchers observed that old images of masculinity based on physical strength have been replaced by new ones – there 'has been a shift towards emphasizing the skills of mastering and controlling complex production lines, which are becoming increasingly digitalized' (p. 1331). Most workers in the control room are male.

The researchers identified different ways in which female operators in the factory adapt to the connotation of technology with male gender:

They use this symbolic connection to describe tasks, tooling and products. For instance, the machines performing tasks previously performed by men are referred to as 'he' by female operators. The operators described the process in which a board equipped with a laser eye moves metal bars to the oven as 'he' reads it into the system. Moreover, materials processed through the factory attain an anthropomorphized shape associated with the male gender, too. We find that these linguistic features, enacted daily on the shop floor, strengthen the symbolic connection between digital technology and masculinity.

(Johansson et al. 2020, p. 1333)

The authors see their findings as making clear that undoing gender in the metal industry is a long and complex process; still, the increased presence of women and the ways they enact femininity differently, making a place for themselves in the industry, are signs of hope.

A similar story emerges in a study of women in the Swedish mining industry (Abrahamsson and Johansson 2020). The impact of advanced digitalization in this industry is impressive: mining becoming 'office work' with parts of it moving from underground to remote-controlled operations being carried out on large computer screens located in a high-rising office tower. Miners now need an overview of the whole flow of production as well as specialized technical qualifications:

> This shift involves contradictory movements of up-qualification, which involves rapidly changing skill demands, more theoretical, comprehensive, and communicative tasks, as well as 'de-qualification', which involves the fragmentation of individual craft knowledge and routinization of work tasks. There is also a form of re-qualification. The new skills and knowledge are in some respects more abstract and theoretical than was previously the case, but in other respects, they are still bodily and tacit: only in a different way with less force and increased precision.
>
> (Abrahamsson and Johansson 2020, p. 7)

The mining company where this research took place has a long-standing commitment to recruiting and training women, including annual pay reviews, and women's networks have been established. However, they have only been partially successful in changing gendered notions of work in the mine; although it may appear more difficult to 'maintain the image of macho mine work in a control room' (p. 8). So, the masculine workplace culture continues to emphasize the difference between the 'real' miners working underground and those in the control rooms:

> The people working underground called, half-jokingly, the remote operations center 'The Seven Heaven', referring not only to its position on the seventh floor in the office building but also to the contrast between this nice, comfortable workplace, and the traditional mining environment. They also gave remote-control workers nicknames such as 'the velour workers', meaning that they are of a soft type of men, almost feminine, and not real macho miners.
>
> (Abrahamsson and Johansson 2020, p. 8)

There is also resistance to technology and the changes it brings about among male mine workers and supervisors. For example, risk-taking and resistance to safety issues are part of the 'old' story of mining that has heavy, rough, and dangerous work.

Given 'the numerical and the cultural male dominance in both mining and digitalization', Abrahamsson and Johansson (2020) see processes of 're-gendering that slowly are changing the mine worker masculinity to suit the new situation' (p. 11) as the most probable scenario for the future. Digitalization 'per se' will not reduce or remove the link between male-dominated workplaces and masculinity, unless more radical moves are made to change the workplace culture and the whole organization deeply commits to distributive justice.

Design Strategies for the Modern Industrial Workplace

We have looked at two types of workplaces for women in industrial companies, in varied transnational settings. Women's work in the factory is often assembly work but also other types of heavy, dirty, dangerous work, in rich as well as in low-income countries. The stories of women factory workers are rather different from women working in the male-dominated areas of industrial companies, where they are few and confronted with strong images of masculinity.

Designing within an Industry 4.0 context with a view of supporting gender equality, researchers and developers will encounter particular challenges. They not only have to find technical solutions that can be appropriated in use, empowering workers, and improving their working conditions. They also have to think about how to widen access for skilled women workers to the emerging new work opportunities. Of course, they cannot do this on their own without support by management and, hopefully, the union representatives on the company level. Given the experiences with digitalization projects in the metal industry and mining, this is expected to be a hard task.

Lewis et al. (2017) have argued,

> There is no consensus about what is it exactly that should be achieved in gender equality change. Changing horizontal and vertical segregation patterns and unequal numerical representations in the workforce is but one part of the agenda. The ambition for change tends to stretch beyond the numbers to non-quantifiable goals such as visibility, access to power and full participation in decision making. . . . Feminist scholars generally consider transformative strategies and interventions, aimed at changing the ways that work is routinely divided, organized, and valued, as the most effective ways to counter gender inequalities and bring about the desired organizational change.
>
> (Lewis et al. 2017, p. 10)

Ideas about the practical measures in support of gender equality at work are rather 'old' and, unfortunately, still timely: they include all that accommodates women's (and men's) family responsibilities, from easily accessible and affordable childcare facilities to worktime arrangements that make family and work compatible, to access to upgrading and training programs for women, as well as mentoring programs and social networks. It seems what needs to be done in the arena of politics and policymaking, as well as the institutional and/or organizational context for action (Gärtner and Wagner 1996), is well known. It is much less clear how researchers and developers can contribute to gender equality on the level of systems and workplace design. At the heart of transformative strategies put forward in the literature is to 'manage diversity' or 'celebrate the difference' – the idea that differences should be recognized and harvested rather than denied or diluted (Liff and Wajcman 1996). But how can this be achieved in ways that make the work organization less gendered, less dominated by images of masculinity, and more open to women flourishing and succeeding?

The experiments at Volvo with teamwork in labour-intense assembly plants were quite unique at their time. They were based on the belief that women's approach to work is different and that this difference would make teamwork more effective. In the words of a production manager,

> From this year we hope to recruit more girls. We do not have a tradition of employing [girls] but we must have girls in this system too for different reasons. The first is that we have to have justice in the [plant]. We have to have girls working otherwise we deny 50% of the population the right to work here. The other reason why I want girls is that it gives you another climate. I have seen it already. Suddenly the guys shave in the morning, they have taken down the pin-up pictures. Suddenly it is more friendly. It gives you another atmosphere.
>
> (Wallace 1999, p. 26)

Including women workers in mixed teams as an example of 'managing diversity' had a positive outcome: more women were recruited onto the shop floor with the possibility to move upward and the teams benefitted from the women's supposed features. However, making teams at the assembly line more diverse 'per se' did not challenge gender stereotypes. The mixed teams worked well on the basis of gendered notions of skills. 'Managing diversity' in this case also implied possible discrimination against women that are not necessarily willing to assume a 'motherhood role'.

Abrahamsson (2014) noted some modest positive changes in a company that had introduced multifunctional autonomous teamwork and other organizational changes as part of a transition to a lean production model. While the results of her study concerning gender equality 'ten years after' are inconclusive, she ventures that a 'continuous implementation of new technology at industrial workplaces, resulting in new types of work tasks, new competence demands, more safety, and a better physical work environment, would (in theory) challenge many older forms of gender stereotypes and gender inequality' (p. 129).

Another relevant example of organizational change, again from Volvo, has been studied by Styhre (2014). The company had set up a concept-car development project that was managed by an all-women team. The project that had a special focus on female customers received much media attention and was highly successful:

> it generated market interest and enabled for a communication with consumer groups Volvo normally have a problem to get hold of; it made use of and exposed the competencies and skills of the female co-workers at Volvo; the concept car per se contributed with some new technical solutions that may be further explored and exploited in new product development projects later on. By and large, for Volvo, the YCC project was a success in terms of internal and external communication and the use of skills and competencies in the company. Women became more visible in the organization.
>
> (Styhre 2014, p. 101)

Styhre is quite skeptical concerning the more long-term effects of the project as long as it remains a singular engagement – 'a gendered carnival?' – without a deeper commitment to distributive justice in the company.

One of the lessons we draw from these few examples is that it is important to, from the very beginning of a project, conceptualize systems development as part of organizational change. This may offer the chance to also systematically think about gender equality in the process of designing system and work practices and all the necessary steps towards the system's appropriation.

Summary

In this chapter, we looked at historical research concerning women in factory work. Our coverage of material here served in part as a vehicle that allowed us to 'see' the pervasiveness of cultures of masculinity in workplaces, and how they seem to be inextricably tied to organizational structures. On the one hand we have stressed that the gendering of organizations and images of masculinity are significant factors that need to be overcome if we are to undo the gendering characteristic of modern organizations. Paradoxically, we also introduced case studies that evidence not only the global nature of contemporary manufacturing, but that also demonstrate that global manufacturing has been feminized in some countries. This last point raises questions about the similarities and differences in women's work in industrial settings throughout the world, and also signals the potential malleability of what Harding (1996) calls gender structures. Although gender structures, gender symbolism, and gender identity may work together to create gendered workplaces, the variability of how that works in different parts of the world also suggests a certain malleability when it comes to gendered expectations, gendered norms, and the gendering of work.

5

Office Automation and the Redesign of Work

In the previous chapter, we addressed issues that arose with the automation of factory work. Factory work was important to consider for at least three reasons. First, some of the early work that addressed computerization of work – although not explicitly focussed on women – was undertaken in (primarily) male-dominated workplaces, and the studies done in those workplaces (e.g., David Noble's (1979) work on numerically controlled machine tools; Kern and Schumann's (1970) case studies in the automotive, tool, and chemical industries) introduced research upon which subsequent work concerned with computerization of women's work built. Second, in some parts of the world (e.g., the Global South) automation of factory work provided opportunities for women and became the focal point for early feminist writing from outside of Europe and North America. Third, these cases were also important to address because they allowed us to see the ways that the division of labour can vary cross-nationally: what is considered women's work in one country may be considered men's work somewhere else.

In this chapter, we discuss the computerization of office work, which in many ways served as a focal point for the emergence of research about gender and technology in the 1980s. Our focus on office automation allows us to explore topics that have been central to the development of feminist perspectives on work. These include the nature of women's work and invisible work. Tracing the automation of office work historically allows us to see the dynamics that guided the gendering of office technologies, and allows us to introduce concepts and debates that emerged (e.g., about whether women's jobs were being deskilled, upgraded or both), which assumed importance not only amongst those studying office automation, but travelled into other intellectual communities, including science, technology, and society studies, PD of computer systems, and CSCW, and became central to more contemporary inquiries in diverse fields. Issues we address include the nature of office work, invisible work and skill, the 'gendering' of office machines, and debates about skill – deskilling, upskilling, and the social construction of skill. These discussions set the stage for us to address issues related to the design and re-design of work. We then move on to a discussion about early PD projects that focussed on gender issues and sought to redesign women's work in automated offices. Material in this chapter both allows us to explore key concepts that have been of concern to the study of both gender and work and system design and serves as a historical orientation to contemporary work in the platform economy.

The Automation of Office Work

Many of the women that pioneered gender and technology studies we interviewed began studying the computerization of women's work around the time that office automation was beginning. This also coincided with the early days of the computer industry, a groundswell of interest in automation of work as a labour issue, the emergence of 'women and technological change' as an area of scholarly inquiry (which had been preceded by feminist historians of technology undertaking groundbreaking studies about technologies used in the home), and critiques of medicine, science, and technology. These developments were all key to the formation of STS. Occurring around the same time – and with some overlapping people – the first CSCW conference was held in 1987, and the first PD conference was held in 1990.

Research about automation and office work started in the 1970s when the first word processors entered the office affecting mostly the work of women typist and secretaries. It was strongly connected to the deskilling debate that understood automation as the transfer of human skills to the machine. Feminist scholars studied women's work in the office with a view towards making women's skills and the invisible parts of their work visible.

Among the best-known studies of office automation at that time was Glenn and Feldberg's (1977) 'Degraded and deskilled: The proletarianization of clerical work' where they examined changes in women's work associated with technological change (and concurrent work organizational/managerial changes). They used the term proletarianization, which

> is said to occur as clerical work loses the features that have traditionally placed it among middle-class, white collar occupations; as narrow, largely manual skills displace complex skills and mental activity; as close external control narrows the range of worker discretion; and as impersonal relationships replace social give and take.
>
> (Glenn and Feldberg 1977, p. 52)

Studies of office automation and women's work portrayed secretarial work as involving professional skills such as abstract thinking, planning, and servicing people from inside and outside the organization in various ways (e.g., Lie and Rasmussen 1985; Silverstone and Towler 1984; Webster 1996; Green 1993). For example, Liisa Rantalaiho (1990) showed that the successful operation of secretarial tasks requires a whole range of technical, interactive, and abstract skills that together form a complex web of practices. While not explicitly focussing on women, Lucy Suchman and Eleanor Wynn's 'Procedures and problems in the office' (1984) addressed technology design issues, arguing that procedural work cannot be fully automated as it involves the ability to flexibly respond to the exigencies of the work as it unfolds. At the same time, the 'deskilling' thesis that had been advanced by Braverman (1974) in a rather general way, without backing up by detailed empirical work, was called into question and a more nuanced view of the effects of automation was developed.

The debate about automation and (women's) skills brought two issues into focus. One was workplace design – how to ensure that office technologies were used to preserve and expand skills (rather than reduce them) and to improve working conditions. The second issue was how to support learning and the appropriation of technologies that were basically purchased by companies seeking rationalization and the reduction of costs. In addition, some of the early work that sought to understand the impact of office automation on women's work (notably Feldberg and Glenn (1983) and Menzies (1981)) also documented changes in organizational structures and the proportion of kinds of jobs, the nature of those jobs, and where women worked. The need to contextualize work beyond a single workplace and look at not only work processes and work practices, but also at organizational structures and changes in occupational structure, remains salient.

The debate about office automation ended in the early 1990s. Although we will never know what led to declining scholarly debate in this area, some possible explanations include that for most the benefits of emergent technologies seemed evident, while the drawbacks (e.g., increasing administrative loads being shifted to all but the most senior workers) had not yet fully materialized. Additionally, as new technologies emerged (such as computer networking; mobile phones, new medical technologies), feminist scholars began addressing these areas.

Although scholarly debates about office or clerical work waned, the work itself – much of it carried out by women – did not disappear. The job of secretary still exists, although the number of secretaries in many organizations has declined, and the tasks they undertake have changed in a world where increasingly tasks previously done by secretaries have been transferred (through the support of technologies) from clerical workers to professionals. The modern office is equipped with all kinds of technologies – networked machines and the software running on them – that have multiple functionalities supporting a wide array of clerical tasks.

Thinking about the future of office/clerical work we can start with Rantalaiho's (1990) definition: 'Office work consists in producing, distributing, conveying, rearranging, applying and interpreting information of various kinds' (p. 68). Much of clerical work today is data work, and data processors, Plantin (2021) argues, are 'not only invisible workers, but also factory workers who follow and subvert a workflow organized as an assembly line' (p. 1). With the introduction of AI-based tools in many work environments, there is 'little or no place' for clerical work as we knew it before, Møller (2018) suggests looking at the work of medical secretaries. Also, new forms of organizing work, as for example mobile or nomadic work, have gained momentum and, with the increasing significance of online platforms of all kinds and the gig economy associated with them, new types of work have emerged. We ask whether these new forms of work reinforce gender-based differences in the workplace and historical conceptions of skill associated with (male) gender.

This chapter focusses on classic clerical work, highlighting numerous issues – notably related to skill and invisible work – which have been central to understanding work in diverse areas. It addresses an important time in the development of research concerned with women and technological change, in part because the issues that surfaced through this work – notably about skill and invisible work – went on to have implications in other fields of inquiry. Our work in this chapter also lays important foundations that helps us understand and address key design challenges for HCI and CSCW research. In addition to a focus on invisible work and skills, it directs attention to issues that reach beyond systems design: work design, learning, design directed at improving working conditions, and the possibilities of supporting labour action through design. Finally, our focus in Chapter 5 on the automated office also lays the foundation and sets the stage for our subsequent discussion of platform work, which we take up in Chapter 6.

Taking a Closer Look at Office Work

Among the feminist scholars that studied office workers, Liisa Rantalaiho's (1985 (with Päivi Korvajärvi) and 1990) work stands out. She starts with the remark that office work in the traditional sense was (and often still to some extent is) considered basically routine work that is carried out by low-paid, unskilled women. Office work (like many other types of work) *IS* often routine, she states, but also not easily standardized because it is undertaken 'often in unpredictable combinations and contexts' (1990, p. 64). This is one of the key insights Lucy Suchman and Eleanor Wynn (1994) formulated in their study of office workers: the ways workers accomplish procedures, they observed, is 'tied to the contingencies of actual cases' and 'managing those contingencies involves ongoing consultation and negotiation' (p. 138). Blomberg et al. (1996) problematized the 'routine/knowledge work' distinction underlying the devaluation of many types of low-paid work:

> The standard organizational icon of the pyramid ... is stratified according to the attribution of progressively more knowledge work as one moves from bottom to top. The bottom layers in this view are made up of relatively large numbers of workers with relatively few skills, engaged in appropriately routine tasks. The top layers comprise smaller numbers of workers with greater knowledge and skills, engaged in correspondingly more knowledge-intensive forms of work.
>
> (Blomberg et al. 1996, p. 251)

They challenged this pyramid using the example of document coding and data entry in a law firm that had been defined as 'routine' although requiring judgmental and interpretive work. The bottom line of these studies is that, even when following routines, office workers need to solve problems and adapt their ways of working to contingencies as they arise. Emphasizing the critical role of workplace studies, Schmidt (2000) summarizes the insights gained by ethnographic studies of office work:

> In particular, they subjected the common-sense presuppositions about the status of office procedures vis-à-vis the actual course of action to a critical analysis and demonstrated that office procedures do not determine action causally; they could thereby show that the design visions of the office automation movement were misguided.
>
> (Schmidt 2000, p. 5)

The Nature of Office/Clerical Work

Liisa Rantalaiho's (1990) work on office automation was based on a study of the introduction of technologies in several organizations. Interviews with office workers gave 'insight not only into the work process, but also into work histories, work orientations, and the meaning of work in women's life as a whole' (p. 65). She emphasizes the heterogeneity of office work as resulting from its dependence on structural conditions: 'Office work at a goods office, furniture factory, insurance company, university faculty, and a child welfare office consists of different kinds of tasks and elements' (p. 66); that means it is highly varied depending on the industry and the organization of work.

Despite this variety, early research on office work largely focussed on the work of secretaries and typists; there have been some exceptions, such as Joan Greenbaum (1996) who studied clerical workers processing phone calls from customers in the insurance industry. Also the focus of Rantalaiho's work was on secretaries. There are few specific skills that may be required in office work (apart from bookkeeping, typing, etc.), she found, and the functional division of labour 'does not go very far'. In many cases the borderline between office work and professional work is not so clear, as office workers may be responsible for preparing documents for decisions and also take over tasks related to the control of procedures and documents. Underlying the many different types of office work is information processing, characterized by its 'invisible and continuous nature' (p. 68) – characteristics it shares with housework.

Referring to Eleanor Wynn's (1979) ethnographic study of office work, Rantalaiho (1990) stressed how the information office workers produce is 'intrinsically dependent on social interactions for its quality, relevance, and appropriateness' (p. 69). An overriding responsibility of office workers is maintaining the infrastructure of the office: 'Office work is women's work precisely as a form of activity that guarantees the continuity of day-to-day praxis' (p. 71) was Rantalaiho's conclusion concerning the nature of office work:

> There is much more to women's office work than its visible routines, and therefore a methodological approach should be adopted which recognizes the workers as genderized subjects of meaningful interaction. What on the surface seems like routine and abstract information processing is in fact work which produces and maintains the social community and common frameworks of interpretation.
>
> (Rantalaiho 1990, p. 64)

It is precisely this overarching role of the secretary that makes it ambiguous, Wichrowski (1994) argues, and some key aspects of the work remain unnamed and uncategorized. Job descriptions normally only cover the 'rational labour' office workers perform. In addition to the rational, well-described part of their work, secretaries carry out various forms of emotional labour – political, latent, and socially supportive – as well as peripheral labour – 'those negotiated tasks hinging on the boss–secretary relationship, office organization, and gender expectations' (p. 35). The concept of emotion work was developed by Hochschild (1983), describing the situation of female flight attendants who have to manipulate their own emotions to please their customers. Transferred to the workplace for a wage, it becomes 'emotional labour', 'a process that

Hochschild refers to as 'the "transmutation" of a private emotion system into the public sphere' (Wichrowski 1994, p. 34). Another relevant category of work performed by secretaries is 'latent work':

> ... there must be someone besides the computer who knows what is going on, a troubleshooter when things go wrong. Bureaucratic channels must often be bypassed in order to maximize efficiency. Instant information may be critical to getting a job done, and rigid rules often make getting it a slow and inefficient process.
>
> (Wichrowski 1994, p. 40)

Secretaries – predominantly women – need to be able to flexibly maneuver an organization and its rules as well as be able to mobilize support of different kinds so as to get the work done timely and efficiently. Historically, secretarial work was often viewed as being similar to work women carried out in the home – repetitive, supporting others, having few 'finished products' to show at the end of it; and requiring skills similar to those of running a family and household. Stereotypes concerning the 'natural' allocation of women to jobs that fitted their specific skills acquired in the home were at the core of the sexual division of labour (see also Balka and Wagner 2021).

Since the 1980s and 1990s when feminist scholars studied the work of secretaries, office work has undergone changes due to the fact that the modern office is replete with technologies that allow secretaries (or administrative assistants as they are often called today) to perform more and different tasks than before. For example, Lesi (2020) describes the job of secretaries at a university as follows:

> Secretaries and administrative assistants use a variety of office equipment, such as fax machines, photocopiers, scanners, and video-conferencing and telephone systems. In addition, secretaries and administrative assistants often use computers to do tasks previously handled by managers and professionals; they create spreadsheets, compose correspondence, manage databases, and create presentations, reports, and documents using desktop publishing software and digital graphics. They may also negotiate with vendors, maintain and examine leased equipment, purchase supplies, manage areas such as stockrooms or corporate libraries, and retrieve data from various sources.
>
> (Lesi 2020, p. 23)

In spite of all of these additional tasks that a secretary may carry out, Truss et al. (2013) contend, 'most secretaries continue to perform traditional tasks and career prospects for all remain bleak. We conclude that processes of role gender-typing are deeply entrenched and that secretarial work remains largely a ghetto occupation' (p. 349). Their findings are supported by Zuin's (2013) ethnographic study of the work of medical and legal secretaries. Although secretaries in these rather different contexts use digitalized systems to do their work, they spend most of their time typing and managing the data in the system, while 'management controls their work by interfering and dictating what they do' (p. 227).

In Harding's (1986) terms, gender structures are evident in clerical work So dominant is the gender symbolism associated with clerical work that it is frequently referred to as 'pink collar work', reflecting the degree to which in most countries it is a profession dominated by women. One of the very few articles that has addressed gender identity amongst male clerical workers provides insight into an unusual aspect of how what Harding would call gender identity works (for male temporary clerical workers). Henson and Krasa Rogers (2001, p. 218) argue that male workers who 'cross over into "women's work," face institutional challenges to their masculinity'. Their failure to live up to the ideals of masculinity are highlighted, and they learn to perform masculinity (often collaboratively in ways shaped by their agencies or clients) to 'reassert the feminine identification of the job while at the same time rejecting its application to them' (p. 218). Henson and Krasa Rogers point out this strategy helps reproduce both the gendered organization of work and naturalize masculinity.

Invisible Work and Skill

A strong motivation behind studies of women's work was to demonstrate the 'invisible skills' in their work, as well as the different valuation of different types of skills. (In)visibility was also a major issue in the early studies of office work. Within CSCW research this notion goes back to a seminal paper by Susan Leigh Star and Anselm Strauss (1999), in which they ask what counts as work. Invisible work is 'expertise often hidden from view (in even seemingly mindless tasks)' (p. 11), they argue, identifying four forms of such work: work that takes place in invisible places (e.g., the 'back office' work that is not visible to those that receive a service, customer support work, work in call centres); work that has been defined as 'routine' although requiring skills (e.g., print or reprographic work, 'micro work' (e.g., Amazon Mechanical Turk and Crowdflower)); work done by invisible persons (e.g., informal carers, domestic workers); and aspects of work that are not part of a job description but crucial to the quality of the work. Much of the emotional labour and latent and socially supportive work that secretaries perform is of this nature; as is Bowker and Star's (1999) example of 'humour' in how nurses perform their work and interrelate with patients (see Chapter 8).

But the notion of invisible work, although the term may not have been used, is much older. For example, in a pioneering study Suzanne Pacaud (1949), one of the founders of Francophone ergonomics, identified '14 difficulties' telephone operators have to cope with in their daily work, including:

> The telephone operator constantly keeps an eye on the lights indicating call and those indicating supervision: it is almost always that whilst talking to a caller she withdraws the cards pertaining to the conversation she just finished; when she is about to establish a communication that a colleague asks her for advice concerning another user; when she sees someone quitting a post that she needs to think to give it to a person that urgently asked for this post.
>
> (Pacaud 1949, p. 216)

While each of these difficulties may be insignificant in itself, their recurrent occurrence makes the work complex, difficult to perform, and exhausting, Pacaud argued.

Work undertaken by German industrial sociologists and work psychologists in the 1980s had a focus on the skills (or qualifications) different types of jobs required. This research was oriented towards the 'humanization of working life' and driven by the idea of designing mentally demanding work, in contrast to low-skilled repetitive work (e.g., Kissler and Sattler 1982). Within this framework, Jakobi and Weltz (1981) conducted a study of the skills involved in typing and the stress that typists experience. They provided a highly detailed list of skills that reach far beyond the sheer mechanical act of typing, among them, the ability to quickly grasp the meaning of larger pieces of text; to actively think whilst reading and typing; and a high degree of concentration.

Roslyn Feldberg (1984), in her discussion of the 'comparable worth movement' in the USA, pointed out the fact that the particular skills required in many women's occupations are not recognized as skill:

> Much of women's work involves recognizing and responding to subtle cues in the work process or in other people, yet women's ability to do so is devalued. For example, the work of housewives, secretaries, teachers, aides, and nurses is geared toward understanding other people's needs and assisting them in realizing their goals. But this work is judged less skilled or less important than that of the persons being assisted.
>
> (Feldberg 1984, pp. 321f.)

Michael Muller's (1999) paper 'Invisible work of telephone operators: An ethnocritical analysis', relates the results of an in-depth study of telephone operators in the USA. Its aim is to make the knowledge work in seemingly 'mindless' forms of work visible, Muller states quoting Lucy Suchman's (1995) paper 'Making work visible'. He identified and described the skills telephone operators need, among them: they are fast and accurate and have 'superior short-term and long-term memory'; they have in-depth domain-specific knowledge 'that includes the computer systems that they use, the business and geographical domains of their customers, and skills in conducting brief but effective conversations' and are able 'to perceive large meaningful patterns in their domain', not least because they possess 'detailed structural knowledge of the database' they use (pp. 39–40). Muller arrives at an interesting methodological conclusion from his research:

> If work is described as 'invisible', then someone must be viewing (or failing to view) that work. This is to say, the work itself is not necessarily invisible: Rather, the work is invisible from a particular perspective or position, and that perspective or position is occupied by one or more human viewers.
>
> (Muller 1999, p. 49)

That is, the (in)visibility of work very much depends on the perspective of the different stakeholders and the task of researchers is to identify these different views. Some aspects of the work may not even be visible to those who perform it, as Blomberg et al. (1993) note arguing in favour of using observational methods in workplace studies: 'People may distort, either knowingly or unknowingly amounts of their own behavior, often simply providing an approximation constructed either for the Questioner's benefit or to match cultural expectations' (p. 130).

Invisible work remains an issue of attention in contemporary studies of work. Whiting and Simon (2020) identify 'digi-housekeeping' as invisible work people perform in their home office. It is the work needed to maintain the digital tools that enable them to work from home. It involves clearing (to remove junk, clear digital space, etc.), sorting and filing, preparing 'devices, software and systems through maintenance, re-installation, keeping them synced, charged and made ready for (mobile) use' (p. 1085), provisioning (buying equipment and software), as well as troubleshooting. Also crowdworkers perform a lot of invisible and unpaid work that is necessary to, among other things, get work and be paid for it, and manage their payments (Chapter 6).

Reflecting on the visibility and invisibility of work in relation to Harding's (1986) understanding of gender, it is important to note that we still have a paid labour force that is largely gender structured. Men are still found largely in some jobs and women in others (gender structure), and jobs where skill is largely invisible are jobs more commonly held by women. The gender symbolism system – the gendering of things – labels these jobs as women's work, which contributes to the invisibility of skills required in jobs symbolically labelled as 'women's work'. Women who cross into predominantly male fields of work and men who cross into predominantly female forms of work, as noted by Henson and Krasa Rogers (2001) and others, experience challenges with gender identity. From the point of view of systems design, identifying the invisible skills – skills that do not appear in formal job descriptions and task analyses – is crucial to building good systems, as this helps both designers and users better understand which aspects of work may be automated and how humans and machines may complement each other. We will return to this point later.

The Different Faces of Office Automation: A Historical View

It all started with what in the 1970s was called office automation when word processors entered offices in the USA. From the very beginning, word processing was viewed as a means to combine dictating and typing (on automatic typewriters) in a centralized unit much in the way of Henry Ford's assembly line. This move was based on the idea of office work being unproductive and costly, hence the need to replace it with machines operated by low-paid women workers, as Hanley (2014) observes in her case study of white-collar automation at GE (General Electrics):

> Geiser (then manager of the business planning operation in GE's Computer Department) refers to office workers as 'non-productive' and 'peripheral' and bemoans the increasing burden of personnel required to generate, ingest and utilize this house of cards, of forms, of reports, inventories, surveys, of bills of sales and bills of lading, of production records, accounting records, shipping records, receiving records, of files and cross files, and of interoffice memos.
>
> (Hanley 2014, p. 412)

Office workers at GE experienced the introduction of typing pools as removing 'nearly all of the rewards of secretarial work', as one of the word processor operators complained in a letter to a business journal:

> MC/ST machines were noisy and the word-processor staff spent their entire working day in cramped conditions looking directly at a wall. But her bigger complaints were cultural. She was paid the lowest salary in the office and cut off from its social life, writing that 'the people in the office regard those of us who run the machines as part of the machines rather than as human beings like themselves!'
>
> (Haig 2006, p. 11)

Word processing formed just a small part of the vision of office automation. Xerox Star, the most advanced word processing system of the early 1980s, was already conceived of as an office automation system for networked workstations. Bravo, which was developed at Xerox Park, was the first machine that combined computerized text processing with formatting 'to create what was soon dubbed the WYSIWYG (What You See Is What You Get) approach to text editing' (Haig 2006, p. 21). It came closer to the vision of 'the paperless office of the future, a multifunction networked workstation with word processing, email, and graphical and voice capabilities would sit on the desks of every manager and every professional' (p. 7). The dedicated word processing machines were soon replaced by the general-purpose computer. However, computer networking was still quite primitive and the idea of

> networked machines, graphically sophisticated machines hooked into databases and sharing electronic mail, only became commonplace during the 1990s. Falling costs, technological improvements, and new software such as Lotus Notes made it possible to add these capabilities piecemeal to ordinary personal computers without raising their costs to an unacceptable level.
>
> (Haig 2006, p. 25)

The office automation tradition, Schmidt (2011) states, was from the beginning based on a widely accepted model 'of tasks and responsibilities or prescribed patterns of communication' (p. 76); a fact that had already been criticized in the early 1980s by Barber, de Jong, and Hewitt (1983):

> In all these systems information is treated as something on which office actions operate producing information that is passed on for further actions or is stored in repositories for later retrieval. These types of systems are suitable for describing office work that is structured around actions (e.g. sending a message, approving, filing); where the sequence of activities is the same except for minor variations and few exceptions. ... These systems do not deal well with unanticipated conditions.
>
> (Barber et al. 1983, p. 562)

The Female–Machine Connection

A second fundamental critique has been that office automation and the organizational changes accompanying it built on the understanding of office work and the technologies enabling it as feminized. This meant, as Juliet Webster (1993) observed, 'that the first generation of word processing, designed and marketed for use by women office workers, was initially targeted at and used by them, rather than being applied to other white-collar tasks involving the handling of text' (p. 115). In a paper, 'typing our way to freedom', Janine Morgall 1981 wrote,

> With groups of five or six female typists working under one male supervisor, the pattern of male supremacy was clearly reinforced in the office hierarchy. Women did not step into the jobs previously held by men. Instead office work was adjusted so that women performed only the routine and subservient functions.
>
> (Morgall 1981, p. 90)

Women were portrayed as being particularly suited to working with machines and to routine work, as Boyer and England (2008) observed, using the example of the Bank of Nova Scotia in Canada. The bank advertised a story – 'The all-girl boiler factory' – about its women employees dealing with checks, deposits, and credit items, emphasizing their keyboarding skills. This is an example of how companies 'strengthened the "female–machine" connection' (p. 248) – in Harding's (1986) terms, altering the gender symbolism system.

ATMs, another technology that was introduced in the late 1960s, were considered another example of the 'female-machine'. A *New York Times* article at that time referred to ATMs as '"the ugliest teller", but with the advantage that they "never get pregnant"' (Boyer and England 2008, p. 251). In general, newspaper articles and advertisements were full of disrespectful remarks about women office workers and often new technologies were praised as offering the opportunity to get rid of them altogether, as Hester (2017) remarks. Unlike a woman worker, an advert ran, the new machines 'can't take maternity leave. Or suffer from morning sickness. Or complain about being tired all the time' (p. 46). These ads both reinforced gender structures and began rewriting gender symbolism.

Deskilling or Upgrading?

Office automation allowed many back-office clerical functions such as data entry, typing, payroll, billing, and claims-processing to be spatially separated from front-office aspects of office work. This process, one of the core arguments was, led to a general deskilling of office occupations.

A definition of skill (or qualification) used by researchers in the tradition of German industrial sociology may be helpful in this context:

> The concept of qualification captures on the one hand abilities and knowledge that are necessary to perform a particular type of work (task-related concept of qualification), the competences and aptitudes of an individual (person-related concept of qualification). As concerns task-related qualifications, a distinction can be made between functionally required and extra functional qualifications, such as loyalty, punctuality, sense of responsibility, mindfulness . . ., but also flexibility, perceptiveness, technical intelligence and technical sensibility. Of more recent origin is the notion of key qualifications. These mainly comprise the abilities necessary for coping with open, undetermined, and complex situations – for example self-reliance, being intrinsically motivated to work, the ability to work in a team, communication skills, the ability to reflect and learn.
>
> (Heidenreich 1997, p. 696)

While skills, as feminist researchers suggested, are socially constructed – 'skill is defined to give priority to traditionally "male" work' (Wajcman 1991,

p. 43) – they also have a material/technical dimension: the 'mastery of technicalities' needed to carry out particular tasks correctly, efficiently, and with care.

As concerns office automation and the 'deskilling' hypothesis, several issues have to be accounted for. One is that skills are conceptualized and 'measured' in different ways. This makes it difficult to interpret the results of studies on office automation, Karen Hughes (1989) remarked in an extended literature review. Given the rather common claim that automation will inevitably lead to a routinization and deskilling of office jobs, she called for a more nuanced critical approach:

> In the debate over office automation, the majority of literature emphasizes downgrading in relation to work content and the focus is on the lower office stratum (i.e. EDP [electronic data processing] operators, typists, secretaries). While upgrading is discussed to some extent, there is uncertainty about the number of upgraded jobs that will be created and the ability of women to move into them.
>
> (Hughes 1989, p. 661)

This phenomenon was also observed in Canada. In workplaces examined, with the advent of automation, some jobs disappeared, some that remained were perceived to be less skilled, and the content of some jobs (typically, a select few) required that the women who filled them gain new skills and competencies. However, this 'upskilling' of jobs often went unrecognized and uncompensated.

Another issue that studies of office technologies brought to the fore was that the effects of office automation vary substantially among type of industry and organization size and tradition and that managerial decisions play a strong role. This, together with the heterogeneity of clerical occupations and office technologies means that we cannot assume that the effect of automation is constant across all cases (Lowe 1987). Silverstone and Fowler (1984) state that

> From the data collected the most likely prediction about the future of secretarial work seems to be that technology will reinforce whatever role the secretary already plays. Therefore, those who have a range of responsible duties will find they are freed from the routine typing and enabled to take on more delegated work, whereas the secretary used basically as a text producer may experience deskilling as presentation is improved and the speed of production increased by the technology.
>
> (Silverstone and Fowler 1984, p. 560)

Evelyn Nakano Glenn and Roslyn Feldberg's (1977) study focussed on five US companies, differing in size, technology, and organizational goals. They found that deskilling is linked to the reorganization of work and is most pronounced in large organizations with proclivity to centralize services such as data entry and typing. In spite of the variations they identify, they paint a rather bleak picture of office automation assuming a general tendency towards clerical pooling arrangements, hence the deskilling of office workers, while the emerging skilled jobs, such as programming, are rarely available to clerks, most of them women. Other studies confirmed the trend towards a deskilling of office work. A case study by Crompton and Reid (1982) of a British treasurer's department found that EDP was deskilled with respect to the complexity of tasks and the autonomy/control of workers. Research on the impact of different applications of technology and work organization (Crompton and Jones 1984) highlighted the link between deskilling and a centralized organization, affirming that in these organizations women were segregated into low skilled jobs. Wharton and Burris (1983) observed that 'by eliminating the need for skill and discretion, word processing also increases the monotony of office work. Some office workers now spend the entire day at word-processing terminals, where their jobs increasingly resemble those of routine machine operators' (p. 120). These studies highlighted the importance of the type of organization on how office automation was implemented and what this meant for the need for skills.

Apart from reducing the technical and social skills required to perform office work, office technologies were used to increase control and push for more output, Gregory and Nussbaum (1982) stated:

> Computer terminals used by data entry operators record the number of keystrokes per minute and lines processed per day. Many of these 'input typists' are paid piecework rates rather than an hourly wage. For claims processors, each claim is coded with the employee's name. The computer rejects any inaccurate forms, keeping track of the number of mistakes along with volume and speed.
>
> (Gregory and Nussbaum 1982, p. 205)

Hence, one of the main effects of office automation was stressful working conditions, exacerbated by low pay and lack of job security. Pacing by computerization was a new control strategy that created an important emerging risk for work stress, as can be seen in Joan Greenbaum's description of 'Sandy's workplace' in her book *Windows to the workplace* (1995):

> ... team trainers, supervisors, and quality control experts – three levels of monitors – listen in to a certain percentage of her calls and give her a monthly rating on how well she is doing. She is evaluated on the number of calls handled per hour, and on a variety of quality characteristics that zero in on her level of courtesy, clarity, and accuracy in giving out information. ... Sandy calls her work 'boring' and 'numbing', but acknowledges that it calls for a whole lot of skills, from listening to and counseling customers to a great deal of problem solving. ... Sandy's manager knows that the job is a high-stress one and that the skill requirements are high.
>
> (Greenbaum 1995, p. 96)

This practice has become fairly common and has been implemented in most call centres.

While office automation was widely used by management in ways that resulted in deskilling and a deterioration of working conditions, studies also identified examples of 'upskilling'. German industrial sociologists (Baethge and Oberbeck 1986; Berger and Offe 1982) argued that technologically induced rationalizations of office work did not necessarily follow Taylorist principles. They found evidence of an upgrading of skills following massive cutbacks of routine tasks. Studying the introduction of word processors in five large organizations in Austria (two banks, one insurance company, and the administrations of two manufacturing plants), Volst and Wagner (1988) drew attention to the complexity of skills involved even in those office tasks that have been classified as simple, stressing the much-needed ability of office workers 'to cope with the unexpected without creating disorder and interruption' (p. 131). They found different types of work organization within the same organization and among different organizations, depending on the pressure for quality of work output and/or volume of operations. Hence organizational units (e.g., in banks, ministries, revenue offices, municipal governments) where routine clerical workers (typists or data-typists) had to carry out a large number of routine administrative tasks or financial operations tended to split up work into standardizable tasks and those requiring personalized judgement. Computerization for typists or other low clerical staff in 'clockwork systems' (Wagner 1987) resulted in deskilling and the narrowing down of opportunities.

> Many of them do not get proper training. After a short learning period that has to be squeezed into a full work day they often have to cope with 6 to 8 hours at the computer terminal: 'Nobody wants to see that we type 8 hours per day. They just told us to make a 20 minute break after every 2 hours. They should tell our bosses too. There are some who give a 3 hour dictation directly into the computer, without a break'.
>
> (Wagner 1987, p. 4)

As concerns secretarial work, office automation also provided women with access to technical work tasks. Secretaries often become their bosses' technical assistants, as the following statement illustrates:

> My normal tasks are purely secretarial like scheduling meetings, preparing the mail; and then the preparation of offers, messages for our regional offices, preparing of charts. And then more skilled work – this special task I got which means surveying prices ...
>
> (Wagner 1987)

Many secretaries enjoyed this expansion of their jobs since it provided them with well-defined tasks that they can carry out independently. At the same time, a tendency to integrate lower-skilled clerical operations, such as data-inputting and typing into more varied clerical jobs was observed and arguably was used to obfuscate the need for expanded skills in lower-paying jobs.

In a study of office technologies in banks, insurance companies, and the legal industries, Pullman and Szymanski (1986) distinguished between two integrative mechanisms: (a) the evolution of lower-skilled clerical workers into higher-skilled positions due to increased technical skills; and (b) direct input of data and texts at the point of origin. While the technologies reduced clerical employment, they 'may have also reduced the need for mid-level skills in sales, policy-writing, and claims-processing functions, which could be transferred to relatively skilled segments of the clerical workforce' (Handel 2004, p. 49).

Also Juliet Webster (1993) emphasized that there was not one best way of implementing office technologies but that these systems have been configured in various ways that reflect local office contexts. But she also pointed to the continuity of how office work is organized and the importance of managerial strategies concerning work and women's employment:

> There are significant continuities in the conduct of office work before and after the introduction of word processor technology. Secretarial workers still have a range of activities. while the regimentation of the typing pool has carried over from the days before office automation. However, many office workers of all categories continue to bring considerable expertise and competence, of both a technical and broader organizational nature, to bear in the course of their work, and these have by no means been eradicated by the introduction of new technologies into the office.
>
> (Webster 1993, p. 116)

In view of her 'many years as a clerical worker, private secretary, shop steward and most recently as a student of sociology', Janine Morgall (1981) described how computers *could* be used in the office:

> Word processing machines can assist secretaries and typists in their daily work. They can increase productivity and bring about a shorter work week. Word processors will save secretaries and typists time in correcting and editing documents. That time should then be used for more responsible and challenging administrative tasks, for the training in new skills and for union activity. Word processors should be a tool in liberating women office workers from low-paid dead-end jobs. Women must insure that it is their brain-power and not their manual dexterity that is drawn on.
>
> (Morgall 1981, p. 95)

The (Re)Design of Work

Morgall's (1981) quote above speaks to the possibilities of consciously designing work in relation to technology – a topic we will address in greater depth in Chapter 10 (where we will discuss the overlaps and differences in designing technology and designing work). Despite the varied and extended discussions about the impact of office automation on women's work, few researchers actively addressed design issues at that time. This likely reflected two things: emergent, more nuanced views of technology at the time (which would come to be known as social constructivist views), and a need to first document gendered differences related to automation, together with the fact that office automation systems were not designed from scratch but rather were purchased.

In reflecting on views of technology during that period in time, Judy Wajcman pointed out that

> it was a very radical thing to talk about: the technical as socio technical, and to talk about the technical and science as a culture . . . Maureen McNeil writing essays on science's culture, and Donna Haraway and others' thinking, that science and technology have got embedded social values, that it's a social practice, that there are cultural practices rounded that.
>
> (Judy Wajcman, interview 03/28/2022)

The focus was on managerial decisions and how to influence workplace design, as well as on how to support office workers to appropriate the new technologies integrating them into their practices. 'When we talk about how computers are changing our jobs', Joan Greenbaum said in the early 1980s,

> it's important to realize that the jobs are changed before the computer comes in the door. To computerize what you do, managers must first find out exactly what decisions you make. First, an efficiency expert comes to set up new procedures which are designed to take your knowledge of the job and put it within the scope of computer programming. Then the computers and VDT's [video display terminals] are brought in. It's this removal of decision-making from us to management and to computer processing which makes us first of all more expendable and secondly, easier to control.
>
> (quoted in Gregory and Nussbaum 1982, p. 200)

Proposing several possible changes of work in the office, Olson and Lucas (1982) described a set of design options to consider when introducing office technologies into an organization, stating 'that some potential problems can be solved by treating the introduction of automated office systems as a problem in work design' (p. 846):

> Task structures and role definitions can be designed to meet organizational objectives and the technology can be configured to support those work designs. For instance, a work design objective may be to increase specialization of administrative and clerical skills and to create a managerial hierarchy to support administrative tasks; a likely strategy would be to centralize word processing and utilize a reduced

staff for other managerial support. On the other hand, increased skill variety and task significance for all support personnel may be a work design goal which would result in decentralization of text processing equipment and training of more personnel.

(Olson and Lukas 1982, p. 846)

In the tradition of CSCW research and PD, Ellen Balka (1987) and Andrew Clement (1990, 1993) were among the few researchers who explored practical ways of supporting office workers in appropriating new office equipment. Both efforts were supported by federal funding in Canada, which allowed unions to partner with academics to explore the impacts of new technology on women's work.

Balka (1987) documented changes in work tasks in two unionized work-places in Canada – a university clerical union and a national airline worker's union. Building on Freire's (1972) work together with approaches adopted by early woman trade unionists, she sought to empower women trade unionists to more deeply engage in workplace design and implementation issues related to technology. In spite of permission to participate in workshops during the workday, participation in workshops was limited, as worked continued to accumulate on desks when clerical workers were attending workshops.

Based on two large research studies of office support groups at a large Canadian university, Clement (1990, 1993) examined 'the difficulties that secretaries confront when attempting to master desktop computing and the cooperative solutions they have developed to overcome them' (1990, p. 223). At the core of the first action-oriented project was the initiation of a unit entitled Self-Managed Office Automation (SMOAP). It consisted of twenty-five support staff,

all women, from six academic department offices, used the center for instruction, problem solving assistance and access to a small library of software and print materials. The focal activity was a weekly meeting in which the representatives from each department discussed the problems they faced with computer use.

(Clement 1990, p. 228)

Shortly after the project ended and the centre was closed, the support staff union went on strike. As an outcome of this strike a staff-run training program was established. Reflecting on the experiences made in this project, Clement spells out a series of recommendations of how to set up a learning process about desktop computing and the kind of measures that have proven useful. He muses why 'the informal facilitation of the basic meta-task of simply learning to use and adapt the technology' (1990, p. 228) had been ignored in the research literature and emphasizes the importance of 'informal, localised processes of collaborative problem solving, development and sharing of local expertise' (1993, p. 323) for accomplishing design work. This is design work that is mostly carried out by the secretaries themselves when appropriating new office equipment running software packages for word processing, spreadsheets, database management, and other office applications. Appropriation means integrating these technologies and functionalities into the everyday work of the office, as well as developing novel work practices;[1] as for example:

> In effect, secretaries (or others close at hand) must create new bridges between document preparation tasks and the generic text processing capabilities of the computing technology. Many of these design decisions can carry over from the previous non-computerised methods. However, the introduction of microcomputers brings new opportunities and constraints that have to be considered. Powerful, but potentially problematic, ways of entering, formatting, editing and correcting documents have to be explored. Apart from the actual text documents produced, new and lingering artifacts often have to be designed. These may include directories for electronic filing, file naming conventions, document templates, 'cheat sheets', reminders and so on. The principal outcomes of the design process, however, are not tangible products but reformed work practices. The new ways of working are seen in the shifting patterns of task sequence, information flow, social interaction, and skill distribution.
>
> (Clement 1993, p. 328)

Redesigning the work practices also meant reorganizing the office infrastructure – another example of work that often remains invisible.

It is important to position workplace design with respect to several strong traditions of (re)designing jobs and the organization in which they are embedded that were developed in the 1970s and 1980s; German action theory and work psychology, with Walter Volpert and Winfried Hacker as their main proponents; the so-called 'socio-technical school' in organizational and workplace studies, which was forwarded by Emery Trist, Einar Thorsrud, and others; as well as PD. The central goal of work design in German action theory was to promote long-term well-being and human growth or personality development. Volpert developed a conception 'of the workplace conducive to personality development' (Oesterreich and Volpert, 1986, p. 504). In parallel, the socio-technical approach formulated a variety of principles for reorganizing work that would allow a move away from the classic assembly line.

---

[1] Domestication (Silverstone and Haddon 1996; Lie and Sørensen 1996) is a related term that is frequently used to describe similar processes when technologies move into domestic spaces. As a strand of the social shaping of technology approach to understanding how technology is created, the term 'domestication' is used to describe the work of integrating digital technologies with the daily routines in the home. It should be noted that in discussions of the domestication of technology, appropriation has a slightly different meaning than that initially put forward by Suchman and Wynn and others.

Experiments with new forms of work, among them job enlargement, job enrichment, and semi-autonomous working groups, were carried out, many of them in Volvo's Uddevalla plant (Sandberg 1995). The idea behind the more ambitious of these new forms of work was to offer workers personally meaningful work that allowed them to regulate the working conditions and influence and actually see the result of their work. Cummings (1978) argued that

> These states are present when the work content is high on the following five core dimensions: (a) skill variety; (b) task identity (i.e., ability to complete a whole piece of work); (c) task significance (i.e., degree to which the job has a substantial impact on the lives or work of other people); (d) autonomy; and (e) feedback.
>
> (Cummings 1978, p. 629)

The early PD projects, such as the 'Iron and Metal Project' (Nygaard and Bergo 1975) and the UTOPIA Project (Ehn 1988), placed work (re)design under the umbrella of industrial democracy. For example, the Collective Resource Approach to design explicitly aimed at enhancing 'democracy and skill' (Ehn and Kyng 1985, p. 56) for the workers. The ambition was to encourage

> workers and their unions to take the initiative from management rather than reacting to management's proposals and demands. In order to do so, workers and local unions must learn about the design and use of new technologies, their likely impacts on jobs and working conditions, as well as possible alternatives.
>
> (Kraft and Bansler 1994, p. 75)

These and other approaches, many of them developed in cooperation with trade unions, sought to counterbalance the desires and efforts of management to reorganize work under the prime goal of (cost) control, seeking to design workplaces that were meaningful, offering workers the possibility to learn and develop their skills.

Summary

Studies of office information in the 1980s and 1990s produced many valuable insights concerning technology, organization, and managerial decisions, with a focus on skill, learning, and the need for workplace design in support of 'well-being and human development'. In addition to raising issues about what we do and don't consider skill, debates about skill helped situate research about technological change and gender within both organizational structures and occupational structures (Menzies, 1981; Feldberg and Glenn, 1983), and also served to reinforce and legitimate the value of ethnographic and qualitative methods in CSCW and PD. The use of observational methods based on fieldwork carried out in actual workplaces contributed significantly to our understanding of invisible work, and the relevance of the taken-for-granted in system design. Broader contexts in which this work was taking place – including the influence of the Tavistock Institute and Scandinavian workplace studies – laid foundations for discussions about the need for work that fulfilled human needs and afforded workers' democratic rights. We consider these earlier approaches to workplace studies as offering orientations for studying modern forms of data work as well as new ways of working 'beyond the office'.

6

Beyond the Office

From Data Work to the Platform Economy

The previous chapter highlighted debates about office automation that ended in the late 1990s. In this chapter, we build on many of the concepts introduced in discussions about the automated office as we discuss data work, and then subsequently platform work in relation to women. By starting with data work, we can see historical continuity from the automation of clerical work in the 1980s and 1990s to contemporary data work and platform work, which constitute an increasingly important part of modern workplaces and economies.

Like clerical work and the work of secretaries before, much of data work is skilled but undervalued, while other parts of data work are highly standardized and repetitive, organized via platforms, and encouraging working from home. The trajectory from office/clerical work to platform work highlights the importance of labour issues connected to modern workplaces, their continuity but also the new forms they take with technological change.

What Is Data Work?

In a paper 'The future of clerical work is precarious', Naja Holten Møller (2018) contends that 'clerical work supports AI [artificial intelligence] rather than being seen as a legitimate occupation in itself' (p. 75). She argues that human data work is critical to ensure the situated registration and use of data and, referring to feminist HCI, points out the responsibility of designers to demonstrate alternatives to having clerical tasks 'disappear' in precarious forms of platform work. There are many reasons to acknowledge the importance of data work, Willcocks (2020) maintains, given the current 'exponential data explosion' and 'the cross-sectoral explosion of audit, regulation and bureaucracy' that goes with it (p. 296). Hence the need to have people who know how to process, store, and analyze data and how to make use of them in different contexts.

Data work is a broad term that includes the work of creating data and making them available for different purposes but also the work involving data scientists, data analysts, and database managers. Data form the basis of administrative and documentation work as well as many forms of accountability work. Increasingly, professionals such as teachers and physicians are expected to spend time entering information into forms in relation to their own work, which become data in other contexts. Having emerged from women's work in the office, here we focus on the work of creating data that (often) have been produced by others and making those data available for the work of others.

Research on different forms of this type of data work in different contexts evokes some of the issues that form a red thread through accounts of women's work, including that it is often intensive, highly skilled work, in most cases badly paid and often invisible. The second issue is that data work is often outsourced and has become part of what Freeman (1993), in a study of women in Barbados processing airline tickets and medical claims, calls the 'global assembly line'. As in office automation, there is an automation agenda, given the design of data-entry tools that supposedly will make people doing this work redundant.

Much data work today is AI-related and organized through platforms; as is service delivery of all kinds. Nielsen and Ganter (2022) define platforms as follows:

> We used the term here to refer to large technology companies that own and operate digital platforms that enable interaction between at least two different kinds of actors (typically users and advertisers) and in the process come to host public information, organize access to it, and create new formats for it, as well as new incentives (or disincentives) for investing in public information about public affairs. A platform company is thus a company that builds its business primarily around operating one or more digital platforms. ... Facebook, Google, and Twitter are all examples of platform companies that are particularly important for news production and distribution. Globally, outside of China, the most important platforms are all US-based – and specifically Silicon Valley- or Seattle-based – publicly traded for-profit technology companies, and most of them rely, in large part, on advertising revenues powered by large-scale data collection.
>
> (Nierlsen and Gsnter 2022, p. 13)

So-called crowdwork platforms – which emerged with improvements in and convergence of computing (especially graphic) and communication technologies, and benefitted from developments in miniaturization, cost reductions, and speed improvements – connect individuals and clients, and very often offer so-called 'microtasks' – that is, 'extremely parceled activities, often menial and monotonous, which still require some sort of judgement beyond the understanding of artificial intelligence (e.g., tagging photos, valuing emotions, or the appropriateness of a site or text, completing surveys)' (De Stefano 2015, p. 474). Besides data entry and clerical work, physical tasks involving transport, couriering, food delivery, cleaning, or beauty work may be organized through platforms. Also, bigger and more meaningful work such as software development or creating a logo and other design tasks, may be done through platforms. Common to the different forms of platform work is that 'workers are provided "just-in-time" and compensated on a "pay-as-you-go" basis; in practice they are only paid during the moments they actually work for a client' (De Stefano 2015, p. 476). In the words of the CEO of a company engaging in crowdwork,

> Before the Internet, it would be really difficult to find someone, sit them down for ten minutes and get them to work for you, and then fire them after those ten minutes. But with technology, you can actually find them, pay them the tiny amount of money, and then get rid of them when you don't need them anymore.
>
> (Quoted in De Stefano 2015, p. 476)

When talking about data, Melissa Gregg (2015) reminds us, it is important to see that data are not 'facts', even though they are often taken as such. She underlines that

> In previous centuries 'datum' was understood as something given in an argument, something taken for granted. Data is something presumed prior to discussion, a framework creating the possibility for discussion. It therefore already contains judgments and decisions about what counts as a prior-ity (both priority and a priori share the same Latin root; priorities are taken from that which comes before). A data 'set', then, 'is already interpreted by the fact that it is a set', according to Travis D. Williams: 'some elements are privileged by inclusion, while others are denied relevance through exclusion'.
>
> (Gregg 2003, p. 41, quoted in Gregg 2015, p. 42)

Hence, data are always selected as representing something (be it a lab value, the result of an exam, or automatically registered sensor data), as well as interpreted, seen through a specific lens. Schuurman and Balka (2009) have pointed out that data have 'an authority that frequently supercedes their quality' and the apparent simplicity of data often obfuscates the complexity of tasks that has contributed to its production (p. 83).

Acknowledging the Skills in Data Work

Data archives are maybe the earliest form of people collecting, organizing, and storing data for later retrieval for different concerns; they reach far back in history. While work in data archives is to some extent still specialized, data work is part of clerical and administrative work and increasingly so due to digitalization and the quest for 'big data'. At the beginning of this development, people doing data entry of all sorts were called data processors, a term that became outdated with improved computer technologies.

Looking back in history, Parolini (2015) studied women who were employed alongside scientists in Rothamsted Statistics Department (UK) contributing to the analysis of agricultural experiments and surveys:

> At first they did calculations with pen, paper, slide rules and electromechanical calculating machines, but after the World War II, when the department underwent an early process of computerisation, their tasks shifted to data processing jobs, such as punching paper tape and cards, and later in time the use of word processors.
>
> (Parolini 2015, p. 105)

From the 1920s until the 1990s, over 200 women worked in the department alongside scientists. In the late 1970s the twelve women engaged in computing work were listed as data processors; they were never involved in programming. In the late 1990s there were still four or five women active in the statistics department and their work was labelled 'data preparation'. Those who stayed at the department for an extended time period had to constantly adapt to new technologies, acquiring new skills. But their salaries remained low, and they never had any career prospective. Although the women were part of the data processing necessary for statistical analysis, their contribution to the scientific results produced by the department was never made visible:

> Gender was not the main element that contributed to the invisibility of the female assistants in the Rothamsted statistics department. It was the lack of authority to preside over scientific work that relegated these women to invisibility. They 'did not have anything to do with the scientific side', they 'just did the punching of the tape and verified it, and the tape was sent off to be run'.
>
> (Parolini 2015, p. 115)

Creating data for others to benefit from professionally and/or financially is a common characteristic of many forms of data work.

One of the few areas where detailed studies of data work are available is health care. They draw attention to the work of medical secretaries, work that was for a long time invisible in research that mainly focussed on the work of physicians and nurses, Bossen et al. (2012) argue: 'Along with other non-clinical hospital staff, medical secretaries seem to be mostly invisible, a fate they share with secretaries and assistants more generally' (p. 922). Further analysis of the study of the work of medical secretaries in two Danish hospitals emphasizes that they are 'deeply involved in medical work' (Møller 2018, p. 76). They have to interpret how to enter the data in the medical record system so that they are ready for coding and analysis: 'It may even be the clerical worker who initiates the appropriate action when errors are discovered' (p. 77). This key role is reflected in the fact that in Danish hospitals medical secretaries 'sit in close proximity to clinicians, patients, and their relatives. Physical workflows were continuously "mirrored" digitally in order for the data to be trusted, valuable, and actionable in practice' (Møller et al. 2020, p. 53). In the USA, some of this data work is carried out by clinical documentation improvement specialist (CDIS) who review the physician's documentation. In Canada, data abstractors are often part of the medical records department, but assigned to specific, ongoing projects requiring domain-specific expertise.

Given the core role of medical secretaries (and comparable types of data workers such as coders or transcriptionists), a simple outsourcing or 'platformization' of this work destroys the context that allows the Danish medical secretaries to accomplish the 'meaningful registration' of patient data. This point is also made by Fiske et al. (2019) who refer to the technological, analytical, and emotional work that is necessary to make data 'clinically and personally meaningful'. They point out the need to make

> the context of data explicit, and asking questions such as: What data was collected, from whom, and how? What do these data represent, and what do these leave out? How has it been made legible for computation, and what has been lost or gained in the process?
>
> (Fiske et al. 2019, p. 4)

Concern about the failure to document these issues led Schuurman and Balka (2009) to propose a qualitative framework for meta-tagging of data.

What may happen when data work is organized as a 'factory' with little time for data workers to apply the knowledge and care that is needed to make data meaningful is described by Plantin (2021), in a study of data processing work in a US archive. He portrays data processors, most of them women, white, and in their early to mid-twenties, as having to work 'along a strict standardized pipeline' (p. 1), at a fast pace. The important point Plantin makes is that,

> By design, data processing concerns only the structure of the data and does not require in-depth analysis of the content, methodology, or results of a study. However, processors have to develop some minimal knowledge about the formal description of the study – typically the author, type of data, and the context of collection. This information is gathered by looking at the various documents coming with the study (such as published papers) and sometimes from searching on the internet. This knowledge is necessary and part of the job, as processors need eventually to write the metadata and other descriptions of the study for the archive's website.
>
> (Plantin 2021, p. 8)

Although they have hardly time for exploring the content of a dataset, some of the data processors manage to do this, which helps them feel confident that they have 'checked all errors' and 'designated all missing values' and gives them the satisfaction that they have created a validated dataset. This is again an example of the skills and care that are needed to create meaningful data, which is made difficult by the organization of data processing under a tight regime.

Who Are the Platform Workers and What Do They Do?

The examples of data work in hospitals, research institutions, and national archives are all about work that is framed by an organization, where people (most of the time) physically convene to work, often in collaboration with others, and that, even if not well-paid, offers stable employment over longer periods of time. This is not necessarily the case with platform work: platform workers are in an individualized position with respect to the platform (or platforms) on which they work and have almost none of the protections that stable employment, if available, would offer them.

Platform work is not necessarily women's work. One of the challenges we face at this particular moment in time is that when it comes to platform work and platform workers, our datasets are incomplete at best, and lacking in consistency at worst, making it difficult to gain a reasonably accurate understanding of who does what kinds of work in relation to which platforms.[1] National and cross-national agencies engaged in collection of data about the labour force often lag behind actual labour-force changes. One result is that there is incredible variation in how the work of platform workers is captured in relation to platforms as contractors (e.g., how do platforms like Uber report data about their 'contracted' labour?). Additionally, there is ambiguity in how people performing 'data work' tasks outside of well-defined job titles (such as 'medical office assistant') report their work on data collection instruments such as national censuses. These and other issues were highlighted in a 2019 report titled Measuring Platform Mediated Workers (OECD, 2019, p. 4). The report – which underlined the need for good data to inform policy – stressed that 'there is a lack of comparable and consistent statistics, over time and across countries, on the number of platform workers, their characteristics, and the characteristics of their jobs and tasks'.

---

[1] This, of course, may change as a result of pressures – now coming from multiple sectors – to better understand the composition of the global platform labour force. However, as we go to press (Spring, 2024), data are still lacking.

The report indicates that after several (unsuccessful) attempts to estimate the number of platform workers and use existing statistics (which yielded varying estimates of the size of the platform economy), 'official statistical agencies of OECD Members have begun to introduce questions on platform workers into labour force surveys and Internet usage surveys'. Although this again yielded varying results – 'these efforts highlight some of the difficulties in measuring platform workers', which include (1) 'difficulties explaining to survey respondents what is meant by platform work'; (2) 'inconsistencies across countries in how platform workers are measured' (e.g., differences between capital and labour platforms, as well as the time period used as reference (e.g., year or week); and (3) small estimates of platform workers leading to small sample sizes which limit the precision of estimates of worker characteristics such as gender (OECD 2019, p. 4).

Although we lack robust data that provides a reasonably accurate description of the platform worker labour force and makes cross national comparisons problematic, we do know from qualitative data that women who engage in platform work often do so because it makes it easier for them to combine work with childcare and other family responsibilities. We also know that there are global differences in the participation of women in platform work. In India, which is the home of 20 percent of the global platform-mediated labour force, only 20 percent are women (Athreya 2021). According to a panel survey by the European Institute for Gender Equality (EIGE), there are somewhat fewer women (42 percent) than men (58 percent) platform workers. However, 'In recent years, the number of women in platform work has been growing. Crucially, COVID-19 led to spikes in platform work, with 36% of women and 35% of men starting or restarting work on digital platforms because of the pandemic' (Thil et al. 2022, p. 13). The fact that the majority of platform workers are young, well educated, and with family responsibilities raises concerns about deskilling, the report found.

The work that is offered by platforms varies. Tubaro et al. (2020) provide examples of work that are highly standardized and repetitive – tasks that 'typically take only a few minutes, require limited skills, are paid on a piecework basis and attract compensation that can be as low as a few cents per task' (p. 68). Platforms offering this kind of work are the so-called microtask platforms (as distinguished from taxi platforms and shopping and delivery platforms). A recent ILO report (2021) observed a shift of types of work offered on platforms over the last few years:

> Globally, a large proportion of tasks are completed in the field of software development and technology, whose share increased from 39 per cent to 45 per cent between 2018 and 2020. Professional, and sales and marketing services also gained

in importance, whereas occupations such as creative and multimedia, writing and translation, and clerical and data entry declined between 2018 and 2020.

(ILO 2021, p. 52)

Many platform workers provide vital services for the AI industry. They

perform the generation and curation of data which is the largest (and most invisible) part of work needed for machine learning . . .. Second, they provide expert knowledge to monitor and moderate machine learning systems, often referred to as 'human in the loop'.

(Mohla et al. 2021, p. 2)

Recent research suggests that significant gender disparities exist in online platform work, including European platforms and workers, whereby women tend to request lower rates but obtain more hours of work. A report by ILO (International Labour Organization) (2021) states that women with childcare responsibilities who do web-based work disproportionately work at night and forgo sleep.

Views about whether platform work is beneficial to those it pretends to serve most – 'workers with under-privileged backgrounds, downward life trajectories, or temporary difficulties due to phases of unemployment or care duties' (Tubaro and Casilli 2020, p. 2), but also workers who due to a disability may have difficulties working in normative office environments – are mixed. Studies about women doing platform work as part of the 'global assembly line' provide some nuanced findings.

The 'Global Assembly Line'

That much of data work is done off-shore is not new. Mosco (1996) has suggested that advancements in telecommunications and computing just prior to the turn of the century led to spatialization – the ability to compress time and space through the convergence of computing and telecommunication technologies, which also offered new opportunities for commodification of services.[2] The globalization debate is extended and carried out from multiple viewpoints; it reaches beyond the scope of this book. Two points seem relevant here though. First, 'globalization does not entrain some single, unidirectional,

---

[2] The third element of Mosco's 1996 study is structuration – 'the process of creating social relations, mainly those organized around social class, gender, and race. For example, with respect to social class, political economy describes how access to the mass media and new communication technologies is influenced by inequalities in income and wealth which enable some to afford access and others to be left out' (Mosco 1996, p. 1).

sociospatial logic' (Cox 1997, p. 16); it results in 'a complex mosaic of inter-linked global city-regions, prosperous rural areas, resource sites, and "dead lands" increasingly cut off from time-space compression' (Agnew 2001, p. 134).

An example of a study of work in the global assembly line is Freeman's (1993) anthropological study of 'off-shore pink collar work' in Barbados. She investigated the situation of women working as data processors in two companies – Data Air and Multitext Corporation,

> ... both foreign-owned off-shore companies, one owned by an American and the other by a British multinational. Both set up shop in Barbados in the mid-1980s, and with the exception of the English general manager of Multitext, they are managed almost entirely by Bajans.
>
> (Freeman 1993, p. 69)

For her the issue was not the invisibility of the women she studied but their 'massive recruitment into the "global assembly line"' (p. 171). She used the term 'pink collar' to express the simultaneous proletarianization and feminiza-tion of the work (again showing how gender structures and symbolic notions of gender are inextricably linked). One of her comments regards the way stereotypes about West Indian women are put upfront by management:

> The young single woman continues to be perceived as the quintessential off-shore worker. Family metaphors that incorporate 'daughter' portray her as a first-time worker, enjoying the freedom and independence that comes from earning a wage, and as a contributing but non-essential earner in her own household. At the same time, 'older' women with children (regardless of their household composition), whose wage-earning roles cast them as the backbone of their families, constitute an alternative stereotype. As the manager makes clear, the expectation is that 'older' women will make up a particularly committed and responsible work force and thus ensure high-quality production.
>
> (Freeman 1993, p. 174)

Although the women could make more money working as domestic or agri-cultural workers, they prefer data-entry jobs because of the ambience of the office spaces they work in together with how they are expected to dress and behave at work, which makes them appear as 'professional' workers. At the same time, they are subjected to excessive forms of discipline and surveillance.

A series of publications (Miceli and Posada 2021; Posada 2021; Miceli et al. 2022) describe the findings of an extensive study of outsourced ML (machine learning) data work in Latin America (Venezuela and Argentina) and Bulgaria by studying several crowdsourcing platforms and a BPO (business process outsourcing) company. BPOs employ data workers from marginalized popu-lations, mainly in developing countries, with the idea of providing the mostly young people with access to the labour market and at the same time offering data services at a low price. The data processors do not work from home but in the company's offices and, 'unlike crowdsourcing platforms, where algorithms manage the labor process ...', BPOs are characterized by traditional and localized managerial structures and business hierarchies' (Miceli et al. 2022, p. 2).

The tasks workers typically perform can be described as interpreting and classifying data. This may include collecting data from websites; producing media content; image segmentation and classification tasks (in the case of platforms specializing in computer-vision projects); or reviewing content flagged as inappropriate by an algorithm and confirming or correcting the output. One of the studied companies uses extensive instruction sheets and carries out briefings when acquiring new projects. The company invests considerable resources in these briefings, which they consider key to data quality:

> These briefings give workers a framework for new projects and are instrumentalized by the company as the first instance of control, aiming at reducing room for subjectivity. Further control instances, aiming to ensure that data work is done uniformly and according to requesters' expectations, take place in numerous iterations where reviewers and team leaders review and revise data and go back to the instruction documents or contact the requester to clarify inconsistencies.
>
> (Miceli and Posada 2021, p. 21)

Another of the companies organizes 'week-long unpaid digital courses called "boot camps" and later evaluation periods called "in-house", with the idea that the workers obey tasks without question' (p. 22).

Although the BPOs' data workers are offered a steady part- or full-time salary and benefits, their salaries remain below the poverty line. Hence, contrary to the stated purpose of the company, there is little evidence that this form of work contributes to the development of poor communities. Posada (2022) uses the notion of 'embedded reproduction' to describe the whole informal support network without which the data processors would not be able to do their work. This support comprises 'domestic labor and economic support that create environments that enable workers to pursue data work, worker organization through social media and the management of common online resources, and the locally managed shared natural resources that workers require for subsistence' (p. 817). This support is highly gendered; sometimes also the children need to contribute.

In their study of AMT (Amazon Mechanical Turk) workers in India, Gurumurthy et al. (2021) argue that digital platforms may offer opportunities, in particular for small-town Indian women. Based on insights gained through interviews with women, they, however, arrive at a rather grim but clear conclusion:

> As a workplace, AMT demands an exacting adherence to the rules of the platform, but enjoys absolute impunity. Women must learn to manage the coercive disciplinarity of the platform, striving to meet its unknowable metrics. Waiting late nights for tasks from US requesters, they must face the exploitative tyranny of an unpredictable wage that may be withdrawn without explanation. With the onset of the pandemic and resultant instabilities in household income, women's work on AMT becomes non-negotiable to making ends meet, even as its harshness is more acute, with reducing work, falling pay, longer hours, and the risk of suspension. The digital economy thrives on gendered dispossession – not only extracting women's digital labor for profit, but also obscuring the care work they must perform in the ostensible flexibility afforded by platform capitalism.
>
> (Gurumurthy et al. 2021, p. 5)

While platforms offer work to women who would otherwise not have access to an independent income, the unresolved key problem remains that women in most cultures (with some variations) are mainly responsible for work in the family – hence the nightshifts make it possible for women to be able to manage both.

Experiences of low-income women with crowdwork in India (Varanasi et al. 2022) complete this picture. Varanasi et al. interviewed women working for Karya, a micro-tasking platform that is designed for low-income, digitally novice communities in India. The task is to collect speech data in local languages. The researchers sum up the 'tremendous challenges' these women face,

> for example, in seeking permission from family members to do crowd work, lack of family support and encouragement, and often working in unfavorable environments where they had to hide their work lives. While crowd work took a toll on their physical and emotional wellbeing, it also led to increased confidence, agency, and autonomy.
>
> (Varanasi et al. 2022, p. 1)

Given the criticisms and barriers they faced, for example with respect to using the phone for their work, the women sought and also found emotional support in other workers, in particular in difficult situations such as delayed payments and domestic troubles. Many women

> were left with no choice but to do crowd work during the night hours when everyone was asleep. Some of them shared how they compromised their sleep time to an average of less than five hours per night in order to do crowd work.
>
> (Varanasi et al. 2022, p. 12)

The authors stress that Karya is not a typical platform, as its ground staff provide a lot of support to workers, addressing their concerns.

These and other studies have suggestions about how to improve the working conditions of platform workers, a topic to which we will return later.

Working Conditions: Labour Issues

Working conditions are a major concern voiced in numerous studies of platform work, and not only with respect to women in poor countries. Political commitment paired with a feminist perspective has led some researchers in the HCI community to take up labour issues seeking to develop support structures with and for platform workers (e.g., Ma et al. 2022; Yao et al. 2021).[3]

At the heart of the problem is the double exploitation of data assets by platform companies, Van Doorn and Badger (2020) argue. These companies not only make profit from the services they provide at low cost but from the value of the data that are automatically produced before, during, and after the service has been provided. The example they cite is from how Deliveroo captures a courier's activities:

> ... to understand from your data (such as your order progress swipes and other Rider App usage, feedback you give about orders and your location data) as well as the data of other riders, what attributes to a positive or negative customer, restaurant or rider experience with Deliveroo and what might cause inefficient deliveries or damage to Deliveroo, and use this data to responsibly design, develop, test and implement new tools, processes, and relationships to improve our business, systems and services ...
>
> (Van Doorn and Badger 2020, p. 1482)

The data they acquire and monitor enable them to progressively increase their profit margins by lowering delivery fees – a classic problem to be addressed by trade unions! In a paper that analyses the gendered and racialized practices of exploiting a 'workforce-as-a-service', Van Doorn (2017) refers to Donna Haraway (1990):

> To be feminized means to be made extremely vulnerable; able to be disassembled, reassembled, exploited as a reserve labor force; seen less as workers than as servers; subjected to time arrangements on and off the paid job that make a mockery of a limited work day; leading an existence that always borders on being obscene, out of place, and reducible to sex.
>
> (Van Doorn 2017, p. 208)

---

[3] The discourse about this topic goes beyond the academic scope, with initiatives like the Digital Future Society working – among other aspects of the digital sphere – to create awareness for gender dynamics that exist in the platform economy, and aiming to specifically bring forward the realities of women who engage in platform work across different economic and social backgrounds.

Here, again, we see the interaction of gender structures and gender symbolism (referred to here as having one's labour referred to as 'servers' not workers, 'reducible to sex'). One of the issues researchers address is not only the invisibility of the workers themselves, but also the considerable amount of invisible and unpaid work they have to do to be able to get work. Toxtli et al. (2021) estimate that the crowdworkers in their study 'spent 33% of their time daily on invisible labor, dropping their median hourly wage to $2.83' (p. 2). The invisible work that took the most time was having to manage their payments, followed by the invisible labour category 'hyper-vigilance, where workers vigilantly watched over requesters' profiles for newly posted work or vigilantly searched for labor' (p. 1). The invisibility of the workers themselves has been emphasized by De Stefano (2015):

> Workers that can be 'summoned' by clients and customers at a click of their mouse or at a tap on their mobile, perform their task, and disappear again in the crowd or in the on-demand workforce materially risk being identified as an extension of an IT device or online platform.
>
> (De Stefano 2015, p. 478)

Another big issue that is particular to the platform economy is algorithmic management – the 'oversight, governance and control practices conducted by software algorithms' (Möhlmann and Zalmanson 2017, p. 4). It allows companies to practice 'just-in-time' scheduling, which results in the unpredictability of working hours, contributing to workers' uncertainty and stress. Digital technologies also make implementing rating systems, as well as reward and penalty systems, possible, which are not transparent to workers. Moreover, workers themselves do not have the possibility to, for example, rate their experiences with clients (Athreya 2021). A study of Upwork, an online platform that facilitates knowledge-intensive freelance labour, Jarrahi et al. (2020) show that the company

> manages through a combination of algorithmic decision-making, technological features, and business rules. We identify six management functions performed by the Upwork platform: (1) managing transactions, (2) channeling communication, (3) resolving conflicts, (4) providing information, (5) evaluating performance, and (6) gatekeeping.
>
> (Jarrahi et al. 2020, p. 14)

Posada (2022) reports the consequences of a form of algorithmic management for workers that do not annotate data according to a clients' directions, whereby the algorithm will ban them from the task and, in the worst case, suspend their account, eventually banning them from the platform. Workers do not have any resource against banning: no explanation is provided, and they may lose their income.

The ILO report (2021) mentions that in particular on freelance platforms 'there is intense competition between workers. They respond through accepting low-paying work (62 per cent); lowering their bids to get work (60 per cent); or performing tasks for free (13 per cent)' (p. 157).

Cedefob's (European Centre for Vocational Learning) Crowdlearn study (2020) looks at an aspect of platform work that it not so much discussed but highly relevant with respect to designing support structures: the possibilities of platform workers learning and improving their skills. It found that crowdworkers in fields with relatively higher levels of task complexity, such as software and technology development, as well as those doing creative and multimedia work, had more opportunities for on-the-job learning than those doing clerical or data-entry work. It seems that those workers benefit more from rapid typing and basic computer skills. More than 40 percent of those workers rated the skill of 'obtaining platform work' as particularly relevant. The report concludes,

> Challenges linked to algorithmic skills matching, to developing continuing training and learning opportunities in line with emerging skill needs, to recognising informal learning and its portability across different platforms and the standard labour market, to understanding better business recruitment practices and reliance on a gig workforce; these all potentially have wider implications for both the gig and traditional workforce in a post-Covid-19 world.
>
> (Cedefob 2020, p. 5)

Design Issues in the Platform Economy

Some HCI and CSCW researchers have started collaborating with platform workers and trade unions in various initiatives to improve working conditions. Such political engagement is not so common in these research communities. While the motivations behind it are manifold, many researchers refer to feminist theory and a deep commitment to design justice (see Chapter 10). We want to highlight three types of initiatives here: support of the documentation of data-work production, support of 'organic' forms of collaboration amongst platform workers, and political work.

In their work with platform workers in Bulgaria and Argentina, Miceli et al. (2022) used a participatory approach in response to a call for

> the professionalization of data work and care (i.e., the careful consideration of the dataset in terms of 'the domain setting where it originates, and the potential questions modeling that data might answer or problems it might solve' [Wolf 2019]), the publication of data documentation, the implementation of institutional

frameworks and procedures to promote documentation, and the consideration of data work as an own subfield of research.

(Miceli et al. 2022, p. 4)

Christine Wolf (2019) conceptualizes the data work carried out by ML developers as 'practices of care', extending the notion of care to technical work. Referring to one of the developers, she describes care as a key element in how

applied ML involves thinking deeply about the domain setting where the training dataset comes from – she doesn't take data at face value, but instead must carefully inspect them to understand the gaps in the perspectives they might provide for a given task.

(Wolf 2019, p. 333)

This is work that also the data processors in Plantin's (2021) study of a US archive tried to fit in their tight schedules.

The concern for extending the documentation of data production to platform workers that do not model but 'just' collect and annotate data used for ML is motivated by the fact that these workers are at the bottom of a hierarchy and are not offered the opportunity to develop their skills and get recognition, including adequate pay for their work. It also reflects a view of data work that fails to acknowledge the role data play as they move from location to location, and that data work is context-laden and often requires the exercise of significant judgement.

This situation motivated Miceli et al. (2022) to carry out a PD project. They interviewed platform workers that were involved in the documentation of projects and ML developers with experience with outsourcing data work to platforms and BPOs. The participatory workshops they conducted in two companies (for which workers received €15 per hour of participation) resulted in vital information about a series of topics, in co-designed prototypes, and a number of insights. Although documentation was seen as an educational resource for data workers, in reality the price for producing metadata for each project and maintaining the documentation was paid by the workers themselves. One main aim of the researchers was to shift attention from what the client may want, to documentation based on the needs of workers. A series of design recommendations resulted from this work, among them: the documentation of data production should be collaborative; it should enable communication; allow 'the co-creation of task instructions with different stakeholders, particularly workers'; 'be integrated in existing workflows and routines'; and 'be adaptable to stakeholder needs' (Miceli et al. 2022, pp. 22–24).

This project demonstrates the possibilities of change with respect to platform work. In particular it shows how to support producing data with care, envisioning future uses, and how to provide data workers with opportunities to learn and professionalize their work. Varasani et al. (2022) identify an enormous potential of crowdwork-based education, arguing, 'A re-imagined crowd work platform would enable women to engage in a diversity of tasks, including peer tutoring and mentoring, and provide them coaching on the skills that are necessary to complete a range of tasks successfully' (p. 15). As articulated by Varasani et al., documenting data work is key to supporting organic forms of collaboration, and also clearly has a political dimension.

A related design issue that Miceli and Posada (2022) as well as Varanasi et al. (2022) propose is to combat workers' alienation by making their contribution to the ML supply chain visible:

> Breaking with the alienation of data workers means much more than rendering them visible. It rather requires making the rest of the machine learning supply chain visible to them. It means providing information and education on technical and language matter that could help workers understand how their valuable labor fuels a multi-billion-dollar industry. This also concerns questions of labor organization and unionizing.
>
> (Miceli and Posada 2022, p. 30)

While on the one hand, platform work is a highly individualized form of work, according to ILO (2021) 17 percent of platform workers indicated that they collaborate regularly. Other studies confirm this finding. For example, Miceli and Posada (2021) describe how data workers used independent social media spaces to 'exchange information about which tasks pay more and are less challenging to complete and warn each other about non-reliable requesters. One of the aspects that workers paid significant attention to was the presence of bugs in the tasks' (p. 23). This is what Gray et al. (2016) term 'organic collaboration', pleading to make space for collaborations that workers develop themselves instead of adding collaborative functionalities to existing platforms (what he calls 'engineered collaboration'). Gray and associates cite many examples of organic collaboration, such as: having a friend help 'avoid online scams by conveying trust'; finding and sharing information about tasks and specific requesters; using different forums, chats, and meetings 'to describe how to manage one's time completing tasks and how to do search queries or execute basic scripts or computing techniques, like copying and pasting, to get tasks done' (p. 142).

A much-publicized initiative in support of platform workers – which also incorporates documentation of data practices, support for organic forms of collaboration, and is a political intervention, is Turkopticon, founded by Lilly Irani and Six Silberman as a review website that allowed Turkers to rate task requesters. Turkopticon was recently developed into a worker-led non-profit organization. It grew out of researchers asking Turkers to write a hypothetical

Bill of Rights, as a way to imagine the conditions of better crowdwork. We Are Dynamo (Salehi et al. 2015), a collective action platform, complements Turkopticon by supporting Turkers in forming public debates around issues and mobilizing them. In parallel to this work in 2015, researchers from several European trade unions, among them the German Metal Workers Union (IG Metall) launched faircrowdwork.org, a website intended to let crowdworkers review various aspects of the working conditions on the platforms on which they worked. While highly visible and attracting a lot of interest, the problem with the numerical ratings provided by workers on issues such as pay, communication, or tasks was that their meaning was often unclear, giving rise to potential disagreements. Based on this experience and other lessons learnt from Turkopticon, Silberman and Irani redesigned the rating scheme and the Fair Crowd website, with the result that the new process

> also allowed the union to more explicitly situate and link the project within its own broader program of activities in support of improving online labor conditions (Silberman et al. 2017). No longer a small project 'just' for a few workers, the website could now be understood as directly connected to ongoing outreach to platform operators and political lobbying.
>
> (Harmon and Silberman 2018, p. 1287)

Looking back at their initiative, Irani and Silberman (2016) emphasize the capacity of AMT workers to assume agency and change their situation.

> Turkers too maintain and repair AMT. They help resolve breakdowns through Turkopticon and through their forums. They advise employers about flawed task designs or bugs. They teach each other how to use tools. In short, they do much invisible work, some of which helps AMT as a system appear to work as intended. In this way, they are like the secretaries making copies, deviating from management rules to achieve management intention.
>
> (Irani and Silberman 2016, p. 4581)

What designers can do, is 'cast technological values into high relief through making . . ., generate controversies around issues . . ., strengthen adversarial positions in public debates . . ., or create infrastructures to support the formation of publics around shared issues' (p. 4575). Realization of Irani and Silberman's (2016) goals requires a broadening of scope in what we consider design work: each of these goals requires that we recast technology design as a series of interlocking activities that includes not only solving problems or addressing issues, or designing technology or redesigning work, but also includes interventions in the processes of design (e.g., engaging workers in design, using design methods that allow us to 'see' both local and global context), as well as its outputs (e.g., new technologies and new forms of work) – issues we will return to more fully in Chapter 10.

What Kind of Work Futures?

Several themes emerge from research done on data work and platform work 'beyond the office' that contribute to thinking about gender and design. One of the key themes is invisible work as well as the invisibility of workers. Invisible work is a hallmark of platform work in the gig economy. Early studies of office work focussing on the work of typists and secretaries broke with the tradition of describing their work as 'mere routine', making the range of skills they need visible. From the point of view of feminist theory, these studies emphasized, among other capabilities such as domain-specific knowledge, the emotional labour and socially supportive work that is part of the everyday work in many undervalued occupations. This perspective has been taken up by researchers studying data work in health care (e.g., Fiske et al. 2019) or crowdwork. For example, Raval and Dourish (2016) looked at the ride-sharing services of Uber and Lyft, using concepts from feminist political economy. They emphasize that much of everyday life is left out of economic analyses – 'domestic labor, emotional labor, care labor, acts of mutual support, everyday community engagement, the landscape of communal life, the natural everyday process of getting along, and informal systems of collective action' (p. 99). With respect to crowdwork they emphasize the immaterial and emotional labour involved in ride-sharing services, arguing that 'this takes on new resonances within the frame of evaluation and ratings that are at the heart of algorithmically-managed ride-sharing' (p. 100). These and other studies demonstrate the influence of 'longstanding traditions in feminist and queer scholarship that attend to how research and theory impacts activism and the lived conditions of those the research concerns itself with', Irani and Silberman (2016) argue.

A second theme is women (and men) working from home and what this means, in particular for women. Feminist theory has contributed to our understanding of the home. Elspeth Probyn (1990) discussed the home as a locale that is built around women, 'a locale of their own design' (p. 181), which simultaneously reflects patterns of domination and provides women with space for positively negotiating and articulating their identities and relations. Feminist scholars have also pointed at women's experience of time as often being ambivalent. Working from home exposes them to contradictory demands: the rhythm of work versus the need to 'let time pass' (in particular when being with young children); being available (the willingness 'to fill in' when needed) versus setting time apart regardless of ad hoc demands, Kompast and Wagner (1998) have argued in a study of early telework arrangements. This makes them particularly vulnerable to pressures arising from work and the demands from family members. An additional point to be made and to be further investigated is to what extend the gig economy becomes a family enterprise where men fill the public roles, and women (and other family members) the private roles, serving as their practical support network?

That COVID-19 led to spikes in platform work is not accidental and has shown that gender inequalities may be reinforced (e.g., Zheng and Walsham 2021). An Australian study (Jenkins and Smith 2021) argues that mandatory working from home could be considered a requisition of people's homes for work (p. 25). They also point out that 'the vital contribution of women's "flexibility" to the economy's resilience against risks and shocks has gone largely unrecognised' (p. 29). They conclude, 'Conversation over public goods, at a minimum, should involve those engaged in household work in envisioning the types of infrastructural development that would make care and flexibility-work better accounted for and better distributed across gender divides (p. 34).

A third theme is the notion of care as a constitutive element of work, an ethical and political obligation for all and as key to non-exploitative relations of co-existence (for the concept of care see Chapters 2 and 8). In the context of clerical work or data work the notion of care points to the normative dimension of practices in the sense of doing things in a 'caring way'. Using the design of a wheelchair as an example, Mol et al. (2010) suggest that 'care, in this setting, is rather to meticulously explore, test, touch, adapt, adjust, pay attention to details and change them, until a suitable arrangement (material, emotional, relational) is achieved' (p. 16). Although developed in a more traditional care context, this notion of care can also be extended to work in general. Related concepts are what Weick and Roberts (1993) observed as 'heedful interrelating' on aircraft carriers or mindful attention (Langer, 1989) or heedful action, or what Ryle (1949) defined as 'noticing, taking care, attending, applying one's mind, concentrating, putting one's heart into something, thinking what one is doing, alertness, interest, intentness, studying, and trying' (p. 136). We would argue that performing an activity with care in a 'heedful way' is both an attitude towards work and a skill.

A final point to be made is about the role of political commitments in CSCW and HCI. There are several important aspects to this issue. One concerns researchers' choice of the topic they want to investigate and what they expect to 'see' and learn when studying a particular area of work, organizational life, and so forth. Blomberg and Karasti provide a clarification:

> As Anderson (1994, p. 155) notes, 'The ethnographer's eye is always interpretive'. It is not enough to simply record what is seen or heard in a straightforward way.

> Accounts are informed by the ethnographer's analytic eye and are shaped by frameworks and theories that both emerge from the 'data' and build on previous research.
>
> (Blomberg and Karasti 2013, p. 401)

Hence, when we study a particular social setting, we want to understand what is going on in it and why practitioners do what they do in particular ways. But we also do this with a framework in the back of our mind that is shaped by, in our case, feminist theory and concepts such as care, invisible work, the genderedness of organizations, and so forth.

Another political and also ethical decision is involved in what designers, in collaboration with users or practitioners, want to design for. The designers of applications such as Turkopticon obviously took sides, seeking to support crowdworkers in improving their working conditions. This is in line with early PD, where workplace democracy was at the centre of PD (Ehn 1988), aiming to provide workers with the knowledge and the tools that would enable them to organize for the purposes of becoming masters of their working lives. Blomberg et al. (1996) formulated a series of requests to designers that are of relevance here:

> Understand the politics of change and where you stand within them; Understand how extended contexts (e.g. institutional, global) constrain the scope of what can be accomplished in a given setting, and attempt to question or take advantage of those contexts as appropriate.
>
> (Blomberg et al. 1996, p. 260)

Concluding with a third politically motivated design aim, we think that, although it is important to work with existing platforms, it is also necessary to help develop alternatives to the dominant platforms run by Amazon, Google, Uber, and so forth in the near future, in order to make platform work attractive, well-paid, and offering workers security as well as space for development. As Benston (1989) pointed out, technology effectively creates a language for social action – meaning that it supports some behaviours and constrains others. Feminist system design begins with an acknowledgement of what women's lives are like, and then seeks to build systems that allow women to better meet their needs. Engaging in the development of alternative platforms has the potential to offer more emancipatory opportunities for women.

The themes we have addressed here will resurface again in the next few chapters, which address AI based technologies (Chapter 7), the computerization of care work (Chapter 8), and the gendering of computer work, which focusses on both the division of labour in computing as well as computing cultures (Chapter 9). With Chapter 10 we begin Part III of the book. We move from considering what is wrong with computing in chapter 9 to revisiting the ethical-political perspective in Chapter 10, which we discuss in relation to design justice. Finally, we end the book with a focus on how in design we contextualize women's work (Chapter 11) and a set of concerns and ideas to take care of in the future from a feminist/intersectional perspective (Chapter 12).

Summary

In this chapter, we began by highlighting the ways that data work is similar to clerical work and the secretarial work that preceded it, jobs that were also predominantly filled by women workers. We briefly defined data work and linked it to platform work. We highlighted some of the skills required in data work (which often goes unrecognized). In our discussion of who data workers are, what they do, and where they do it, we highlighted the difficulties in obtaining accurate and robust data about data work and data workers. We then turned our attention to the global nature of data work, the experiences of women data workers in numerous national contexts, and a focus on working conditions and labour issues. We consider how gendering works in relation to platform work and the gig economy before turning to design issues in the platform economy. We end the chapter by looking at what a focus on data work and platform work 'beyond the office' can contribute to our thinking about gender and design. Here we highlight three design aims. Throughout the chapter we have touched on AI, as much platform work is undertaken in support of AI applications. In the next chapter, we more fully address a range of issues related to AI and gender.

7

AI-Based Technologies

New Forms of Invisibility and the 'Ironies of Automation'

In this chapter, we build on concepts concerning the ethics of care (Chapter 2), data work, complexities involved in it, and its organization via digital platforms (Chapter 6) in our discussion about AI-based technologies, bias, and algorithmic harm, as well as AI 'at work'.

We begin by introducing concepts that capture bias in datasets and algorithms from a feminist data ethics of care approach, using a series of examples in discussing lines of action to avoid or countervail bias. Ideas about care together with the notion of trust lay the foundations for a discussion about data justice, and the relationship between data, artificial intelligence, and ML. We then turn to work and the question of how to make AI-based technologies work in practice. Examples, most of them from IT development and health care, help understand the centrality of care, trust, and human–algorithm collaborations, what is often called 'the human in the loop', as key elements determining the usefulness of AI-based systems and tools to work. Regrettably, gender as a focus of concern in studies of AI-based technologies in work contexts has not been thoroughly addressed yet. Judy Wajcman pointed to the 'big gap between educating ... women in data science and AI and actually see them thriving in workplaces' (Judy Wajcman, interview 03/28/2022). At the same time, feminist theory informs our view of AI-based systems, emphasizing care and trust and highlighting the repair work and emotional work that are needed to make systems work in practice.

AI: Points of Concern

From its inception, AI research has put forward a vision of technologies that will have the ability to learn and gradually take over many human activities. Following the development of Frank Rosenblatt's Perceptron (a computer model based on human brain neural networks, which ran on an IBM 704), articulations of this vision have predominated. In 1958 a *New York Times* article about Perceptron 'called it an "Embryo of Computer Designed to Read and Grow Wiser"', while *Popular Science* went with the shorter 'Machines that learn' (*Popular Science*, May, 2022). The myths that are being created around the potential of AI technologies are not new. As Judy Wajcman remarked, 'AI is used very broadly as a marketing tool for companies and lots of things are shoved under that label' (Judy Wajcman, interview 03/28/2022).

The 'hard' version of robotics, one instantiation of AI, aims at equipping machines with an equivalent of the human body and the ability to learn and to enable them in the future to develop real emotions and social behavior (see Chapter 8). Although there is and probably always will be a large gap between this vision and the realities of how AI is and can be used in practice, AI-based technologies – from food-serving robots in restaurants to programs that will generate varied texts, advertising campaigns, and more – are already present in many areas of life and need careful consideration from the point of view of design and use.

From the perspective of gender (and race), the 'representational and alloca-tive harms' (Gray and Witt 2021) caused by 'data decisions' based on algorithms is one of the most discussed topics. It captures the bias in datasets used in, for example, screening technologies, hiring and promotion practices, law enforcement or health care, and aims to understand and avoid bias and its effects on vulnerable people.

Gender has been noticeably absent from studies of AI-based technologies in work contexts for several reasons. For example, both Lucy Suchman and Judy Wajcman identified gaps in data about women in AI that make it impossible for us to currently situate women in the broader contexts of AI workplaces. Judy Wajcman pointed out that we need

> to collect the data on how many women are in those fields. [I] did a report and actually found that there was very little, a lot of data gaps. . . . [W]hat people document is the number of women in education, doing PhDs, publishing in journals . . . What I've been trying to do for three years and haven't succeeded, is to get the big tech companies to be transparent about where women and men are within the big corporations and at what level.
>
> (Judy Wajcman, interview 03/28/2022)

Lucy Suchman spoke about where women are likely located:

> . . . gender and work is in the outsourcing of labeling and categorization in machine learning. I think that women are massively involved in AI and machine learning, when it comes to the invisible labor, of creating the datasets that those systems rely on.
>
> (Lucy Suchman, interview 04/22/2022)

However, despite these shortcomings in data, feminist ethics can contribute to thinking about how to make use of big data and ML in ways that support human actors rather than replace them, constrain them, or obfuscate those places where human agency arguably should be present and supported. The well-known request for keeping 'the human-in-the-loop' can be enriched by the concepts of care and trust: the value of caring involves 'attentiveness, responsibility, nurturance, compassion, meeting others' needs' (Tronto 1993, pp. 2–3; see Chapter 2). From the perspective of 'feminist black scholars', Raji (2020) calls for 'a slowness data scientists are not accustomed to, a carefulness that many technologists are not taught'. She adds,

> ... people are no less deserving of care when represented by a data point than at any other point in their lives. Humans are no less fragile and their experiences no less meaningful when housed in digital identities or bookmarked into a spreadsheet than if they were to stand right in front of me. Data are most beautiful when they are alive – when they grow, compound, and evolve. When predictions are wrong and the limits of the image become clear.
>
> (Raji 2020, p. 2)

Trust has an interpersonal aspect but 'may also be conceptualised as generated "in action", built up in some form of situated or contextual practical engagement of a work routine, often in contexts when people have a responsibility to build trust in new technology' (Winter and Carusi 2022, p. 3).

While one aim of this chapter is to discuss various examples and scenarios of bias in datasets and algorithms by examining their sources and how they affect women's and other genders' (work) lives, it will also take up a topic that Gray and Suri (2017) characterize as the 'ever-moving frontier of AI's development, the paradox of automation's last mile: as AI makes progress, it also results in the rapid creation and destruction of temporary labor markets for new types of humans-in-the-loop tasks' (p. 2). Some of the real people behind AI are called micro-workers, many of whom are women mainly recruited through dedicated platforms (see Chapter 6). Among the real people are also physicians, nurses, ML developers or caseworkers that appropriate AI-based systems making them work. Studies of AI in real-life contexts, many of them of an ethnographic nature, focus on making the work of getting AI-based technologies to work in practice visible, demonstrating 'how the concept of invisible labor can expose the significant human efforts required by our automated systems' (D'Ignazio and Klein 2020).

(Gender) Bias and the Harms It Causes

While recognized as one of the problems of AI in combination with big datasets early on, bias as a topic of concern has spread widely giving rise to organizations such as the Algorithmic Justice League (www.ajl.org), 'Black in AI', and 'Data for Black Lives', which aim at raising public awareness of the injustices that bias in computer systems create and to move toward an 'equitable and accountable AI'. The organization is a follow-up of a documentary *Coded bias* directed by Shalini Kantayya. In this film MIT Media Lab researcher Joy Buolamwini reports her discovery that facial recognition does not see dark-skinned faces accurately, and her journey to push for the first-ever legislation in the USA to govern against 'bias in the algorithms that impact us all' (www.codedbias.com/about).

The notion of bias in computer systems goes back to Friedman and Nissenbaum (1996) who proposed three types of bias: 'Preexisting bias has its roots in social institutions, practices, and attitudes. Technical bias arises from technical constraints or considerations. Emergent bias arises in a context of use' (p. 330). They also provided a working definition of biased systems as 'computer systems that systematically and unfairly discriminate against certain individuals or groups of individuals in favor of others' (p. 332). AI in combination with very large datasets and ever more complex models have revived scholarly debates about bias, prompting a discussion about how automated tools might introduce bias or entrench existing inequity – especially if they are being inserted into an already discriminatory social system. Discriminatory bias either results from the fact that the training data that are used for refining an algorithm do not represent the diversity of populations ('bias of the sample'); or due to prejudice and stereotyping having influenced the collection of the data ('prejudicial bias'). From the perspective of Black feminism, Hampton (2021) argues that the term bias obscures what she describes as 'algorithmic oppression' (see also Noble 2018) and the need to analyze 'the ways that technology has violent impacts on marginalized people's lives' (p. 2). Klumbytė et al. (2022) have suggested we use the term algorithmic harm instead of bias. Birhane (2021) points to the need to discuss the wider picture underlying biases in datasets, 'such as unquestioned or intuitive assumptions in datasets, current and historical injustices, and power asymmetries' (p. 1).

In the next few sections, we discuss these varied forms of bias, with a focus on highlighting those parts of design processes that may prove useful sites of intervention aimed at mitigating bias, which disadvantages women and other equity-seeking groups.

Biased Datasets: From Diagnostic Tools to Screening Technologies

The existence of bias in large datasets is not surprising, as these data reflect medical, law enforcement, and other practices and the often-biased classification systems around which datasets are built. Consequently, there is also implicit gender bias that has characterized these practices for decades (e.g., Pot et al. 2019). In the medical field, 'big data' analyses do not only use data from clinical trials but, increasingly, new kinds of data sources, including 'DNA sequences, MRI scans, electronic health records (EHR) or social media posts' (Pot et al. 2019). EHR data about a patient, for example, are generated in different clinical situations and settings and are therefore 'inherently biased by the patient population structure, frequency of healthcare visits, diagnostic criteria, and care pathways' (Prosperi et al. 2018, p. 10).

There are many well-known examples of gender bias connected to medical practice. As Gabrielle Jackson states in a presentation of her book *Pain and prejudice* (2019), 'Centuries of female exclusion has meant women's diseases are often missed, misdiagnosed or remain a total mystery'. For example, it is well documented that the concept of depression has been framed in a gendered way (Hirschbein 2016). As researchers studied mainly women, more women fitted into the descriptions and were diagnosed with depression. An algorithm for the diagnosis of depression that has been trained on a set of gender-biased data will replicate and perpetuate this bias. Gender bias is particularly pronounced in the area of mental health. Examples include how pain is expressed by women and men and how this is interpreted by the treating physicians. Many studies suggest that women's expression of pain is taken less seriously by physicians than those of men, and that they are coded as 'pain in the absence of diagnostic evidence' or 'pain without organic pathology' (Samulowitz et al. 2018, p. 9). Exploring the relationship between gender and the experience of psychological distress, Becker (2019) states that three times more women than men are diagnosed with BPD (borderline personality disorder), which is used as 'the most pejorative of personality labels', which is 'little more than a shorthand for a difficult, angry, female client' (p. 423).

A related problem emerges when illnesses that are primarily related to women (e.g., what was at one time referred to as chronic fatigue syndrome, or CFS) lack legitimacy – what Leigh Star (Balka and Star 2015, p. 432) called 'diseases without passport'. People who presented at doctor's offices for several years with symptoms related to CFS were classified as having myriad ailments, including depression, hysteria, and more. These designations remained in patient records (which might be used to train datasets), as medical understanding of the disease matured, and it gained legitimacy as a bona fide illness. With its new-found legitimacy, CFS was given a new name: myalgic encephalomyelitis (ME), sometimes also referred to as myalgic encephalomyelitis/chronic fatigue syndrome (ME/CFS). Such data reclassifications – often undertaken without retrospective correction of data – may further introduce bias into data.

These and many other studies show that sample bias as well as prejudicial bias potentially impact a wide range of illnesses and their representation in big datasets. Sanchez-Martinez et al. (2019) speak of 'inherited bias':

> This inherited bias occurs because we ask ML (machine learning) solutions to predict which decisions the humans profiled in the training data would have made. Thus, we should not expect the ML method to be fair or impartial or to have the slightest idea about what the clinical goal is. The challenge is to find the way in which ML overcomes human bias, as this is crucial for successful decision-making applications that do not learn the mistakes that we have committed in the past.
>
> (Sanchez-Martinez 2019, p. 19)

Pot et al. (2019) argue that the availability and use of more and more digital data does not necessarily reduce the invisibility of gender; on the contrary, 'The "data bodies" that digital medicine operates with often have no explicit gender attribution anymore' (p. 14). That means that the non- or underrepresentation of women and gender minorities remains invisible and unrecognized.

Although a biased database poses many largely unresolved problems, 'a deeper dimension of unfairness lurks within algorithms' (Courtland 2018). While there is increasing evidence of this unfairness, Dourish (2016) points to the dangers of supporting an 'essentializing view of algorithms'. In broader discussion of digitalization 'the concern is not with algorithms as such', he argues, 'but with a system of digital control and management achieved through sensing, large-scale data storage, and algorithmic processing within a legal, commercial, or industrial framework that lends it authority' (p. 3). A widely discussed example of such a system is face recognition and the bias present in automated facial analysis algorithms and datasets with respect to phenotypic subgroups (Buolamwini and Gebru 2018; see also www.codedbias.com/about).

With respect to the problem of workers being discriminated against by data-driven practices, Raub (2018) discusses gender and racial bias in predictive hiring algorithms and its impacts on hiring practices of high-tech firms. However, she also argues that 'if developed in a responsible, comprehensive way, they have the capability to increase diversity, advance the interests of minorities, and fight discrimination' (p. 565). Kim (2017) proposes legal responses to data-driven discrimination that negatively affect workplace equality, using the term classification bias. She argues that 'if the goal is to discourage classification bias, then the law should not forbid the inclusion of race, sex, or other sensitive information as variables, but seek to preserve these variables, and perhaps even include them in some complex models' (p. 867).

We, however, must account for the fact that in certain countries (e.g., in Germany and France) collecting data about race and ethnicity is not allowed, for historical reasons but also because they are fundamentally flawed ('Races do not exist, but racism does', Introduction). The changing gender identities and realities complicate the situation.

The list of studies pointing to gender bias is long. For example, Guiterrez (2021) makes a fascinating case concerning gender bias embedded in advertising, film, music videos, and television that 'take on a new life when the platforms make biased algorithmic decisions, potentially multiplying prejudice, and establishing a vicious cycle that is not apparent' (p. 440). She concludes, 'Blind spots happen when women are absent in audiovisual content, leading to invisibilization; meanwhile, hotspots ensue when women are differentiated, leading to discrimination' (p. 446).

Examples of potential algorithmic harm abound when it comes to the 'informatization of the body'. A study by Katyal and Jung (2021) examines the difficulties transgender travelers face when exposed to screening technologies at airports or when subject to ID checks. They call attention to the 'misgendering' of trans people, which often means that they have to undergo lengthy and potentially humiliating search procedures. Another example Katyal and Jung discuss is the difficulties transgender drivers experience when attempting to pass Uber's mandatory ID checks, with the risk of being expelled by their app when their photos don't match their identity documents. They point to the danger of being denied access to certain social and medical services and, more generally, the risk of 'censorship, erasure, and self-censorship' posed by technologies that are used to categorize people and keep them under surveillance. McNamarah (2021) considers (intentional) misgendering as a form of gender policing, 'meant to reinforce a binary, discrete, stable notion of gender, and to punish and censor those who challenge it' (p. 50).

Keyes et al. (2021) point to technologies such as AGR (automatic gender recognition) as a source of misgendering trans and non-binary people, arguing that there is 'no way to make a technology premised on external inference of gender compatible with trans lives' (p. 14) (or, for that matter, the experiences of masculinized or 'butch' women, or effeminate men). They suggest that 'designers and makers should quite simply avoid implementing or deploying AGR' (p. 14).

AI border technologies, such as iBorderCtrl, are another compelling example of technologies that potentially discriminate against LGBTQ+ persons, persons of colour, and asylum seekers. Being introduced by the EU to speed up border crossings of third-country nationals, they include facial recognition and deception detection, with all the pitfalls identified in other studies (Hall and Clapton 2021).

Relating this back to Harding's (1986) understanding of gender, the gender symbolism reflected in AGR algorithms enforces a dichotomous view of gender that prohibits those whose projected gender identity (gender identity perceived by others) may not neatly map onto their subjective gender identity (how an individual sees themselves in gender terms) from moving through the world with ease. The AGR algorithms and the dichotomous views of gender they are built upon serve to reinforce dichotomous (rather than non-binary or gender queer) views of gender.

Avoiding or Countervailing Bias

While D'Ignazio and Klein (2020) in their book *Data Feminism* provide a discussion of the relationship between data and power, Dencik et al. (2019) dig deeper into the notion of data justice, which they define as examining 'how our understanding of social justice is changing in the context of datafication, what concepts and practices are needed, and how social justice can be advanced in a datafied society' (p. 873). Both pieces of research are driven by intersectional feminist thought.

Several strands of thought stand out in the debate on data justice. First, the need to document and analyze the positionality of people involved in generating and making use of datasets. As the details of proprietary ML models are often not transparent, Shadowen (2017) argues, who developed them for which purpose becomes important:

> A machine learning model is architected from the programmers that create it, the algorithm and metrics used, and the data it takes as input. When a development team programs a machine learning model they must choose carefully: what type of algorithm is used, how the algorithm is set up, what metrics and parameters are used, and on what data the algorithm is trained and tested. Creators' influence can show up in unexpected ways.
>
> (Shadowen 2017, p. 9)

The quest for transparency of decision-making that guides research on data justice is influenced by standpoint theory, which goes back to Dorothy Smith (1987) and Sandra Harding (1986) (see Chapter 1). Gray and Witt (2021) consider identifying who is behind an algorithm as a means to not only identify the interests that are shaping the ways data are collected and put together but also as providing a lever to understand gender power relations and other substantive inequalities and how to possibly change them. They define a feminist data ethics of care approach that has as its aim to 'identify opportunities for improving workplace diversity; identify real decision-makers in the machine learning pipeline to understand the potential biases they are at risk of embedding; and hold real actors to account' (p. 11).

A second, proactive, approach pushes for more geodiversity and demographics in datasets – 'tipping the balance' (Zou and Schiebinger 2018). While taking up this approach to increasing diversification of datasets and sources, Draude et al. (2020) stress the need to not overlook historical power imbalances when collecting data. They point out that certain marginalized groups may not want their data to be collected, for example when they are used for the purpose of surveillance – for 'certain groups, the claim for participating power could also entail the right to refuse being a source for information' (p. 334).

Finally, data justice is also about 'fostering the recognition and the exploration of ways of thinking and using data from the margins' (Decik et al. 2019, p. 874). Milan and Treré (2021) build their vision of data justice on the distinction between 'data at the centre' and 'data at the margins'. They point to the invisibility of people such as undocumented migrants in datasets that are used to regulate access to important services; but also at the fact that many of the data collected at the margins remain 'out of sight' or absent, if people lack the resources and skills to collect and share them: 'Journeying into data at the margins is "stepping into the land of otherwise"' (Rodriguez 2017, p. 49). One example is the sharing of health insurance numbers by citizens with non-citizens migrants, to give them access to services. This is another form of 'data at the margins' that remains out of sight.

While addressing the exploitation of data collected in poor countries at the margins 'in the complex ecosystem of data extractivism and commodification' (p. 4), Milan and Treré (2021) also refer to examples of 'social actors engaging in resistant data practices' (p. 7) and to 'alternative imaginaries' and practices that are informed by a feminist data perspective. Among the examples they provide are indigenous data sovereignty initiatives (Walker et al. 2021); or an art project by Caroline Sinders (2020) – 'an intersectional approach to datafication: it purports to collect cultural material about feminism to train AI systems to locate feminist and other intersectional ways of thinking across online media content' (p. 10).

There is a broad discussion of algorithmic fairness that builds on different definitions of fairness, some of which focus on groups/populations while others focus on individuals (e.g., Collett and Dillon 2019). Klumbytė et al. (2022), among others, argue that fairness as a criterion may be too weak, proposing to aim at 'accountable and contextualized systems that go beyond fairness towards equity and justice' (p. 1528). Pot et al. (2019) propose a set of questions that might help make gender bias in data visible. Schuurman and Balka (2009) argue that all data should be meta-tagged to avoid the myriad of issues that arise as we take data out of context – and of course this is especially important when it comes to attempting to eliminate bias. Data that have been collected for a specific purpose are used in other contexts. Ferryman and Pitcan (2018) refer to this general phenomenon as 'lack of data empathy', a term that goes back to computer scientist James Faghmous, one of the informants in their study of fairness in precision medicine. He described this lack 'as a distance between these analysts and the data, specifically their lack of knowledge and direct experience of how, why, and where health data were collected' (p. 21). This and other approaches, including for example the notion of 'situated algorithms' put forward by Draude et al. (2020), reflect Donna Haraway's notion of situated knowledge.

The Work to Make AI-Based Technologies Work in Practice

I always wonder what we're actually talking about when we talk about AI. What we talk about AI outside of academic computing, research and development labs, big tech, [is] the assumption that AI and machine learning have been widely deployed. I have a lot of questions about that. I'm keenly interested to hear examples of where AI and machine learning are actually implemented in worksites. . . . Data analytics, that's all over the place. But more specifically, AI, and some versions of AI and/or machine learning – I am very skeptical. And I'm really struck by how rarely the people that I'm following, which are mainly in the military, ever actually specify what they need.

(Lucy Suchman, 04/22/2022)

Suchman's skepticism concerning the promises and pretensions of AI to make human labour and human ingenuity at work dispensable is well founded. Recent in-depth studies of machine-learning applications in practice confirm this skepticism, drawing a rich picture of 'human–algorithm collaborations' (Blomberg et al. 2018). Before discussing some of this research that examines the use of data analytics and ML in different fields of work, a few clarifications may be helpful.

Big Data and Machine Learning: Some Definitions

Data analytics applies statistical analysis and technologies to data to find trends and solve problems. Although data analytics is widespread, it still meets considerable difficulties when it comes to supporting complex work practices. AI reaches beyond that: it involves data analysis, making assumptions, aiming to make predictions that are beyond human capabilities and to push automation to a level that makes a machine independent of human interventions.

Machine learning is one of the most successful forms of AI. It enables analysis of massive quantities of data – so-called 'big data'. Learning in this context means that the computer program (an algorithm) is able to explore these big quantities of data, identify patterns in them, discover errors, and modify the algorithm to produce accurate (and sometimes also unexpected and new) outcomes (e.g., a particular diagnosis). The accuracy and plausibility of the outcome of such a process depends on the quality of the data and the algorithm (the 'model'). 'Deep learning', a subcategory of ML based on artificial neural networks, refers to algorithms that have achieved a special accuracy in solving numerous problems. They are

> inspired by the early models of sensory processing by the brain. An artificial neural network can be created by simulating a network of model neurons in a computer. By applying algorithms that mimic the processes of real neurons, we can make the network 'learn' to solve many types of problems.
>
> (Krogh 2008, p. 195)

ML raises big questions concerning the interpretability and plausibility of its results, one of the reasons for keeping the human-in-the-loop.

'Big data' is a term that covers multiple phenomena. First of all, it stands for large datasets that are much larger than those for which earlier databases and software systems were designed. They are larger in terms of volume, velocity (i.e., the speed with which they are generated and move through systems), and their variety (e.g., Kitchin 2014). They are so large that they exceed existing capacities for collection, storage, and analysis (Brown et al. 2011). 'Big data' does not just describe large datasets and the associated technologies, it is also strongly connected to 'datafication' – the capture, storage, and processing of more and more data concerning our social lives and our bodies.[1] The fact that big data have become highly valuable economic assets raises multiple concerns about ownership and privacy. 'In this spirit', an opinion of the Austrian Bioethics Commission states, 'we understand big data as a socio-technical

---

[1] As anyone who has used a smart watch, an RFID-based scanner, or compared measurements from two devices (e.g., a GPS-enabled smart watch to the pedometer algorithm in a phone, or an RFID-enabled ski pass to measurements captured by a smart watch with a ski algorithm built in) can tell you, data collected by consumer-based sensors is incredibly variable and lacks consistency even when two devices proport to measure the same thing.

practice that should be seen in connection with the political, economic and social factors that enable it' (BEK p. 23).

The 'Ironies of Automation' Revisited

Automatons and their construction are a long-standing object of fascination. In an essay on mechanization, Simon Schaffer (1996) describes the automatons Charles Babbage built in the nineteenth century, remarking on their supposed intelligence:

> The intelligence attributed to machines hinges on the cultural invisibility of the human skills which accompany them. In Babbage's devices, the skills which surrounded automatic mechanization were systematically rendered invisible. Then and only then might any machines seem intelligent. ... If such machines look intelligent because we do not concentrate on where their work is done, then we need to think harder about the work which produces values and who performs it.
>
> (Schaffer 1996, p. 13)

While Schaffer refers to human work with respect to a machine that has been made invisible in 'automatic Turks, mechanical elephants, and clockwork women', an experience that precedes AI, Lisanne Bainbridge (1983) points to another phenomenon that is crucial to understanding the relationships of humans with machines. The 'ironies of the classic approach to automation', she argued, 'lie in the expectations of the system designers, and in the nature of the tasks left for the human operators to carry out' (p. 775). In her paper, she discusses examples from chemical production, steel manufacturing, and the flight deck in aviation, identifying several types of work human operators have to perform, so that these systems work properly: manual control skills, cognitive skills needed to intervene in an automated process when things go wrong, and, generally, the monitoring of automation. She also showed how transferring easily automated tasks to machines may make the remaining activities more difficult for human beings. Bainbridge concluded her paper that is still much cited in discussions about the need to keep the human in the loop: 'The more advanced a control system is, so the more crucial may be the contribution of the human operator' (p. 775).

This insight has been confirmed many times by research that looks deeply into the practices that evolve around different types of IT artifacts. Reflecting on technologies in support of care work, Bratteteig and Wagner (2013) have taken up this insight. They argue that many of these technologies build on separating the work that can be carried out by a machine from the work that cannot be automated, and hence is left to human actors. Thought of as 'residual work', it is often devalued as not requiring special professional skills. They discuss an example of homecare technologies that split a complex activity such as 'watching over' (monitoring a person's health status), distributing it between a human caretaker and a machine:

> 'Watching over' becomes partitioned into an automatable part, which is 'faceless' and disembodied, leaving the social part of 'watching over' to become a task of its own ... [T]his 'social part' may consist of different kinds of work that are not just 'add-ons' but crucial for the 'watching over' to be done in a caring, safe and heedful way.
>
> (Bratteteig and Wagner 2013, p. 157)

This example points to the need to carefully think not only about what to automate but also to design the 'interface' between humans and machines in ways that they complement and support each other. This is hardly a new insight, and it is astounding that developers of AI-based technologies tend to ignore it (with some exceptions, as we will see).

Underestimating the Complexity of Work Practices

Two well-documented projects at IBM Almaden Research Center shed light on the challenges of developing human–algorithm collaborations. The Cloud Services Analytics Project (Blomberg et al. 2018) aimed at providing an internal group of sellers and their managers working in the global cloud IT infrastructure-as-a-service (IaaS) business with data analytics that would help them improve their selling performances. The Intelligent IT Configuration Project (Wolf and Blomberg 2019a, b) aspired to support IT service designers (called 'architects') within IBM as they prepared architectural solutions and created bids in response to requests for proposals from clients.

One of the key problems the researchers in the Cloud Services Analytics Project encountered was the sellers' difficulties 'intuitively' making sense of the predictions provided by the algorithm:

> ... the results of these models were difficult to reason about as some of the features were abstract and not easily mapped on to the sellers' everyday experiences ... [I]t was difficult to see the direct link between the revenue data and the predictions, and impossible to explain in everyday language exactly how the model arrived at the predictions. ... The analytics found patterns in the data that humans could not 'see' requiring a level of 'blind' trust on the part of the sellers.
>
> (Blomberg et al. 2018, p. 292)

Given these difficulties, the prospective users continued to make sales decisions based on information beyond what the system knew: 'Actually, we observed that they continued to take their decision outside the system as they didn't see enough advantage in using it' (Blomberg quoted in Simone et al. 2022, p. 205). Moreover, the system was of little help when it came to predict potentially risky situations, as it did not account for all the factors that could lead to such a situation.

The Intelligent IT Configuration Project responded to a genuine need of the 'architects' at IBM, promising to diminish the effort required by a time-consuming activity (requirements extraction) and it had their full commitment. Despite extensive user support, it met issues that in the end were not resolved. Much of the effort to improve the tool went into developing a deeper understanding of the work practices of architects. The fundamental problems that the development team were unable to resolve had to do with the complexity of the architects' work practices and the difficulties of shaping data analytics in accordance with them. This resulted in users having problems engaging with the results. One of the main problems was that the tool did not account for the fact that the architects often collaborate with their colleagues to align their choices and make each other aware of critical decisions. In addition to that, Blomberg et al. (2018) argue, 'Realizing the full potential of data analytics requires awareness of the technical and organizational complexity of acting on analytics in the enterprise' (p. 297). Wolf and Blomberg (2019a) comment on the experiences:

> What makes a smart system 'explainable' for a given context? What are the key enablers (and inhibitors) to end users' contextual understanding of such system? . . . Scholarly attention is needed to chart the interacting aspects of ML interpretability and how sense making and coherence dynamically emerge thorough interactions between users, smart systems and their deployments.
>
> (Wolf and Blomberg, 2019a, p. 1)

The examples of human–algorithm collaborations we briefly present here point to several fundamental problems, including the interpretability and trustworthiness of a system's predictions and its limited ability to capture the decision-making of knowledgeable workers who have developed the skills required to (cooperatively) manage large amounts of data. The examples also speak to the importance of context – how it is drawn on by experienced workers, and the context of presenting findings from AI and ML to those who are asked to make decisions based on the material produced by AI and ML. Simone et al. (2022) conclude, 'When the complexity involves the capabilities of knowledgeable workers, such as their intuition and creativity based on an experience that is difficult to formalize, this technological innovation meets serious difficulties' (p. 294).

The complexity of work in an industrial context is different from the complexity involved in producing medical diagnosis. Several small but rather detailed observational studies in clinical settings describe how physicians and nurses successfully integrate AI-based tools into their daily work. The issues they address are: how trust in an algorithm is built; how to strengthen the human-in-the-loop; and how human–algorithm relations are not fixed but need to be configured and reconfigured.

Building Trust in Algorithms

Studies of AI-based technologies in health care place the notion of care and trust in the centre of analysis. These technologies, the argument runs, deeply affect the relationship between physicians (and other caretakers) and patients, a relationship that is based on dialogue and deliberation in which findings, observations, and decisions are communicated, justified, and discussed not merely with regard to 'facts' but also values, preferences, and attitudes (e.g., Wirtz et al. 2006). Also in the past, technological innovation and medical specialization have brought about changes in these relationships. What is deemed new though is a gradual displacement of a relationship based on dialogue und trust by quantitative-mathematical approaches to medical justification. Few studies look deeper into this process and examine the extent to which this is happening in practice.

The centrality of trust in algorithm-based predictions that influence decision-making is an issue that is increasingly being raised by researchers (e.g., Clarke et al. 2019). Trust as a fundamental condition of human relationship has been addressed by feminist scholars, among them Annette Baier (1986) and Trudy Govier (1992), who argued for a whole new approach to ethics centred less on legalistic contractual relations and more on trusting relations such as those existing between parents and children. Fisher and Tronto (1990) emphasized the relationship between caring and trust, arguing that

> ... caring also embodies a sort of justice and inspires a type of trust. Caring is seen as just when it refers to a shared standard by which each gives and receives her 'due'. Trust results because these standards are shared, and one can count on other community members to maintain them.
>
> (Fisher and Tronto 1990, p. 46)

Baier also proposed that we understand interpersonal trust relationships as embedded in networks of trust. This, Peter and Morgan (2001) argue, enables us to situate them politically, hence address issues of oppression – 'Optimum trusting relationships may not be possible on a one-to-one level if either party is oppressed by others in the network' (p. 6).

Trust in one-to-one relationships is different from trusting that a dialysis machine works properly, or an algorithm has come up with a trustworthy diagnosis. This may be a complicated matter that is often understood as correlating with information and risk calculations. Leighton and Roberts

(2020), in a multidisciplinary collaborative project in Mexico City about water quality, public trust, and health, come to a different view. Seeking to understand 'how people trust or distrust water', they argue that,

> In regards to trust itself, as anthropologists and feminist technoscience scholars, we do not assume 'trust' is something immutable that can be tracked as a presence or absence. Instead, we have structured the project to understand how it is enacted, or not. In theorizing trust this way, we work against a 'common sense' understanding of trust that sees it as a problem arising from a lack of knowledge or inappropriate calculation of risk.
>
> (Leighton and Roberts 2020, p. 4)

Trust (or mistrust), in this understanding, is worked out collaboratively as part of people's experiences and practices of dealing with a phenomenon. Taking up this insight, Winter and Carusi's (2022) study of the validation of three AI-based diagnostic systems for the early diagnosis of pulmonary hypertension (PH) describes the building of trust in an algorithm. They use the term practice-oriented trust (in addition to interpersonal trust), which can be 'conceptualised as generated "in action", built up in some form of situated or contextual practical engagement of a work routine, often in contexts when people have a responsibility to build trust in new technology' (p. 3).

The study provides detailed descriptions of the activities the team (of PH clinicians, consultant PH nurse, radiologist, computer scientist, data scientist, and biomedical scientist) engages in querying datasets, building the software, and training the model. Querying involves the practical work of questioning how and by whom the datasets have been labelled or coded, eventually relabeling features on images so that the radiologist can trust the datasets the algorithm will built on. Bossen et al. (2019) have pointed out the complexity of such a process in which data are repurposed to be used in another context of use. Trust-building in the outcome of data analysis also involves further steps of validation in which the algorithm gradually gains 'meaning, interpretability and comparability in the real-world context of use' (p. 15). Conceptualizing trust in a technology as collaboratively achieved in practice over time has methodological consequences, as this is a process that can only be captured by observing what people do in a particular context.[2]

---

[2] Over time it became clear that pulse oximeters (put on the tip of a finger to measure oxygen levels in a person's blood) had been designed to produce accurate results for those with skin pigmentation typical of 'white' people. Measurements of more heavily pigmented people (basically, anyone not 'white') were incorrect (Balka et al. 2007). Manufacturers began altering devices and algorithms over time to increase the accuracy of measurements for a greater diversity of people. As hospitals acquired the newer, more accurate models, a mix of the newer pigment-sensitive pulse oximeters alongside the older models led to confusion about which were which (since no one bothered to label them).

Even after trust in the algorithm has been successfully built, Winter and Carusi (2022) argue, physicians do not take the algorithmic outcome for a patient at 'face value': they interpret what it is 'saying', questioning 'its "truth", a potential withholding of belief' (p. 12). Hence, observations in this study suggest that physicians still engage in reasoning about an outcome (in a dialogue with the patient, a colleague, or just themselves). A similar observation was made in a study of radiologists engaging with a detection and diagnosis tool (CADe) for screening mammographs. 'The prompt', Randall et al. (2021) state, 'required that readers deploy their professional vision to make sense of and make accountable what the machine was showing as a lesion or a calcification and requiring a decision to recall or not-recall' (p. 207).

Strengthening the Human-in-the-Loop

Several other studies focussing on human–algorithm collaborations in a clinical context corroborate the finding that physicians' and nurses' professional vision is not simply delegated to a machine. Beede et al. (2020) studied the introduction of a deep learning system for the detection of diabetic retinopathy (DR). The research is based on interviews and observations in several clinics in Thailand that perform an AI-assisted screening process for eye diseases. It focusses, among other issues, on the screening workflow operated by nurses, in each of the clinics in slightly different ways. Images produced by a camera operator are sent to an algorithm in the cloud and returned in real time to the nurses with an assessment of the presence/absence and severity of DR, including a recommendation for whether the patient should be sent to an ophthalmologist. Apart from problems with the consistency and quality of the images in this particular case, this seems like an easily automatable process. One of the most interesting observations concerns how the nurses perceived and used the system. Not all the nurses were equally confident in assessing images for the presence of DR, in particular its severity. Hence, they valued the system as offering a learning opportunity – 'improving their ability to make accurate DR assessments' – and to '*prove* their own readings to on-site doctors' (p. 589). That a PD approach is critical to the design of AI-based systems is another insight of the study. It points to the importance of practitioners – nurses, camera operators, and clinicians – collaboratively designing their own workflows and fitting in AI-technologies in ways that serves them best.

Also Sendak et al.'s (2020) study of Sepsis Watch, a tool that is based on a deep learning model, focusses on the importance of designing appropriate workflows. The tool has not been purposed as a diagnostic device; it identifies patients for further evaluation by a physician. Nurses are the primary users of

Sepsis Watch, which has been fully integrated into clinical practice. The researchers observed how the rapid response team (RRT) nurses developed 'expertise and practices' with the tool over time that helped them contextualize 'the information displayed by Sepsis Watch and facilitated the integration of the tool into existing clinical practices. These practices ranged from emotional labor around communication with physicians to drawing on their own clinical expertise' (p. 106). Observations of clinical practice over time revealed that 'RRT nurses and ED physicians retained professional discretion to diagnose sepsis' (p. 106). Hence, instead of pushing human expertise into the background, the tool served as a support, widening the opportunities of nurses and clinicians to watch over patients. Most importantly, it helped the RRT nurses to expand their professional expertise. The authors also describe how trust and accountability in the tool's design was developed over time, in a project with strong participatory features. 'We found that although model outputs do not need to be explainable, clinical decisions do require explanations and justifications and there is significant labor required to map between model outputs and clinical decisions' (p. 108), Sendak et al. (2020) conclude their analysis.

Jussupow et al. (2022) looked into how radiologists use an AI system for stroke diagnosis in support of their own professional 'seeing'. Also, this system meets a real need, as most radiologists 'agree that it is necessary to adopt AI systems in order to cope with the increasing workload, case complexity, and required diagnostic accuracy' (p. 295). The research points to the role of diagnostic self-efficacy – how confident radiologists were with respect to their own diagnostic ability, with professionals with low-to-medium confidence making intense use of the system. They used the system as an important backup that helped them to not overlook any critical fact, especially in judging damage severity – the system as 'a control mechanism and as an immediately available second opinion' (p. 302). Moreover, the radiologists integrated the information the tool provided into their own diagnostic work:

> ... for creating a detailed diagnostic report, these physicians used the information provided by the AI system in an iterative process to dig deeper into potential damages in different brain areas. The detailed, quantified views on different segments of the patient's brain were seen as especially helpful to decide between alternatives and in case of boundary decisions when classifying the severity of the stroke.
>
> (Jussupow 2022, p. 301)

The studies point to intense forms of human–algorithm collaboration that are developed when technologies based on ML become integrated into a real work context. Instead of getting automated, diagnostic work is augmented through offering practitioners an analysis (and the associated alerts), often paired with a recommendation that supports them in situations of stress, an ambiguous diagnostic finding, providing a 'second opinion'. The studies also highlight that with ML systems, which are continuously taking into account data from use, the skill/sophistication level of the user matters in terms of what the system trains to do – if more trainees use a system than expert users, this has implications for how the system is used in the future. Yet at the moment we don't have ways of tracking how the corpus of data – and hence what the system trains to do – changes over time.

Configuring Human–Algorithm Relations

The notion of configuration work goes back to a long-standing interest within CSCW research and systems design in how to support users in adapting an IT artifact so that it can be integrated into their specific work context. Different terms have been used to describe this process, such as tailoring (Trigg and Bødker 2004), appropriation work, domestication, and customization. Appropriation has been used to describe the activities that allow a technology (typically designed at a distance from use) to be taken up in specific work contexts. The same technologies may be appropriated in different ways in varied work environments, reflecting differences in work practices, scope of practice, work organization, and so on, which vary across workplaces. One of the key arguments in the debate about appropriation is that it is a process that goes beyond the mere 'adoption' of a technological artifact (Pipek 2005, p. 30). Bentley and Dourish (1995) define customization as implying 'not only the ability to mould and manipulate structures within the system, but also the ability to appropriate them and use them in new ways; support for customization is support for innovation' (p. 137). Houben and Bradram (2013) define configuration work as 'the amount of work required to set up an environment, so it enables the user to perform a task or activity. It is the effort required to control, manage and understand information, applications and services that are distributed over all used devices' (p. 722). Balka and Wagner (2006) have used the concept of configuration work to indicate the range of things that needed to be configured when technologies are appropriated into specific settings: not 'just' the technology itself but 'organisational relations, space technology relations, as well as people's connections to other people, to other places, and work materials' (p. 229).

Configuration work is also necessary when AI-based tools meet the realities of a specific work context. In a paper on how patients and physiotherapists appropriated an AI-based system in support of rehabilitation, Schwennesen (2019) refers to 'recent work on the fragility and incompleteness of algorithms' suggesting 'that the algorithmic system needs to be creatively "repaired" to build and maintain enabling connections between bodies in-motion and professionals in arrangements of care' (p. 176). At the core of the smart phone application that patients use at home is the algorithmic transformation of movement data. The practices that patients developed while interacting with the device point to active processes of appropriation, with patients learning how to arrange themselves in their home space so that the system can produce and process data about their bodily movements and how to cope with other limitations of the system.

While this example describes the configuration work involved in adapting the environment to make the algorithm work, it does not touch on the algorithm itself. Grønsund and Aanestad (2020) present an example that describes configuration work in a global ship-brokering company that introduced automated algorithmic support for data analysis and prediction work. The system is based on the global Automatic Identification System (AIS), which contains information about ships, their identity, location, and cargo. They found that 'humans and the algorithm were configured and reconfigured in multiple ways over time as the organization dealt with the introduction of algorithmic analysis' (p. 1). They, more specifically, describe the activities needed to prepare 'clean' AIS data and classify them, which was done by an experienced researcher and involved many sessions to clarify anomalies. Once the algorithm was running, manual and algorithmic output had to be compared, systematically training the algorithmic system. Grønsund and Aanestad provide a highly detailed description of these lengthy processes of monitoring and evaluating (which Beede et al. (2020) term validation). From our perspective, the most interesting finding is that these activities do not end at a certain point but are part of living with AI-based systems. Although the algorithms that were developed were relatively simple, 'the data input or the presentation mode had to be continuously improved – or altered. As a collective, the team's work of auditing and altering the algorithm comprise what we call "augmenting work"' (p. 16). They distinguish two types of augmentation work: auditing the algorithm and altering it.

A study of software automation (Shestakofski 2017) provides additional insights into what happens when a company introduces and further develops AI-based software development tools, describing how 'managers continually reconfigured assemblages of software and human helpers' (p. 4), changing the company's organization. The software itself was not able to solve the problems the company, a digital marketplace for local services, faced, at any stage in this process. One of the main insights of this study was that 'full automation of every task was impractical given the instability of the firm's environment and product' (p. 115). As a consequence, there remained a place for human expertise carried out by 'complementary workers'. The tasks these workers carried out changed with progressing automation, as 'outdated labor processes were typically replaced by new functions that supported new innovations' (p. 115). Shestakofski also points to the emotional labour that was necessary to build and rebuild buyers' and sellers' trust in the broker company throughout periods of technological changes: 'Phone agents struggled to keep up with and understand the innovations originating in the San Francisco office. At the same time, they were tasked with supporting users who were angry or confused about the changing product' (2018, p. 55).

It seems that, whether AI-based or based on more traditional technologies, automation that reaches beyond simple processes aiming at complex professional practices sets a 'never-ending story' of configuring, reconfiguring, and other developments in motion. The work this involves varies, reaching from purely technical work to workflow redesign and other organizational changes, and includes all kinds of support and emotional work that working in such a demanding environment requires.

Practices of Care

The various findings about what happens when tools based on ML are designed, developed, and integrated into a real-use context can be seen as illustrations of what Christine Wolf (2019) in her observation of the work of ML developers termed 'practices of care' – 'the ongoing ethical struggling and striving to make a given situation better' (p. 2). She asks how a focus on situations of care with respect to work that is normally not understood as such, 'push[es] forward our understanding of sociotechnical care', adding,

> This case provides not only an alternative site to see caring practices (adding ML to more traditional zones of care like nursing). It also allows us to think through 'local' configurations of care, and their relation to more 'global' sociotechnical systems and regimes of formalization.
>
> (Wolf 2019, p. 2)

The journey through several studies of AI in real-life/work contexts highlights a diversity of practices of care. The first is the care of datasets, which involves querying the 'who' and 'how' data are collected and for which purposes they are used. It also entails an engagement for data justice – to diversify data in terms of geodiversity and demographics as well as pay attention to the imbalances in power relations. Care is also an element of the work that seeks to make the complexities of work processes visible, including activities and people performing them that may have been overlooked in accounts of the work. Hornecker et al. (2020) have studied such technical care settings as a triadic interaction and propose 'to take account of this in the future design of care technologies, in particular for robotic solutions' to prevent breakdowns in interaction among the technology and the involved stakeholders. This was further elaborated on in a study by Carros et al. (2022), focussing on the use of social robots in a care home. They emphasize the importance of a close linkage with the existing everyday practices of care, in such a way that the social robot can clearly become an improvement of the quality of care, instead of a replacement of direct human interaction. Elish and Watkins (2020), in a report on Sepsis Watch, point to the importance of repair work when it comes to integrating an AI-based technology into a particular work context. Their notion of repair echoes the notion of care: 'Repair work can take many forms, from emotional labor to expert justifications, and involves the labor of integrating a new technology into an existing professional context' (p. 4). Recognizing repair work, they continue, brings work that often remains invisible (and undervalued) to the centre of attention:

> If only the work of initiation and theoretical construction, typically elite and masculine forms of work, are valued when it comes to the future of AI and society, then so much of the actual day-to-day work that is required to make AI function in the world is rendered invisible and undervalued, further contributing to conditions of social inequality.
>
> (Elish and Watkins 2020, p. 4)

Elish and Watkins (2020) emphasize the disruptive nature of technological interventions in an organization as well as the different interests and perspectives of the participating and affected stakeholders. They point to the key role of RRT nurses in carrying out the repair work that the disruption of professional hierarchies and traditional workflows had made necessary. This involved a great deal of emotional labour – 'constantly negotiating their tone and approach based on the affective reactions of the doctors they called' (p. 37).

In this light, many of the activities that studies of AI in practice highlight have an element of care: the building of trust in an algorithm; all the efforts made to develop human–algorithm relationships that are respectful of workers' skills and attentive to upgrading them; but also the work that goes into the auditing and altering of algorithms to develop them into truly supportive tools.

Summary

In this chapter we began by discussing historic visions of AI, and how these have persisted over time. We briefly touched on data gaps related to gender and work in AI, which constrain our ability to better understand where in AI women work. We identified some of the places women are likely to be working in AI. We returned to feminist ethics as the ethics of care, which allowed us to identify some of the consequences of gender-biased data in AI and ML and the potentially deleterious consequences that may result from the use of gender- and race-biased data. Here we build on the work of Friedman and Nissenbaum (1996) and others to outline different types of gender bias in data that can permeate AI and ML applications. This set the stage of our coverage of gender and other forms of bias and harm in algorithms. We reflected on how different aspects of gender work together to reify gender-based norms in relation to automatic gender recognition software.

We revisited the ethics of care and demonstrated how care is central to issues of addressing bias in data in the context of data justice. We discussed the relationship of data, ML, and algorithms, and through examples from health care and the business world identified some design failures resulting from what are arguably failures of caring, when it comes to designing work and particularly allocating tasks between humans and machines. Through our examples it becomes clear that trust and care are central to data and algorithmic stewardship, which will need to be mobilized in relation to AI and ML if we are going to achieve gender justice in future work processes. We point to some studies where human–algorithm collaboration worked well: in these circumstances, work carried out by predominantly women workers was accounted for in work design, which sought to preserve autonomy and skill. We discuss configuration work and augmentation work, the latter of which is particularly relevant to algorithmically mediated work. Throughout the chapter we have considered the role of 'role of the human(s) in the loop', who increasingly must respond to numerous developments in motion. These we framed as another aspect of care work. That means that, although women as designers and users of AI-based systems are not explicitly present and thematized in the studies we described, feminist theory makes a major contribution to how we understand the systems and what making them useful in practice requires.

8

The Computerization of Care Work

In this chapter, we focus on the computerization of care work. It provides a rich lens through which to view issues related to women's paid work, gender, and technology, for several reasons. Often referred to as a 'quintessentially female profession' (Goan 2001, p. 196), nursing has had a persistent division of labour based on sex (what Harding (1986) calls a gender structure). As a profession, nursing work has been symbolically gendered as feminine or women's work, no doubt related to the perception among many that women possess an innate ability to nurture, making them better suited to care work in general and nursing work in particular.

Modern hospitals are dense with technologies that deeply affect the work of health professionals and patients. Literature describing these changes abounds. It shows how the profession of nursing, has progressively been shaped by technologies that have far-reaching implications for the practice of care work: IT-based nursing documentation systems, including nursing protocols and other documentation systems, as well as care robots. Writing about 'gender–technology' relations in nursing, Sandelowski suggested that

> Current efforts in the field are directed towards explaining the nature, ethics and politics of the Western cultural association between technology and masculinity. Scholars increasingly seek to understand how gender and technology are constitutive of each other, how Western technology embodies or consolidates masculine identity, practices and values, and how technology can be an equalizer in societies characterized by gender, class and race inequalities.
>
> (Sandelowski 1997, p. 2019)

In light of the strong association of technology with masculinity (in Harding's (1986) terms, gender symbolism) and the prevalence of technology in nursing (not to mention the gender structures characteristic of hospital settings),

199

nursing work offers a unique lens through which we can examine women's work in relation to technology. As caring work, nursing work also serves as a means through which we can explore notions of care.

We begin this chapter by elaborating these points and expanding our understanding of care. After providing an overview of the computerization of care work, we highlight four areas that have received attention in diverse settings, which have implications for the design of ICT-based systems to support nursing. We then address these issues through a focus on two areas in which nursing care has been the focus of computerization: nursing information systems and robotics and the automation of care.

Background

Care is a constitutive element of many professions and services. Social work and community work have a strong care dimension as well as a democratic-transformative one (Meagher and Parton 2004). Education is based on care in the ways teachers relate to their students taking care of their (special) needs (Goldstein 2002). So does research with a participative or action-centred character. Toombs et al. (2017) discuss 'how researchers and participants navigate a complex set of roles and reflexively engage with interpersonal vulnerabilities and needs for care' (p. 1). Reflecting on participation in diversity research, Howard and Irani (2019) describe 'how care, vulnerability, harm, and emotions shape ethnographic and qualitative data' (p. 1). Krüger et al. (2021) use the concept of care in analyzing their co-design work with migrants and refugees. Maria Puig de la Bellacasa (2011) proposes that we consider caring as an ethical and political obligation for all and as key to non-exploitative relations of co-existence.

Predominantly filled by women, nursing is arguably the most prominent area in which care work has been professionalized. It is also an arena in which women's professional work very closely mirrors those attributes that have historically been viewed as feminine attributes. Care relations are particularly vulnerable to exploitation and social injustice and in many countries, women, immigrants, and racial minorities disproportionately perform the work of caring. Moreover, with the rise of managerial power in health-care systems all over the world, care work has become subject to rationalizing with a view of controlling expenditures and increasing efficiency.

Nurses work in hospitals and care homes, also visiting patients at home. Based on extensive (ethnographic) studies of hospital work and care work in the home, Strauss et al. (1982) have pointed to the normative dimension of caretaking – to interact with patients 'in a caring way', show respect for their feelings, avoid exposing their fragility, perform procedures with care, and pay attention to safety in their work. From a care-ethical approach (see Chapter 2), care relations are seen as different from other systems of social relations, as they follow the values of caring – attentiveness, responsibility, nurturance, compassion, meeting others' needs (Tronto 1993, pp. 2–3). Tronto also disentangles the four dimensions of care we refer to: Caring About, Taking Care Of, Care-Giving, and Care-Receiving, later including Caring With (Tronto 2013). However, Orupabo (2022) draws attention to a 'problem with viewing care work as requiring a specific disposition and being inherently different from other systems of social relations' –

> it detaches care work from its physical aspects and being recognised as manual labour and body work similar to many male working-class jobs. The work is heavy, dirty, repetitive, low paid and framed by difficult conditions created by others in the occupational hierarchy.
>
> (Orupabo 2022, p. 60)

This association of care work with a specific disposition seen by many as innate to women serves to establish it as feminine work. This in turn undermines the ways that this work is otherwise like men's work (manual labour, heavy, dirty, etc.), and worthy of levels of compensation typically granted only to those jobs gendered as men's jobs and filled predominantly by men.

Another key aspect of the work of nurses derives from their special position in a strongly hierarchical system that is characterized by an increasing diversification of patient trajectories, medical specialization, and the fragmentation of services. It is

> their all-round availability – their willingness to 'fill in' combined with their capacity for professional judgement, when needed. Nurses mostly view themselves as working partly in routinized schemes, partly under doctors' instantaneous orders, and partly 'à la demande du patient'. There are two sides to this ad hoc availability. On one hand it reflects power relations and the hospital's politics of invisible work; on the other hand, some of the distinct quality of care-giving as being 'much concerned with rectifying the more depersonalized aspects of hospital care' (Strauss et al., 1985, p. 99) rests upon nurses' availability for comfort and sentimental work.
>
> (Wagner 1995, p. 309)

As a major part of their work is about responding to the needs of others – both those of patients and other care providers (particularly physicians) – nurses are only able to plan part of their time. Based on a temporal analysis of the work of nurses in three hospital wards, Theureau et al. (1979) point to the skills nurses display in juggling the exigencies and expectations of patients, doctors, and others:

> The work of nurses has its own characteristics: it has a conscious design aspect (activities are constantly adapted to new situations), it is sequential, preprogrammed and interrupted, it is team work, and all these characteristics confer an important methodological value to the nurse's introspection.
>
> (Theureau et al. 1979, p. 34)

The integration of ICT in the practice of nursing in hospitals started in the 1990s, when the first nursing documentation systems were developed as a way to influence nursing practice. They were defined as a record of nursing care that was based on planning and provided to individual patients by qualified nurses. While not bringing about radical changes of nursing as a profession, they introduced new elements in the daily work of nurses that continue to pose challenges that are not easy to manage. In a recent study of health information systems (HIS) in Swedish hospitals, Salminen-Karlsson and Golay (2022) observe that

> All nurses interact with their patients' electronic health records, both documenting and looking for information. In addition to the electronic health records, there are systems for recording patient and process data (e.g., during surgery) and systems for planning (such as allocating staff), record keeping (such as showing what material/medications can be found, where) and information retrieval (such as providing guidelines for different situations). . . . The implementation of HIS has met with problems, however: the healthcare staff who are the intended users do not always welcome them; the expected benefits may fail to appear; and, sometimes, productivity, communication between staff, and patient safety may actually be reduced . . . . Furthermore, HIS often appear to be poorly adapted to everyday clinical practices.
>
> (Salminen-Karsson and Golay 2022, p. 2)

While HIS form the core of ICT-based systems in hospitals, other digital tools such as decision-support systems, simulation tools for learning, automated drug dispensers, as well as care robots have entered hospitals and training institutions.

Accompanying these developments is a rich academic, professional, and political discussion of several key issues:

- The nature of care work – and the limits of automation.
- Standardization and modelling – how they influence what counts as relevant care measures.
- Data work – whose work it is and how to balance caregiving with the demands of articulation work in a complex organization.
- Responsibility and control – how they are distributed and practiced in human–machine interactions.

Each of these issues has implications for the design of ICT-based systems and tools in support of nursing.

Nursing Information Systems

A Historical Account

When nursing became a research topic of interest for feminist researchers in the late 1980s and early 1990s, not least in relation to the introduction of IT-based nursing documentation systems (e.g., Bjerknes and Bratteteig 1986, 1988), researchers were committed to making the skills that nurses deploy in their work visible. In a paper on the 'comparable worth' movement in the USA, Roslyn Feldberg (1992) made a strong argument about the invisibility of nurses' work, emphasizing that they 'are treated as if their work was only to "carry out orders" undervaluing their professional skills' (p. 182). Moreover, as Wagner (1993) in her study of early nursing information systems in France and the USA observed,

> Nursing takes place in organisations which are shaped by the diversity of their occupational 'milieux', strong hierarchies of knowledge and power and intense collaborative relationships. The problems of positioning themselves within such a complex professional field nurses encounter are made more difficult by the fact that they are interwoven with gender inequalities.
>
> (Wagner 1993, p. 297)

The nursing information systems that were installed in hospitals from the early 1990s onwards in most cases, notably in the USA, were introduced in a top-down process, while for example in France, pressure by management was in part counterbalanced by the organized interests of professional nurses.

Looking back at these early nursing information systems and the debates surrounding them, two different and partially overlapping approaches can be distinguished. On the one hand, professional nursing associations saw computers as helping to make nursing more 'scientific' against the view of caregiving as a residual activity; on the other hand, the management of hospitals drove computerization with the aim of improving planning and increasing control over the work of nurses, with the intention to ultimately cut the costs of caregiving, a major expense in health care. Both approaches resulted in changing the position of nurses in a complex field of professional relationships (Feldberg 1992; Acker 1997).

Françoise Acker, who for several decades studied nursing in French hospitals and its development as a profession under the influence of health policy and the introduction of IT-based nursing documentation systems, points to the role nursing documentation systems played in the 'gender project' of professionalizing nursing (1997). Indeed, nursing associations that were involved in the introduction of nursing documentation systems hoped that computerisation might help nurses to make the high level of their skill and the complexity of nursing activities more visible, and thereby attain a level of systematisation of nursing knowledge that makes it 'scientific' (based on theoretical models, empirically tested knowledge, scientific reasoning).

(Wagner 1993, p. 298)

The computerized nursing protocols in use in the cardiology department of a French hospital in the early 1990s, for example, built on an analysis of hundreds of patient folders, a task that was carried out by the unit's nurses. They used a list of ten nursing objectives that included the patient's autonomy with respect to eating, sleeping, moving around, and other specific goals that mark the healing process. These objectives were translated into detailed lists of indicators, contraindicators, and required nursing activities. One example refers to the changing of bandages:

> This introduces a certain degree of rigor. The bandage, this needs to be done at a specific stage, when it is done earlier, the computer asks why, why are you changing the bandages? There (pointing to an example on the screen) it has been changed because it does no longer fit closely or even leaked, because the patient's temperature rose, or an anomalous tension or pain, then she has the possibility to enter why ... And as a consequence, everybody does the same things, in a well-defined way.
>
> (Surveillante, Service de Chirurgie Cardiaque, quoted in Wagner 1993, p. 301)

The French nurses had a clear aim in mind: to make their skills and the complexity of their work visible and to be able to bargain for lower workloads and better pay – in fact the opposite of what new management principles in hospitals intended to achieve.

This 'gender project' of professionalizing nursing was a difficult process, Acker argues in her analysis of 'La coordination infirmière', a spontaneous movement organized by nurses in 1988:

> One of the issues of the movement of 1988 was the difficult construction of a relationship to the notion of skill, the transition from the merits of the person towards professionalism, towards the expertise needed for a function ... articulating the professional nature of the work. How to manage, as professionals and no longer as women, the emotions, the sentiments of the ill and one's own, which develop with the experience of an illness and medical care? How to break through a reactivity which is individual, personal and profane or through what P. Corcuff (1996) terms compassion and rely on defined entities, on knowledge, on theories that help work through the experiences and behaviours.
>
> (Acker 2000, p. 67)

At the heart of these efforts was the classification of nursing diagnoses and care interventions in the form of protocols. In their study of a Nursing Intervention

Classification System (NIC) that had been developed bottom-up by a grassroot network of nursing researchers in Iowa (USA), Bowker and Star (1999) showed that there are aspects of nursing that are difficult to capture in a classification scheme. They discuss examples of nursing interventions such as 'anticipatory guidance' and 'mood management', asking,

> How can one capture humor as a deliberate nursing intervention? Does sarcasm, irony, or laughter count as a nursing intervention? To be measured? When do you stop? How to reimburse humor, how to measure this kind of care? No one would dispute its importance, but it is by its nature a situated and subjective action. A gray area of common sense remains for the individual staff nurse to define whether some of the nursing interventions are worth classifying.
>
> (Bowker and Star 1999, p. 30)

The higher visibility of activities that are taken for granted and are often considered 'residual' is one side of the NIC. The other side is that precisely these invisible aspects of care work tend to escape categorization: 'There are continuing tensions within NIC between just this kind of common sense and abstracting away from the local in order to standardize and compare, while at the same time rendering "invisible work" visible' (Bowker and Star 1999, p. 30).

ICT and the associated standards and categories define what counts as work that is socially valued. By participating in the building of classification systems and the development of standardized nursing protocols, nurses and their associations worked on arriving at adequate representations of their work. They sought to gain control over problem specifications and work performance standards, hoping that in doing so they would make themselves more independent of doctors' orders. This, however, was not an easy task. 'One reason is 'the lack of a "culture d'analyse", as one nurse put it. An expert nurse will operate from a deep understanding of a situation without necessarily being able to spell out the rules which she had interiorized' (Wagner 1993, p. 301). Only 'when alternative perspectives are not available to the clinician, the only way out of a wrong grasp of the problem is by using analytical tools' (Benner 1984, 34). That researchers were able to 'see' the parts of work that remained invisible to health administrators and often also medical doctors, that were not only missing in official job descriptions but also invisible to nurses themselves, as they were taken for granted is a result of the methods they used: observation-based work, in particular ethnomethodologically informed observation that is part of the CSCW tradition of studying the work practices of nurses.

The other side of standardized reporting in the form of nursing documentation systems was that they introduced a managerial perspective into the work of nurses, making their work accountable in terms of 'measurable' care activities, impelling them to develop cost and time consciousness. Based on case studies in Canadian hospitals, Marie Campbell (1990) argued that building a knowledge of nursing in which time (as an indicator of costs) is the unit of measurement affects nurses' work practices:

> Nurses who have used such structured information about their work have gradually adjusted their thinking to match it. ... It seems apparent that with cost-accounting embedded in care planning, hospitals expect to bring the standpoint of cost-efficiency to the very heart of the organisation, to grasp and organise nurses' clinical decisions.
>
> (Campbell 1990, p. 9)

Drawing a parallel between nursing information systems and the introduction of DRGs (Diagnostic Related Groups) in the USA, Feldberg (1990) saw nursing practice as becoming increasingly shaped by the necessity to comply with regulators' and employers' definitions of 'billable categories', asking,

> Will 'costing out nurses' services mean that nurses are subtly pressured in similar ways? What categories of activity will be 'billable' and who will decide? If back rubs and talking to patients are billed at a lower rate than giving injections and starting IV's, will nurses be 'free' to decide how to care for their patients?
>
> (Feldberg 1990, p. 43)

Hence, by ensuring the integration of management criteria and organizational priorities into the work of nurses, nursing documentation systems stand for a gradual transformation of activities that used to be predominantly embodied, highly interactive, and strongly experience-based. Notwithstanding this transformation process that also aimed at making the skills of nurses and the many facets of their professional activities visible, the reality nurses face in many countries is still one of (increasingly) high workloads, low pay, and poor social status.

How to Address Issues of Standardization in Care

Historically, the early nursing information systems can be seen as a first step in providing nurses with a 'new language' for discussing their patients and ordering their work.

> This includes: making judgements about the relevance of information and writing it up; making a diagnosis; working with objectives and 'projects' in mind; managing multiple and distant sources of information; setting time apart; developing cost and time consciousness; making their own role explicit and visible.
>
> (Wagner 1993, p. 306)

For systems designers the question is how to balance the values (and practices) of caring – attentiveness, responsibility, nurturance, compassion, meeting others' needs (Tronto 1993) – with data work and the demands of articulation work in a complex organization. This is a challenging task, as standardization projects in the form of care plans and nursing protocols are not 'per se' detrimental to the quality of care. However, standardization may contribute to the documentation burden and leave less time for caring work.

Empirical evidence suggests that nurses (and also many doctors) continue to experience tensions between the exigencies of working with ICT systems and what they perceive as the core of their work. For example, analyzing nurses' experiences with HIS in a large university hospital in Sweden, Salminen-Karlsson and Golay (2022) identify a strong resistance against having to integrate the system into their work:

> The main clashes between electronic patient recording and the daily work and responsibilities of nurses were that the information retained, although extensive, was not adapted to nurses' needs; that the documentation work required a different time regime than the nurses had; and that patient safety, a core value in nursing care, could be set aside for the sake of electronic documentation.
>
> (Karlsson and Golay 2022, p. 7)

Also Kirchhoff et al. (2021) report from a study in a high-tech Norwegian hospital that doctors and nurses see ICT systems as impairing contact with patients and the quality of care. While simplifying some tasks and routines, 'standardization is found to increase the number of routinized work tasks, organizational control of health care professionals and threaten the logic of care' (p. 2946). An analysis by Wisner et al. (2019) of studies from the USA (13), Scandinavia (2), Australia (1), Austria (1), and Canada (1), found that 'the EHR provided insufficient support for activities like collaborative decision-making, conveying updates aimed at establishing a shared under-standing of the clinical situation, or contextualizing certain clinical findings relative to a patient's case' (p. 81).

One of the problems that seems to persist relates to difficulties to account for key aspects of professional care in nursing information systems, for a variety of reasons. A study of an electronic triage system at the emergency department of a Canadian hospital by Bjørn and Balka (2007) found that the system favored a narrow biomedical view of patients making it rather difficult for nurses to follow their professional intuition:

> Standardization makes it theoretically possible to monitor deviations from anticipated workflows, but in a manner that fails to take the continuous exception-handling of work into account. Standardized categories do not have the power to

capture the invisible, but often critically important, aspects of work. Standardization of nurses' work reflects a shift back to a narrow biomedical view of patients and neglects the holistic perspective of nursing, thereby reducing the professional discretion nurses have worked so hard to gain.

(Bjørn and Balka 2007, p. 375)

These observations are in line with Smith (2013) finding that electronic triage tools support mainly one of several modes of thinking: system-aided judgment, which builds on triage guidelines using algorithms and severity indices. She emphasizes the importance of experience and intuition in triage decision-making, as well as patient- and peer-aided judgment. The reliance on intuition or 'instinct' has also been underlined by nurses of a cardiac medical unit in the UK (Rycroft-Malone et al. 2008). An interesting observation in this particular case is:

While several standardised care approaches were available for use, in reality, a variety of information sources informed decision-making. The primary approach to knowledge exchange and acquisition was person-to-person; decision-making was a social activity. Rarely were standardised care approaches obviously referred to; nurses described following a mental flowchart, not necessarily linked to a particular guideline or protocol. When standardised care approaches were used, it was reported that they were used flexibly and particularized.

(Rycroft-Malone et al. 2008, p. 1490)

In this hospital individual nurses had some discretion over how they made use of nursing protocols; they were given the space to find the right balance between standardized practices and their own clinical judgment.

Standardized triage tools are also used in health call centres, as in an example from Perth, Australia (Larsen 2005), where 'nurses' advice is "computer-derived" from 149 guidelines or algorithms adapted from American prototypes by the medical directors who oversee the clinical content' (p. 137). During a call nurses must allot the patient to a distinctive category. Only in exceptional cases are they allowed to deviate from the prescribed path, which has to be justified in writing. 'Responses to standards will always be ambivalent and compliance piecemeal', Larsen concludes, adding,

Whatever the standards, most nurses experience a mixture of relief that they can trust the guidelines, and annoyance that the guidelines do not allow for diversity, that the process is slow, cumbersome and tedious when the most appropriate disposition is obvious to an experienced nurse early in the call.

(Larsen 2005, p. 142)

Nurses working in a health call centre in British Columbia, Canada struggled with two areas of standardization. The system they worked with had been imported from the USA and had been poorly localized, which often resulted in difficulty related to terminological differences between the USA and Canada. They also found the scope of their work more limited than it would be in face-to-face clinical settings. Many argued that this resulted in patients being unnecessarily sent to emergency rooms (Balka and Butt, 2008).

Studying the importance of informal information in a clinical setting, Zhou et al. (2009) describe the use of CPOE (Computerized Provider Order Entry) as detrimental to nurses' understanding of 'how a patient was doing during last several shifts' (p. 2067). They see this as a consequence of the system leading to a reduction of informal working documents that are 'rich with psycho-social context' (p. 2067). While before, the patient record in its physical form (the Kardex) and the 'Shift Sheet' were 'on the table' and could be easily linked, this link was broken with the electronic version. Moreover, they found 'that computerization of the nursing data led to a shift in the politics of the information itself – the nurses no longer had a cohesive agreement about the kinds of data to enter into the system' (p. 2061).

These findings not only suggest that standard forms of providing care and documenting have to be developed 'with care'. They also point to the need of nurses for multiple sources of information, as well as the inclusion of not easily standardizable forms of knowing. When information that is vital for the process of care does not fit the electronic record, the work that goes into it is made invisible, with the consequence that other health professionals that take care of a patient do not have access to it. This echoes Geraldine Fitzpatrick's (2004) notion of the 'working record' as a document that is not just a repository of information but actually a key element of the workplace of nurses (and physicians). It consists of various formal and informal documents – the EPR (electronic patient record) together with observation sheets, changeover notes and the like – that 'are brought into play together and become actively embedded in the very doing of patient care' (p. 296). She also observed how nurses (and others) appropriated forms differently depending on personal preferences, overlaying them with Post-its and personal annotations or adding functionality.

An additional functionality to consider in designing ICT systems in support of care work is redundancy, Cabitza et al. (2019) argue, in particular with respect to the coordination of activities. They see redundancy as a positive feature of information systems that could also be built into their electronic version. They make a case for considering

> how the knowledge that is distributed among individuals and embedded in their work practices could be integrated and shared with others, not by dividing the

situation into elemental parts but by focusing on the entire situation and providing intensive feedback about the accuracy of clinical judgements.

(Cabitza et al. 2019, pp. 68–69)

The second main concern with regard to nursing information systems – they integrate a managerial logic into care work – continues to be voiced throughout the research literature. McIntyre (2020) summarizes this concern, arguing that nurses'

'customer' ... is not only the patient, but the organization and even the greater regime of data collection and surveillance. In addition to documenting their own activities in an increasing level of granular, real-time detail, nurses are frequently serving as the eyes and ears of the institution's general regime of surveillance and control.

(McIntyre 2020, p. 3)

At the core of ICT-based systems, McIntyre observes, is the aim to manage individual variation in nurses' and doctors' practices in the name of 'patient-centered care' and 'evidence-based practice' with a view towards the hospital's financial interests, all of which Balka (2010) observed in relation to the assignment and subsequent use of triage data. She documented how the assignment of a triage acuity score to patients contributed to numerous resource allocation and other managerial decisions. Pine and Mazmanian (2014) stress the institutional logics of the EMR. Based on fieldwork in an obstetrical unit, they found 'that the institutional logics of "safety" embedded in the EMR create negative organizational outcomes, effectively undermining coordination and necessitating inaccurate accounts of work' (p. 283). The main reason for that was that the EMR was programmed with permission structures that 'placed large barriers in the way of nurses attempting to manage orders' (p. 286). At the roots of such a system, they argue, is a notion of 'safety' that is primarily technical rather than 'social, situated, and agentic'. It relies on a layered system of permissions and protocols to follow instead of 'collective responsibility and adaptation' (p. 291).

Systems such as the one described by Pine and Mazmanian (2014) are an example of technical rationality (Schön 1983) that restricts 'one to the use of a single type of knowledge, preferably scientific, to solve problems, instead of using that knowledge as one component in a reflective practice', Salminen-Karlsson and Golay (2022, p. 4) argue. They refer to the work of Wise et al. (2017) on nursing protocols that are based on algorithmic rules, allowing nurses to undertake medical tasks previously considered too complex. However, these protocols 'restrict nurses' autonomy to patients with lower acuity, non-complex conditions and limits their discretion over the choice of medications or investigations (p. 507). Technical rationality is in conflict with the ethics of care, Salminen-Karlsson and Golay resume. It requires 'thoughtlessness' in the sense that it leaves little space to individual reflection and decision-making (Goodman 2016).

Given the complexity of health-care systems, with their multiplicity of worksites 'that differ in terms of the involved professions, medical devices, and technologies, as well as patients' illnesses and the care activities performed' (Simone et al. 2022, p. 97) it is hard to argue against standardization, as there is the need to facilitate collaboration and coordination across professional and organizational boundaries. Also, there are (even though relatively few) positive examples of ICT-based systems that effectively support local practices. Pedersen et al. (2011) have studied nursing-care plans that include a Nursing Intervention Classification (NIC) as well as a decision-support system for nursing that is used by nurses for silent (instead of oral) handover. They come to the conclusion that,

> With the introduction of electronic nursing documentation, the information work has shifted from a chronological status note to process-oriented, structured documentation where the EPR care plan, especially the standardized plan, is positioned at center stage.
>
> (Pedersen et al. 2011, p. 174)

Bossen and Markussen (2010) describe standardized electronic medication plans (EMM2) in a hospital that, in contrast to the paper-based plans, 'support the ordering of information according to the task for which the table is being used' (p. 631). They also stress the usefulness of so-called ATC codes (a drug classification system), as

> there is a fortunate resonance between two different artefacts with which nurses have to work: the order of drugs on shelves, and the order in which information on drugs is displayed in EMM2. This kind of transartefactual ordering, which we may call 'composite ordering', is rarely supported.
>
> (Bossen and Markussen 2010, p. 631)

This finding contrasts with a study of the introduction of ADS (automatic drug dispensing machines) in a Canadian hospital (Balka et al. 2007) as an access point to prescribed drugs for nurses. Here standardization in the form of generic drug names (among other characteristics of the system) made access cumbersome for nurses:

> The generic nomenclature is not in common use among floor staff who must now translate doctor's orders (which are often written in trade names) into generic names. Staff may spend more time looking up drug names than they did in the past. Standardizing the location of drugs within the ADS was intended to make it easier

for staff who move between floors to use the ADS. However, staff on some floors were frustrated by having to retrieve commonly used drugs from the bottom drawer. In both cases it is not clear if the benefits gained from standardization outweighed the costs.

(Balka et al. 2007, p. 240)

This is a good starting point to think about the design of ICT systems in support of care work. We see several points of discussion. First, while standardization is an essential part of nursing documentation systems, nursing protocols, and care plans, the question is how to make space for, in Smith's (2013) words, judgment based on experience and intuition, as well as patient- and peer-aided judgment (in addition to system-aided judgment). This also requires thinking about the consequences of emphasizing too strongly the unique, local, and contextual solutions or a too uniform solution – how is the boundary between the global and the local drawn and maintained.

Our second point concerns the managerial logic that is built into many ICT systems and often seems to be the dominant one. It in many ways contradicts the very concept of care based on values of caring. Activities that are guided by these values are focussed on the patient and they require time. The account that Martin and Bouchard (2020) provide from a study of Canadian nurses suggests that new management methods in hospitals make this difficult to achieve: 'Most of the participating nurses said that they are being contaminated by a managerial culture and getting bogged down in a clutter of documents and hospital procedures that are imposed on them' (p. 317). In deeply collaborative work arrangements, documentation work is important but it costs time. It requires asking 'whose work?' and how to best support the work making it less cumbersome and time-consuming. Another question is how to support nurses in dealing with the contradictions between what the managerial logic requires them to do and what they think is their responsibility as the patients' caregivers.

Robotics and the Care Profession

Connected with the design of ICT-based systems is the question of automation: Which aspects of human activities can and should be automated for which purpose? There are many different types of robots in development to support the work of health-care professionals: surgery and diagnostic robots that manipulate instruments inside the human body; rehabilitation robots that directly move users' impaired limbs; telemedicine robots that a remotely located physicians can move to the patient bedside and communicate via video; courier robots that can grasp and transport objects; personal care robots that assist with eating, drinking, bathing, toileting, lifting; and so-called companion robots that support activities such as learning, cognitive training, reading, writing, as well as keeping company and entertaining (including robotic pets for those suffering from dementia). However, many of these robots are not yet at a stage where they could be used reliably in practice:

> Currently, there are no care robots capable of fulfilling functional care tasks with direct contact to a human body (in contrast to transport tasks, entertainment purposes, or pet-like behaviors). Nevertheless, it is important to determine the requirements for integrating any future robotic technologies into care practices.
>
> (Hornecker et al. 2020, p. 2)

One of the best-researched topics to date is nursing robots in the care of old people, which may assist them and their caregivers, monitor and survey them and/or their health parameters, or act as 'companions'. We look at the research literature from a more general point of view of care work.

Human–Machine Interactions and the Nature of Care

The discourse on robotics, big data, and ML is taking up the 'old' issue of what is needed to 'rectify the more depersonalized aspects of hospital care' (Strauss et al. 1985). It at the same time radicalizes the question of what is genuinely human, and which parts of human action could/should be delegated to machines, often exaggerating the potential of AI while severely underestimating the complexity of work.

There is the normative dimension of care: dealing carefully ('in a caring way') with those receiving care, not exposing them in their vulnerability, respecting their feelings. At the same time caregiving requires a high degree of professionalism, which manifests itself in precision in the execution of procedures, in meticulous adherence to safety standards, and so on, as well as the ability to act – communicate, coordinate – in a complex organizational context (Strauss et al. 1982).

It is useful to look at a variety of scenarios of robots supporting the work of caregiving. A study of how robots are embedded in a functional care task that is an everyday heavy workload for nursing staff – the transfer of patients from bed to (wheel)chair – Hornecker et al. (2020) – describes the ways in which 'functional and emotional as well as social aspects of care are ... closely intertwined' (p. 1). They argue for a processual and collaborative understanding of a seemingly simple 'mechanical' task:

> Instead of conceptualizing robots as task-executioners and humans as sentient interpreters, actual HRI is enacted in an interplay between such entities. We have

shown how the use of these machines requires activity from both sides as well as collaboration between caregivers and people to be lifted. None of the lifting devices can function without such collaboration – and be it for the resident to remain motionless while hanging in the net. Our analysis has shown that the communicative and emotional practices performed by caregivers are just as crucial in enabling lifting functionality as the manual tasks.

(Hornecker et al. 2020, p. 8)

A similar argument has been put forward by Beane and Orlikowski (2015) who studied the night rounds in a post-surgical intensive care unit with and without a telepresence robot. They point to the need to carefully study how the coordination of complex, dynamic, and distributed work is materially enacted 'through the multiple participants, objects, devices, monitors, spaces, documents, and bodies that accomplished the work of intensive care in the SICU' (p. 1571). They also emphasize the importance of nurses' direct observation of a patient's condition, quoting a physician:

They know what to do. They know how to take care of these patients. They may not know why but they know. They have good judgment. They know when patients are sick and when they're not sick, and that's the important thing that I need to know because in the middle of the night, I don't need to know specifics, I need to know when somebody is getting better or they're getting worse. If they're getting worse then I have to come in.

(Beane and Orlikowski 2015, p. 1558)

These examples strengthen an approach taken by CSCW research: to study robotics in nursing as a phenomenon requires direct observation; as well as an understanding of technologies not as an independently working machine but one that is embedded in collaboratives requiring interaction work. These examples also point to the importance of emotional work, observing directly, having eye contact, and touching the patient so that functional (and other) tasks can be accomplished 'with care' and keep the patient safe. This has, for example, been observed by Van Wynsberghe (2013) in a study of a robot that plays an assistive role in lifting patients with the support of a HAL (Hybrid Assistive Limb). The study demonstrates the importance of touching and eye contact in caregiving:

Touch is an important action in care that is valued on its own as well as a means for manifesting other values like respect, trust and intimacy. Touch is the symbol of vulnerability, which invokes bonds and subjectivity . . .. Touch acts to mitigate the temptation for objectification. . . . Using the value of touch as an example, we can see how a certain technology might impede its manifestation.

(Van Wynsberghe 2013, p. 414)

Another scenario of robot-assisted care is feeding people who, due to specific disabilities, for example, a stroke or dementia, are not able to eat by themselves or, as is often the case with very old people, simply forget to eat and drink. Robot Brian keeps old people in a care home company stimulating them to eat and drink. Brian uses 'natural' forms of communication: language, gesture, facial expression. He welcomes the person with her/his name, invites her/him to the table, makes simple jokes, and positive and encouraging comments. He is always in a good mood, entertaining and patient. There are few (if any) studies of mealtime in care homes. In an observational study of 22 patients aged 60–94, Davies and Snaith (1980) identified a series of problems that they saw as a consequence of high workloads and lack of time; among them: wheelchairs were placed in a row so that patients did not see each other; food and cutlery was often not within easy reach; food was often no longer warm when it arrived, portions too big; and food was readily taken away without motivating patients to eat and drink. Compared to this situation having Brian certainly represents some 'progress'.

In a much newer study of feeding assistant robotics (FAR), Nickelsen (2019) offers some interesting observations. He articulates the differences between 'feeding as task' and 'feeding as relationship', noting,

> During the last decades, feeding is eliminated from nurses' responsibilities and relegated to non-professional staff because they see it 'an efficiency task' and not a valued opportunity of 'the art of nursing'. It has, in other words, become low status and thus, it is now robotized.
>
> (Nicelsen 2019, p. 75)

He describes two cases, one of a young woman suffering from cerebral paralysis who manages to eat independently with the help of FAR. The other woman who cannot use her arms and also cannot speak for herself likes eating with the help of the FAR but is less successful in the eyes of the human assistant at her side, as much of the food lands on her face or is spilled on the table and floor – according to the assistant '"dirt" during the meal is disrespectful' (p. 82). This woman started losing weight and had to leave the program. One of Nickelsen's conclusions from his observations is that

> The FAR presupposes a specific human. Engineers have envisioned humans, who have low or no functions in their arms and hands, but not humans who suddenly turn their heads when something catches their attention, neither have they envisioned humans who do not understand when to press the button and when to open the mouth.
>
> (Nickelsen 2019, p. 94)

A third scenario concerns robots that can grasp and transport objects in a hospital – seemingly simple tasks. One of the core insights from studies of their use in a hospital setting is that their introduction often requires a reorganization of work – the spatial organization of a ward, the sequencing and timing of activities, and so forth. The weaknesses of technology design that disregards these issues are illustrated by the example of a transport robot in a US hospital (Mutlu and Forlizzi 2008). The robot was perceived as a nuisance wherever patients required a lot of attention – for example when the robot brought food or fresh laundry while nursing staff did not want to or could not interrupt their work. In cases where a sample had to be taken to the laboratory quickly, the robot was often not readily available. There were frequent collisions between the robot and hurrying doctors or nurses, or a wheelchair left standing in a corridor. The study also found that the expected savings did not materialize; on the contrary as the quote from an interview with the director of a medical unit shows,

> The package was sold as that it was going to save time and effort. And it has on someone else's end but not from this unit, did not, so yes . . . Did it save hiring a dietary person to pick up carts? Did it save the linen person to come pick up linen? Yes, it did . . . Where did that land? It landed with my people. And so while it's a nice thing, nobody gave me more because a person wasn't doing that anymore . . . Well, it didn't save any for me. It cost me, and I didn't get that to replace it. So, yes, I don't like it for that reason. It's not that I dislike the technology.
>
> (Mutlu and Forlizzi 2008, p. 6)

The example demonstrates the degree of detail to which workflows and spatial constellations must be observed and how important it is to coordinate automated activities with those of the hospital personnel. These varied considerably in the different departments examined.

A similar observation has been made by Tietze and McBride (2020) who studied the impact of Moxi, a service robot with a functional arm, on nursing practice. They draw attention to the importance of workplace redesign, adding that,

> in order to redesign workflows . . . and provide clean linens and essential supplies, tasks had to be explicitly mapped out on the unit in order for Moxi to be programmed to support nursing services in the delivery of clean linens. In addition, it was critical to fully standardize how things were done related to linen and supply delivery.
>
> (Tietze and McBride 2020, p. 19)

Robots need a structured environment to function well, allowing their programmers to anticipate possible situations. For example, the typical living environments of many elderly people – small, cluttered rooms – are often unsuitable for robots, Sparrow (2015) argues. They also need patients to behave in fairly standardized ways in order to function properly, as Nickelsen's example of FARs demonstrates.

The studies of human–robot interaction also point to the often underestimated work to be done by humans to make robots work properly. In a study of mobile service robots in support of a hospital's kitchen staff, Tornberg et al. (2021) identified numerous 'visible and invisible procedures underpinning human–robot cooperation' (p. 381), among them 'minding' the robots as a new type of task. While 'consistently having water available at the bedside and consistently having critical supplies such as IV flushes in the patient rooms' (Tietze and McBride 2020, p. 24), is in fact a positive aspect of having robots take care of these tasks, attention needs to be paid to all the (additional) work that makes robots work in a work environment.

How to Approach Robotics in the Caregiving Professions from an Ethical-Political Perspective

Feminist scholars have a long-standing interest in humanoid or anthropomorphic robots. Suchman (2011) in her analysis of 'three stagings of human–robot encounters (with the robots Mertz, Kismet and Robota respectively)' asks,

> If objects, as Haraway reminds us, are 'boundary projects' (1991: 201), the figure of the humanoid robot sits provocatively on the boundary of subjects and objects, threatening its breakdown at the same time that it reiterates its founding identities and differences.
>
> (Suchman 2011, p. 133)

Her reflections on these stagings focus on human–machine intra-actions with two points in mind: how 'humans and nonhumans together can perform different intelligibilities'; and 'while affect is clearly present in these "e/motional" assemblages ..., the relation of humans to machines is explicitly that of evocation and response between different, non-mirroring, dynamically interconnected forms of being' (p. 137).

With respect to robotics in care settings, there is an enormous amount of literature on robotics and the ethical issues at stake. These debates are deeply influenced by a feminist notion of care. At their core is the question of whether or not activities performed by a robot can and should be considered 'genuine' caretaking. In a paper 'In the hands of machines?', Sparrow and Sparrow (2006) emphasize 'the importance of the social and emotional needs of older persons – which, we argue, robots are incapable of meeting – in almost any task involved in their care' (p. 141). Care, they emphasize, presumes recognizing the individuality of those we care for, acknowledging their frailties (as something we potentially share), treating them with respect, and seeking to understand their needs. They conclude, 'Robots would therefore have to have a similar set of capacities and frailties as human beings in order to be capable of genuine emotional responses' (p. 154).

Wynsberghe (2021) adds thoughts about reciprocity to this debate, starting out from Joan Tronto's (1993) concept of care as being strongly interrelated with social justice, which emphasizes the need to 'reciprocate to human care workers across society' (p. 6). Reciprocity, Wynsberghe argues, is 'instrumental to good care and an "indispensable duty" for the just society' (p. 1): 'reciprocity is about recognizing the care work being done across society and to insist on "broad social responsibility" to return care to those who have provided it' (p. 4). Clearly, reciprocity towards a robot that may need changing the battery or repair is not the same as reciprocity towards a human. Wynsberghe's asks how to embed values in robot design, concluding that 'robot designers, when designing for reciprocity, ought to conceptualize it as a value to be established between humans rather than as a value to be established between the human and the robot' (p. 6).

This debate ties in with how affect is framed in feminist studies of service work. Dobrosovestnova et al. (2021) discuss the example of service robots and affective labour within a feminist tradition, asking

> how professional service robots may contribute and disrupt individual emotional labor, and the collective socio-affective structures in service sector workplaces. In this regard, we highlight three points: (1) the relationship between the narrow repertoire of social and affective behavior of service robots and the potential burden on emotional labor of human employees that may arise from such limitations; (2) the contribution of service robots to established corporate 'feeling rules' and (gendered) stereotypes about service work'.
>
> (Dobrosovestnova et al. 2021, p. 6)

Their concern is that (women) service workers may feel constrained by reductionist models of 'proper' (and often sex-stereotyped) social and affective behaviour. Jutta Weber (2014) develops a critical view of how human emotions and social behaviour are translated into algorithms, implementing 'rules of feelings and of expression as well as (problematic) stereotypes of behavior – for example with regard to social hierarchies, ethnicity or gender ... into artefacts' (p. 190). Isbister (2004) questions reductionist models of human–machine interaction as potentially resulting in turning social relations into a commodity.

Another key ethical concern with robots in sensitive contexts such as care, is control. 'Who controls the robot?' Sharkey and Sharkey (2012) ask, in a discussion of a series of fictitious examples. A robot might register a potentially dangerous situation and alert the client that the cooker is still turned on;

prevent her/him from climbing on an unsteady chair to reach for an object; but also prevent a person with health issues from drinking another glass of wine. While the first two examples seem unproblematic, interfering with a person's preferences regarding alcoholic drinks appears much less acceptable. The critical question is if these robotic interventions are based on the person's consent, are controlled by her/him, and can be changed by her/him. In case a person's control is compromised (temporarily or as a result of a cognitive impairment), the question is, does a potential harm to a person's safety and health justify restrictions to her/his personal freedom? The problem is often presented as finding a balance between protecting a person from harm on the one hand, and (authoritarian) control and a paternalistic attitude on the other hand. Who decides if the balance has been kept? Would the problem be different if not a robot but an (authoritarian) nurse would exert control? Here, it could be argued that control exercised by a caregiver is at least directly understandable and open to question, while technically implemented control is not transparent and understandable: it happens behind the back of the person. The challenge for robot design is to enable care receivers themselves to control the robot, also making them easily configurable and adaptable to changing needs.

Jutta Weber (2005) sees the question of control as social robotics being purposely designed in ways to instill rule-oriented behaviour in their human counterparts:

> Obviously, recent research in the field of social robotics is not primarily about making machines social as most researchers suggest. Rather it seems to be about training humans in rule-oriented social behaviour between caregiver and infant, owner and pet, etc. Only relying on the latter can make the interaction with these machines intelligible.
>
> (Weber 2005, p. 214)

Hence, control is not just a question of a robot directly intervening in people's behaviour but, more generally, a matter of in which ways computational modelling of a robot's range of behaviours shapes and disciplines the range of potential human responses to it.

Which Aspects of Care Can/Should Be Automated?

Behind the rich debate about robotics and the nature of care are imminent practical questions for designers to address. The first question is *what* to automate. It is common practice in the development of machines to 'split up' complex activities and transform them into tasks that can be easily automated, leaving 'residual activities' to human beings (see the example of 'watching over' discussed by Bratteteig and Wagner (2013) in Chapter 7). Hornecker et al. (2020) as well as Van Wynsberghe (2013) insist on the need for designers to consider that the functional aspects of an activity such as lifting a patient from the bed onto a wheelchair are closely interwoven with its emotional and social aspects. Referring to value-sensitive design, Wynsberghe asserts that

> ... the practice of lifting requires much more than the action of lifting the care-receiver from one place to another. In order to call this a 'good care practice' according to the care orientation, many other values need to be expressed throughout the practice – values like attentiveness to the care-receiver responses or eye contact for establishing trust in the practice (and technology in this instance).
> (Van Wynsberghe 2013, p. 15)

As part of this, designers of robots are also called upon to counterbalance what Kitwood (2019) in his work on people with dementia called 'objectification' – treating a person as if they were a lump of dead matter: to be pushed, lifted, pumped or drained, without proper reference to the fact that they are sentient beings' (p. 52).

Santoni de Sio and Van Wynsberghe (2016) develop an elaborate argument about what kind of tasks to possibly delegate to a robot, based on what they call the 'nature-of activities' approach. Making the distinction between goal-directed and practice-oriented activities, they take up the argument that a fine-grained description is needed to be able to decide if a robot is a legitimate solution. They bring the example of urine sample collection from pediatric patients undergoing chemotherapy, which involves a potential health risk for the nurse. In this case, they argue, it seems 'permissible to remove the nurse from a portion of the activity of sample collection, namely the goal-directed and harmful to the nurse portion; provided that a connection between the nurse and the activity of sample collection is maintained' (p. 1756). The argument here is that delegating the activity of urine collection to a machine does not disrupt the care relationship, as both goals are achieved – 'the (external) goal of the safe and efficient collection of a sample to be tested and the (internal) goal of the realization of the values of attentiveness and responsibility on the part of the nurse' (p. 1758).

This approach echoes Coeckelbergh's (2010) distinction between deep and shallow care. It refers to the fact that many aspects of human care are routinized involving little if any emotional exchange (such as simply picking up a urine sample). In these situations, where 'there is little time for emotional, intimate, and personal engagement', there is the possibility 'that replacement with regard to one care task may actually make room for more and deeper human care with regard to other care activities' (p. 183). A limit to using robots in care settings for Coeckelbergh (2015) is when they undermine good care. These are situations where 'the machine is perceived as "taking over" the task of care and as taking on the role of the human care agent' (p. 273). These are also situations where a robot promotes illusions, creating discomfort with its deceptive qualities, its potential of displacing human intimacy, as Lynch et al. (2022) contend using the example of robots in therapy sessions with children with ADS (autism spectrum disorder).

Going back to the example of lifting a patient, Santoni de Sio and Van Wynsberghe (2016) also introduce the perspective of the patient as a relevant criterion, arguing that there may be people for whom

> the presence of other people is not a part of the activity of lifting. . . . [A]n elderly person who endorses this view of the nature of lifting may reasonably prefer to be enabled by a machine to safely, efficiently, autonomously lift as opposed to be caringly, compassionately, empathetically assisted by a human carer in lifting.
>
> (Santoni de Sio and Van Wynsberghe 2016, p. 1753)

The question what to automate also has a clear political dimension. Much has been written about considering robotics a 'solution' to the shortage of healthcare workers, in particular nurses and resources (instead of making nursing more attractive by improving working conditions and offering better salaries):

> The traditional Marxist notion of labor displacement is evident in research on care economies, interrogating the gendered and racialized commodification of care through strategies to manage care costs, maintained by precarious, mobile workforces.
>
> (Lynch et al. 2022, p. 685)

At the same time, it may indeed be desirable to many caregivers that unpleasant activities, for example those that are physically exacting, will be carried out or supported by robots in the future. But why would nursing staff want to hand over to a robot the very activities that are at the core of their work? This concern is also voiced by Welfare et al. (2019) with respect to manufacturing – 'it is possible that preferred work tasks will be replaced, human interaction will be reduced, and work paces will increase unsustainably' (p. 76).

How to Address Power Issues in Nursing

Care ethics and intersectionality are closely connected with issues of social justice, Olena Hankyvsky (2014) reminds us. She also draws attention to the fact that Patricia Hill Collins, who introduced the 'matrix of domination' to the debate on power, gender and race, and other potentially marginalizing characteristics, proposes to shift away from 'a simplified binary of power versus powerlessness':

> Oppression is filled with such contradictions because these approaches fail to recognize that a matrix of domination contains few pure victims or oppressors. Each individual derives varying amounts of penalty and privilege from the multiple systems of oppression which frame everyone's lives.
>
> (Collins 1990, p. 559)

Individuals occupy multiple partially overlapping locations and they can experience discrimination and advantages at the same time (Balka, 2009).

We have seen that ICT-based systems and machines (such as robots) may have varying consequences for the practice of nursing. While on the one hand they may help make the skills of professional nurses visible support them in managing routine tasks and potentially alleviate some of the heavy, dirty, and sometimes hazardous parts of their work, they also introduce new kinds of constraints and pressures. Orupabo (2022) maintains that 'care is especially vulnerable to exploitation and social injustice' and it is central to 'reproducing existing power relations':

> ... the least well-off in society, such as women, immigrants and racial minorities, disproportionately perform the work of caring. Cost-cutting pressure followed by the aim to deliver equivalent care with fewer resources, as well as the standardisation of care and introduction of systems of accountability to control expenditure and increase efficiency, are two major sources of rationalisation in current political economy.
>
> (Orupabo 2022, p. 59)

Hence, one of the key problems is the establishment of new public management in health-care institutions. It often results in computer-based technologies being primarily introduced for the purpose of exerting control over nursing practices and increasing efficiency, to the detriment of nurses gaining time for 'deeper human care'. Examples are the regimes of auditing and regulation that nurses are increasingly subjected to (McIntyre et al. 2020); the institutional logic around safety implemented in EMRs that 'place barriers in the way of nurses attempting to manage orders' (Pine and Mazmanian 2014, p. 283); or what Martin and Bouchard (in a 2020 study of Canadian nurses) refer to as 'a deprofessionalization of nursing and a drift toward authoritarianism' (p. 306).

Nurses traditionally are subject to a hierarchical power structure, with physicians often unwilling or unable to perform certain tasks, and asserting an expectation that nurses will follow their orders: 'the traditional hierarchical discourse still dominates the interprofessional dynamics within many rooms and situations at the hospital' (Lokatt et al. 2019, p. 7). ICT-based systems often contribute to cementing hierarchical power relations, Marc Berg (1999) has argued, using the example of standard reporting forms in a Dutch clinic, that technologies, such as an EMR, contain scripts that lay out the relevant actors and their respective roles. Systems design, one could argue, has the possibility of contributing to changing these scripts instead of hardwiring them.

This leads to the question of who designs the systems and models the robots. For social robotics, Coeckelbergh (2021) contends,

> The robotics lab is not excluded from this pervasiveness of power. Together with others who make decisions about robotics and employ or use robots in various contexts, those who develop and design robots have some power to shape the meaning of practices, the stories of people, and the goals we set ourselves as humans.
>
> (Coeckelbergh 2021, p. 11)

'Categories do have politics' (Suchman 1994), and they reflect the perspectives and values of the people who define them. Each standard or algorithm embodies an ethical choice, and it valorizes some point of view while excluding others. While systems design is becoming somewhat more open to women, other genders, and people of colour, AI and robotics are predominantly in the hands of white males. This is partly to do with the 'old' question of how to make space for women in science and technology. Examples are Borau et al. (2021) who describe how injecting women's humanity into AI objects may make these objects seem more human and acceptable; or Women in AI & Robotics (www.womeninairobotics.de). Partly the complexity of the technology makes it difficult to see how and where we can exert agency (a topic that has been explored in Chapter 6).

Summary

The focus on the computerization of nursing work allows us to clearly see how an association of caring with femininity (strengthened by gender structures in the health-care labour force, as well as gendered dynamics of health-care work) reinforces stereotypes about nursing work as feminine/women's work. Seen as women's work, the complexity of nursing work is underestimated, which in turn leaves it vulnerable to standardization efforts. Many attempts to standardize nursing work have fallen far short of expectations: the failure to recognize the complexity of the work has often resulted in the inclusion of inadequate classification systems and related categories in ICT-based systems, making them cumbersome and difficult to use. Efforts to standardize nursing work also result in the standardization of data. Although well intentioned, standardization of data may contribute to its use in managerial agendas (which often reduce the agency of nurses and undermine their ability to carry out caring work).

The devaluing of caring work (achieved partly through its symbolic gendering as feminine or women's work) in combination with an insufficient understanding of the complexity of care also contributes to the design of poorly conceptualized care robots. Bad design reflects gendered politics that fails to recognize the significance of women's contributions, particularly with respect to the varied dimensions of caring.

Reviewing the computerization of nursing work highlights the need to accommodate experience, intuition, and judgement while maintaining an awareness of too strongly emphasizing either contextual or universal aspects of work. It also raises fundamental questions about power, autonomy, and control in relation to robotics and the automation of care. Computerization of nursing work also foregrounds power issues and the need to address them through a focus on intersectionality, and attention towards Collins' (1990) matrix of domination.

9

The Gendering of Computer Work

The underrepresentation of girls in school and leisure-based computing activities and women in the computing professions – with some important exceptions when we think of the (for a long time) forgotten but outstanding contributions of women to computing – is a fact; and the reasons why women are not attracted to computing in great numbers 'are subtle and complex defying mono-causal explanations and solutions' (Adam 2001). Most of the newer research literature on women ICT professionals internationally ends in 'distressing scenarios' (Vitores and Gil-Juárez 2016). 'Why are there so few female computer scientists?' Much of the literature seeking an answer to this question is dedicated to the potential sources of this situation in the educational system (often referred to as the pipeline), as are the numerous programs to attract more girls and young women to computing, and work environments that in many places are hostile to women.

But it was not always so, as research on the history of women in computing has demonstrated. The names of the pioneering women in computing, foremost Ada Lovelace and Grace Hopper, are well known, as are the contributions of 'women computers' to the development of the ENIAC and Univac machines in the USA. Much less is known about the history of women IT specialists in other domains (such as gaming)[1] and in other parts of the world. An intriguing question is, what stopped women from entering careers in computing from the 1980s onwards, in particular in Western countries? The answers are multifarious. Trauth (2002) has looked at socio-cultural influences on the career choices of women, showing that 'women who work in the IT profession represent considerable variation. Women who are IT professionals do not all experience the same influences, nor do they all respond in the same

[1] Pioneering women in key working positions in gaming were long forgotten, as we have learned from Pernille Bjorn and her Atari Women Project.

ways' (p. 114). Women IT professionals enter a masculine field, Corneliussen (2021) (among many others) argues, where they have to 'find ways of empowering themselves' and establish 'their own sense of belonging' (p. 47).

Of special concern are the obstacles experienced by women of colour and by gender minorities in computing (e.g., De Oliveira Lobo et al. 2019; Rankin and Thomas 2020; Erete et al. 2020). With respect to poor countries in the Global South, ICTs are seen as an opportunity for development, poverty reductions, gender equality, and social justice. In many of these countries – India, Malaysia, the Philippines – the field of computing is not deemed 'masculine' and women, mostly from a middle- or upper-class background, are much more highly represented in IT professions.

In this chapter we are interested in the experiences of women IT professionals. It also focusses on women acting as designers of technologies in different socio-cultural contexts, arguing 'that we must pay analytical attention to women who enjoy and derive pleasure from computing and programming "in itself"' (Boivie 2010, p. 21).

We discuss women's careers in relation to three questions. First, we ask where women have been in computer science. We take a historical and transnational approach to this question, which illustrates the malleability of gendered divisions of labour over time and across national contexts. By looking at where women have been in ICT-related careers, we can also see where their contributions have been erased, only to be discovered years later. Next, we go beyond questions of why there are so few female computer scientists and critiques of the 'pipeline problem', to consider what kinds of questions arise and insights emerge from looking beyond the numbers. Here we outline the diversity of pathways women take to computing careers, and what kind of working conditions and career opportunities women can reasonably expect in computer science. The chapter ends with the question 'What is wrong with computing?', and points towards research about how to use feminist theory in designing ICT systems. This last question in a sense sets up the final three chapters of the book, which focus on gender and design – what we can do to positively influence the gendering of system design so that it reflects principles of the ethical-political perspective, design justice, and feminism.

A Historical Perspective

From Punch-Card Operators to Programmers

In a paper titled 'Making programming masculine', Ensmenger (2010) suggests that while computer programming was unusually 'open' to women during and after WWII, the professionalization[2] of computer work that started in the 1960s turned it into a stereotypically male field. In the early days, programming was not yet a science, 'but a black art, a private arcane matter ... each problem required a unique beginning at square one, and the success of a program depended primarily on the programmer's private techniques and invention' (p. 125). The development of professionalized structures – formal educational programs, standardized development methodologies, mathematical models to build software and hardware systems, professional bodies, journals, and conferences – changed that.

Computer work in the early days inherited the gender hierarchy of the punch-card system (invented by Herman Hollerith for the first automated US 1890 census), which was introduced in governments and businesses in the early 1920s and was widely used by the 1940s. For ordinary people who received their bills and social security checks in the form of punch-cards (together with the warning 'Do not fold, spindle or mutilate') or students whose class registrations or grades were stored on them, punch-cards became the symbol of alienation: 'They stood for abstraction, oversimplification and dehumanization. The cards were, it seemed, a two-dimensional portrait of people, people abstracted into numbers that machines could use' (Lubar 1992, p. 44).

The punch-card operators were all women, van den Ende and Van Oost (2001) state in their analysis of the introduction of the system in the Dutch Central Bureau of Statistics (CBS) in the 1920s. The room where the incoming data were checked and encoded was staffed by men only. The machine room 'was "mixed" but dominated by women. They operated the tabulating machines and the desk calculators' (p. 495), whilst the men operated the sorting machines. This gendered division of labour also applied to repair jobs:

> ... the management of the CBS and the minister reserved the technical knowledge and skills for (small) repairs to the machine for the male employees: The male employees should be taught the construction of the card punching-, sorting and counting-machines and be able to remedy small problems.
>
> (van den Ende and Van Oost 2001, p. 497)

This gender hierarchy also dominated early computer work that originated in female clerical work; with the difference that the 'women computers' in the

---

[2] Professionalization is an attempt by an occupational group to achieve occupational closure, and thus a 'shelter' from the labour market. It involves the proliferation of objective standards of work/professional norms, the spread of tenure arrangements, licensing, or certifications, the establishment of bodies that control adherence to standards and admission procedures, and so forth.

1940s were highly skilled but completely undervalued mathematicians. A famous and well-researched example are the so-called ENIAC women who worked in the US Army's Ballistic Research Laboratory and the Moore School of Electrical Engineering (at the University of Pennsylvania). These women possessed a high level of mathematical skill, which included solving nonlinear differential equations with several variables. However, these women's contributions to the development of the ENIAC computer and to programming were not acknowledged at that time. Jennifer Light (1999) states that

> In a number of laboratories, scientists described women not as individuals, but rather as a collective, defined by their lab leader ('Cecil's Beauty Chorus') or by their machines ('scanner girls'). Likewise in the ENIAC project, female operators are referred to as '[John] Holberton's group' or as 'ENIAC girls'. Technicians generally did not author papers or technical manuals. Nor did they acquire the coveted status symbols of scientists and engineers: publications, lectures, and membership in professional societies. Ultimately these women never got a public opportunity to display their technical knowledge, crucial for personal recognition and career advancement.
>
> (Light 1999, p. 459)

The ENIAC project made a fundamental distinction between hardware and software: designing hardware was a man's job; programming was a woman's job. However, the work women actually did in this project challenges this widespread notion: to program at the machine level, the women had to understand the hardware. In the words of one of the programmers of the ENIAC computer,

> We spent much of our time at APG [Army Proving Group] learning how to wire the control board for the various punch card machines: tabulator, sorter, reader, reproducer, and punch. As part of our training, we took apart and attempted to fully understand a fourth-order difference board that the APG people had developed for the tabulator ... Occasionally, the six of us programmers all got together to discuss how we thought the machine worked. If this sounds haphazard, it was.
>
> (Light 1999, p. 471)

The women at ENIAC significantly influenced the design of this and the following computers, as the following episode demonstrates: when 'ENIAC programmer Betty Holberton ... convinced John von Neumann to include a "stop instruction" in the machine: although initially dismissive, von Neumann eventually recognized the programmer' s legitimate need for such an instruction' (Ensmenger 2010, p. 122). However, these successes were systematically erased from accounts of the development of the field.

There were other, less well-known, women at that time who were employed by the national bureau of standards (NBS) that 'directed the transfer from hand driven computing machines to the modern Computer era' (Schinzel 2017, p. 88): Gertrude Blanch, Mina Rees, Ida Rhodes, and Thelma Estrin, all of them having fled antisemitism and prosecution against Jews and Eastern Europe; as well as the Austrian actress Hedy Lamarr who used her knowledge about telegraphy 'for steering torpedos, which could not be tracked. This method today is used for every communication between mobiles, radio communication, bluetooth, mobile internet, etc., in order to make it secure' (p. 88).

Based on a new historical dataset comprising 50,000 individuals, Misa (2021) argues that the decline of the number of women entering computing – a worldwide phenomenon (with some exceptions) – is not only a consequence of the professionalization of computing: it also reflects 'cultural changes in the 1980s [that] led to today's gender bias in computing – a contingent (not inherent or permanent) result of professionalization' (p. 76). In order to arrive at a clearer picture of the underrepresentation of women and of the diverse ethnicities living in the USA, the different reasons behind this phenomenon (many of them cultural) have to be considered. For instance, quoting Kendall's (1999) piece, Misa points to the 'nerd image, which had been previously ambiguous, flexible, and rhetorically situated distant from power, which "gets rehabilitated and partially incorporated into hegemonic masculinity" beginning in the 1980s' (p. 81).

A Diversity of Early Developments: (National) Informatics Cultures

Most (if not almost all) historical studies of women in computing are about the situation in the USA, which was at the forefront of computer development. Taking the cultural argument seriously requires looking at the situation in other countries. From the few in-depth studies from other countries we derive some understanding of cultural variations and their effects on women's participation in the computer field: historical research on women IT professionals in the UK civil service (Hicks 2010); Marja Vehviläinen's (1999) paper on the 'the legacy of the pioneer culture in relation to the gendering processes in computing' in Finland (p. 45); the situation in France where women gained access to the engineering schools relatively late (Morley and McDonnell 2015); and women's participation in the pioneering stage of computing development in Russia (Khenner 2019). Questions common to all these historical studies are: When did masculinity/femininity become part of the cultural vocabulary of IT? What other reasons led to the undervaluation of women's contributions to computing?

The situation of women in computing in the UK during WWII very much resembles the story of 'women computers' in the USA:

> The story of British computing starts in WWII with the codebreaking and
> cryptanalysis apparatus at Bletchley Park. Kept secret for decades after the war, the
> work conducted at Bletchley is now understood to have been crucial to the allies'
> victory, shortening the war by at least two years and saving hundreds of thousands
> of lives (Hinsley, 2001). The success of D-Day invasions at Normandy, for example,
> was largely made possible by the intelligence decoded by the Colossus computers –
> and, as Hicks points out – the women who were responsible for operating them.
>
> (Miltner 2019, p. 165)

After WWII computerization was at the heart of British government agencies
and programs – civil services, the National Health Service, and the many social
insurance and welfare programs – which required an increase in data-
processing power. Before computers were introduced at a larger scale, numerous technically skilled women operated and programmed the machines that
performed payroll and accounting tasks. Some of them also did difficult
scientific computations. All these jobs were considered low-skilled and
received much lower pay than executive jobs that were mostly held by men.
Machine work was not yet considered a male domain within the UK civil
services, Marie Hicks (2010) argues:

> This association of women workers with technical, machine work might seem to fly
> in the face of cultural stereotypes. Yet, by constructing technical work as being at
> odds with the intellectual work of government officers, managers' association of
> women with this work did not break down any barriers.
>
> (Hicks 2010, p. 162)

The Equal Pay Act in 1954 was used not to increase women's salaries nor to
lower those of men; instead management changed their job titles, thereby
creating 'a formal division between the managerial classes and the workers
responsible for the calculation and tabulation work' (Miltner 2019, p. 166).

When the number of computing projects in the public sector increased in the
early 1960s, the government ignored the large pool of technically skilled
women and hired from the mainly male 'executive classes' to run the new
computers. They had no technical training but were recruited because managers perceived computing work to be of increasing importance. The fact that
these new hires were inexperienced and required substantial training soon
turned into a major stumbling block, with the effect that managers showed
an 'increasing willingness to hire and train an entry-level, gender-diverse
workforce' (p. 174).

Although this move offered opportunities for technically skilled women that
found computing fascinating, this complex story (more details can be found in
Hicks 2010) did not end well for women. The government was more concerned with finding the right candidates for 'their professionalizing cadre of

management-oriented technocrats' (p. 178) and found that women programmers earned too much:

> The Central Computing Bureau's hiring manager suggested that 'a fundamental and
> searching examination of the grading and pay of the machine class is badly needed',
> if such young recruits were rising so quickly through the ranks and earning so much.
> Meanwhile, young men of the same age, earning the same amounts, were not
> subjected to such scrutiny.
>
> (Hicks 2010, p. 181)

Following Hicks, the story of women in computing in the UK seems less one
of gendered images of technical work taking over than one of excluding
women from the most well-paid and powerful positions in the economy.

The case of Finland, which installed its first computer rather late, in 1958 in
the Post Bank of Finland, is different. The computerization of the country,
which at that time was considered a project of national progress, was driven by
the ADP club – a club of men. The most important pioneering force behind it
was Otto Karttunen, the first director of the State Computing Center. He had a
background in the military and was dedicated to management from above and
ideas of scientific management. Marja Vehviläinen (1999) provides a detailed
description of this pioneering phase, in which the ADP club, in fact a small
'secret society', assumed the leading role:

> The country needed, in Karttunen's and his colleagues' minds, computers. In the
> ADP club, they, in a small group, among brothers (their letters started with the
> words 'my good brother'), figured out the preconditions of computing and also tried
> to arrange these prerequisites for 'our country'.
>
> (Vehviläinen 1999, p. 46)

IBM was the most important computer supplier in Finland in the 1960s. While
mainstream ideas about programming dominated, a discussion that was unique
to the Nordic countries at that time raised the issue of information systems.
It helped develop new ideas about systems design that eliminated the boundary
between programming and systems design, focussing attention on organizational
and work practice issues. In this notion of how to develop systems there was also
a place for women who were attracted by the new university curricula. During
the 1970s the share of women in computer science studies increased from 20 to
30 percent, growing even larger in the 1980s. Vehviläinen stresses that

> women gained space as experts and project leaders in practical information
> technology because: 1) the Finnish information technology culture emphasized
> systems design; 2) in Finnish society, even before computing, women participated in
> the labor market and education; and 3) there was increasing support from the welfare
> state's child-care services.
>
> (Vehviläinen 1999, p. 47)

However, in the 1990s the computing professions became more male again. Vehviläinen describes a particular development: a 'world without women' that was built by male computer pioneers alongside 'women's spaces' that were opened by the new systems development methods, in which women supported by a strong welfare state successfully participated. The problem she diagnosed in 1999 was that 'The pioneer culture intertwined with women's space. Women were able to use alternative methods or practices only by relating them to the methods created by the male pioneers' (p. 50).

The case of France is interesting not only because of the major role the state played, both politically and economically, in the creation and mergers of computer manufacturing firms, but because of its elitist educational system. Women were not only absent from power positions in companies taking a lead in computing. They had to wait until 1972 to be admitted to the prestigious engineering schools and even then were prevented from accessing the 'engineering corps' whose members were the main decision-makers in key industries: 'It was not until the 1980s that a few female engineers were admitted to the influential "corps des mines" or "corps des telecommunications"' (Morley and McDonnell 2015, p. 4).

However, also in France a few exceptional women managed to make substantial contributions to the computer industry in the late 1950s; among them Alice Recoque who was put in charge of the design of the rather successful mini-computers:

> These mini-computers were not within the scope of the 'Plan Calcul' [launched in 1966] which may explain why a woman was placed in charge of research in what was then termed 'small computers'. Despite her achievements, Alice Recoque never reached a position of responsibility either in the public or private sector.
>
> (Morley and McDonnell 2015, p. 6)

At the beginning of the 1980s more and more women graduates from engineering schools chose computing and entered a large range and variety of jobs. In 1982, 35 percent of all computer scientists were women. However, numbers started to drop again in the late 1980s, replicating a common trend in Western countries.

This did not happen to the same extent in Russia, where a significant number of women were included in the development of computing in the period from 1960 to 1980; and they were highly visible. They worked in the computing centres of universities, research institutes, and industry, although they rarely held key positions. Some of these pioneering women became well known for their special contribution; such as Kateryna Yushchenko, who developed 'one of the world's first high-level programming languages with indirect addressing' and also was a founder of the first Soviet scientific school of theoretical programming; Rosetta Zhilina who 'headed the development of many algorithms and program-solving problems in the field of physics, mechanics, heat conductivity, and ballistics of complex structures in the national defense industry' (Khenner 2019, p. 248); Elena Glivenko who participated in the design of a powerful multiprocessor computer system; or Elena Paducheva who began the first systematic research in the USSR on logical analysis of natural language (Smolevitskaya 2021).

Khenner also provides information about several computer companies today that employ women computer scientists; such as Cognitive Technologies, a company that is in need of high-level programming skills and has increased the number of women employees to 35 percent; or Technoserv Consulting, where the ratio of women to men is 50:50, 'since the company deals not so much with classical programming as with introduction of large systems, where deep knowledge of business, processes, and approach to analysis is required' (p. 254). While Russia may not have experienced the sharp decline in women's participation in computing common to Western countries, the current status of women in the computing field is not so clear. Khenner offers some facts, such as that in '2012 women made up 27% of the total number of applicants taking the Unified National Examination in Informatics' (p. 257). He also refers to observations that women in computing experience discrimination; according to a survey conducted by the Institute for Internet Development in 2016, women mention the 'lack of career development, 24%; getting a wage lower than male employees in the same position, 24%; other factors, 15%. At the same time, 36% of respondents emphasized the absence of specific difficulties' (p. 257).

Britta Schinzel (2017) attributes the differences in women's participation in the computing field in different countries mainly to cultural factors. For example, with respect to Russia she remarks,

> ... I think of the common conviction of women and men, that men are incapable of organizing everyday life, giving women a fairly self-conscious gender identity. Therefore, in these countries a self-respect stemming from being a woman as well as from being a man as such is kept up. So there is no necessity for boys or men to hold their ground nor to compete with women intellectually. Therefore women easier can consider themselves as of equal mental power, also in subjects like informatics. And boys and men need not take up the computer in order to stabilize their male identity.
> (Schinzel 2017, p. 96)

Sure, gender attributions exist all over the world and they influence what women and men think they are capable of and how this shapes their career choices as well as the types of jobs that are accessible to them. However, there are other factors to account for, as Durndell et al. (1997) contend in a comparative study of the situation of women in Romania and Scotland. While stressing the cultural and economic differences between Eastern European countries, they state that in all of these countries gender equality was more an ideology than a lived experience. However, 'even with all the cautions and caveats, a situation seemed to exist in these countries whereby any negative connection between being female and choosing involvement with technology was relatively absent' (pp. 272–273). Taking the example of Romania, they found that even the disintegration of the Communist regimes has 'not altered the situation whereby females take it as quite unexceptional for females to be interested in technology, specifically computing in this case' (p. 279). Other relevant facts are the relatively poor quality of technology in these countries and the need after WWII, to mobilize all young people with mathematical skills, including young women, to contribute to the development of their country by entering an engineering profession. Becoming an engineer was not always a matter of choice for women at that time but a result of decisions made by state agencies.

Last but not least, there are power issues that determine women's opportunities to enter a career in the computing field, as Abbate in her book *Recoding gender: Women's changing participation in computing* (2012) emphasizes:

> When it comes to individual workers, assessments of skill are colored by assumptions about the capacities, interests, and appropriate spheres of action of different social groups. Since technical skill conveys power – including prestige, access to well-paid employment, and the opportunity to shape the tools used by a whole society – the dominant groups in society tend to assert their 'natural' superiority in these fields.
>
> (Abbate 2012, p. 40)

Taken together these cases illustrate that gender structures that have resulted in computing being a predominantly male occupation in some countries (such as the USA, Canada, and the UK) are malleable. From looking historically at the emergence of computing we can see how in many cases women played significantly important roles, often erased from history. From looking at computing cross-nationally, we can see how in some cases computing was masculinized, while in other cases the demand for (and short supply of) talent combined with state interventions left computing open to women. This suggests that symbolic gendering of occupations as well as the gender structures and divisions of labour that characterize these highly gendered occupations, often appearing fixed, in reality are malleable. If this is the case, what then explains why in many parts of the world there are proportionally few women in computing?

Numbers, Numbers ...

Numbers, numbers – why are there so few female computer scientists? Numbers *do* matter but 'Getting in is an interesting question, but not enough. Because what does the field look like? Does it open up? Does it provide other opportunities? What are the jobs like?' (Joan Greenbaum, interview 05/05/ 2022).

So, there are several questions to address, beyond the 'numbers': Why, in the first place, should young women be interested in a career in computing? Why do comparatively few of the young women who start an education in computer science find their way to a job in the computing field? Why and where do they get lost? What kind of working conditions and career opportunities can they reasonably expect?

The questions that are voiced today somewhat different from the diversity discourse that researchers and practitioners have been leading during the last decades. It implied that women computer scientists, by virtue of being women, would speak critically to trends in the field that support patterns of control and dominance and the exclusion of different voices. Toni Robertson refers to this argument that was quite popular – 'that if we had more women in computing, everything would be alright. And computing would be better because the women were there. And I was never particularly convinced of those, and they worried me' (Toni Robertson, interview 05/18/2022). Sørensen (1992) presented a nuanced view of this debate based on Norwegian findings that support 'a modest claim that caring values may affect R&D through the presence of female researchers under special circumstances where women are able to and/ or find it productive to assert the female gender as a resource' (p. 23). He also takes up the argument that as women in science and technology disciplines are selected and socialized, they become more similar to men with respect to their values, the ways they shape research problems and seek solutions. Studies at that time suggested that many of the young women choose an engineering education for the same motivations as their male colleagues: 'for the adventure of abstract thought, for the intellectual pleasure that analyzing a problem, looking for details, isolating, and manipulating variables provide' (Wagner 1993, p. 257). Another strong reason for motivating young women to embark on a career in computing we should not forget was (and still is) that the computing (and other engineering) field(s) offer women well-paid jobs as well as access to positions of power.

The other issue with respect to bringing more women into science and engineering concerns the problem of the 'pipeline discourse', a metaphor that has been much criticized. 'What's wrong with the pipeline?', Branch (2016) asks: 'Everything. The pipeline assumes a passive flow of women (and men) from one stage to the next culminating in a scientific career. Women's under-representation in science results then from their leakage from the pipeline' (p. viii). Women (as well as people of colour and gender minorities) are portrayed as passive 'resources' to be mobilized for a STEM career. In this model, they 'fail' to enter and successfully navigate a pipeline that is on principle open to them (Vitores and Gil-Juárez 2016). The problem with this view is not only that women's agency is disregarded but that the pipeline represents the classical (male) career model. Women more often than men do not follow a straight career path, for many reasons, in particular when they decide to have children. Moreover, a computing career does not necessarily start with a classical computer science education. There are other computer education sites than computer science programs and women (and others) often access jobs in the computing field from different disciplines and professions (e.g., Cukier et al. 2002; Birbaumer et al. 2007; Corneliussen 2021). Misa (2021) suggests that we conceptualize women's diverse career paths as 'non-linear pathways'.

The third question to ask when considering the numbers of women in IT professions – that in Western countries are around 20 percent, while they are higher in India (35 percent), the Philippines (30 percent), and Malaysia (more than 40 percent) – is: What kind of working conditions and career opportunities can women reasonably expect?

Women's Work Experiences in the IT Professions

In May 2017, the Wall Street Journal caused a commotion when it reported that women software engineers at Facebook were 35 percent more likely to have their code rejected by the company's internal peer review system (Seetharaman, 2017). The results of the original study, conducted by a former Facebook employee during her tenure at the company, suggested that the rejection rate implied more intense scrutiny when it came to the code of women engineers.

(Miltner 2019, p. 161)

IT companies as well as computer workplaces at other sites are gendered and the experiences of women professionals working in computing are similar to those in male-dominated industrial companies – in construction, mining, oil and gas, and the automotive sector (Chapter 4). However, as computing is a wide and heterogenous field, also women's career paths and working lives vary considerably. This section looks into the biographies of women IT professionals in different cultural and organizational contexts; it describes the gendered division of labour in the computing field as well as the working culture in IT companies, small and large ones, also from a global perspective; and it addresses racism in IT education and at work.

A Diversity of Biographies

In the framework of the project WWWICT (Widening Women's Work in Information and Communication Technology (Wagner et al. 2003), researchers conducted biographical interviews with 107 women working in the ICT sector in seven European countries – Austria, Belgium, France, Ireland, Italy, Portugal, and the UK. Although this project was carried out twenty years ago, it resulted in key insights that have been mostly confirmed by newer studies, as we will discuss in the following. The project in particular demonstrates the diversity and, in many cases, non-linearity of pathways women IT professionals traverse.

One of the insights from this study was that attachment to computers does not always begin at an early age, although some women mentioned early interests in computers, and that as young girls they preferred technical toys and liked tinkering and using tools. Some women received special encouragement from their parents to enter a STEM career, namely from fathers who had a scientific or technical background. There were also family circumstances that did not remotely signal a career in ICT. Interestingly, mothers (in particular in Austria and in the South of Italy) had a strong influence on their daughters' personal development and ideas for the future. These mothers

> are described as role models – strong, admirable, and supporting, expecting their daughter to be strong and independent. These mothers' backgrounds differ – some are teachers, others homemakers, and only a few work in the area of math/science, 'naturalizing' mathematical and/or technical skills. There are several cases of mothers who run their own business, representing a strong incentive for their daughters to get independent.
>
> (Wagner et al. 2003, p. 9)

Young women that enter a career in the computing field are highly motivated. For example, Corneliussen (2021) stresses that many of the Norwegian women in IT professions she interviewed 'expressed pleasure, fascination, and becoming "hooked" on programming, as well as sadness for not having learnt it before' (p. 54). In a survey study of students of computer science, Guzman and Staton (2008) found 'that women in IT enjoy learning and getting involved in activities that would allow them to acquire more IT knowledge and skills' (p. 221). An earlier case study by Clegg and Trayhurn (2000) of women and men who took applied IT courses, stresses the importance of intrinsic (in addition to instrumental) motivations:

> Some of them had embarked on other careers but found that it was their glimpse of computer systems that excited them and also the discovery that they were good at systems. ... [F]or them intrinsic pleasure was embedded in the instrumental and by doing a degree they hope they will have job choices with the power to do the things they enjoy.
>
> (Clegg and Trayhurn 2000, p. 83)

Along similar lines, the well-received project to '*unlock the clubhouse*' at Carnegie Mellon's School of Computer Science by Margolis and Fisher (2002) rather successfully aimed to multiply the number of female undergraduates in computer science. A key factor here was the insight that comfort to enter the field goes hand in hand with perceived freedom to not need to live up to specific (predominantly male) role expectations. Other works later focussed on the structural specificities and lived character of computing education programs, such as Borsotti and Bjørn (2022) exploring the role of humour and stereotypes at a computer science department.

Wagner et al. (2003) summarize the factors that the participants in the WWWICT project mentioned as making a career in ICT attractive:

> It is challenging work, offering the opportunity for learning and perfection, and for being creative. It is fascinating, satisfying the urge to 'solve riddles and generally the curiosity to get to the bottom of things'. Being able to work with customers, translating their needs into software or a web site – this may even include a care-taking aspect. It is an open world, with a wide horizon. It offers jobs in a respectable area and status.
>
> (Wagner et al. 2003, p. 10)

The researchers identified several 'life story patterns' in the women's biographical interviews that were identified on the basis of a cluster analysis (Birbaumer et al. 2008). These patterns represent a diversity of career paths, motivations, and strategies. The women that had been included in this analysis worked in rather different areas of computing, in small or large companies, in highly skilled jobs but also in more modest positions, several of which are described below.

Straight careers in ICT: These women entered the computing field, having developed a strong interest in science, math, and/or technology. For some of them, the fact that ICT is a field with good job prospects was the main motivation. All of them followed one of the predefined trajectories in ICT. They were driven by a strong notion of excellence and in some cases showed ambition to reach the top. They tended to accept the conditions for having a successful career in computing, including long hours, stressful working conditions, a competitive environment, and (in many cases) hierarchical structures.

From the margins to a field of opportunities: For these women ICT offered the chance to move out from their milieu – a rural background (Austria), an area with limited job opportunities (the South of Italy), or an ethnic background (UK) – into jobs that offer good pay, a high level of job security, and the opportunity for learning. While for a few of the women this move was the result of rebellion against their home environment, most of them remained emotionally attached to their homes. Their entries into ICT varied. While some already were interested in ICTs in school, others took an engineering or computer science degree or encountered ICT in their (clerical) jobs, seizing the opportunity to qualify themselves, either through learning by doing or through additional training. While the women maintained their interest in computing, one of the prime movers of these careers is the chance to get a well-paying job offering security, possibly in a large company.

Building one's own environment: Some of the women were strongly goal-oriented and took steps to realize their career goals and life themes. This led them to actively create an environment that correspond to their ideas and attitudes. Most of these women came from a supportive environment and had chosen supportive partners. However, not all of these careers were straightforward. The strong will of these women to shape their own environment took them in different directions. These included going abroad as a single woman to be exposed to other cultures, being in charge of their own life from a quite young age on, founding their own company, carving out their own field of expertise, building things on their own, and fighting for a good position.

Combining art with technology: These women (almost all of them from Italy) started out with a background in art, graphic design, or journalism. Typical of these careers is the ease with which the women integrated ICT into their work, developing a passion for both fields, but with their artistic interests and ambitions staying in the foreground. Regarding their lifestyle and way of working they are more artists than computer professionals.

Some of the women have found good work in the IT field, but their ambitions are limited. There are other important perspectives in life for them, such as having more time for their family or for hobbies. They have jobs at the lower end of the hierarchy of ICT but felt competent and respected. Some of the career paths, mostly those of the younger women, were (still) rather open and they had not yet arrived. Most of them had a good start in working life, liked their job in ICT, and worked hard; taking up opportunities where they offered themselves, not always sure where to go.

There were also cases of women who met considerable difficulties – *struggling but not giving up*. Among the difficulties were adverse working conditions, problems managing work and family life, or limited job perspectives in their region. Coping strategies were to look for alternatives or start additional training to make up for the lack of qualifications and/or a degree, or train for other types of jobs. Finally, there were *fragile or broken careers*: women who did not have a good start in working life due to a lack of qualifications and/or a degree, unsatisfactory working conditions, limited job possibilities, having made a wrong career step, or just not liking work with ICTs. They lacked motivating and realistic alternatives, and, in some cases, felt discouraged and that they had failed and/or experienced unfulfilled ambitions.

These findings show that women who work in the IT professions have had varied experiences. This has also been found by others, such as Trauth (2002) who states that women are shaped by their backgrounds and the culture in which they live and respond to these influences in individual ways. Corneliussen (2021) adds that once women have empowered themselves,

> belonging in this new ICT field can be claimed, not only on the basis of early interest in gaming and programming, but also based on an interest in mathematics and sciences, social challenges, languages and creativity, and more, all of which are defined as relevant once a wider image of ICT is recognized.
>
> (Corneliussen 2021, p. 56)

A Gendered Division of Labour

Computing is not a homogeneous field. As computers are highly specialized and varied, there are a great variety of jobs, which are connected with a diversity of career trajectories. Women (as well as people of colour) are not equally represented in all job categories and in all levels of the hierarchy. For example, Panteli et al. (2001) state about the situation of women in computing in the UK in the late 1990s that

> ... women are under-represented (relative to their overall proportion in the workforce) in management, technical, network support, and operations. They are disproportionately highly represented in systems and analysis-programming work, and in help desk (user support) work.
>
> (Panteli et al. 2001, p. 9)

Women in management positions were mostly employed in administrative or customer service jobs and, among systems workers, more in organization-oriented analysis work than as leaders of software development projects or hardware-oriented jobs. Hunter (2012) found that women working in computing careers in New Zealand were clustered 'in occupations associated with the "soft" side of ICT, for example administration, marketing, sales, customer service, training, [and] helpdesk support' (p. 134).

This pattern does not seem to have changed much over time and it does not vary much across different parts of the world. Ruiz Ben (2007) presents data about IT specialists in software companies in Germany. Jobs in the computing field are divided into IT core tasks (1) that include software development, system analysis, databases; and IT core tasks (2) that include IT organization, IT consulting, or IT service and support. While for the former category a university degree in computer science is required, there are more entrance routes to core tasks (2). This offers people who do not have a university education – hence also women – the possibility of entering the computing field through other educational programs. In big companies, women are typically employed in quality management and project management, meaning 'that the soft skills necessary for integrating diverse requirements of the market into software production are concentrated in particular areas in which women are especially welcome' (p. 324).

Interviews with professors of computer science and personnel managers of software companies demonstrated differences in how women and men IT specialists understood their expertise and brought it to the fore. For example, 'while men often arbitrarily use the term "technology" to describe their work, women tend to distance the description of their tasks from technological terminology' (Ruiz Ben 2007, p. 323). Also, women's and men's approaches to software development seem to differ, the study found:

> Men focus more on product and process aspects, while women are more interested in the clients' requirements. . . . Male software developers, for example, considered first price or time priority and then including customers at every step of the process to avoid misunderstanding. . . . Women sought to ascertain the customer's needs or, in other words, for them the requirements analysis forms the crucial part of the software development process.
>
> (Ruiz Ben 2007, p. 324)

It looks as though women would find employment in computing jobs that are not only less technical but closer to the realities of workplaces in organizations, responding to the need to adapt, maintain, and repair software in use in those places. These are jobs that are valued and paid less than those in the more technical areas. Interviews with fifty-seven technically skilled female IT professionals in the UK corroborate this experience (Kenny and Donelly 2020). While the role of the technical expert is clearly connoted with masculinity, signalling strong technical skills, independence, and competitiveness, women are seen as possessing strong communication and organizational skills:

> These skills were perceived to make them better suited to so-called 'housekeeping roles'. Women . . . are sort of split into two areas. They tend more to be in project management . . . or operations . . . Operations is basically like the wives of the office, they make sure that food happens . . . And then, on a project, the people that keep it ticking over [are] the wives of the project. (Abigail, IT Consultant).
>
> (Kenny and Donelly 2020, p. 9)

There is, however, a big difference between big and small IT companies, which has also been noted by Ruiz Ben (2007). Due to the specialization of tasks, there is a much more pronounced division of labour in large companies than in small ones for which the ability of their employees to 'multitask' is essential. The study carried out by Wagner et al. (2003) identified about a third of the women they interviewed as working in small (some of them very small) companies. These companies offer the possibility to acquire a broad range of skills through learning on-the-job; they have flat hierarchies but also a limited range of jobs:

> A career here means to move on to other companies and types of work. Within the software industry, inter-company mobility is seen primarily as a way of acquiring new knowledge, of increasing one's experience and grow in one's profession.
>
> (Wagner et al. 2003, p. 12)

Although there is a lack of detailed data about the division of labour in the computing field worldwide, the situation is not so different in other countries.[3] For example, in India, where women make up 35 percent of the workforce in computing, women are absent from managerial roles in most technology teams and they are 'provided with less critical and complex projects and more trust lies on the male professionals' (Maji and Dixit 2020, p. 3072). In Brazil, as of 2010–2011, women made up just 17.6 percent of computer science students. with the percentage of women working in computer science-related professions having dropped from 35 percent to 15 percent. Women are 'utterly unrepresented as database administrators, games developers, and in information security. Women have a slight majority as desktop/full stack developers, designers, and quality/test engineers' (Kohl and Prikladnicki 2018, p. 38). An exception is Malaysia, where computer science is 'dominated by women' for a variety of cultural and political reasons (Mellström 2009).

Looking into the possibilities for change, Roan and Whitehouse (2007) critically discuss the assumption that 'mixed skills job[s]' will be the future of IT companies that are going to be 'increasingly dependent on workers who are able to liaise effectively with end-users and make computers "user friendly"' (p. 22) and that women will benefit from this development. They problematize the fact that, again, the 'mixed skills' argument builds on an essentialist notion of the suitability of women for certain work in IT. Drawing on evidence from Australia, they state that to date women have not made much

---

[3] There are organizations like the Anita Borg Institute that provide regular statistics: https://anitab.org/research-and-impact/top-companies/2020-results/. But many of these statistics are not national but concern tech companies; see for example https://daoinsights.com/exclusives/unleashing-womens-potential-in-chinas-tech-industry-an-interview-with-xiaoman-hu/.

progress in career paths for which communication and organizational skills are important, while core technical development functions as well as top management positions remained a male domain.

More recent studies suggest that women may find niches for themselves where the proportion of women leading internet entrepreneurial projects is very high (Zhang/Yin 2019). Other research points to spaces that some women IT professionals find for themselves. For example, Canedo (2020) studied women working as core developers in OSS (open-source software) communities, where they are few but successful; Panteli and Urquart (2022) investigated the job-crafting experiences of women in IT who had left permanent employment. While some of the reasons behind these rather varied conditions that led women to pursue a professional career in computer science are cultural, others, more specifically, have to do with the working culture in IT companies.

The Working Culture in IT Companies

IT companies are likely to be gendered organizations and women entering them have the same experiences as women working in other male-dominated fields, where they are confronted with strong images of masculinity and exposed to working conditions that may be hard to reconcile with their family responsibilities.

Studies examining the working conditions for women in IT companies all seem to agree that a 'macho culture' makes it difficult for women to stick to a career in computing. It is a culture that 'militates against women … because it is insular, self-reinforcing, intimidating, alienating, discriminatory and misogynistic' (Tassabehji et al. 2021, p. 1300). Among the aspects of work that potentially discourage women is the ideal of a good programmer as one who merges with the machine through 'plugging themselves in' to write code all day. Coding 'is a head down, know your job, that's what I've been tasked to do, I've got to build this, and I'll just sit and build it' (p. 1307). A Brazilian study about what repels women from participating in hackathons (which offer good opportunities for learning and networking) concludes that low self-esteem and toxic masculinity – 'which involves misogyny, rudeness, sexist and inappropriate behavior, which ends up promoting an unfriendly environment' – were the main problems for women (Paganini and Gama 2020, p. 11). Kenny and Donelly (2020) found sexism as the principal reason of women in the UK for leaving the industry, where women are facing a climate that 'continues to be hostile and unwelcoming' (p. 3). It is not clear, though, whether these findings are representative of IT companies in general. For example, Wagner et al, (2003) in their study of women IT professionals in seven European countries arrived at the conclusion that

> Our findings do not support the view that women generally find hostile work environments in engineering firms. There are cases of supportive work cultures as well as those of exclusionary and unsupportive ones. No clear pattern emerges, with work cultures being organization-specific, location-specific, and even team-specific.
> (Wagner et al. 2003, p. 18)

A recent Norwegian study at an international consulting organization active in the IT industry (Holgersson and Romani 2020) presents some encouraging findings. Although its core professional group is strongly male dominated and performance-pressure high, gender awareness is high among employees and women have 'a strong agentic role' in 'defining the company's practices' (p. 649). The researchers portray this company as 'a case of an organization that not only exposes and challenges the implicit masculine norm; it also aims to replace it with a gender egalitarian one' (pp. 657–658). This is what Toni Robertson found in the small IT company run by women where she did her research: 'they were women, and they lived with women's bodies in a patriarchy and they had developed certain kinds of skills, which happened to enable them to work very well over distance at a time when the blokes were not able to do that' (Toni Robertson, interview 05/18/2022).

What are women's coping strategies when confronted with an 'unfriendly' environment? One is denial of the experience of not being equally valued and treated inappropriately – a strategy that has been observed in many cases of women in other male-dominated work environments (see e.g., Bagilhole et al. 2002 about women in the construction industry in the UK). With respect to women IT professionals, Hunter (2006) describes 'the day-to-day practices of the self' of women who 'disavow their femininity and any disadvantages flowing from it' (p. 91). This is a survival strategy that seems to work for some women, but at a cost. In Harding's (1986) terms, these women may have an internal gender identity as female, but as a coping strategy they adapt an external or projected gender identity that stresses their congruence with a male gender identity.

Research on gender in male-dominated fields of work generally points to the difficulties that working mothers with young children in particular have with long hours including availability during evenings and weekends. Interestingly, the women in Hunter's (2006) Australian study did not identify the difficulties that resulted from 'long hours, unavailability of part-time work, vulnerability to dismissal' as a form of discrimination but just 'as things are' (p. 99).

A study carried out by Canedo et al. (2021) in Brazilian IT companies adds observations about women's situation in software development teams. Their study confirms that only few women have leadership roles in gender-diverse teams and that men are given the more complex tasks. It also shows the 'fragility' of women's positions in these teams: the fact that they have to demonstrate their ability to carry out tasks that had been allocated to them and, more generally, the lack of 'gender-equal communication'. Men tended to not talk on equal terms with their female colleagues who often found it difficult to make themselves heard, even when they were in a team leader position – 'when a woman joins a men's team, men do not trust immediately and their trust has to be earned' (p. 384). Another issue was that women did not always receive credit for their contributions, as the examples of the 'Atari women' demonstrate (Bjørn and Rosner 2021). 'Some men have harmful attitudes, for example, stealing my ideas or reducing my participation in meetings and product deliveries' (Canedo et al. 2021, p. 384). This has also been observed by Nafus (2012) who studied the experiences of women in open software development teams: 'Men monopolize code authorship and simultaneously de-legitimize the kinds of social ties necessary to build mechanisms for women's inclusion' (p. 669).

Hunter (2012) summarizes these experiences of women in the IT industry as being an 'outsider-within social location', a term that Collins (1986) used to describe the ambivalent situation of Black women domestic workers in white families: a mixture of belonging and not belonging. A related observation about women IT professionals in Norway has been made by Corneliussen (2021) who describes

> how women still approach ICT as a highly masculine field that they receive relatively little support to enter, thus leaving it to women to empower themselves to gain a sense of belonging. . . . [T]he women's post-understanding of ICT produced by their self-empowerment opens a more spacious ICT field that is populated by 'normal people' and 'people like me'.
>
> (Corneliussen 2021, p. 56)

Women entering the computing field are well aware of the fact that it is largely male-dominated. However, through a process of self-empowerment they expand their view of ICT and learn how to make a space for themselves that fits their strengths.

Other studies support modest optimism that women may be able to carve out a place for themselves in IT, most of the time without being supported in this process. Canedo et al. (2020) studied OSS communities using a dataset of 711 open-source projects as well as a survey with women core developers. Despite vertical and horizontal gender segregation, the majority of the women that worked as core developers (only 2.3 percent) in these projects did not seem to have experienced gender discrimination. Moreover, the researchers did not find substantial differences between the work practices of female and male developers, raising questions about whether or not women experienced acceptance in large part because their external or projected gender identity at work mirrored that of men. The women that responded to the survey described the benefits of gender diversity (that included gender minorities and people of colour) in OSS teams; such as the availability of different experiences, perspectives, and 'sensibility to different ways of working and communicating', or an enlarged design space that may make a product 'more generic and inclusive' (p. 7). However, there was also evidence of gender bias with women's contributions sometimes not being equally valued, though most of the women core developers stated 'they never had any problems with their contributions and never suffered gender bias' (p. 9).

Another path for women is to practice 'job-crafting', which means to (re) design their own job on the basis of contracting; this implies being self-employed and losing the job security and benefits a permanent job may provide. Panteli and Urquart's (2022) study of twenty-four female IT contractors in the UK presents some interesting findings. First of all, women that decide to give up permanent employment do this to gain the flexibility and autonomy they need to master the logistics of a life with family responsibilities and to also find personal satisfaction in a male-dominated world. The women participating in this study used different strategies to develop a career, foremost networking and building a reputation. They also actively engaged in enlarging their resources and skills through 'on-the-job learning, training and stretchwork' (selecting work that builds on previous work experiences but helps them 'stretch' their repertoire of skills), but also 'metacognition as well as avoidance practices' (p. 120). Metacognition means the practices of self-reflection that lead to a better understanding of one's own thinking and learning. One of the main motivations of women IT professionals to practice job-crafting was 'having distance from organisational politics as well as from gender bias that hindered their internal promotion and career development' (p. 116).

The research on what kind of work environment women find in IT companies in different countries/cultures demonstrates the persistence of gender bias and lack of support structures for women that may take the form of more or less open misogyny and hostility and prompt many women to leave computing. But it also shows how women with time empower themselves, carving out a space that helps them deploy their skills and grow, and take control of their own careers.

Gendered Racism and Other Marginalizing Forces 'At Work'

In her book *Hidden Figures: The American dream and the untold story of the Black women mathematicians who helped win the space race* (2016), Margot Lee Shetterly describes the contributions of Black women mathematicians that have been obliterated from the early history of computing (just as the work of the (white) 'ENIAC girls'). Gendered racism still plays out in computing education today and prevents Black girls from engaging in a career in the field of computing. There is a powerful 'false message', Rankin and Thomas (2020) state, which attributes the underrepresentation of Black women in the field of computing to their lack of interest in computer science.

While most studies deal with the situation in the USA, De Oliveiro Lobo et al. (2019) provide an account of a number of programs, internationally and in Brazil, that seek to increase the number of Black women in computing (and other engineering fields). They refer to Nilma Lino Gomes' work on Black identity and, more generally, emphasize the importance of the community for learning and development and the need for female community leaders. Among the successful programs directed at Black girls and women are: 'Meninas Digitais Regional Bahia (Digital Girls Program – Bahia)', which seeks to specifically engage Black LGBTQIA+ women; 'InfoPreta', a company created by Black women in 2015 that 'offers technical restoration services, mainten-ance, and assembly of computers. It also offers to recycle notebooks, desktops and electronic devices in general, which are donated to women who live in the outskirts' (p. 10); and 'Black Rehabilitation', which provides training to Black women who are homeless or have been in jail, in cooperation with Microsoft Brazil. All these programs seek to give voice to women, their experiences and perspectives, connecting them, and provide access to training and jobs.

Gendered racism is discussed within the CSCW and HCI communities within a social justice framework that emphasizes the complex and varied social issues that women of colour – Black women, Latina women, indigen-ous/native women, and Asian-American women – face. Much of this work is about the need to break through the silencing of Black women's voices, 'particularly through testimonial quieting and testimonial smothering'; strat-egies that Kristie Dotson (2011) has identified as used to suppress the ideas of marginalized groups. The paper by Erete et al. (2020) provides space for three testimonials of Black women in which they describe their experiences of violence as well as being overlooked and forgotten in CSCW and HCI. Ogbonnaya-Ogburu et al. (2020) have argued that 'the human–computer interaction community has made some efforts toward racial diversity, but the outcomes remain meager'. They maintain that 'racism is pervasive in everyday socio-technical systems'; that the HCI community is prone to 'interest convergence', where concessions to inclusion require benefits to those in power; and that 'the neoliberal underpinnings of the technology industry itself propagate racism' (p. 1) They introduce critical race theory and adapt it for the HCI community in an effort to 'lay a theoretical basis for race-conscious efforts, both in research and within our community'. While these studies heighten awareness of gendered racism in the field, much political-practical work needs to be done to make space for women (and men) of colour.

While the experiences of Black women or, more generally, women of colour in IT education and at work in IT companies is given more and more attention, accounts of the situation of gender (and other) minorities are still scarce, with some exceptions. For example, Alegria (2020) compares the situation of Black and Latinx workers in high-tech companies with those of Asian descent. She pays special attention to findings suggesting that

> White and Asian women who disrupt normative femininity felt a greater sense of belonging at work than their more heteronormatively feminine counterparts, an approach that did not produce the same benefits for the Black woman in their gender-fluid group.
>
> (Alegria 2020, p. 6)

This and other studies describe a 'gendered spectrum of belonging', Alfrey and Twine (2017) argue: women may experience different forms of inclusion or exclusion, depending on their race and sexual orientation. In a study by Miller et al. (2021) on students with minoritized gender identities, they report their experiences with a hostile learning environment. They felt exposed to a demonstration of hypermasculinity and anti-LGBTQIA+ discourses and were treated 'as if they are not smart or invisible' (p. 340). Brown et al. (2022) conducted a study of minoritized identities in AI teams. Those workers who left their team did so for reasons related to the team's work culture and climate. The authors argue that a high pressure to outcompete other products on the market as well as prejudices result in what participants in the study qualified as a toxic work environment. 'AI teams in which minoritized workers thrive', they contend, 'tend to foster a strong sense of interdisciplinary collaboration, support professional career development, and are run by diverse leaders who understand the importance of undoing the traditional White, Eurocentric, and male workplace norms' (p. 1).

The studies highlight the fact that being different on top of being a woman – Black, coloured, lesbian, gender-fluid – exacerbates the problems girls and women face in computer education and, later, at work, in situations where they have access to professional IT jobs in academia or in industry.

Women IT Professionals in Developing Countries

In-depth studies about the situation of women IT professionals in developing countries are scarce. Most of the research on gender and IT has been done in Asia, namely India, Bangladesh, Malaysia, and the Philippines, where women occupy a large share of jobs in computing and where technical work, apart from some types of hardcore engineering tasks, is not strongly associated with men. The generally positive view of a woman being skilled in computer science is also reflected through cinema. For example, Pal (2010) describes South Indian films, where 'we see a burst of female software engineers on screen, including films with a reversal of roles, with the female lead being an accomplished technologist and the male lead as professionally subservient' (p. 185).

However, access to jobs in the computer industry in these countries is reserved for middle- and upper-class women; and these women seem to experience the same kind of barriers as IT professionals in Western countries. Women are mostly employed in software development, in jobs that are less well paid; and there exists a glass ceiling that restricts women's access to management positions. According to Raghuram et al. (2017), the majority of women working in the Indian IT industry are aged 30 years or below and are usually single. A large proportion of women leave employment after five years (Gupta 2020).

The main barrier for women is the working conditions in IT companies. Long hours, sometimes also weekend and night shifts, and having to be available for frequent travel make reconciling a job in IT with the women's traditional responsibility for the family, which is particularly strong in these cultures, difficult for them. Arun and Arun's (2002) study of women software developers in Kerala, India, documents their problems conforming with the notion of 'working flexibly' and 'working under pressure' (p. 45). Women's difficulties of complying with the typical working conditions in IT companies have also been documented by Dhar-Bhattacharjee and Richardson (2018), who found that in the Indian IT sector 'women are more likely to negotiate their flexible working patterns or provision for time off to undertake caring responsibilities for the family than negotiating salary packages or promotions' (p. 582). They also point to unexpected travel and the importance of participating in informal networks as preventing women negotiating for higher salaries or looking for more attractive jobs. An additional issue is safety, which is a reason why many IT companies provide secure transportation facilities. Hence, researchers studying women's situation in IT companies stress the need to create more favourable working conditions for women, with the list of measures including family breaks and training opportunities (in particular for women from rural areas and disadvantaged classes) and extending social security benefits (e.g., Mehta 2016).

While women IT professionals in India (and other Asian countries) may not necessarily be exposed to a toxic male-dominated work environment, there are other barriers, such as class, caste, and religion. For example, Sarkar's (2016) ethnographic study of 'the computer girls of Seelampur' (New Delhi) that receive training in an ICT centre shows that the centre primarily attracted women from higher class and caste positions, although it aimed at girls from marginalized poor Muslim families. The study also demonstrates that ICT skills, although providing access to employment, did not level out the structural constraints that members of marginalized communities experience. Here it is not 'just' gender, but also class and religion that prevents women from accessing professional positions in IT companies.

A similar observation has been made by Saifuddin et al. (2022) in Bangladesh. In interviews with female high-tech professionals, they identified socio-cultural norms that also affect organizational practices as the main barriers to women's careers. The women, with a background in computer science and other engineering disciplines, found that they may have to act in ways that violate gender norms to be accepted at work, as expressed by two of the study participants:

> Shushmita is rejecting the norms while Preety is negotiating the boundaries of acceptable behavior. Preety is aware that being overly open and direct in Bangladeshi culture can taint her femininity. Therefore, while she undermines gender norms by maintaining rapport, she also does gender by enacting limits on her behavior.
>
> (Saifuddin et al. 2022, pp. 681–682)

Referring to the notion of 'undoing gender', the paper shows how highly skilled women demonstrate 'agency and resilience while conforming to macro-societal norms of respectability to avoid negative repercussions' (p. 682). In Harding's (1986) terms, undoing gender requires an awareness of gendered norms on the one hand, and an ability and willingness to alter one's projected gender identity in a manner that is both congruent enough with normative gender roles to not offend, and at the same time allows women to exercise agency in relation to their work, on the other hand. This may require some departure from one's internal gender identity, or an awareness of the need to maintain a difference between one's internal gender identity and projected gender identity. There is no single way to do this, however.

There are cultural and political differences between Asian countries that also affect the situation of women in high-tech. For example, Saloma-Akpdeonu et al. (2005) show that the Philippine ICT industry created jobs characterized by 'disciplinary hybridity' where women find well-paid and highly valued positions. She perceives a momentum towards gender equality in the industry, based on notions of technical competence and professionalism, and explains the existence of 'female spaces' in the industry by three features: '1. Presence of fields in the ICT industry that require a business background; 2. Absence of gender tracking in the compensation structure of some fields in the ICT industry; and 3. Recognition of women's epistemic privilege and standpoint' (p. 102). The last point is particularly interesting, as it suggests that in the industry women's experiences and perspectives are identified as a specific asset. Saloma-Akpdeonu and colleagues point to the fact that women in the Philippines have a relatively high status, resulting from its enormous cultural variety with 111 linguistic, cultural, and ethnic groups, some of which have more egalitarian gender groups than others.

Mellström (2009) offers a nuanced culturally situated intersectional analysis of gender and computing in Malaysia, where women dominate the IT sector, with leading female professionals within ICT-related businesses occupying an impressively high proportion of executive positions. Malaysia is a multi-ethnic society, dominated by Malays (58 percent of the population), 27 percent Chinese, and 7 percent Indians. Despite efforts to emphasize national unity, 'Chinese and Indian people have been marginalized, as non-Muslims, while the Malaysian state has been promoting a "national culture" based on indigenous Malay culture, combined with a distinctly Islamic "governmentalism" as a central feature' (p. 890). Connected with this is a Pan-Malaysian identity that builds on development and technology. The introduction of a race-based quota system for university admission has opened computer science as a field of study for Malay girls. Mellström describes how

> the very idea of an extended national 'family', implying paternalistic family and kinship relations at a national scale, also supports gender relations that are important for how computer science and IT work was viewed with techno optimism by many Malay women.
>
> (Mellström 2009, p. 902)

A job in computer science is associated with indoor spaces that are thought suitable for women and compatible with traditional gender roles; while hardware network jobs are perceived as masculine as they are more physical and involve outdoor exposure. These cultural perceptions are supported by the fact that Malay men are often 'portrayed as effeminate . . . and not "men" enough to cope with a modernity ruled by a globalized market economy, glossy consumerism and financial nationalism' (p. 898). The highly qualified female IT professionals co-exist with the many 'nimble-fingered' docile female workers in factories (Chapter 4). 'Race has become more pertinent than gender' (p. 894) and women's jobs in the computer industry co-exist with paternalistic family relations.

Unfortunately, there is little known about the situation of women IT professionals, apart from numbers, in Africa with its many different countries and cultures. Okwach Abagi et al. (2009) characterize the situation in Kenya as one in which women, despite being skilled computer experts, are placed in 'female'-oriented service jobs; in the words of one respondent, they have been completely 'swallowed in the male-dominated work environment and are wasting their knowledge and skills in ICT because they are doing irrelevant things' (p. 176).

These mixed findings from a handful of countries with vastly different historical, cultural, and political backgrounds point to the need for more research that does justice to these differences with the aim to understand why some of these countries are much more open to educating and employing women IT professionals than others (including most Western countries).

What Is Wrong with Computing?

In spite of lots of similarities with other areas of male-dominated work cultures – the key question with respect to women in ICT professions to address here is 'What is wrong with computing?', as Clegg and Trayhurn (2000) argue:

> ... computing has become characterised by a reliance on mathematical formalism. Precedence is given to areas such as AI, formal methods and computer vision. This emphasis is misplaced. More creative approaches which approximate art-based skills are more likely to meet the real needs of organisations. ... Bricoleurs and mature women with organisational experiences may give us a very different view of what is desirable. The recognition of a plurality of phenomenologically-based ways of knowing in computing and the uncoupling of computing from a reliance on mathematical verification might produce better educational experiences for both men and women since it would force us to think through the tacit theories-in-use involved in doing computing.
>
> (Clegg and Trayhurn 2000, pp. 78, 88–89)

This view is not new; it has been forwarded by feminist researchers in computing. Karen Frenkel (1990) argued that computer science curricula put too much emphasis on formal planning in formal languages, with the result that 'women lose interest' (p. 41). When using software packages that 'do real work real soon', 'women, who perceive computers as tools rather than toys, would see the purpose of computers' (Danielle Bernstein, quoted in Frenkel 1990, p. 41). Marja Vehviläinen (1999) saw in the Nordic approach to systems design a possibility for women to find a space in IT. However, this other sphere of computing (that includes PD) always had to define itself in relation to the dominant top-down, highly formalized one. Approaches that advocate for giving more weight to hybrid forms of systems development and to jobs that require 'mixed skills' in the IT industry, though much needed, present the danger of gender stereotyping and do not change the fact that hardcore technical jobs are still difficult to access and maintain for women who would love to work in these jobs.

The main material for working out alternative visions of computing are feminist theory and pedagogy as well as queer and decolonial approaches. For example, Corneliussen et al. (2018) see feminist pedagogy and 'hands-on work within digital environments' (p. 5) as one way of counteracting the problems women encounter in the field of computing. Amrute and Murillo (2020) propose approaching computing from 'unexpected angles' – 'a view from the South pays equal attention to contests over knowledge and over materials and desires that take place within and across multiple sites' (p. 2).

Summary

In this chapter, we consider two aspects of computer work. First, we take an historical look at the gendering of computer work, tracing its emergence from the female domain of punch-card work to the male domain of programming in some countries. We consider the gendered dimensions of labour characteristic of computing work, and by examining computer work cross-nationally, we can see that the extent to which computing jobs are considered 'men's jobs' varies from country to country. History too has shown us that not only have women filled important roles in the history of computing work, but that current gender structures that have characterized computer jobs in the West since the 1980s have not always been as they appear today. We have looked at pathways of women who entered computing work, which are quite varied; and we have looked at the culture and challenges women face as workers in the computer industry, highlighting how race, sexual orientation, and gender identity all influence women's experiences at work. Women may experience different forms of inclusion or exclusion, depending on their race and sexual orientation. Our closing section – which addresses what's wrong with computing – serves as a bridge to our final three chapters, which shift out focus from what we have learned from looking at the past, to things we can do to influence the future.

PART III

Gender and Design

10

Revisiting the Ethical-Political Perspective
in Technology Design

This chapter revisits the ethical-political perspective on technology design, with a focus on designing IT artifacts and systems. It explores how to use feminist/queer theory and intersectionality in designing ICT systems, examines different approaches, and considers how we can put insights from feminist thinking into practice in software and system design. This means taking a step back from describing women's work in different contexts to considering the approaches, methods, and tools that will support us in designing more equitable systems. With work as the main focus of this book, this chapter will mainly look at workplace technologies.

Design Justice: The Context of Participatory
and Practice-Based Design

Design justice aims 'to ensure a more equitable distribution of design's benefits and burdens; fair and meaningful participation in design decisions; and recognition of community-based design traditions, knowledge, and practices' (Costanza-Chok 2018, p. 5). We recognize this aim as an important part of the tradition of PD (Simonsen and Robertson 2012), (participatory) action research ((P)AR) (Reason and Bradbury 2001, Cahill 2007), and practice-based design (Wulf et al. 2011). What does a focus on feminist/queer theory, intersectionality as well as postcolonial approaches add to these traditions? Our first step in this chapter is to explore these connections.

'Practice-based' or 'grounded' design, which has grown out of research in CSCW, HCI, and PD, is carried out in iterative cycles of ethnographic fieldwork, concept-building, and artifact creation. Fieldwork provides an in-depth understanding of people's practices based on 'naturalistic' studies of what they are doing (and why), and helps designers get a 'feeling' for the larger context in which those practices are embedded. PD methods and techniques are used to generate ideas for design, take design decisions, and evaluate the different materializations of the design artifact in practice by involving future users in all stages of the design process. An important part of this process is to observe the appropriation of the design and its continuous use in a real (work) context over a long period of time. This reflects the insight that a design is completed in use over time and that understanding its appropriation, including the novel practices that evolve around a design, is a crucial part of the design process (Suchman and Jordan 1988; Wulf et al. 2011 and 2015; Stevens et al. 2018). From a feminist perspective, this can also be seen as responding to a 'desire to design for the Other, which we will never be able to know fully' and 'to do justice to the Other' (Van der Welden and Mörtberg 2012, pp. 678–679). The concepts that are developed in this process are 'grounded' in the sense of resting on data collected in a phase of intense engagement with users and their practices in a particular context: they are instruments to guide the research and design activities.

Practice-based design also takes up the emancipatory drive of PD and (P) AR. The latter offers a framework for inquiry that 'seeks to bring together action and reflection, theory and practice, in participation with others, in the pursuit of practical solutions to issues of pressing concern to people' (Reason and Bradbury 2001, p. 1). Action is an explicit part of the inquiry in an action research project. This implies seeking to elicit dissenting views, as it is through those that new and unexpected aspects of a phenomenon may come to the fore. For participants to be able to express such views, a safe space is needed. Many action research projects aim at involving marginalized groups in the research, seeking their knowledge and abilities. While facilitating dialogue, engagement, and fostering mutual learning is also at the core of PD, action research (AR) puts particular emphasis on developing the practice of reflection, where 'the researcher and participants engage in collective interpretation of the findings and contemplate what can be learned from the experiences' (Lau, 1997, p. 52). The credibility of the data that are produced in a process of collaborative inquiry is ensured by the inclusion of multiple perspectives, and it is supported by 'members' checking the accounts that are produced, commenting and eventually modifying them. This process is complemented by what is called 'standpoint analysis' – the reflection on the various positions that contributed to the knowledge that has been generated: 'AR reminds us that no singular account with one voice can describe the myriad complex viewpoints in any research setting' (Hayes 2011, p. 158). Because of the strong link between inquiry and action, 'the credibility and validity of AR knowledge is measured to a large degree by the "workability" of solutions – that is, their ability to address real problems in the lives of the participants' (p. 158). Damodaran (1996) advocates assessing the validity and credibility of AR in relation to whether or not there is evidence of participants' contributions visible in project outcomes.

We can see here an analogy to PD, where the quality of the IT-based solution reflects on the process of arriving at it: good participatory practices help arrive at a participatory design outcome. In a similar way, a good practical solution to a problem points to a successful participatory inquiry process: 'When evaluating a PD result it should . . . be possible to recognize the users' voice in decisions that have consequences for them – including those decisions that are materialized in artifacts' (Bratteteig and Wagner 2016, p. 142). While the focus of PD is on the design process – how participants' choices move the design – and its result, AR emphasizes the research process – how the inclusion of the research subjects moves the research – and the resulting action.

Feminist approaches to design position themselves in this tradition, contributing to it a focus on gender/intersectionality. They also, Angelika Strohmayer emphasizes, bring a more personal stance towards issues of inclusion and a different kind of politics to PD:

> I think it brings a new kind of criticality. And it brings, I think, a new interrogation of power structures. . . . Because PD is also incredibly political, like, you know, stemming from the union work and all of that stuff. But it brings a different kind of politics into it that is perhaps more personal. And that allows us to address different topics and relate to people in more real . . . in slightly different ways . . . it is also that move away from only looking at gender, and from broadening our understanding of gender and broadening our understanding of interconnected forms of oppression and violence.
>
> (Angelika Strohmayer, interview 10/06/2022)

Taking seriously that gender(s) and forms of marginalization in the work process matter reaches beyond practice-based and participatory forms of designing in an emancipatory spirit. The focus on 'gender' specifically warrants the inclusion of women and of all those who are overlooked, excluded, and undervalued in design. It provides a specific analytic perspective, helping to understand the gendering of technologies and the organizations in which they are embedded. It often also involves a political/activist mission towards more equitable working conditions. Angelika Strohmayer makes a distinction between gender research and feminist research: 'So gender to me is very much we're looking at this very specific topic, whereas feminism is the *how* are we looking at this topic' (Angelika Strohmayer, interview 10/06/2022); hence feminism is about methodology. This distinction between gender research and feminist research differs from Harding's (1986a) focus on the three aspects of gender, which point to how gendering works (in relation to the gender structures, or divisions that revolve around gender, gender identities, and gendered symbolism). Harding's articulation of gender can be seen as a tool of feminism as methodology, in that it helps us see how gendering processes work. Yet it is only one piece of a feminist methodology, which can also include other foci such as intersectionality.

A focus on gender/intersectionality enlarges and transforms the design space, while feminism/queer theory helps to find ways of realizing gender/ social justice in design. It helps ascertain how much diversity there is in the place in which we design, recognize the sources of difference, and identify the experiences, sensibilities, and knowledges of people with whom we design. The ethical-political perspective directs attention to norms and values, such as care, reciprocity, social justice, and agency/enablement. It is concerned with creating the conditions for these values and norms and the basic capabilities they entail to develop, be critically reflected upon, and used in the design process in creative ways. We have to be able to do more than see that differences exist: we also need to understand how differences have historically been overlooked (often as a result of failing to explore the broader contexts in which technological change is occurring), as well as used to perpetuate inequalities. Focussing on the norms and values which the ethical-political perspective forefront is critical to going beyond seeing difference. Another key point is the need to look globally and to focus on context as part of a feminist design justice method. This is also stressed by Arora et al. (2023) who, based on an inquiry on women's work in India and Bangladesh, argue, 'To imagine feminist – or in other words, inclusive – futures of work requires us to see, think, and feel from the perspective of those who have been historically marginalized, across geographies' (p. 20). They add that 'drawing the contours of a concept from locations considered peripheral can make it more inclusive and more broadly applicable than designing from the narrow view of the centre' (pp. 20–21).

The following sections develop these perspectives, in several steps:

- We first describe feminist/queer approaches to design that have experimented with different approaches to inclusion, with a focus on norm-critical, norm-creative, and social justice-oriented design, and with questioning, critically assessing, and 'de-gendering' practices and technologies.
- We then direct attention to the technologies themselves, asking, 'What is wrong with computing?' Our aim here is to identify ways of designing systems that do justice to 'the Other(s)' – ways that are open to other ways of thinking and doing (work), hence inclusive of diversity on many levels.

• And, finally, we take up the design challenges that have been identified in the chapters about women's work in different domains, discussing how these can be addressed from a feminist/intersectional perspective.

Feminist Approaches to Design

Much of current feminist research in HCI and CSCW pays tribute to the writings of Shaowen Bardzell (2010) who in her paper 'Feminist HCI' encouraged researchers to take a step from critical analysis to 'generative contributions' that 'involve the use of feminist approaches explicitly in decision-making and design process to generate new design insights and influence the design process tangibly' (p. 1308). Referring to PD and its achievements, she emphasized the need to understand design contexts and pointed to the contributions of feminism to 'help identify needs and requirements, discover opportunities for design, offer leads toward solutions to design problems, and suggest evaluation criteria for working prototypes, etc.' (p. 1308). She also articulated feminist values, such as 'agency, fulfillment, identity and the self, equity, empowerment, diversity, and social justice' (p. 1301) and their importance in finding alternative ways of designing. Bardzell presented a program of feminist design 'in a nutshell'.

There are inspiring examples of design that have been guided by feminist thinking. They reach from designs for and with women concerning women's health and intimate care (e.g., Almeida et al. 2020), design work with refugees (e.g., Krüger et al. 2021a) to impressive large-scale projects, such as the Archive of Our Own (AO3), which was mostly designed by women and developed into a 'queer female space' (Fiesler et al. 2016). An important body of design-related work was produced, most of it during the last two decades: work that emphasizes the need to make the design of computer technologies visible as a gendered process; norm-critical and norm-creative design as a way of counteracting gendered inscriptions; social justice-oriented design that takes a step from tackling immediate issues to long-term structural problems; methodological work to create more equitable participatory engagement when working in a project; as well as decolonial approaches that not only critique Western models of computing but experiment with 'unexpected views' as a form of resistance.

Identifying Gendered Scripts: Encouraging Critical Alternatives

Feminist approaches to design are firmly anchored in the pioneering work of feminist scholars that produced feminist standpoint theory and the notion of 'situated knowledge', together with numerous empirical studies about the gendering of technologies that helped develop a feminist/intersectional perspective. Most of these approaches are analytical, critically examining technologies that are already in place or the 'gender scripting' of technologies as they are developed. They question the assumptions underlying design choices and make alternatives visible (e.g., Draude and Maaß 2018; Bath 2009). For example, Chivukula (2020) promotes a 'feminism through design' approach that encourages 'critical alternatives, by considering affective dimensions, and by using feminist values as problem frames' (p. 39).

Norm-critical design is another approach that feminist researchers engage with:

> It's really around where did the norms come from that get inscribed into technologies? And how can you design things more consciously? Or how can you kind of change designs to de-emphasize or emphasize certain values and norms that are seen to be inclusive or seem to be representative?
>
> (Ingrid Erickson, interview 03/30/2022)

Norm-critical design often uses ethnographic studies to challenge social norms that contribute to inequalities and social exclusion in a field (e.g., Isaksson et al. 2017). It is complemented by 'norm-*creative* design thinking – developing design solutions that counteract such norms through reflection on what might be' (Nilsson and Jahnke 2018, p. 376). A similar approach was articulated in the 1970s by Arnstein and Christakis (1975) in their 'futures creative paradigm' approach to technology assessment, which sought to more explicitly include notions of desirable social outcomes into technology assessments in order to challenge norms and set an agenda for more desirable futures. While the norm-critical phase challenges designers to question (hidden) assumptions that put anyone outside those norms at risk of 'being forgotten, disregarded, neglected, or otherwise discriminated against' (Nilsson and Jahnke 2018, p. 379), the next phase consists in laying the grounds for design alternatives.

One of Nilsson and Jahnke's (2018) examples is the gynecological examination chair, which puts a woman in an uncomfortable position 'with her feet placed in stirrups that separate her legs and expose her genital area' (p. 386). The design team explored a radical alternative based on women's experiences – the 'Andro Chair' designed for men. It elicited strong reactions, as it made the potentially humiliating situation of pelvic examinations clear, encouraging the male observers to think about design alternatives. Another design example Nilsson and Jahnke present is the waiting room situation in a hospital, where the most active patients, mostly men, received faster attention. Using PD techniques, the design team arrived at two design solutions: an app that allows patients to describe their symptoms when they arrive at the emergency unit 'in a neutral way'; and displays offering information about wait time and available staff to patients in the waiting room. Another example of norm-critical and creative design is d'Ignazio et al.'s (2016) work on the 'breast milk pump'. They engaged with the ideas of over 1,000 women to improve an artifact that many women hate having to use, and collected stories expressing 'feelings of shame, guilt, humiliation and anxiety' (p. 2619).

What distinguishes these examples from classic PD projects is their strong emphasis on a critique-based feminist approach with its focus on gender(s) and on how to counteract the gendering of technologies. What they share with PD is a strong moral and political commitment. Realizing such a commitment under real-world circumstances poses challenges, which we discussed with respect to hospital work, where the prevalence of a managerial logic results in computer technologies that are introduced for the purpose of exerting control over nursing practices, 'hardwiring' hierarchical structures and reducing the space for care-related work (Chapter 8). While sympathizing with a feminist approach, Donia and Shaw point out that 'even those E + VID (ethics and values in design) approaches that embraced the most critical view of the world, such as design justice and feminist HCI, did not embrace a "low agency" view of the designer' (2021, p. 57). In most real-world contexts, including large technology companies where much design work happens, designer's agency is constrained and, to make feminist and participatory approaches successful, these constraints must be well understood and possibly also resisted with strategies aiming 'at corporate management, regulators, or others implicated in the design and development ecosystem' (p. 57). Often such approaches require an engagement beyond what we typically think of as the boundaries of design.

The Challenges of Engaging in Social Justice-Oriented Design

A commitment to social justice through design requires that we enlarge the design space, asking designers 'to move beyond individual action and toward designing for collective action, by focussing on regional and national contexts; activist groups, and/or nonprofit organizations', Dombrowski et al. (2016, p. 661) argue. They define the goals of social justice as including 'transformation, recognition, reciprocity, enablement, distribution, and accountability' (p. 657). Design in this view is part of a larger endeavour to counteract social injustices.

The project with sex-work charities by Strohmayer et al. (2017) is of this kind. Its main aim was to support women sex workers in the reporting of and alerting to incidents of violence and crime using digital technologies.

Technologies were not in the foreground, although they were used in innovative ways. The researchers engaged in intense conversations with volunteers and sex workers who saw their common work as

> stand[ing] in solidarity with sex workers who had experienced violent crimes, and as a chance to spread positive messages around staying safe, the positive emotions that come out of reporting a crime and the support that is available if someone were to report a crime committed against them.
>
> (Strohmayer et al. 2017, p. 3356)

At the same time, the project contributed to addressing the wider structural issues of sex work. Safe reporting of and alerting to violence and crime is one important step towards enabling sex workers to do their work in a safer and more supportive environment, the researchers argue. The 'technologies for harm reduction' they provided play an important role in the charity's efforts to mobilize activists in the sex workers' rights movement, remove the taboo of making crimes committed against sex workers public, and ultimately create a space for policy change based on data. Moreover, 'the chance to share intelligence with police also allows direct empowerment through the criminal justice process' (p. 3358). These goals cannot be addressed by an external design team all alone but require building alliances with the main actors in the field. In our increasingly complex world where system integration is expected, alliance building between actors is increasingly important.

Social justice-oriented design almost always seeks to engage with underserved and marginalized populations. An example is Schorch et al.'s (2016) design work for 'those that are overlooked' – chronically ill people and their informal carers. Such 'equitable engagements' (Harrington et al. 2019) entail risks that need to be openly addressed and reflected upon. One of these risks has been highlighted by Bennett and Rosner (2019) who critically examined the 'promise of empathy', an emerging trend in HCI studies in working with people with disabilities.[1] Their study refers to well-known design techniques such as simulation and personas. Empathy may go wrong, they argue, illustrating how designers may focus on their own interpretation of the disabled experience, displacing the experiences and emotions of the disabled persons with and for whom they design. This observation points to the need to recognize 'the range of emotional, political, and historical relationships of which empathy is a part' (p. 299). This is an important insight to reflect on,

---

[1] The term disability, although widely used with good intents, is criticized because it is connected with deviance from what is considered 'normal' and often based on a deficit discourse.

in particular when engaging in social justice-oriented design work with marginalized populations.

The dangers of ethnocentric bias have for a long time been an issue in anthropology and cultural studies. Erdheim (1984) has pointed to the blind spots associated with one's own biography, the unconscious distortions of 'otherness' caused by an unreflected, naive, often good-willed ethnocentricity. Without a larger understanding of the historically shaped experiences of being in the world as a disabled person and the resources that come with it, designers may 'distance themselves from disabled people, framing the disabled identity as one distinct' from their own (Bennet and Rosner 2019, p. 298). They may end up with disabled people serving as 'spectacles for designers to look upon for inspiration' (p. 298). Bennet and Rosner propose to work on imagining and apprehending in 'partnerships' and looking at developing mutual understanding as 'a process of ongoing attunement' (p. 298). Starting out from standpoint theory, Brulé and Spiel (2019) critically reflect on how, in the context of PD, identities in relation to gender and disability shape relationships between researchers and marginalized children in a participatory project. One of the recurrent conflicts they identified is 'that the external assessment of disability does not necessarily match children's self-identity' (p. 7). They point to the difficulties of disentangling the communities and standpoints that influence the children's identities and the conflicts arising between them.

Harrington et al. (2019) take up this larger concern pointing to the importance of reflexivity for a feminist/intersectional approach. Their experiences in a series of community-based PD workshops with underserved populations in the USA led them to understand the importance of considering the history of a research site. They define developing such an understanding as a method of trust-building among researchers and community residents. Research engagements often lead to 'participants recognizing that the data, information, and stories collected will tell a narrative over which they are not in complete control' (p. 18); a fear that may result 'from the intergenerational trauma caused by academic and government institutions that have historically caused harm to these communities. Additionally, the fear of disclosing illegal or stigmatizing information can be felt deeply' (p. 18). Harrington et al. also point to the danger of devaluing the existing resources in underserved communities and a 'valorization of technical innovation along with corporate notions of design' (p. 19). Connected with this was the insight that what we often have contextualized as 'personal' was in fact frequently 'political' (p. 18). Harrington et al. also point to the danger of devaluing the existing resources in underserved communities and a 'valorization of technical innovation along with corporate notions of design' (p. 19).

Social justice-oriented design is often not only action-oriented but activist (Leal et al. 2021). Both approaches use participatory techniques to directly address social problems. However, activist research is more overtly political. An example can be found in Strohmayer et al. (2020) who co-organized a local activist march of sex workers, presenting 'reflections on the use of digital technologies during the public activist march, a private service for commemoration, and the development of a semi-public archive to collect experiences of the day' (p. 87). Historically, much of feminist thinking was (and still is) strongly connected with activism. Consequentially, also much of current work from a feminist/intersectional perspective is deeply action-oriented and activist. The research and design with and for platform workers is of this kind (Irani and Silberman 2016; Harmon and Silberman 2018).

When engaging with marginalized and particularly vulnerable populations, much of the work is not about design, as Strohmayer explicates: 'the nature of the discipline is to design a technology that will solve a problem. That's the underlying premise of a lot of work. And I just don't think that works in a lot of spaces' (Strohmayer, interview 10/06/2022). It is important to move away from a solutionist approach to what she calls 'crafting safe spaces'. She experimented with crafting and working with textiles as an important element of a feminist approach to design. It allows building 'solidarity and sisterhood', acknowledging the value of silence and of doing things alongside other women in complex life situations. Technology comes in with, for example, digital augmentation – 'you can add new layers to things, right? Like stitching as activism has done, ... or as documentation of community knowledge or [a record of] oppressed knowledge' (Strohmayer, interview 10/06/2022).

'Crafting safe spaces' is part of what Asad (2019) calls 'prefigurative design'. It grew out of women's (and other genders') experiences of oppression, which may make collaborating in a research project difficult. Maria Menendez Blanco expresses the need for safe spaces, saying that she would put funding into creating a research group from a feminist perspective:

> I think ... the nicest collaborations I ever had, they were not like, with women, ... but they were with people who care about inclusion or care about democracy or ... but really, from a feminist perspective. ... [H]ow do you talk with people? I think all these matters in research. So, I will put my money into making these groups like nicer. Nicer, more welcoming, more caring. I think and then every time the research will come after.
>
> (Maria Menendez Blanco, interview 03/03/2022)

'Safe spaces' is an old concept that stands for having a space for resistance and the freedom to organize; it denotes 'safety from any emotional harm or othering (being treated as abnormal or alien)' (Scheuerman et al. 2018,

p. 39). While it is used to indicate the need to counterbalance harm experienced by vulnerable users of technologies, such as transgender persons or women refugees (e.g., Hedditch and Vyas 2023), it proposes a more general strategy of preparing the grounds for social justice-oriented technology design. Lewis et al. (2015) suggest a distinction between 'safe *from* and safe *to*, demonstrating that once women are safe *from* harassment, abuse and misogyny, they feel safe *to* be cognitively, intellectually and emotionally expressive' (p. 105).

Ahmadi et al. (2020) have conceptualized feminist living labs as a research infrastructure for HCI work that provide a safe space for participants. The living lab situation allowed women employed in the German video game industry to freely exchange experiences, to critically reflect, and to build a community. The researchers describe how 'the openness of the "geeky" corporate culture and quite young personnel with a similar age-range between researchers and participants as well as shared mindsets towards feminist ambitions' also helped to build trustful relationships' (p. 20). Their study shows how a safe space can help 'understand and challenge dominant practices of technology design and give voices to design (of any kind) to otherwise marginalized groups'. Although not always considered at the core of design, the work of setting up and maintaining a living lab infrastructure has relevance for design outcomes, as it fosters processes of social co-creation that can lay the grounds for 'confidence and skills which are undoubtedly design relevant' (p. 10).

Decolonizing Approaches

Decolonizing approaches can be seen as a continuation and rephrasing of feminist/intersectional approaches to design in the context of Southern locations. They combine a deeply critical and liberating perspective on colonialization and power asymmetries with sometimes radically novel ideas about computing: 'Approaching the field of computing from unexpected angles, a view from the South pays equal attention to contests over knowledge and over materials and desires that take place within and across multiple sites' (Amrute and Murillo 2020, p. 2). While not being able to do justice to the richness of the research and design work done in countries of the South, it is important to note that this work reaches beyond the critical analysis of 'the complicated and complicit relationships that computing projects have to the development and settling of Indigenous lands and the continued imperial relationships such projects support' (p. 7).

Among the remarkable examples of practical design work is a study by Andrade et al. (2021) who have worked with Maori IT professionals to describe the specific cultural elements underlying their practices, with a view to enhancing the representation of indigenous computer scientist and communities in design projects. In Brazil, which has a large computer science community that is dominated by (white) men, numerous initiatives seek to involve Black women in computing (Chapter 9). Free software-based digital infrastructures and networks have been developed in Brazilian communities serving as 'situated models of resistance' (Roussel and Stolfi 2020, p. 1). These projects work with communities of Black people and involve technologists, international artists, and activists. Russel and Stolfi describe a Latin American feminist server as an example of 'minoritized decentralized technological practices that convey integral organizational models opposing capitalist hegemony' (p. 1). There are also joyful and provocative forms of using technologies, such as the feminist drones that convert their original purposes 'tak[ing] advantage of gaps in legislation to distribute abortion pills across borders' (Sued 2018, p. 104); or 'a drone called Droncita, which records the social protests in Mexico City, providing counter-information on the power and number of attendees at the protesting marches' (pp. 104–105; see also Suarez 2016).

Decolonizing approaches also have a place in Western societies where researchers from other countries receive their education in computer science, engage in design projects, and seek to get access to important publication venues. Marisol Wong-Villacres' account of the difficulties she and her colleague encountered in the HCI community as a researcher from Ecuador is an example. She articulates her experience with using the concept of intersectionality (and, in general, the feminist literature) in ways that were not considered 'appropriate' by reviewers:

> ... not being an American, I didn't fully understand ... the importance for it to be always related to black women. To me, it was an interesting academic tool to understand this data that had nothing to do with black women, it had to do with vulnerability – extreme levels and different kinds of vulnerability.
>
> (Marisol Wong-Villacres, interview 09/30/2022)

She felt criticized as not having the appropriate view of concepts of importance for her agenda, such as care and intersectionality – 'the way we looked at it was more like intersecting and interacting systems of oppression'. These experiences are also expressed in a paper by a group of researchers from five Latin American countries (including Marisol Wong-Villacres: Reynolds-Cuéllar et al. 2022). It addresses the potential of 'intellectual dialogues between dominant forms of understanding PD and Latin American epistemic perspectives and cosmologies' with the aim to 'analyze the alternative trajectories they suggest for PD practice and knowledge-making' (p. 1). The authors propose an alternative approach to reviewing PD papers that they based on five principles – 'citational justice, epistemic justice, emancipation, relationality and positionality'.

Feminist/intersectional/decolonizing approaches often have the character of resistance; their focus is local but their critical vision global and directed at the ways computers are used to cement oppressive power structures, marginalizing parts of the population, discarding their needs, disrespecting their knowledge. This leads us to return to the question 'What is wrong with computing'?' that was raised at the end of Chapter 9.

What Is Wrong with Computing?

There are numerous and ongoing critiques of the ways IT artifacts and systems are made and deployed in practice. At the core of these critiques is the computing field, which 'still sees its realm as mainly in technical artifacts and their mathematical foundations, a view that tends to ignore the social practices these artifacts are embedded in' (Simone et al. 2022, p. 317).

(Exclusive) Reliance on Mathematical Formalisms

Let us go back to an influential paper by Joan Greenbaum, 'The head and the heart' (1990), where she elegantly analyzes what is wrong with computing. One of the core sentences in this paper is, 'the use of gender-biased dichotomies [what Harding (1996a) might call gender structures] strongly influences both the questions system developers ask and the way questions are asked' (p. 8). The scientific tradition of 'technical rationality', which in turn is based on 'gender-based myths' (what Harding might refer to as gender symbolism), obscures those parts of the world that are outside what can be broken down 'into manageable and controllable descriptions' (Greenbaum 1990, p. 11). While the process of developing design specifications is clearly effective for certain kinds of processes, it leads developers to 'simply cut away the parts that don't fit into formal descriptions' (p. 14). The result is systems that do not capture and support many salient aspects of work and the contexts in which it is embedded, which remain invisible.

These insights have been taken up by feminist scholars and practitioners of PD. German feminist computer scientists, such as Britta Schinzel (2004), questioned the objectivity in modelling and formalization that is at the heart of computer science. She described software as based on formalized – 'supposedly objective orders of reality' (p. 253) – that exclude other viewpoints and alternative ways of knowing. Draude and Maaß (2018) discuss how the 'semiotization, formalization, and algorithmization' underlying computing inevitably leads to selectively blending out important aspects of real-world problems. Marsden and Haag (2016) problematize the increasingly common use of personas in a design process, showing how this runs the risk of reinscribing existing stereotypes and following more of an I-methodological than a user-centred approach.

Feminist scholars also demonstrated that computer education in schools and colleges that emphasized mathematical formalism deterred women from computing. Frenkel (1990) argued that 'BASIC, Pascal, and the emphasis on step-by-step division of functions, and formal planning in formal languages' (p. 41) tended to discourage women who were more interested in using computers for solving practical problems. Clegg and Trayhurn (2000) criticized curricula that relied on mathematical formalisms, giving precedence to areas such as AI, formal methods and computer vision' (p. 78) as failing to recognize 'the plurality of phenomenologically based ways of knowing in computing' (p. 88). The emphasis on mathematical formalism reinforces gender structures, which in turn fortify gender symbolism.

Several types of answers have evolved alongside these criticisms: one is participatory design that explicitly starts from the experiences and practices of the participants involved in the design, before any kind of system is developed; the other one is (ongoing) research concerned with how to build more open and flexible systems. While they have not originated in a feminist critique of the ways technologies are conceived and built, they are essential building blocks of a feminist/intersectional approach to design. Both approaches are essential: PD allows us to articulate designs that give voice to the real-world needs of those often silenced, while more open and flexible systems are required to implement those designs and allow them to change over time.

Changing Practices of Systems Design

PD from its very beginning recognized that laypeople are not trained to understand specifications written in a formal language. As part of the UTOPIA project, Pelle Ehn and Morten Kyng (1985) presented the 'tool perspective' to systems design. These tools were simple mock-ups that the graphical workers could use to simulate page makeup, so that the designers could observe them and get a better understanding of the technical and practice-related issues the workers experienced. Cooperative prototyping became a common approach in PD. It allows designers and users to explore the problem space and possible solutions in a design project. This was an important step in bringing designers closer to the world of users, preventing them from 'simply cut[ting] away the parts that don't fit into formal descriptions' (Greenbaum 1990, p. 14). In a PD project, Bratteteig and Wagner (2014) argued,

> the running prototype tested 'in the wild' by users in a real use context may replace a specification document. Also, key to the practice of PD is that the analysis of an application area or problem space and the construction of the solution are inseparable (Schön 1983). Building a prototype is an intricate part of doing the analysis.
>
> (Bratteteig and Wagner 2014, p. 3)

Prototyping requires understanding and integrating practices and materials from the specific place of design; hence the knowledge workers have developed. Moreover, a prototype does not 'simply speak for itself, but must continually be "read" for its significance and lessons' (Blomberg et al. 1996, p. 259).

Techniques such as cooperative prototyping help deal with one of the dilemmas of computer science: while categories or models cannot give a full account of real life, building systems is not possible without them. Unfortunately, computer scientists (and others) often tend to mistake the partial and simplified for the whole and find it difficult to see and acknowledge the political in the artifacts they build. PD seeks to open and enlarge the design space until the design decisions that are made are well grounded in the experiences and knowledge of those who participate. Recent works on methods and techniques such as (digital) storytelling (Waycott et al. 2017) recognize the importance of 'voice' in the design space, and the need to ensure that designers as well as other stakeholders/prospective technology users have a shared language and understanding of their topic as well as of each other. They have organized the design space they are sharing in a manner that is capable of leveraging what Wilson et al. (2020) have labelled 'communication differences'.

Another key challenge is to design for 'flexible use', which is a long-standing issue for researchers engaged in PD. Toni Robertson expresses the need for flexible designs and for PD as a path towards achieving this flexibility:

> ... if you're going to use the basic principles of people had a right to have a say in their technology design, if you're going to test it, if you're going to make it flexible, all of those things, in theory ought to be covered by that kind of design approach.
>
> (Toni Robertson, interview 05/18/2022)

Working critically in design is knowing how to make a design flexible, Robertson argues, so that it can be appropriated by people that are different.

Indeed, a specific characteristic of IT-based artifacts or systems that have been developed in a context-aware and participative way is their technical flexibility and malleability. This notion reaches back to the 1990s when researchers that were connected to the PD community developed a strong interest in what at that time was called the tailorability of systems. Researchers started studying people who worked as 'user-designers' customizing software to the needs of users in companies (Trigg and Bødker 2004; Gantt and Nardi 1992). This interest in tailoring, customizing, or configuring has stimulated a research stream referred to as 'end user development' (Lieberman et al., 2006; Paternò and Wulf, 2017).

In a paper entitled 'Malleability in the hands of end-users', Cabitza and Simone (2017) define malleability as 'the capability of interactive systems to empower end users in tailoring them in different ways' (p. 5) (see also Chapter 1). They refer to the work of James Moore (1985) who connects the logical malleability of computer systems with ethical concerns. It makes them

> less rigid 'political artifacts' (Winner, 1980), that is artifacts that do have politics by either imposing or reflecting political and moral values, e.g., in the categories (Suchman, 1993) they afford and disseminate, and in the behaviors that they promote and constrain. This is because the designers' politics can be confronted and modified (at least to some extent and in principle) at run time, by the end users themselves, if they do not fit the users' worldview or if changes made them no longer correct or applicable.
>
> (Cabitza and Simone 2017, pp. 5–6)

Cabitza and Simone emphasize malleability at the semantic level of work practices. Malleability on this level includes the possibility to extend and modify the basic building blocks of a system 'if new digitized practices made this necessary'; that means it supports appropriation. Based on their work in hospitals, Cabitza and Simone define a 'logic of bricolage', a complex conceptual framework, which 'conceives of malleability as a first-level affordance to be put in the hands, i.e., in full control of the end users to empower them in appropriating and adapting their applications at different (potentially any) level of detail' (p. 1).

There is a key lesson to be drawn from the work on how to design flexible systems that are open to end-user development: the importance of technology construction in terms of architecture, malleability/flexibility, and how to balance requirements that change with the context of use for realizing the potential of a feminist/intersectional approach to design.

Repurposing AI from a Feminist/Intersectional Perspective

AI-based technologies pose additional challenges that Alison Adam addressed in her seminal book *Artificial knowing: Gender and the thinking machine* (1998). She put forward the notion of feminist AI (FAI) as an approach that explores 'how AI can be informed by feminist theory and be used for feminist projects' (p. 157). Toupin (2023) refers to some still unfinished projects that attempt to realize the idea of an FAI. Caroline Sinders (2020) initiated the development of a feminist dataset to feed an FAI-powered chatbot with whom a user can converse about feminism. The NGO DataGenero is about to create an open-source AI system that 'will collaborate with criminal court officials in Argentina and Mexico to bring more transparency to the judicial treatment of gender-based violence (GBV) cases against women and LGBTIQ + people' (p. 9). While Sinders' project is about 'facilitating the invisible, slow, and nitty-gritty work of creating a community-led data set' (Toupin 2023, p. 6), the work of DataGenero is led by the question of how to use AI for a feminist engagement for social justice:

> How can AI algorithms help us understand the phenomenon of GBV, its subtypes and their contexts? What happens with the less visible types of violence such as the psychological or the economic? How can we use these algorithms to show how judges rule, guaranteeing the protection of people's sensitive data? We hope that starting to answer these questions through our project contributes concretely to, in the long term, facilitate access to justice to women and LGBTIQ+ people who suffer GBV, and increase people's trust in the justice system.
>
> (Feldfeber et al. 2022, p. 3)

The research team of DataGenero has developed a prototype based on AI techniques that will support the publication and maintenance of data from GBV cases. These and other emergent activities led by feminist researchers are about how to appropriate and repurpose AI and ML techniques from an 'intersectional feminist, anti-solutionist stance' (Feldfeber et al. 2022, p. 1), with the ambition to, ultimately, push for a reform of the judicial system. With its projects, DataGenero pursues a political/activist mission.

Specific Design Challenges at Work: How to Address Them

The chapters about different areas of women's work have described different kinds of design challenges, which this section takes up from a feminist/ intersectional perspective. A good starting point is the notion of prefigurative design, which Mariam Asad (2019) defines as meant to frame conversations and negotiate boundaries around what kind of work needs to be done and to set goals and expectations across researchers and partners for the outcomes and impact of the collaborative work. . . . [P]refigurative design tries to articulate opportunities for researchers to engage with and support justice work in three ways: through *social relationships, distribution of resources,* and by *building counter-structures.*

(Asad 2019, p. 2)

While Asad has formulated her approach based on fieldwork with activist organizations, the notion of prefigurative design also applies more generally to design. It emphasizes the need to set up the conditions for participation and collaboration on different levels – 'from the emotional to the administrative and bureaucratic to the ethical' (p. 13).

We have identified four issues that a feminist/intersectional approach to design should attend to in different areas of work:

- making women's work visible and fighting marginalization;
- combining design with professionalization and upskilling strategies;
- designing for improved working conditions; and
- designing with care in mind.

Making Women's Work Visible and Fighting Marginalization

Making invisible aspects of work visible has been and still is a prime concern of feminist studies of women's work. Roslyn Feldberg (1984) pointed out the fact that some of the key skills required in occupations that are primarily performed by women remain invisible and undervalued; hence, they are not recognized as skills and are not remunerated. These invisible skills – skills that do not appear in formal job description and task analyses – are not only crucial to building good systems; making them visible is key to achieving social/design justice.

Examples of the invisibility of skills in areas of women's work abound. Clerical work and data work have notoriously been described as routine and low-skilled, while studies of feminist scholars have brought the professional character of the work to the fore. Non-clinical work, in particular the work of medical secretaries and their key contributions to the documentation of clinical cases, is mostly invisible. Platform or crowdworkers remain invisible to their clients; so are their vital services for the AI industry and the unpaid work they need to do to get work. Maintainability and repair work of all kinds tend to remain largely invisible. In highly automated work contexts, where workers are often thought of only performing residual tasks, the numerous activities and procedures they have to engage in to make the machines work tend to be overlooked. Workplace marginalization is often combined with sexual and other forms of harassment. Bias in diagnostic tools and screening technologies reinforces and/or results in marginalization. The same holds for large groups of people or communities, such as non-binary people, refugees, and migrants whose culture, perspectives of life, and needs remain unaccounted for.

From a feminist/intersectional perspective, a commitment to making visible and fighting marginalization requires action on several levels. First, as we have argued with respect to nursing information systems and nursing protocols (Chapter 8), standardized categories do not have the power to capture the invisible, but often critically important, aspects of work. While modern organizations have to rely on standardized systems and procedures, designers have to be mindful of local variations and those aspects of work that escape categorial schemes: aspects that are based on experience and intuition, emotional labour, relationship management, and so forth.

On a methodological level, the aim of recognizing invisibility and marginalization gives leverage to PAR and an ethnographic approach. While this has also been emphasized in PD and CSCW research, a feminist/intersectional approach draws attention to the need for researchers to care for their research subjects. Toni Robertson's story about her research in a small design company that was founded by a group of women describes a situation of mutual caretaking between researcher and research subjects. The women mainly worked from home and held weekly meetings:

> And I went and interviewed each of them in their home and got access to all the communications on the bulletin board. And then, really interesting things happened because they just treated me like another work person, because they saw me as often as they saw each other. And then they started keeping notes for me and ringing me up, because I'd also tell them what I was doing. And they'd gather stuff for me. And then someone said, I recorded this conversation for you between two of them that they'd had through the week, because they were working on something together. And, and she gave me the tape of it.
>
> (Toni Robertson, interview 05/18/2022)

Howard and Irani (2019) describe 'how care, vulnerability, harm, and emotions shape ethnographic and qualitative data': 'Care orients researchers to embodied sensitivity, experience, affect, and the provisioning of resources and knowledge' (p. 3). They also point to the possibilities of researchers to 'make contacts and circulate stories people otherwise would not share widely' (p. 7). This can be especially important when working with participants from 'the forgotten margins' who may have experienced a loss of control over their stories, once researchers or others have used them for their own purposes.

Research with these persons presents the opportunity to 'elevate' their stories, preserving their authenticity (Harrington et al. 2020). In other circumstances, researchers may be able to give voice to important stories when hierarchies and consequences may leave worker participants at risk if they share their own stories (Balka and Wagner 2006).

Finally, engaging with research subjects in social justice-oriented design requires designers to address the wider structural issues of work. Issues of invisibility and marginalization cannot be resolved without building alliances from the start of a design project. Such alliances help widen the design space and engage 'more explicitly with precisely the key concerns of social justice – the multiplicity of stakeholders, power relations, and the unevenness of social and political systems' (Dombrowski et al. 2016, p. 659). One recent example of social justice-oriented design is Ismail and Kumar's (2018) study of health data work performed by social health workers (ASHAs) in underserved communities in Delhi, India. The researchers sought to understand the ASHAs' institutional roles and responsibilities and unpack their 'relationships and power dynamics with various actors involved in data collection' (p. 6). They describe the ways in which the ASHAs' data-collection practices evidence sensitivity to social norms; how the women 'navigate social barriers in a patriarchal society' and how their data-collection practices 'reflect and foster feminist solidarity' (p. 2). Key to the research was a deep understanding of the structural issues shaping the work of social health workers in rural India and how solidarity meant working with other workers in the health-care system and with the local communities despite numerous conflicts and 'despite little recognition by the incentive system of the physical and emotional labor involved' (p. 17).

Ismail and Kumar (2018) refer to Chandra Mohanty's postcolonial feminist approach as having helped them focus on the 'micropolitics of context, subjectivity, and struggle and the macropolitics of political systems and processes' (2003, p. 501).

Combining Design with Professionalization and Upskilling Strategies

Making invisible skills and knowledge visible is a first step, designing work-places that allow women and other marginalized workers to deploy their skills, learn, and grow is a next step. Let us go back to Toni Robertson's story of her research in a women-run business:

> ... it was about this little company of eight, seven of whom were women, ... or the two women who ran it and left their previous employer because of being taken over by a multinational, who had basically made it horrible to work in, they did dump

computer-based learning, basically, in the CD ROM days, the very early days of that, and they decided to set up their own company that made it nice to work in. And the partner of one of them was this kind of really nerdy folk who set up a company with modems, and early bulletin board technology, and they all worked from home. And they had made of their own volition a CD, on contraception for family planning. . . . [T]hey met weekly and they had data processes that had worked about maintaining the interaction between them, while they were separate, where they were basically doing a whole lot of relationship repair and maintenance work, which she was describing to me in terms of checking that other people were alright, and looking forward, and so on.

One of her main intentions was

> . . . just trying to understand and articulate the skills that these women had in communicative work. That yes, we explained because of the position they occupied in relation to men, but not necessarily essentialist ones that the blokes I was working with could use an excuse to not have them themselves.
>
> (Toni Robertson, interview 05/18/2022)

One of the challenges in this research was to recognize the women's skills without falling into the trap of gender stereotyping. There are numerous examples that demonstrate how the skills that women supposedly tend to develop may be appreciated in specific contexts, while at the same time being contrasted with highly valued masculine skills. Including women in teams in male-dominated areas of work, such as manufacturing or computing, is often thought of as improving performance due to women's social skills 'such as conflict resolution, humane decision making, the ability to build a pleasant and relaxed atmosphere' (Wallace 1999, p. 29). The 'mixed skills' argument in the IT sector builds on the idea that women are particularly suited for certain types of computer work (an essentialist position, which also reflects deeply held views of gender symbolism); and the notion of care as a specific female quality contributes to the highly unequal distribution of care responsibilities.

Unfortunately, skills are often redefined in a gendered way in the process of computerization/automation. Women are often relegated to the low-paid jobs, as for example Brumley's (2018) study of a manufacturing plant demonstrates; or the introduction of IT systems is used by management to de-professionalize an occupation such as nursing (e.g., Martin and Bouchard 2020). Ensmenger (2010) argued that the professionalization of computing that started in the 1960s had an excluding effect on women (reinforcing gender structures) as it made programming masculine (reinforcing gender symbolism).

There is a fine balance between making women's skills visible and locking women in particular job categories. Norm-critical design with respect to gendered skill definitions would require designers and the organization or community involved in a design project to not just develop an IT artifact but to engage in workplace design with the aim of ensuring that the technology is used to preserve and expand skills (rather than reduce them). This also requires supporting (women) workers in learning and appropriating the new technologies and advocating for fair compensation for their new work. Varasani et al. (2022) have made this argument with respect to crowd-based work. This is another step in a process that widens the design space in view of accomplishing design justice.

Improving Working Conditions

A burning issue concerning work in highly developed as well as poor countries is working conditions. Bannon et al. (2011) argued that

> issues of working conditions, issues of workload and stress, of dependability and safety, of the debilitating effect of monotonously repetitive work without scope for learning, of professional autonomy in making decisions – are, if not essential or ubiquitous, then surely typical. Or to put it differently, these issues are regular features of working life in contemporary society.
>
> (Bannon et al. 2011, pp. 226–227)

This also regards workplaces that are traditionally occupied by men; but women tend to be more severely affected by adverse working conditions, as most of them have to combine work with childcare and other family responsibilities. Examples of adverse working conditions from all areas of work abound – hard and sometimes dangerous and unhealthy work, long working hours, time pressure, and hostile work environments, in particular in male-dominated areas of work.

Claiming agency over working conditions is a traditional goal of trade unions that, historically, have not always cared for women's work and women's health. Ingrid Erickson claims that 'even in this tightest space we have some agency', which she considers something 'universal' (Ingrid Erickson, interview 03/30/ 2022). How technology design may contribute to improving working conditions is rarely an explicit design issue. A concern for how work and working conditions affect a person's personal life is considered outside the design space of most design projects, including those that are based on an ethnographic study; and this although, Lucy Suchman argues, 'at least within anthropology, ethnography is just inextricably connected to the wider engagements that people have' (Lucy Suchman, interview 04/22/2022). However, the recent work done to improve online labour conditions for platform workers shows the growing commitment to orienting design to issues of social justice (Harmon and Silberman et al. 2019). Another example is Matilal's (2020) study of the Indian software industry where she points to the need to support women to exercise agency over the scheduling of working-time.

There are research traditions that have working conditions as their key concern. One of the main aims of workplace design in the tradition of German industrial sociology is to widen workers' space for responsibility and control over stress-relevant working conditions. Francophone ergonomics has a strong focus on redesigning work with the aim of improving working conditions. One of the early French studies of the work of telephone operators – all of them women – found evidence of intense stress (a consequence of having to read micro cards on viewers and to search for information under time pressure) resulting in sleep disturbances, digestive problems, and even personality changes that affected those close to them. 'The operators' general opinion was', Dessors et al. (1979) found, 'that the work is mindless, that they themselves are just talking machines, robotized, as they are forbidden to have personal conversations with clients or colleagues during work, and that this robotlikeness stays with them after work' (p. 497). Quebec-based Francophone ergonomists have women's occupational health and safety as one of their main research foci (e.g., Messing et al. 2021). Messing and collaborators observed strategies of what they call 'work–family articulation', among them schedule choice ('bidding'), which also involved receiving and exchanging schedules; and health protection where the concern was that women do not 'sacrifice their health to keep or advance in their jobs' (p. 234). Quebec ergonomists also 'hypothesized that work organization as it affects work–family articulation (WFA) might be a collective dimension of work and therefore part of the purview of conventional ergonomic intervention' (p. 230).

Feminist/intersectional approaches to design can take up these and other experiences and, for example, push for the integration of gender into ergonomic analyses, which 'remains a conceptual, methodological and political challenge' (Messing et al. 2021, p. 219).

Designing with Care in Mind

Care is maybe the concept that has been most influential in design-oriented research communities. Maria Puig de le Bellacasa (2011) has suggested that we take responsibility for the artifacts we design, turning them into 'matters of care'. She adds, 'Potentially, matters of care can be found in every context; exhibiting them is valuable especially when caring seems to be out of place, superfluous or simply absent' (p. 94). For Ingrid Erickson the concept of care is one way of thinking about women's work:

> Because it has traditionally been either given up for as not relevant because it couldn't be tracked or traced or improved or managed or something like that. And in that obscurity, and in that invisibility, ... there's something about this idea of it not being measured. I think that sort of the gender or the feminist move there is like, like preserving room for a diversity of ways of knowing and ways of working without it being seen as slow or inefficient or optimal or optimized.
>
> (Ingrid Erickson, interview 03/30/2022)

She also insists on not looking at care work as just a gendered activity:

> There's something that is more valuing of randomness ... it's not around profits ... and efficiency is what I'm trying to say, it's often around kind of being able to sort of deal with students and all of their complexity or being able to deal with patients and all of their complexity. We can call that care work, we can call that inefficiency, right, or slow or something like that.
>
> (Ingrid Erickson, interview 03/30/2022)

This is another norm-critical and norm-creative move inspired by feminist theory. It seeks to defend care against the managerial logic that drives much of IT development, making space for experience and intuition, fighting against the replacement of caring people by machines, but also standing up against the dictate of efficiency by making space for activities that are slow and may not be 'measurable'.

The case studies in different areas of women's work encourage us to delve more deeply into caretaking as an aspect of the many small and overlooked tasks work may require; to ask who the caretakers are and how they are remunerated. But also, they ask us to understand and acknowledge the care it takes to review and maintain databases and algorithms or to forge collaborations with robots, fitting them into grown practices and the temporalities of human activities. Care, Krueger et al. (2021) argue, may mean 'paying attention to a potential difference between intended beneficiaries of a technological artifact and those that maintain it' (p. 11). They look at designers as carers and at carers – in their case community collaborators that assist refugees and migrants in their efforts to settle in Germany – emphasizing that it is legitimate to ask, 'do I want to be involved in caring for the designed artifact too?' This insight underpins the need to design not just artifacts but also work trajectories that include new skill acquisition. It demonstrates the importance of considering who will care for the designed artifacts after they have been handed over to their users, advocating a view of design that is broader than just the artifact and its immediate context.

Designing with care in mind requires attention to all these issues concerning the nature of the work to be supported by technologies, including the complexities involved in human–machine collaborations. The concept of care also must be critically examined, as it may, unthinkingly, be regarded as an expression of personal attention and commitment ignoring the 'normalizing strictures' in which care often happens, Ahmed (2004) and Murphy (2015) have argued. They plead to unsettle care by 'historicizing and situating' and creating 'moments of unease that might prompt the possibility of feminist, queer, anti-colonial, non-nationalist politics' (Murphy 2015, p. 721). As much as care work needs to be acknowledged, supported, and more equally distributed, it also should not be romanticized: care work can be dirty, it can be physically and emotionally exhausting: hence the need to understand and possibly remove the 'normalizing strictures' under which care is practiced.

Summary

Feminist/intersectional approaches to the design of IT artifacts build on practices developed in PD and PAR, enriching them with norm-critical, norm-creative, and social justice-oriented perspectives. Practice-based design adds experiences with designing flexible, malleable systems that are open to end-user development, offering technological tools for designing systems that are open to other ways of thinking and doing (work), and hence are inclusive of diversity on many levels.

A focus on gender/intersectionality enlarges and transforms the design space on various levels. Questioning the gender scripting of technologies, the underlying design choices, and the norms they present helps generate design alternatives. Social justice-oriented design draws attention to the wider structural issues on which gendered, race-based, and class-based processes of creating inequalities and injustices are based. They enrich participatory approaches to design with experiences of how to work with marginalized populations, avoiding the pitfalls of an ethnocentric bias. Doing justice to parts of the world that experienced oppression and marginalization, discarding the needs of people and disrespecting their knowledge are also main contributions of decolonizing approaches that often have the character of resistance. Among the important lessons to be learned from norm-critical, social justice-oriented, and decolonizing approaches to design is the need to critically reflect on the historical roots of injustices and 'normalizing strictures'.

Among the specific challenges of a feminist/intersectional approach to design is the need to make invisible aspects of work visible and fight marginalization; to recognize women's skills without falling into the trap of gender stereotyping; and to engage in improving working conditions, addressing the wider structural issues of work. The notion of care has a special place in feminist/queer theories. With respect to design, it means to defend care against a managerial logic, to address and take care of the many overlooked and undervalued aspects of work in design, including the complexities involved in human–machine interactions, but also to care for research subjects and create safe spaces.

11

Contextualizing Women's Work

One of the main strengths of studies of work from a feminist and intersectional perspective is that they consider the larger context in which work is embedded. Understanding the contextual conditions that shape gender technology relations and power relations in these contexts is key to achieving social/design justice. In this chapter we go back to the arguments about the importance of context for design-oriented research on women's work. Here we address questions such as: What are the most relevant aspects of context, how much do designers need to know about them, and what are the methods that can help them understand and deal with contextual elements in their work? Addressing these questions places the final foundational pieces in place, which then allow us to turn, in our final chapter, to what we think of as central tasks for a feminist/intersectional perspective on design from a future-oriented perspective.

Understanding Context as Key to a Feminist/ Intersectional Approach

Why look beyond the workplace? Early studies of women's work have done this from the beginning. They brought the intersection of paid work and unpaid work in the home to scholarly attention. Famously, Dalla Costa and James (1973) argued that it was not sufficient to look at women's work but that it was necessary to account for women's reproductive work in the home, which they defined as a form of exploitation distinct from and complementary to wage labour in production. Feminist researchers in Germany described the experience of ambivalence of working mothers in the automotive industry, which they saw as resulting from the contrasting requirements of the work sphere and the reproductive sphere (Becker-Schmidt et al. 1984). In her study of women at

'StitchCo', Sally Westwood (1984) observed that the women, most of them confined to the 'typical' low paying semi- and unskilled jobs of machinists and finishers, had developed their own 'culture of resistance' that reflected their private lives. Heidi Tinsman (2004) in her study of women agricultural labourers under the Pinochet regime in Chile portrays them not only as subject to the most despicable forms of labour exploitation, she shows 'how wage work impacted women's understandings of themselves, negotiating power with the family, or willingness to challenge labor exploitation or authoritarianism' (p. 264).

Also research in the tradition of Francophone ergonomics on (women's) work and health emphasized the relationship between salaried work and women's personal and social lives. Its focus of attention is on health issues that originate in harmful working conditions. Dessors et al.'s (1979) study of the work of telephone operators (see Chapter 10) not only found evidence of health issues resulting from intense stress but 'a general hypersensitivity, an aggressiveness towards their entourage, but also as a form of apathy, and increasing disinterest' (p. 497). Instantiations of what Walter Volpert (1985) called 'the long arm of work' can be found across studies of women's work and they demonstrate that 'context' needs to be considered in the design of workplaces and systems and that working conditions deeply affect workers' personal and social lives.

The relationships between work and people's personal and social lives that have been documented many times point to the personal histories and experiences of women and gender minorities as an important aspect of context to be considered in design. Kristie Dotson (2011) has identified strategies of 'testimonial quieting and testimonial smothering' being used to suppress the experiences and ideas of marginalized groups. She defines 'epistemic violence 'as the failure, owing to pernicious ignorance, of hearers to meet the vulnerabilities of speakers in linguistic exchange' (p. 236). Being included is not just a question of having a voice but of being heard; and this presupposes that others acknowledge the speaker as a 'knower'.

From a design perspective, the larger context shapes the object of design. Lucy Suchman's story about Andrea, the engineer at *CalTrans* who was working on a particularly difficult intersection of a bridge design, is an example:

> The argument that I made based on her relationship to the place that she was working on was informed not only by the work that she was doing at her CAD workstation, but by a whole lot of other knowledges that she had, ... from the fact that she walked around at the site. But she had also been in many, many meetings where it [the object] was discussed; she looked at many, many documents. So, she

had this sort of much fuller embodied understanding of the fate of the object that she was working on than the rendering of it on her workstation.

(Lucy Suchman, interview, 04/22/2022)

The bridge is not just an artifact that has to be designed and fitted into a representation of the terrain, observing all the engineering knowledge that makes the bridge stable and safe. It is a part of a larger context of the site and its history, negotiations with different stakeholders, and political and economic circumstances (Suchman 2000).

Concepts That Help Understand Context

We have used several key concepts throughout the chapters on women's work in different domains and areas of the world that help us understand context: skill, care (which includes communication, relationship management, maintenance, and repair), working conditions, the genderedness of organizations, and intersectionality. While some of these concepts are familiar to researchers in HCI and CSCW, they are not necessarily used in design-oriented research.

An attention to skill as a gendered category has played a large role in early studies of women's work. It spurred the insight that many of the skills that women deploy in their work are invisible and undervalued. Skill is a concept that is used by job analysts and management to evaluate different work activities and determine how they should be compensated. In the late 1970s in the USA, the comparable worth movement was founded to challenge conventional definitions of skills in response to a separate and lower wage hierarchy for women. Seeing 'skills and interests that men are encouraged to develop as a form of cultural capital that is arbitrarily rewarded' (England and Dunn 1988, p. 237), women activist and academics fought for pay equity. As Roslyn Feldberg has (1984) pointed out,

> ... paying jobs according to their worth requires only that whatever characteristics of jobs are regarded as worthy of compensation by an employer should be equally so regarded irrespective of sex, race or ethnicity of job incumbents. The theory rests on the argument that compensation should be independent of the social characteristics of the workers.

(Feldberg 1984, p. 319)

Despite its liberal origins, the comparable worth movement has the potential of far-reaching changes for women of colour and white women, Feldberg argued.

The invisible aspects of some work – particularly work carried out largely by women – are crucial to its accomplishment. This phenomenon can be observed in almost all work contexts, be it office and data work, nursing, or computer work. The ethnographic orientation to doing fieldwork in CSCW research has highlighted the concern with invisible work:

> background work ... articulation work ... that is one of the most gendered forms of work that the history of social science has documented ... and it's in my mind one of the core dimensions of understanding these work practices.
>
> (Luigina Ciolfi, interview 03/31/2022)

Related to the invisibility of skills is the gendered mapping of skills that stands in the way of achieving gender equality. Numerous examples demonstrate how the reference to stereotypical notions of women's skills – particularly those skills that were thought at one time to map neatly onto cis-gender[1] categories of womanhood (and historically were referred to as essentialist views of women) – serve to assign women to lower-paid jobs that often prevent women from accessing new higher-skilled work. Male-dominated and well-paying industries, such as for example the automotive sector, are based on the gendered mapping of skills. Gendered notions of skill also regulate opportunities for learning in present as well future work contexts. Technological changes, particularly the digitalization of physically heavy and dangerous work (as examples from the mining and metal industry show), are not sufficient to 'undo' gender in the ways work is perceived and organized, unless connected to dedicated efforts to implement gender equality are put in place.

Connected to the notion of skills and their potential invisibility are the care aspects of work. Care is a core element of the professional work of nurses as well as the informal carers in the context of the family or residential homes for older people (Schorch et al. 2016). These forms of care are deeply connected to social justice, raising questions about who does the work of care – often women migrant workers – and how it is compensated. Care also describes a more general characteristic of work. Joan Tronto defines care as involving 'attentiveness, responsibility, competence, responsiveness, and integrity' (1993, p. 136). To identify care aspects of work is particularly important in connection with digitalization. Automation often drives standardization, with systems-aided judgment replacing judgment based on human experience, intuition, and collaboration (Smith 2003). Both concepts, skill and care, help identify limits of automation and standardization; a deep knowledge about how persons accomplish sensitive work activities in a particular context is not only crucial to achieving design justice but is also essential to the design of better systems.

---

[1] Cis-gender (an antonym of transgender) refers to persons whose gender identity corresponds with the sex registered for them at birth; not transgender. It does not say anything about a person's sexual orientation though.

In reflecting on the unique aspects of focussing on women, work, and technology, several of the women we interviewed spoke about other aspects of care work, often in conversations about invisible work. Communication, relationship management, maintenance, and repair work were frequently identified as invisible aspects of women's work. They are also aspects of care work. We might think of skill as an aspect of caring and caring being a requisite of skill in a kind of circular relationship.

Identifying stressful, sometimes dangerous, and hostile working conditions is a concern that runs through many studies of women's work. Much of women's factory work traditionally has been and often still is heavy, dirty, highly repetitive, and strenuous work. Other forms of work may be physically less demanding but subjugate workers to conditions of pacing, behavioural control/surveillance, and time regimes that women find difficult to cope with. From an ergonomic perspective, Karen Messing identified five aspects of working conditions to pay attention to in studies of women's work:

> ... the unexpectedly heavy physical and mental workload involved in occupations traditionally assigned to women; showing the consequences for women's health of their precarious relationship to the work force; demonstrating the health effects of the double workday; studying the effects of work on those aspects of biology that are sex-specific; suggesting ways to remove ergonomic barriers to women entering non-traditional jobs which have been designed in relation to the typical male body.
>
> (Messing 1992, p. 1)

A concern with working conditions also pays heed to the personal responsibilities of women and their difficulties in managing work–life balance. Here we come back to the insight that life outside work needs to be viewed as a context for women's regulatory strategies at work.

Context also includes the genderedness of an organization as well as the power structures that maintain it. Most work contexts are highly gendered. In this book we have taken a closer look not only at areas of work that typically employ women, but we have also looked at male-dominated work environments in factories and the IT sector. The gendering of an organization is closely interrelated with experiences of harassment, from (sexualized) violence to degrading remarks, and with different forms of marginalization. Going back to Sandra Harding (1986a), gendering has a structural aspect – the sexual division of labour. It has the aspect of gender identity or individual gender that 'we were taught to despise; around the globe we insist on the importance of our social experience as women, not just as gender-invisible members of class, race, or cultural group' (p. 659). The third aspect is gender symbolism – the culturally varying images of masculinity, femininity, and non-binary forms of being and the ways they are ingrained in an organization, community, or the wider society. Gender symbolism reinforces our sense of a gendered world, full of behaviours and things that are gendered. Gender symbolism is an important part of what 'normalizes' gender structures (a division of labour based on the dominant view of sex and gender) as well as individual gender (e.g., gender symbolism may tell us that the technical world of computing is male and helps normalize a division of labour based on cis-gendered roles). Gender symbolism – through its prevalence – also reifies traditional notions of (cis-)gendered norms. The prevalence of (cis-)gendered norms also serves as a constant reminder to non-binary and gender queer workers that they are not quite what is expected of them in the paid labour force (Grant 2023).[2]

Intersectionality can also be considered a tool for exploring contextual aspects of work, helping to understand the interplay of gender, ethnicity, social class, and education in how work is defined, made accessible, and compensated. It draws attention to the gendered and racialized understandings of job categories, to forms of marginalizing and of making contributions, and the people that made them invisible. Intersectionality also helps identify bias in databases and algorithms and (workplace) technologies that discriminate against LGBTQ+ persons, persons of colour, and other marginalized groups of people.

Different Epistemological Traditions

Feminist/queer theory and an intersectional perspective and their contributions to understanding context have been referred to throughout the book. However, there are several other traditions we wrote about that we deem relevant for design work. That an ethnographic approach is important to design is evident. Many of the studies of work and participatory design projects we have presented are based on ethnographic observations that have yielded some of the most significant insights – for example, about invisible work – of concern for system designers. An ethnographic account describes how people carry out work in natural settings, in which it usually occurs. The main method used by ethnographers is participant observation of what people do and how they do it. Connected with this is what Blomberg and Karasti (2013) call a 'holistic view': taking account of the context in which work practices unfold, and not abstracting the observations from this context. While assuming a practitioner's view of the work as it unfolds, ethnography is also

---

[2] Ali Grant, *Not quite that* (documentary film), https://notquitethat.ca/, consulted 06/21/2023.

concerned with providing an analytic account of events and activities as they occur, without attempting to evaluate the efficacy of people's practices. These descriptive understandings however enable the possibility of more interventionist agendas.

(Blomberg and Karasti 2013, p. 374)

Lucy Suchman thinks of the attention to work detail common to ethnographic studies of work as a 'political move'. Anthropology was always also a political project, she argues, and an ethnography that ignores people's relationships and engagements as well as their gender exercises 'a kind of deliberate marginalization ... of the politics of work and of the gender politics of work' (Lucy Suchman, interview 04/22/2022). Paying attention to how we undertake ethnographic work, together with her thinking 'about responsibility not in terms of control, but in terms of relationship', are all congruent with feminist thought and its connection to politics.

Action research is another tradition that can be considered complementary to an ethnographic orientation. It is anchored in multiple epistemological traditions. Lake and Wendland (2018) refer to some of these traditions:

Rieken [et al.] (2005) grounded their work in a Bakhtinian analysis of voice and dialogue and a Freirean understanding of dialogue as a radical 'method of action' ..... Jackson's (2013) 'indigenous research' concept calls for use of postcolonial theory, subaltern studies, historicity of imperialism, and critical Whiteness studies .... Gustafson and Brunger (2014) insisted on a 'woman-centered' feminist participatory action research approach that shapes the design of the project and requires reflexive, discussion-based methodologies.

(Lake and Wendland 2018, p. 17)

Some researchers also adopt a systems theory perspective of change. All these theories have in common that they help articulate and practice a commitment to empowering the communities they work with. In a design research context, it is important, however, to focus not only on empowerment during the process of design, but to also focus on how the outcome of design processes will also support empowerment.

Another important tradition that is less well known in feminist research is Francophone ergonomics. This approach to studying working conditions is strongly connected to ideas about how to 'humanize' working life by engaging in sustainable workplace transformations. While researchers in this tradition engage in observational work, their orientation is not necessarily ethnographic. In their paper 'Observing gender', Messing et al. (2021) reflect on which aspects of gender can be captured by ergonomic research. Gender, although not always observable, is 'embedded in observable phenomena such as work and task organization, organizational violence, and work–family conflict' (p. 232). Although this work may also include measurements, the need for specific measurements results from the context of the work that researchers capture by using observational methods and interviews (Messing et al. 2005).

A Range of Work Contexts

Contextual issues of relevance for a feminist/intersectional approach to design vary, depending on the specific domain of work; but there are also some aspects of work that we find across workplaces. Chapters 4–9 offer a historical view of a range of work contexts, and they do this in a specific way. They provide an account of the main characteristics of work in a domain that is largely carried out by women, and how feminist scholars addressed them. They also demonstrate how insights from empirical studies of women's work shaped the key concepts used in the analysis. They also trace the development of workplace technologies, from classic machines to new technologies, analyzing how the technologies were introduced, and used to change the work and its organization.

Factory Work

Types of work: Women have traditionally been employed in factories as cheap labour for manual work, such as assembly work in the electronics industry or for all kinds of dirty work in meatpacking. Globalization has opened factory jobs for women in the South, providing them with a basic income but also creating a gap between the demands of 'feminine domesticity' (Barua 2021) and work lives in the factory. Women have also entered well-paid male-dominated industries – among them car production, metal work, and mining – but in small numbers. Pathways to move out of ghettoized roles to other forms of work and workplace culture remain areas of concern for women.

The organization of work: Automation is expected to make assembly lines shorter without fully replacing them in the near future. Including women workers in mixed teams as an example of 'managing diversity' has positive outcomes. However, making teams at the assembly line more diverse does not necessarily challenge gender stereotypes.

Key concepts, gender symbolisms, and identities: In all these industries, skills have always been and still are mapped as gendered and connected with traditional images of masculinity, foregrounding connotations with physical strength, particular (craft) skills, and the ability to cope with dangerous working conditions; thereby disregarding and devaluing the skills of women and the hardships they withstand. Many women factory workers were (and are) immigrants and of colour; hence there is also a racialized understanding of job categories in the industry. Historically, idealized images of masculinity were used to legitimate men's rough behaviours, physical aggression, verbal abuse, and harassment. In male-dominated industries, a masculine culture at work poses a threat to women's femininity. Women experience different forms of marginalization that made/make them feel different, unwelcome, and uncomfortable.

Influence of technologies: Technologies have made many factory jobs physically easier to perform and have created new types of qualified jobs. However, women's access to the new types of jobs is limited, as management often manipulates gendered notions of skills and capabilities to the advantage of the company; thereby also adapting images of masculinity to the new conditions.

Clerical Work: Data Work

Types of work: Studies of clerical work – the work of typists and secretaries – early on demonstrated the range of technical, interactive, and abstract skills women need in organizing an office, while arguing that these skills largely remained invisible and underpaid. Data work or data processing (as it was originally called) is the work of creating data and fulfilling requirements to make them available for different purposes. Similar to other forms of clerical work, it is often intensive, highly skilled work, in most cases badly paid and often invisible. Moreover, there is a tendency of organizations to outsource data work to what is called the 'global assembly line'. Much data work today is provided through platforms, where workers are provided tasks on a 'just-in-time' basis and remunerated on a 'pay-as-you-go' compensation model. Most platform work is highly standardized and repetitive. Clear evidence that platforms benefit workers with underprivileged backgrounds, downward life trajectories, or temporary difficulties due to phases of unemployment or care duties, and persons with disabilities is not available.

The organization of work: Office automation helped to spatially separate and centralize many back-office clerical functions such as data-entry, typing, payroll, and billing from front-office aspects of office work. This strengthened attention to the need for workplace design in support of well-being and human development. Platform work, on the other hand, is a highly individualized form of work, although a considerable proportion of workers engage in 'organic collaboration' (Gray 2016).

Key concepts, gender symbolisms, and identities: Word processing helped to cement the view of clerical work and the technologies enabling it as feminized.

Historically, data work, most of it done by women working in statistics departments or as medical secretaries, was labelled 'data preparation', making the need for interpretation and analysis invisible. Data work also makes the person doing this work invisible. Recent research also makes the immaterial and emotional labour as well as the care work involved in algorithmically organized service provision visible.

Influence of technologies: Office automation made clear that it was largely a management decision whether this technology was used to preserve and expand skills and improve working conditions, or if office automation was designed in a manner that reduced the skill content in jobs. This directed attention to the need for workplace design. Platform work has renewed interest in labour issues and brought them to the attention of researchers and designers. Studies explore the possibilities the technology offers to strengthen the collaborative aspects of work, help workers mobilize in support of better working conditions, and to improve access to education.

AI-Based Work

Types of work: As AI-based tools and systems proliferate and are gradually put into practice, the types of work that result from these developments are rather diverse. Data analysts and ML developers are highly qualified professionals that collect and organize data, develop hiring algorithms, diagnostic tools, screening technologies, and so forth. Only about 10 to 20 percent of these jobs are occupied by women. Other skilled professionals such as physicians, nurses, craft workers in manufacturing, or caseworkers in public administrations cooperate in appropriating AI-based systems to make them work in practice. Finally, there are millions of platform or crowdworkers engaged in the numerous 'microtasks' (e.g., tagging photos, valuing emotions, or the appropriateness of a site or text) – extremely parcelled activities – that make AI work.

The organization of work: AI-related types of work are to be found in all types of organizations. AI-based tools have led to new professions, such as data analysts and ML developers, some of which work for specialized service companies, while others are integrated into different user organizations. Platform or crowdworkers are often dependent on finding work with the dominant platforms.

Key concepts, gender symbolisms and identities: AI is predominantly in the hands of white men. However, an increasing number of women are engaged in critical work on data justice and on how to combat gender and racial bias in algorithms, insisting on transparency (who is behind an algorithm) and pushing for more geodiversity and demographics in datasets. Of specific concern is the 'misgendering' of transgender persons as a kind of gender policing. Care and trust are fundamental to algorithmic stewardship: the building of trust in an algorithm; the care that goes into developing human–algorithm relationships that are respectful of workers' skills and attentive to upgrading them. Making AI work also requires invisible work, such as the invisible and unpaid work platform workers must do to be able to get work; or the emotional labour involved in establishing trust in an algorithm.

Influence of technologies: The 'ironies of automation' as a warning also applies to AI-based tools and systems pointing to the need to carefully think not only about what to automate but also to strengthen the 'human-in-the-loop'. Intense forms of human–algorithm collaboration (e.g., for the auditing and altering of algorithms) are needed to make AI work in practice. Concerns about the potential threats that AI-based technologies pose have recently escalated,[3] which may lead to opportunities for more nuanced questioning of technology design that incorporates AI, as well as opportunities to open discussions more generally about the role of humans in human–algorithm interactions and the need for auditing of algorithms and greater transparency of algorithms.

Care Work in Hospitals

Types of work: Care work in hospitals encompasses a wide range of profes-sional nursing tasks. Women, immigrants, and racial minorities disproportio-nately perform the work of caregiving. Hence, these groups are especially vulnerable to exploitation and social injustice.

The organization of work: Hospitals are hierarchical organizations, in which nurses traditionally are perceived as following doctors' orders. With the rise of managerial power in health-care systems all over the world, care work has become subject to rationalization with a view of controlling expenditures and

---

[3] The introduction of ChatGPT late in 2022 seemed to stimulate significant public debate about the potential perils of AI. Increasingly, computer industry leaders from companies heavily invested in AI including OpenAI, DeepMind, and Anthropic, and executives from Microsoft and Google, as well as executives from related industries (such as Elon Musk, founder of Tesla) have publicly spoken about the social risks of AI and the potential risks it poses to society, as well as the need to better regulate AI. See for example 'Artificial intelligence poses 'risk of extinction', tech execs and experts warn', *CBC News*, posted May 30, 2023, viewed 05/31/2023 at www.cbc.ca/news/world/artificial-intelligence-extinction-risk-1.6859118, or 'Hit pause on AI development, Elon Musk and others urge' (Thomson Reuters, posted 03/29/2023, viewed 05/31/2023 at www.cbc.ca/news/world/chat-artificial-intelligence-safety-protocols-1.6794454).

increasing efficiency. ICT systems reinforce this propensity to cement power hierarchies. Poorly designed systems can also compromise patient care.

Key concepts, gender symbolisms and identities: Historically, nurses that were portrayed as following doctors' orders have had difficulties having their work acknowledged as professional work. As a result, much of their work with patients remained invisible and undervalued. Care, as the key aspect of nursing, combines a high degree of professionalism based on clinical judgement, precision, adherence to standards, and so forth with 'nurturance, compassion, meeting others' needs' (Tronto 1993). It is often perceived as fitting gendered stereotypes.

Role of technologies: ICT-based systems, such as nursing protocols, have reinforced a tendency to subject caregiving to standardization and modelling, bringing a managerial logic into care work, resulting in a deprofessionalization of nursing. Care robots, on the other hand, have stimulated a wide debate about the nature of care and the ethics of care.

Professional IT Work

Types of work: Computing today encompasses a wide range of jobs – from 'hardcore' technical jobs to jobs that require 'mixed skills'. Moreover, there are many entries into a career in computing, apart from a computer science degree.

The organization of work: In IT companies, there is a highly gendered division of labour, with software development projects or hardware-oriented jobs being mainly in the hands of men. Women are more likely to find employment in computing jobs that are closer to the realities of workplaces in organization, responding to the need to adapt, maintain, and repair software in use. Few women have leadership roles in gender-diverse teams and men are given the more complex tasks. There are marked differences between small and big companies though. Women's main problem is the working conditions in IT companies.

Key concepts – gender symbolisms and identities: One key observation is the invisibility of women's and Black women's substantial contributions to the development of computing prior to the 1990s. The current gender bias in the industry is seen as going back to the professionalization of computing. The mapping of skills as gendered is pronounced; also the 'mixed skills' argument builds on an essentialist notion of the suitability of women for certain work in IT. However, in many countries of the Global South the connotation of hardcore technical work in computing with men is not so strong; access to those jobs is mostly restricted to middle- and upper-class women. Women in

IT companies often find themselves as 'outsiders-within', exposed to an unfriendly/hostile work environment. They put weight on 'prefigurative design' as a condition for achieving learning how to make a space for themselves that fits their strengths. Women may experience different forms of inclusion or exclusion, depending on their race and sexual orientation.

Role of technologies: Technologies are at the core of computing work, and they are rapidly changing. The question 'What is wrong with computing?' points to a general problem: the dominance of mathematical formalisms, AI, and computer vision at the expense of alternative approaches likely to expand the diversity of those working in computing, as well as the approaches to design they bring to their work.

Commonalities and Differences and the Need for Detail

In these brief descriptions of the contexts in which women and gender minorities find themselves in different areas of work, several commonalities and differences stand out:

- There is a low skill – low pay divide across areas of work or industries. Women find themselves mostly but not always in the low-skill segments, often facing bad working conditions, with few possibilities for learning, advancement, and little recognition.
- A gendering of skills is a persistent and common feature of all areas of work. Gender stereotypes are the dominant means through which gendering of skills occurs. However, it also occurs in areas in which women dominate the paid labour force.
- 'Toxic masculinities' in some industries define women, non-binary people, and people of colour as outsiders, subjecting them to different forms of harassment, and making it difficult for them to live their gender as well as racial identities.
- Invisible work is everywhere, especially in the care aspects of many types of work, and along with emotional labour is stereotyped and not acknowledged as an essential part of the work.
- There are substantial differences between women's work opportunities and experiences across the world (and historically) that need to be accounted for.
- With respect to a feminist/intersectional perspective, technologies in and of themselves are not sufficient to change gendered notions of skills and provide equal access, as most organizations continue to build on and perpetuate these gendered notions of skills.

Compounding these challenges, as new areas of work emerge and are increasingly carried out in new forms of organizational settings, the collection of data that might allow us to know who is working where, doing what kinds of work and for what rates, is being eroded. In addition, as gender norms have changed, confusion has emerged about how best to collect data to reflect emergent gender norms. This will likely result in a period of time where confusion about the use of the terms sex and gender alongside efforts to introduce new categories for collection of data reflecting non-binary views of sex and gender have neither been standardized across data collection instruments nor in respondents' minds. Data collected during this period may lack validity, and at least until data collection and linguistic norms stabilize, will compromise our ability to understand the complex interplay of gender in relation to technology and work. In the absence of robust data, it will be increasingly difficult to evaluate how women are faring as computerization of work continues to evolve.

While this book provides historical context and many empirical studies that offer insight into the specifics of the different areas of work, including some encouraging developments, it also demonstrates that a search for (ethnographic) studies of work can fill in many details of the context an IT project enters, help develop a nuanced view, and identify problems. The following sections suggest several approaches to contextualizing a project that go beyond a more general understanding of the work context.

Dealing with Context in Practical Terms

Understanding context can involve a formidable amount of work, requiring researchers to adapt a variety of methods. This poses numerous practical problems, given the time and resource limitations most design work must cope with. It also begs the question of how much contextual information is needed to achieve a good design result from a feminist/intersectional perspective. The emphasis is on the methods and techniques a design team may want to use to explore the relevant aspects of context in a specific project. Some but not all these methods have strong links with a feminist research tradition.

Learning about the History of a Place and Its Culture

Research with marginalized people and communities, as well as decolonizing approaches, has emphasized the importance of knowing the history of a place. Paying attention to where people come from, what shaped the space they live in and their culture, helps us recognize and respect their experiences and knowledge.

Designers may want to consult research done by labour historians in order to develop knowledge about the history of a place. There are numerous historical studies of women's work, which provide designers with a deeper knowledge about the field of work they are entering. In this book we have made use of a range of historical labour studies. Another possibility is to engage in oral history, a method that has been used by feminist scholars. An example is Joan Sangster's (1994) oral history research on wage-earning women in a small Canadian manufacturing city (for a critical appraisal of feminist approaches to oral history see Gluck and Patai (eds), *Women's words: The feminist practice of oral history* (1991)). In many regions of the world including the so-called Global South, in addition to understanding the history of women's work, it may be just as important to understand the history of aid organizations in a region, particularly those related to computerization or automation, as aid and 'development' organizations often have significant reporting requirements that affect the technologies used at work as well as workers' jobs.

Numeric data concerning the composition of labour forces at a macro-level as well as changes over time in organizational structures (the meso-level) are often overlooked by designers. However, work by Feldberg and Glenn (1983), Menzies (1981), and Balka (1995 and 2002) are examples of how varied numeric data (including census and other data collected at a national level; organizational data often available in corporate reports), and other data can be used to understand the broader context in which women's work exists. Data can be used to develop insights about which job categories are shrinking and which are growing, and who is in which kinds of jobs. Corporate reports are an excellent resource for learning about a company's short- and medium-term plans, as well as changes in employee levels from year to year.

While a participatory and action-oriented approach provides space for participants to talk about their background and personal lives, learning about the culture of a workplace and its genderedness may require a more structured approach. Cynthia Cockburn (1993) thought of 'culture as a medium between the material world, say of the workplace, and gender identity'. Cultural studies, she argued, was of enormous value 'in bringing to view and giving value to the sub-cultures of oppressed groups'. Feminist scholars started investigating women's subcultures; they also examined 'masculine cultures anew with eyes that could, and none too soon, see in men sex as well as class' (p. 151). Margaret Somerville (2005) suggests narrative techniques as well as involving workers themselves in their own cultural analysis as ways to understand a workplace culture. Examining the masculine workplace culture in mining, she has taken mine workers' stories – of forming a 'close knit' community, of aggression, competition, and risk-taking – as 'mutually constitutive of individual subjectivities and workplace cultures' (p. 18).

A related method for learning about workplace experiences and workplace cultures is the biographical interview. It aims at developing an understanding of a person's biography or trajectory – their development as based on opportunities, choices, and individual coping strategies. This may include how a person is juggling the demands of work and private life; steps that a person takes in order to prevent marginalization; being differently treated (from men); avoiding exposure to harassment and/or particular expectations; experiences of transitions (e.g., changes of field of work, occupation, life situation, etc.), which allow a person to redirect her biography, define new challenges, and find better opportunities. Silvia Gherardi's (1996) narratives of 'women travellers in a male world' come closest to this notion of biographical interviews. She started collecting stories of women pioneers in male occupations, looking in them for 'the presence of a common plot, the outsider, the journey, the unexpected encounter with the different' (Gherardi 1996, p. 190). Her idea in interpreting the women's stories is to 'demonstrate how a story relates to the social order that allows us to progress beyond the individualistic account of narrative construction' (p. 191).

Understanding Politics, Policymaking, and the Institutional/ Organizational Context

Understanding the political and organizational context of a workplace can be a huge endeavour. For example, the so-called case-study approach in German industrial sociology uses a wide range of classic sociological instruments for describing the wider context in which workplaces are embedded. This includes analysis of the sector, knowledge about markets and customers, about legal regulations and collective wage agreements, available data about a company's organization and occupational structure, and so forth. This knowledge is deepened and complemented through expert interviews with management, union representatives, and technology specialists, workplace observations, surveys, and worker interviews, partially standardized, partially qualitative (Nies and Sauer 2010).

While this makes perfect sense for a long-term study of work, a design project is most unlikely to have the resources for an in-depth sociological study. As an alternative, we suggest conducting an arena analysis. The concept of social arena goes back to Anselm Strauss; it denotes a place in which different actors meet to discuss shared or overlapping projects and concerns. Strauss has discussed these concepts primarily in relation to organizations that he sees as being rooted in different social worlds and as participating in 'politicized arenas – of various sizes and types – characterized by discussion, debate, positional manoeuvring, and inevitably also by negotiation among the participants' (Strauss 1982, p. 351). Balka (2006) takes up the distinction between different 'arenas' in which systems design occurs (see also Gärtner and Wagner, 1996): the arena of work practices, the organizational context that frames these practices, and the arena of legal and policy measures.

One of the virtues of arena analysis is, Adele Clarke (1991) contends, that it allows understanding and handling a mixed world of worlds and organizations: 'Thus voluntary and involuntary worlds, formal and informal aspects of organizations, profit and non-profit organizations, social movements, professional groups, labor unions, and so on, each and all participate in arenas' (p. 12). It focusses on the different actors that are directly or indirectly connected with a design project, their vested interests, and resources, with a view onto enlisting them as allies. Adele Clarke (2021) also proposes 'situational analysis' as a tool to capture 'the broader situation' in which actors in a particular context are embedded.

> Situational analysis is based on pursuing four mapping strategies and memoing the maps in detail: situational maps, relational maps, social worlds/arenas maps, and positional maps. Data for making the maps may include transcribed interviews, memos of ethnographic observations, and analyses of extant (found in the situation) discursive materials (documents, visual and historical materials such as websites). A situational map including all the elements tentatively in the situation is useful even at design stages of research (then much revised as data are gathered). All maps are done and redone across the trajectory of the research.
>
> (Clarke 2021, p. 223)

Apart from understanding important characteristics of a place of work, arena analysis helps recognize and possibly interlink the different social arenas in which a design project is embedded: the arena of technology design and social practices, the arena of organization or community development, and the political and policymaking context. Such an analysis can also help designers understand which contextual conditions may escape their control, or with whom they need to work to achieve a particular outcome. This information in turn may prompt new iterations of design or point towards the necessity of forming new alliances or partnerships to support justice-oriented design.

Getting a Hold on Working Conditions and Skills

While a focus on working conditions requires specialized knowledge and techniques, it is an approach worthwhile considering from the perspective of design justice. Although the ergonomic studies carried out in the Francophone tradition are mainly qualitative, using observations and interviews, they also include quantitative data (Messing et.al. 2005). Some of them are based on measurements of time, workload, strain caused by particular postures, weights to lift, noise, or lighting conditions, frequency of interruptions, and so forth. Among the strengths of this approach is its focus on solving workplace problems (which may or may not require a technological solution), and its ability to identify and document new insights about the gendered dynamics of jobs. As is the case with other methods, the strength of this method in uncovering gender dynamics rests in a willingness to 'see' gender. In other words, this method – like many other methods we discuss – can be used to uncover gendered dynamics. However, doing so requires a desire and willingness to focus on gender.

The skills needed to perform certain types of work well can be identified through observational methods, as for example the numerous studies of office and data work or nursing demonstrate. However, they need special attention and conceptualization. German work psychology uses measurements of skills that are based on a categorical scheme rather than observing work as it unfolds situationally. These rather detailed schemes provide an alternative method to identify (invisible) skills, compare skill levels needed for different work activities, and, ultimately, to think about how to design 'mentally demanding work', in contrast to low-skilled repetitive work.

Making Space for Intersectionality

Design justice begs the question, 'Are we collaborating with the right people?' In part this question is answered by the place – group, community, organization – that a design team chooses for a project or is called in to work with. However, a commitment to intersectionality may require specific efforts. To come back to the example of mining, the question would be 'How do we include women and gender minorities in the design?' In the first place, this is simply a question of 'numbers', especially in male-dominated areas of work. But it is also a question of context in the sense of the background and personal experiences of potential participants in design. Michael Ahmadi and colleagues have focussed on these contextual aspects when studying the gendered nature of working environments in the game industry, seeking to understand the barriers regarding equality and career chances for women. Their study of a video game companies explores the social drivers of such contexts and discusses 'flexible structures and a welcoming corporate climate' as factors required to achieve and sustain more gender-sensitive working environments (Ahmadi et al. 2019).

In her work with people with mental health problems, Paola Pierri (2016) refers to 'the *internalised domination* that makes marginalisation not simply an explicit violation of equality, but something more subtle that deprives individuals themselves of the capacity to demand equality in the first place' (p. 4). Pierri describes the difficulties of understanding and acknowledging the context she encountered; among them incorrect assumptions (e.g., 'assuming that the depression of an elderly immigrant woman must be due to homesickness') thereby perpetuating stereotypes or creating new ones; 'transforming descriptive categories into normative ones and pathologizing those who depart from that norm'; or blindness for differences among participants. Pierri explicitly encourages 'outsider' ways of seeing 'which are drawn on personal and cultural biographies of people with lived experience of mental health as significant sources of knowledge' (p. 7).

Making space for intersectionality implies openness to the history and culture of 'outsiders' – members of marginalized and/or underserved communities, as well as people that are different and whose voices need to be valued in design. Dori Tunstall (2023) has coined the term 'Respectful Design' for an approach that requires 'forgoing vast emotional experiences that validate privilege, and instead amplifying the voices of the oppressed by repatriating the ownership of aesthetic cultures instead of the oversimplification of how such cultures are represented through design' (Onafuwa 2018, p. 11).

Design justice also includes awareness of power relations and the role and impact of design research itself. Angelika Strohmayer described to us how a feminist methodology raises consciousness 'of the potential of research but also the harms that it can cause and will cause', calling for a practice that

> allows for not having the answers and allows for exploration and picking up the nuances; and recognizes the exploration as the research practice, not always necessarily having to have solutions. Like Donna Haraway's rallying cry of staying with the trouble, [the] ability to stay with it and to stay with the complexity and unpick it and constantly critique and self-critique, hear critique and respond responsibly to what is happening.
>
> (Angelika Strohmayer, interview 10/06/2022)

In a joint publication with Débora de Castro Leal and Max Krüger, Strohmayer has elaborated this argument further, suggesting that this can mean we choose 'participatory ways of researching as a way to include different standpoints into our work or through care for research collaborators and their perspectives and commitment to understanding, which at times might include the *un-learning* of our own knowledge' (Leal et al. 2021, p. 3).

Contextualizing Design Work: Opportunities and Challenges

We decided to do a retrospective analysis of two of our own design/research projects, looking into how we dealt with context. The first project is about designing digital tools and information that should serve refugees and their helpers. The second project is the effort to design a system for adverse drug-events reporting and install it in the province of British Columbia. These projects could not be more different; they point at several challenges and how they were dealt with.

The *nett.werkzeug* Project

The *nett.werkzeug* project's aim was to design and build a digital platform that provides a set of digital tools and information to serve the orientation, information, and communication needs of refugees and their volunteers as well as professional helpers. Following an action-oriented approach (Small and Uttal 2005), the project directly relied on the creative potential of the people themselves, fostering their participation in the overall design of the platform as well as the creation of information and content. The project's explicit commitment to supporting digital empowerment (Mäkinen 2006) and working towards enhancing citizen participation in the community entailed several concrete actions and considerations for the design process.

First, these were concerned with the development of a shared language: How do we talk about the technology that we jointly create? In the project's socially and culturally diverse setting this did not only concern the level of national languages. It rather meant all stakeholders' linguistic possibilities to express what needs, ideas, and possibilities there are and need to be. As part of the PD process, this shared language, as well as the confidence to use it, first had to evolve. This happened for example, in workshops with refugees and volunteers that were organized to develop a feature that – ultimately in the form of a wizard – simplified the restrictive and bureaucratically complicated path to a language course, not least by making it possible to find language courses offered by volunteers (Weibert et al. 2019).

Second, and building on this, a shared understanding of the realm of digital possibilities is needed – What opportunities can be enabled by means of digital technologies, and what specific skills and knowledge are needed to put these opportunities into practice? In the socially and culturally diverse setting of the project, people's experiences with IT and their skills were rather heterogeneous – for example, when it came to login procedures and input options. Developing a common basis here was therefore an important challenge on the way to enabling participatory technology design.

Third, it was important to acknowledge how the diversity of the group itself (e.g., regarding legal status, cultural background, age, gender, education) as well as the relationship with different stakeholders outside the immediate design process was rooted in power dynamics that were also influential regarding the joint design work. The systematic disadvantage or advantage of certain participants, such as the ability to have a legal form capable of acting, has a direct influence on design decisions. Such context may appear at the periphery of the actual design process but directly influence its outcome and sustainability. It affects for example, who can take legal responsibility for jointly developed content, and based on this, how access to and control over designed tools and content can be distributed. Relatedly, the question of how much visibility the technical and content designers themselves want to have needed continuous consideration. The experience of refugee participants with censorship and control on the Internet in their countries of origin appeared as a strong and repeatedly determining contextual element, as well as the general need in the group to keep a low profile vis-à-vis right-wing groups.

Last but not least, one of the very early steps of the design process for the project involved consideration of the envisioned platform and its set of digital tools as situated in a specific context, and at a specific point in time. This laid the groundwork for subsequent and continuous networking with initiatives, actors, and projects – locally and beyond – with the overall aim of bundling knowledge and engagement, to exchange and to collaborate. Thus, it was possible to not only design the digital platform but to understand and locally sustain it as a socio-technical means of support for refugees and migrants in the process of making themselves at home in a new place (Krüger et al. 2021).

The ActionADE Project

The ActionADE project was a PD project that resulted in an adverse drug-event reporting system that we designed from scratch, pilot-tested, and implemented (thus far) in nine hospitals in British Columbia, Canada. ActionADE is also being used to meet mandatory federal adverse drug-event reporting

requirements. It is a software system that was designed to support collaboration between physicians, pharmacists, and potentially nurses.

The system was designed to support the collaborative work of physicians
and pharmacists who work together over time (e.g., because they often have to
wait for lab results or imaging results or see how a patient's symptoms change
with time) to determine whether or not an adverse drug event has occurred.
ActionADE allows practitioners to record information about a potential
adverse drug event as it unfolds. Once a definitive diagnosis of an adverse
drug event has been made, it is noted in the software, which then sends
information to the provincial drug-dispensing system used by all hospitals
and community pharmacies (drug stores) in the province. Anecdotal evidence
suggested that in other hospital settings (such as emergency departments that
were smaller and/or in rural areas), pharmacists may not be present and nurses
may play a greater role in bringing possible adverse drug events to the
attention of physicians. Sometimes even when pharmacists were present,
nurses played a greater role contributing documentation related to an adverse
drug event than was acknowledged by doctors.

In Canada, the scope of work (specific activities that various health practitioners are allowed to do) is governed provincially and varies from province to
province. This is particularly true for nurses (who are not allowed to prescribe
in British Columbia but may prescribe in some other provinces) and for
pharmacists (whose ability to prescribe also varies from province to province).
Although our primary physician designer was a woman, she was also a doctor.
In the world of medicine doctors are primarily men (69 percent of emergency
room physicians in British Columbia are men) and nurses are predominantly
women (91 percent of Canadian nurses are women),[4] reflecting what Harding
(1986) would call gender structures, and others might refer to as a sex-
segregated labour force. The gender structures themselves are supported by
gender symbolism and the gendering of things: caring is seen as feminine;
taking fast action and interacting with lots of technology (as in emergency
departments) is viewed as a masculine activity. It is this gender symbolism that
helps maintain gender hierarchies.

Balka (2009) suggested that when women hold jobs typically dominated by
men their allegiance to career hierarchies (e.g., that doctors – a predominantly
male labour force – are culturally held in higher regard than nurses who are
predominantly women) may supersede their allegiance to gender hierarchies
(which generally value men over women). In the case of ActionADE, as a

---

[4] www.cna-aiic.ca/en/nursing/regulated-nursing-in-canada/nursing-statistics, checked 03/28/
2023.

senior member of the design team and project co-lead, I advocated for inclusion of a role for nurses within the system that we were designing, although my physician colleague insisted that nurses would not use the system (because they were not central users in our primary design context).

Although I felt we could have – and should have – undertaken more extensive analysis of nursing work as it related to documentation of adverse drug events, my efforts in this regard fell short: we never did extensive fieldwork looking at emergency department nurses and their interactions with patients related to medications. However, I was successful in making sure that the software design included the capacity for nurses to contribute to adverse drug event documentation, so that over time as ActionADE was implemented in more diverse work settings, the software was designed to support a nursing role, and appropriation of ActionADE functionality by nursing staff in varied settings. In this case (as in many others), our workforce was characterized by what Harding (1986) would refer to as a gender structure, where in general men fill some jobs and women fill others, and that fact had an impact on whose work was 'seen' and whose work remained invisible. I was ultimately only able to get the nursing role built into the software because of my awareness of context – that in other jurisdictions nursing work allowed nurses to prescribe (and hence it would be appropriate in those settings for nurses to have similar access and privileges within the software as pharmacists). I was also motivated in my efforts to ensure that a nursing role was written into the software by the antidotal information I had gleaned from speaking to nurses about their jobs informally over the life the project. It became clear to me that in other settings – such as a geriatric unit – that while nurses were not able to prescribe or withdraw medications without a physician's orders, that it was often a nurse on a unit who realized that a medication problem existed. Use of ActionADE would provide a potential avenue for nurses to communicate concerns about prescribing to physicians.

Hospital unit clerks who registered a patient when they first arrived at the emergency department and prepared patient records for physicians, pharmacists, and nurses to see, were not intended or primary users of ActionADE. However, depending upon how we designed and implemented the software, their work might be altered. Maintaining gender sensitivity during design allowed us to acknowledge the role this predominantly female labour force played in relation to adverse drug events: they downloaded a fourteen-month drug dispensing history from the provincial drug dispensing database and attached it to each patient's record. This allowed all of the emergency department care providers to see what drugs had been dispensed to a patient, which was an important step in determining whether or not an adverse drug event had occurred. Had we not been aware of these 'off stage' workers, we might have insisted that they perform the task of importing a patient's dispensed drug record into ActionADE. We were aware of the workload burden the health unit clerks shouldered and determined that we could not add the importation of a patient's dispensing record into ActionADE (where the information it contained – and particularly the patient's demographic and past dispensing history – would pre-populate the ADE record in ActionADE). Particularly during iterations of our prototype – during which time our system was not fully integrated – we supported the work of unit clerks by having research team staff members undertake the importation of dispensed drug data, in order to avoid adding that task to the work of unit clerks. Recognizing how use of the system prior to full integration might negatively impact the unit clerks allowed us to preserve their workflow, and not add to it, during system development. This recognition kept them onside through the fully integrated implementation.

In designing ActionADE, we had to make numerous decisions about what classifications systems were incorporated into the software, and what the behaviours of various fields would be (e.g., auto-populated, auto-complete as a user typed, pick lists, etc.). We were very aware that a lack of attention at this stage could easily add to rather than reduce the documentation burden associated with identifying and tracking patient-level adverse drug events. Consequently, much of our design work focussed on discussions with our primary user group – hospital-based pharmacists (mostly women), evaluating classification systems, determining how varied nomenclatures behaved in relation to pharmacists' work, and so on. We were facing pressure from a powerful (man) operating at a distance who was championing the use of a different classification system than the one our users had identified, at a provincial level. Along with our user participants, we were concerned that use of the other system would prove problematic. We took the proactive step of conducting a sub-study using retrospective chart review to compare the efficacy of three different classification systems (including the one championed by the powerful man), so we would have data to rely on in making a case for the classification system that our pharmacist participants (largely women) felt best supported their work. This was an interesting example of recognizing a gender-based problem (although we had a solid rationale for our choices, we were not being heard: we were women and we were advocating for the needs of a predominantly female group of workers) and coming up with a creative means of protecting the interests of the pharmacists whose needs we were representing.

A focus on gender was also important in a few other areas of our design practices. First, when we held design workshops and focus groups we attempted to schedule with a high degree of awareness of women's commitments outside of work. During workshops we captured data about the gender or participants so we would be in a position to determine whether or not any of the input we received from participant designers appeared to relate to gender. Finally, during design activities, we occasionally had to manage gender dynamics during design workshops. During one workshop in particular we had to reign in a (male) participant in order to ensure that the majority of those in the room (women) had an opportunity to speak.

Taking Account of Gender Issues in Technology Design

The common themes that brought us together as co-authors – which include a shared commitment to designing computer systems that will support women and other marginalized groups in just ways at work – can at times feel overwhelming. It is easy to lose sight of the forest through the trees, particularly as we have made an argument for considering context in design in a way that goes well beyond what many would consider the purview of traditional design. Keeping this in mind, it is perhaps useful to unpack design processes and think about how and where in design one can begin to address the myriad issues we have raised in an effort to give people the rationale, background, and conceptual tools to improve technology design through a focus on women.

For our purposes here (of supporting readers in developing strategies that will maintain a sensitivity towards gender issues in technology design), it is useful to think about different aspects of the design process, and what kinds of steps (or activities) are carried out at various points during technology design processes. Gender sensitive design is not the result of singular grand acts, but rather can only emerge through the alignment of many smaller interventions undertaken over time at varied points in design processes, with a consistent focus on gender issues.

The approach or *process* of design needs to, first, ensure an *attentiveness to gender*. Questions that help achieve and maintain this attentiveness are:

• Concerning gender structures / the gender division of labour: Who fills what kinds of jobs? Historically, which jobs have been held largely by men or women? Has this changed over time? If so, how? How can activities undertaken as part of the design process be scheduled with a sensitivity towards unpaid work and family responsibilities? Are gender structures likely to interact with work hierarchies in a manner that adversely influences design processes? If so, how can these challenges be mitigated?

- Concerning gender identity: How do the people doing these jobs feel about them? Do cis-gendered men feel the jobs or technologies emasculate them? Do cis-gendered women feel the job or the technologies they work with enhance or challenge their femininity in any ways, or give them access to previously denied male worlds (e.g., ease in commanding technical conversations)?
- Concerning gender symbolism: Are the jobs typically seen as 'male' or 'female' jobs? Are the technologies typically used on the job gendered (seen as primarily male or female)? How do these varied aspects of gender interact and reinforce or challenge one another?
- In terms of a commitment to give voice to the marginalized: What are the emotional, political, and historical relationships that need to be accounted for when working with marginalized groups? How can designers ensure that the knowledge and resources of marginal groups be identified and valued? How can safe spaces be created for the project participants?

A second issue to clarify is the *work problem or issues* that a project is trying to solve and how does the problem or issue relate to gender. This requires asking:

- Who has defined the problem (researchers? front-line workers?), and does the problem definition presuppose a technological solution (which may or may not be the only or best solution)? Does the problem formulation address the needs of workers in jobs held primarily by women or men (and those who are non-binary and/or gender queer)?
- Who are the primary people whose work will be impacted? Are they men or women? Cis-gendered, gender queer, and/or non-binary?
- Are there any indirect or off-stage system users (e.g., in a medical setting, doctors and nurses may be the direct users but changes to a system they use may impact unit clerks and the hospital records department, or any number of staff elsewhere in a hospital). Are indirect users primarily men or women?
- Do all groups of workers define the problem or issues the same way? If not, is there a gender component to how different groups view the design issue or problem? If so, what can we learn from exploring those differences? How do other stakeholders or actors (e.g., managers? the occupational health and safety office?) view the problem or issue? Will bringing varied stakeholder groups together to develop a shared understanding of the domain, issue, or problem contribute to more positive outcomes?

Another level of attention in pursuit of gender-sensitive design is on *the output of design processes*. Focussing on the outcomes of a design project is import-ant as it helps develop a deeper understanding of what can possibly be achieved in a particular context and under specific conditions. An important aspect of thinking about outcomes is that they can be maintained after a project has come to an end. A critical perspective is needed to recognize the power structures of the use situation and hence be able to address them.

There are different categories of outcomes to consider: the system or artifact, the work processes or work practices, and work/employment trajectories. Although the design of the artifact and design of work may overlap, it is useful to think of them together as each indicates different potential points of intervention in design. For example, the artifact may address issues such as suitability to a wide range of bodies and/or learning styles or interaction patterns often associated with men or women (but in reality, are as diverse within groups as they are between groups), while designing work may include things such as what classification systems are incorporated into a system and how fields work (whether responses are free text, drop down menus, predictive entry, etc.), all of which influence a person's experiences of work, and reflect either observations of or assumptions about skill.

Designing work and designing artifacts covers a lot of ground: everything from details about which classification systems are incorporated into software and how they are implemented, to who assumes responsibilities for emergent and new tasks related to new workflows need to be addressed. The process should include discussions about skill (are there tasks that require skill that are not immediately visible, which, if overlooked could prove problematic for design?), and identification of the places for which a 'human in the loop' is essential, because certain kinds of judgement are required. Discussions about skill should also address the parts of the job workers would like to keep or see automated. Questions to ask are:

- Are insights reflecting the needs of women users/workers in a diversity of positions evident in the final system or artifact? This might include an awareness of decisions about classification systems and how data fields behave in computer-based systems, and how choices might impact the work of varied groups, for example. Are technologies (e.g., in computerized factories) equally able to accommodate the diversity of bodies, from stereo-typically female to stereotypically male? Does machine design equally well accommodate the majority of body sizes, strength capacities?
- In terms of a system or IT artifact: How can we make sure that the technical outcome is not gendered? How do we design a flexible/malleable system or IT artifact?
- In terms of work: What can be done to make sure that the design outcome helps improve women's working conditions? How can we help women and

other marginalized workers have access to training programs that qualify them for higher-skilled, better-paid positions? How can support be secured for organizational change that enables these outcomes? What policies need to be developed and put in place to secure these outcomes?

- In terms of data: What kinds of data need to be collected over time in order to ensure that desired outcomes are achieved in practice (e.g., data about the access to training programs and job gains for women and other marginalized groups in an organization; the incidence of gender-based discrimination and harassment)? What kind of data might we need to understand the experiences of non-binary and gender-queer workers? Or whether or not improvements of working conditions have been realized?

- In terms of an orientation to social justice: What are the immediate issues that could be addressed in the project? What are the more long-term issues that require planning beyond the initial project timeline? Which alliances need to be built to secure social justice-related outcomes?

Being able to address these (and other) questions related to design processes and outcomes presupposes that the design team has studied the context they are entering with a design project. These questions can also be used to study those contextual aspects that matter for organizing a good process and achieving the planned outcomes.

Summary

In this chapter we have focussed on issues and challenges that arise in relation to contextualizing women's work, which we have argued is a crucial step in designing workplace technologies in a manner that supports women and other marginalized groups at work. Among the points we've made throughout the book and have returned to here are that we need to look not only at women's paid work, but also at their work in the home, including what are often perceived by women themselves as personal struggles (which upon further investigation are more widely shared and rooted in politics). Francophone ergonomics reminds us to consider health impacts and gives us tools that allow us to identify and address health issues that occur in paid work as well as at the intersection of paid and unpaid work.

Concepts such as epistemic violence (Dotson, 2011) and feminist analyses of PD (e.g., Balka 1997; Bardzell 2018; Bratteteig and Wagner 2014) underscore the need to go beyond inclusion during design processes and grant marginalized speakers voice and authority as knowers. Doing this may require that we identify varied forms of invisible work such as communication, relationship management, as well as maintenance and repair as essential aspects of many jobs and broader work processes they support. In addition to acknowledging these specific kinds of care work, we also need to recognize care as a core element of many traditionally women's professions, as well as the roles women fill – often without recognition – in traditionally male jobs. Turning our attention towards skill and investigating the ways in which skill has been conceptualized in relation to work and technology, and considering both in relation to gender and compensation, are important and often overlooked aspects of context.

We need to understand the broad context in which emergent technologies and jobs we are designing for will be embedded. This means assessing the genderedness of organizations, industries, and the types of jobs within them, and anticipating how the devices and systems we are creating may alter or reinforce the existing gendered patterns. Of particular importance is culture, and the need to tend to cultural changes that will create work environments more welcoming of women. Adopting an intersectional approach will be crucial to identifying and understanding how workplace experiences differ for those whose gender expressions differ from traditional masculinity and femininity and vary in relation to one's ethnicity. These may be overt or subtle, and care must be taken – and in all likelihood strategies developed – that will allow us to untangle the complex ways in which different kinds of difference contribute to relative advantage and disadvantage in workplace settings. Our approach to design is built on epistemic understandings that are rooted in identifying differences, which in turn necessitate ethnographic work.

We've shown how in different areas of work (e.g., factory work vs. healthcare work) women have traditionally undertaken specific types of work. As we move forward, automation of work will influence the organization of work in particular ways, each of which will draw on aspects of gender differently. The influence of technologies has varied across sectors and in different regions of the world. The future of work for women has yet to be determined. We have highlighted the need to incorporate an attentiveness to gender issues throughout design processes. This means structuring design processes with a sensitivity towards gender issues, thoughtfully addressing how the articulation of a design problem or issue may be gendered and focussing on the output of design processes – in terms of the artifacts or system produced, the emergent work practices, and employment trajectories.

As the cases we have briefly described towards the end of the chapter suggest, not all design projects draw on all of the concepts we have identified here, and not all of our efforts will be wholly successful. Change is often incremental and slow. However, Arnstein and Christakis (1975) advocated for designing consciously for futures we aspire to – for identifying a desirability criteria – rather than being bound by what seems immediately doable or simply seems to follow on from the present.

12

Pathways to Gender Equality in Design

At the end of this journey through much theoretical work and many empirical studies of women's work as well as design-related research, this chapter presents future-oriented reflections on key questions and concerns. Our aim here is to not only to draw conclusions but also to highlight what we think of as central tasks that need to be addressed to support the further development of a feminist/intersectional perspective on design. Can it ever become 'mainstream', inspiring design work across scientific communities and technologies as we think it should? While our focus has been on work, that the points and principles we raise are just as relevant to other contexts (particularly given the constant movement of technology into the home), and the insights we raise are also relevant for home contexts as well, we hope is evident.

Strengthening Intersectionality in Computer and System Design

Increasingly intersectionality is receiving attention in computer science and software design communities. A quick search in the ACM (Association for Computing Machinery) digital library yields a plethora of articles on varied aspects of intersectionality. Recent papers include explanations of what intersectionality is; how an intersectional lens can be used to reduce selection bias in computing, computing education and mentoring; how an intersectional approach can improve designing for accessibility; how it can help us to make data activism meaningful; and how an intersectional lens can allow us to identify biases inherent to automated computational systems. Intersectionality has been addressed in relation to ML systems, differences in views of data, ethics, and fairness, and how to go beyond retroactive audits of datasets. There are many calls to implement intersectional approaches.

An important step in strengthening intersectionality in computer and system design will be to review work that has been undertaken and determine how – from our varied positions and social locations – we can influence change. Change is uneven and messy and occurs across multiple social, temporal, and institutional settings, which means there are varied ways that each of us can engage in relevant interventions.

We also need to monitor our efforts to make change. And, although there are many forms that making change as well as assessing change can take, we need to have a sense of where we are starting from, and whether or not the interventions we make are achieving desired results.

Intersectionality is not only but also about numbers. As long as there are so few data about the work and life situation of gender minorities, persons of colour, and persons with disabilities, it is difficult to gain acceptance for the need to design with a focus on those populations. Additionally, with so few of them included as participants in design projects, the possibilities of engaging in comparative research and analysis are limited, and so are the opportunities to open design to the full spectrum of people's needs and knowledges. We need data to help us understand the needs of more diverse participants in design, and we need data to support evaluation of the extent to which design meets or falls short of needs articulated by diverse populations.

Garcia Johnson and Otto (2019) have developed a 'model for women and LGBTQ+ equality in the workplace' and present a diagnostic tool that could be of use in an ICT project. They suggest various ways of measuring the incidence of gender-based discrimination and harassment and evaluating the organizational culture, in particular those elements that reinforce 'hetero-sexist values', using qualitative (interviews and focus groups) and quantitative measures. They also suggest action, such as, 'Engage key members in the organization (visible and/or powerful) to serve as champions to inspire cultural change. Identify excluding and otherizing communication practices' (p. 11). We think of such a tool not just as an opportunity to perform a diagnosis of one specific work organization but also as a tool for thinking about how to share equality-related data across organizations.

'Finding' those who should be part of research can be more complicated than it may appear, as there are all kinds of reasons why people may remain invisible, and a myriad of obstacles may make it difficult for them to participate. Hence, supporting intersectionality requires reflecting on appropriate methods for involving marginalized people. First, this means carefully reflecting on how gender and other categories are 'encoded and operationalized' (Burtscher and Spiel 2020). Are these 'labels' assigned or self-selected? What are the words we choose to describe people? This is a particularly sensitive issue, given that in many cultural contexts (for example in many European countries) the term 'race' is avoided due to its racist heritage. Also 'disability' is a contested term as it is often based on a deficit-based discourse. Secondly, Burtscher and Spiel remind us

> to be mindful about participants' lives outside of a given project context. This begins by actively including marginalised groups and goes all the way to offering lunch during workshop days and tweaking the project schedule to accommodate for care responsibilities . . ., as well as making counselling available for participants.
>
> (Burtscher and Spiel 2020, p. 438)

Much has been written about how to create 'safe spaces' in a project, value the resources that participants bring with them, and make sure that they remain in control of their stories (see Chapter 10).

All this may be difficult to achieve in an IT-based design project where funding agencies provide few resources for preparatory and supporting activities. It can be done. In Canada, increasingly health research projects require patient participants to contribute. With this expectation, provincial and federal supports have been developed to assist in the recruitment and training of patient participants and research teams to work together, policy has been developed to guide compensation of patient participants, and strategies have been developed to ensure that they are not tokenized in projects or isolated.[1] A commitment to intersectionality requires resources, and hence as an aim must be negotiated upfront with funding agencies and all stakeholders in a project. It also may be difficult to access a work context without the support of trade union representatives and others committed to gender equality and diversity. Longer periods of collaboration with a work organization may be necessary before measures to promote women, gender minorities, and other marginalized groups are in place.

Intersectionality in design can also be strengthened by looking back in history and making the contributions of women and other marginalized groups to design visible. Pernille Bjørn and Daniela Rosner (2021) uncovered 'the hidden history of Atari women', seeking

> to challenge the contemporary predominantly masculine representation of computer game development through design encounters; and we do this by re-working current historical ('retro') celebratory memories of gaming to include hidden stories about women's contributions.
>
> (Bjørn and Rosner 2021, p. 2)

---

[1] More information is available at Strategy for Patient Oriented Research (https://cihr-irsc.gc.ca/e/41204.html) and Patient Partner Compensation Guidelines (https://cihr-irsc.gc.ca/e/53261.html), both viewed 06/22/2023.

Pernille Bjørn, Maria Menendez-Blanco, and others also developed the 'Grace artifact', an 'interactive installation' that brings women's contributions to early computing to life. This kind of design-based work complements historical research on the contributions of marginalized people, making it visible to a much larger audience.

'Publics': How Do We Take a Feminist Perspective on Engaging in Discourse?

Design justice is about making space for 'outsiders' – members of marginalized and/or underserved communities, as well as people that are different in various ways – and have their voices valued in design. Here we want to reach beyond the numerous examples of design work carried out in this spirit (Chapter 10), adding more general reflections about how to engage in discourse from a feminist perspective.

Engagement in discourse goes hand in hand with a recognition of the power of words, and of the publics these can create, foster, or diminish. Schlesinger and colleagues (2017) remind us that how our views on communities we design with and for come with categories, and how these are used in language to represent, but also 'sacrifice some of our ability to produce complicated, boundary-pushing representations of gender, race, ethnicity, and class' (p. 5419). They focus on identities and on how to acknowledge and represent the complexities of these identities from an intersectional perspective as a precondition of discourse – who are the people we engage with in discourse, be it research or design or both? This is important since the words with which we describe these people should reflect the context and conditions of their lives, where they come from, with what kinds of barriers they are confronted, and which kind of openings they come across. Even within communities, lived experiences vary, which is often reflected in differences in terminology and discourse within communities as well.

Marisol Wong-Villacres emphasizes a cultural perspective on engagement in discourse. She suggests that we

> look at problems more from a cultural base – what are the strengths that people have; what are the cultural roots of those strengths; what are the systemic . . . roots of those strengths? And also the way systems are preventing those strengths to be mobilized to actually produce the impact that communities want to produce or have.
>
> (Marisol Wong-Villacres, interview 09/13/2022)

To start from people's 'cultural base', taking strength from the diversity of their roots and lived experiences is one key element of engaging in discourse.

The other element she emphasizes is resistance – 'like across the US and other places, and what I've seen indigenous women, in the way they engage with a lot of the issues that take place … for me the commonality is resistance'.

Marisol Wong-Villacres' position reflects a feminist concern with power, agency, and resistance. Going back to 'the personal is political', Thompson et al. (2018) express their concern that 'already marginalized voices can become obscured in the very processes of knowledge production that seek to understand them' (p. 94). 'Prioritizing the personal is a political act; it is part of the political project of resistance', they state, and failing to recognize this 'can prioritise the researcher's interpretations of structural oppression over the voices of participants' (p. 95). Gillian Rose's notion of 'paradoxical spaces' is helpful here. We have discussed the notion of safe spaces for women and other marginalized groups to raise their voices and tell their stories (Chapters 10 and 11). Rose suggests the notion of paradoxical spaces as representing a position of 'elsewhere' in the margins of hegemonic discourses of masculinism: 'The simultaneous occupation of centre and margin can critique the authority of masculinism … help[ing] some feminists to think about both recognizing differences between women and continuing to struggle for change as women' (Rose 1993, pp. 152–153).

Spatiality is an important element of feminist thinking; it leads back to the power of words. In her work with women of 'mixed race' Mahrani (2001) notes that their 'mixed race' identity 'represents a paradoxical space where several social categories and spaces overlap at once' (p. 301). Exploring feminism in digital spaces, McLean et al. (2016) reflect on the participatively designed online group 'Destroy the Joint' – an open space for people 'who are concerned about sexism and misogyny to do something to counter them' (p. 169). They emphasize the importance of spaces that contain paradoxical possibilities.

These three approaches to strengthening a feminist perspective on engaging in discourse are strongly interrelated. The words we use to represent complex identities matter and researchers/designers need to allow for overlapping categories. The importance of prioritizing the 'personal' (people's personal stories that go back to their cultural roots) needs to be recognized as a political act of resistance to hegemonic discourses; and the need to not only create safe spaces for discourse but spaces with paradoxical possibilities needs to be foregrounded.

How to Move towards Gender Equality in the Workplace

The de-gendering of organizations and male-dominated professions is a long-term project; and thorough studies of what it takes to achieve gender equality in the context of ICT projects are scarce. First, it is important to be clear about what we mean by gender equality. A study in a large French company argued that gender equality is a multidimensional concept and that the awareness of workers and management of inequalities and their ideas about what to do about them largely depends on what gender equality means to them: gender diversity, access to positions with management responsibilities, equal pay, and/or support in managing work-life balance (Coron 2019). Lewis et al (2017) emphasize that 'transformative strategies and interventions, aimed at changing the ways that work is routinely divided, organized, and valued' are the most effective means of achieving gender equality. A study of the American Sociological Association over a period of ten years demonstrates that 'de-gendering involved both larger social forces and feminist agency' (Robyn 1992, p. 22). This also holds true for contemporary organizations. Structural issues cannot be resolved as part of an intervention that is limited not only in time but also in access to decision-makers and resources, as is usually the case in a design project. This doesn't mean though that we should not attempt to address structural issues. Rather, it is imperative that we identify structural issues and build alliances with those who are in positions to influence change.

'Feminist agency', the 'situated equality' approaches in ICT provide some directions. Vehviläinen and Brunila (2007) base their approach on Donna Haraway's notion of situated knowledge and Ruth Lister's feminist citizenship. In a joint publication with Irene Bruegel and Ginny Morrow, Lister (2005) emphasizes the 'transformative capacity' of women's citizenship that is developed through collective experience. She uses it in conjunction with the notion of social capital that Bruegel redefines from a feminist perspective as the resources that 'can furnish women with a degree of power that enables them to challenge the status quo, through solidaristic social networks' (p. 3). Both Lister and Bruegel focus on the informal as the key stage of women's agency – 'informal politics embraces both local community or neighbourhood-based action and national/international social movement' (p. 21).

This collective dimension of women's citizenship and their social capital is at the heart of gender equality, Vehviläinen and Brunila (2007) argue: 'agency is communal rather than individual and deeply rooted in the societal technically mediated orders'. Their 'cartography' of gender equality in ICT projects in Finland demonstrates that most of these projects focus on individuals, attempting to shape girls' and women's interests in technology and increase their competences. In contrast,

> ... in situated equality, equality starts from locality where people define their space in global ICT. This understanding is part of the social constructivist and more

specifically technofeminist research traditions. It further connects features from equal treatment (rights), positive action (local communal agency) and mainstreaming (institutional and societal development).

(Vehviläinen and Brunila 2007, p. 388)

Approaching gender equality as an aim in the framework of an ICT project needs to pay attention to these three interrelated features, emphasizing positive collective action as well as measures on the institutional and societal level. Vehviläinen and Brunila also stress the importance of equality work to focus on the 'practices of doing equality and gender' (p. 393). In our view this provides leverage for thinking about how these practices can not only be maintained and further developed but also shared and transferred to other contexts. For example, early feminist attempts to include women in participatory design projects yielded a wealth of information, which may be relevant to the inclusion of other marginalized groups in design.

Another avenue to take is to use changes in an organization to push for more gender equality. Lena Abrahamsson's (2014) study of what has changed over a period of ten years in eight Swedish companies she had done research in provides some valuable insights. Focussing on four processes (structures, symbols, interactions, identities), she found that organizational changes also result in changing patterns of gender equality that are worthwhile observing. This made her think that 'gender equality can, at least in part, be seen as a prerequisite or perhaps even a side effect of the modern organizational concepts'. At the same time, she observed the 'restoring power' of gender constructions: 'The changeable nature of gender constructions is a central, although perhaps somewhat inaccessible, restoration mechanism within the gender-segregated working life' (p. 131). This mixed message is helpful as, while stressing that organizational change in itself does not decrease gender inequalities, it can serve as leverage for 'positive collective action' in the context of an ICT project.

How to Build Alliances in Support of Gender/Social Justice in Design

'We got to make the struggles visible, too, not just the heuristics of the work or the job' (Joan Greenbaum, interview 05/05/2022). Alliances are needed for struggles to succeed. Joan found them first in a collective called Computer People for Peace, and later engaged in union-organizing. Others, such as Ellen and Toni, were part of women's collectives. Grassroots groups in HCI, such as Fempower.tech and AccessSIGCHI, work for changes in their research community in an effort to build 'respect, inclusion, fairness, and transparency', highlighting the insight formulated by Reshmi Dutt-Ballerstad, that 'failing to interrogate institutional decision-making processes while claiming to work towards social justice is one way individuals (un)consciously sustain white supremacy'. Many of these initiatives are cases of feminist advocacy:

> Advocacy that is specifically feminist in nature is designed to advance women's rights through reforming gender discriminatory policies, laws, corporate behaviour, and cultural practices which affect women around the world. Feminist advocacy is intimately connected to – and grounded in – the local struggles of real women, and takes its legitimacy and direction from these women, who are experiencing injustice and inequality of different kinds at first hand.
>
> (Evans 2005, p. 11)

Hence, feminist – and we would add queer – advocacy stands for the 'spirit' in which networking activities are undertaken, rooting them firmly in local experiences and struggles; but also ensuring that these local agendas are being connected to the regional, national, and international levels. Angelika Strohmayer emphasizes the creation of safe and comfortable spaces for people to work and collaborate in as important – 'where all the regenerative work and all the community work is valued for what it is and where critique is taken as love and care' (Angelika Strohmayer, interview 10/06/2022).

Such networking and discourse acknowledge the long-term character of the process and see technology and its development as deeply rooted in social relations, locally, regionally, nationally, and internationally. 'I'm not going to create a perfect system, definitely not by myself', Angelika Strohmayer imagines:

> ... I would build a team that cares deeply about kindness and justice; and gets into the nitty-gritty of what technologies are or what they mean, how they support, how they hinder, how they oppress. And how the processes that are used to create them are powerful and amazing and hurtful and offensive and how it all fits into the global geopolitics – kind of capitalist hetero-patriarchy. Like I'm burning that down maybe and then rebuild[ing] from the ashes. Things that could be different, because they can, they are. People are doing that work already in their own little ways. Just connecting all of that up, I think, is a good place to start.
>
> (Angelika Strohmayer, interview 10/06/2022)

While often being reserved more generally for political campaigns, feminist/ queer advocacy can also be connected with the work of participatory infra-structuring in ICT projects. Bødker et al. (2017) use 'the concepts of knot-works, relational agency, and symbiotic agreements' to 'bring into focus activities and processes in which participants are not only engaged in designing technology, but in creating the structures, networks, and agreements that are crucial to creating sustainable outcomes' (p. 269). While their focus is on sustainable outcomes – IT artifacts and practices that will be appropriated, used, and eventually further developed in real-life/work contexts, participatory infrastructuring as a practice is also needed to advance design and social justice in a project. Huybrechts et al. (2017) specify some of the work involved – it requires 'legislation-checks, policy-checks, fund-raising, partnership-forming, reporting and assessments in relation to all parties involved' (p. 151). They also point to the need to expand participation by engaging in 'institutioning' – including institutions 'as political platforms and sites of change' (p. 151). This involves recognizing the potential of design projects to bring about 'institutional change in terms of policy frames, institutional action frames, and metacultural frames, primarily at the meso-level of the institutions involved' (p. 155).

The challenge is how to find the important stakeholders to collaborate with and how to extend the networks and alliances with a view towards contributing to the long-term aims of gender and social justice in design. There are examples to learn from. The Fablab@school.dk project (Bødker et al. 2017) is not about gender equality. It, however, describes how the research team systematically expanded the reach of a single project in one school to introducing digital fabrication technologies and design thinking in the Danish school curriculum. This was done in the form of workshops that gradually engaged a wider set of stakeholders, starting with headmasters, teachers, and representatives from the municipality, to 'also include a public hearing with parents, national stakeholders, and other interested parties' (p. 262). Much of the work involved in participatory infrastructuring was political. Similarly, Strohmayer et al. (2017) expanded their collaboration with a sex-work charity, connecting with the sex workers rights movement, journalists, and other academics with a view to influence policymaking and law. Ellen Balka chose to accept a position 'in the belly of the beast' – a large public hospital – in order to be able to influence how technology design and implementation were carried out in health-care workplaces – a sector she began working in specifically because it was full of women and full of technology, and hence would serve as an excellent 'living lab' where she could try to effect change (Balka 2006). Over what became a more than two-decade affiliation with the hospital, many of the projects Balka worked on surfaced women's voices during design and implementation while simultaneously engaging in 'political infrastructuring' (e.g., Balka and Kahnamoui 2004; Balka 2009).

Historically, the trade unions have been an important ally for change. However, they have been challenging for women to work with and the relationships between women workers and trade unionists have been ambivalent. Reporting on 'The First International Conference on Women and Work' in Turin, Italy, in 1982 Cynthia Cockburn (1984) noted,

First, women's struggle within the unions cannot succeed through the initiative only of feminists in influential positions. It requires a very difficult choreography involving a simultaneous mass movement of women rank and file members. Second, women, once their needs are expressed and their strengths unleashed, inevitably pose challenges about openness and democracy in the trade unions and so ally with the left in a combination that is threatening to the traditional union leadership.

(Cockburn 1982, p. 44)

The Italian women's movement in the 1970s was particularly powerful, as the example of union-led labour struggles at Fiat shows (Chapter 4). In the same time period in Canada, working-class and socialist-feminist activists 'developed a strong feminist presence in the labour movement and a significant working-class orientation in the women's movement that both continue to influence the current women's movement' (Luxton 2001, p. 63). Women trade union activism has expanded with a 'focus on the oppressive power of capital over workers to include gendered concerns, experiences, and demands of women workers' (Kennedy-Macfoy et al. 2021, p. 522). Women outnumber men in trade unions in many countries, in Eastern and Northern Europe, Canada, Australia, Ireland, and the UK, and the number of women union members still on the rise in 'nearly all countries' (ILO 2020, p. 5). Bronfenbrenner and Warren (2007) emphasize that in the USA, 'workers of color, especially black men and women, are organizing successfully at disproportionate rates, even though they have been the hardest hit' by job losses in manufacturing and the public sector (p. 144). Given the informality of women's labour in many countries, they are marginalized in trade unions and pushed to devise strategies of their own. An example is the activism undertaken by female rank-and-file workers in industrial zones, which was informal, but 'played a crucial role in the progressive changes to labour relations in Vietnam' (Chi and van den Broek 2020, p. 1145) (see Chapter 4).

With respect to design, these and other strategies help enlarge the agenda of an ICT project to achieve gender equality. They do this by engaging stakeholders that are relevant to this goal, horizontally and vertically, moving in circles of more immediate design work and political work on different levels. Doing this necessitates long-term engagements that go well beyond traditional notions of research and traditional notions of design.

How Do We Connect with Moves to Decolonize Discourses and Practices of IT Design?

Moves to decolonize discourses and practices are not accidentally connected with a feminist/intersectional perspective on design. As Luiza Prado stated, 'I believe that decolonization must emerge from an engagement with feminist and queer theories', adding, 'A decolonial politics must be a feminist politics; otherwise, we risk reinforcing the same structures that we set out to deconstruct' (Schultz et al. 2018, pp. 16–17). Key themes common to both are: showing respect of other people and cultures; being mindful of 'othernesses' of different kinds; providing space for other experiences, ways of expressing, and developing ideas about computing; being aware of over-layering systems of oppression and their historical roots. Both are also deeply internationalist: seeking connections to advocacy groups and research teams internationally, thinking about what design/social justice mean in other social, cultural, and political contexts.

Specific to decolonization is the aspiration to 'think from and at the margins/ borders/periphery of the world system' (Ali 2014, p. 1). While such a move is essential to design justice on a global scale, considering Haraway's (1988) notion of partial translations adds a helpful caveat. She argued that 'Science has been about a search for translation, convertibility, mobility of meanings, and universality – which I call reductionism only when one language (guess whose) must be enforced as the standard for all the translations and conversions' (p. 187). In writing about the standardization of technology production, Lucy Suchman (2002) explores the possibilities of replacing 'universal languages' for translation across devices by 'densely structured islands of customization' (p. 100). Apart from posing theoretical challenges, such a program requires collaboration across borders – what Winschiers-Theophilus et al. (2019) call transcultural engagement approaches. They add that such an approach also 'opens up a controversial debate about protecting versus integrating local epistemologies' (p. 1).

We think of decolonization of IT design practices as a multilayered endeavour that requires addressing several interrelated issues.

'Ownership' of concepts: Marisol Wong-Villacres met difficulties when she started using 'Western' concepts, such as intersectionality and care, transferring them to her own context: 'But for me, it was like, there might be things that we get excited about, because they seem so promising for our own agendas' (Marisol Wong-Villacres, interview 09/13/2022). While it is important to take a historical view and be respectful of where concepts come from, we also think that concepts can/should be transferred to other contexts where they may take different meanings. As an example, Adair et al. (2006) use the term 'indigenization' of psychological knowledge, by which they mean 'the blending of an imported discipline with the generation of new concepts and approaches from within a culture' (p. 155). Nicola Bidwell adopts the notion of 'meshwork' to characterize 'inhabitant' and 'occupant' knowledge and to

discuss their differences and mutual interplay, as well as the different temporalities they follow (in Simone et al. 2022).

Respect for 'other' knowledges, values, and resources: Related to this, researchers from other (non-Western) cultures emphasize the value for HCI to develop practices that are informed by other knowledge systems, as these not only are more appropriate for people developing and using technologies in these contexts but also enrich the dominant (Western) ways of designing. In this spirit, Bidwell (2016) emphasizes the need to make African HCI research and practice visible. She mentions 'Mbembe's (2001) reference to the "nothingness" ascribed to Africa' that 'builds on Frantz Fanon's recognition of the sense of nonexistence that colonized black and African people experience in everyday interactions with the world' (p. 24). She highlights the problematic primacy of the visual in HCI; whereas 'drama, song, and oral performances [are] closest to the way African cultures share meanings in ordinary life' (p. 26). Chilisa et al. (2016) argue that evaluation, which they consider 'the worst instrument of epistemological imperialism' (p. 314), should be led by African worldviews and values; among them, 'sharing and collective ownership of opportunities, responsibilities, and challenges ... the importance of people and relationships over things ... participatory decision-making and leadership' (p. 322). In a study of repairers of mobile phones in Kenya, Wyche et al. (2015) point to mismatches between the design of mobile phones and the contexts in which they are used, mentioning among other things dirt or sand getting inside the phone and damaging the parts that receive and emit sound, and broken screens; Jackson et al. (2012) emphasize the importance of acknowledging what they call 'broken-world thinking' for design.

Avoid potentially exploitative relationships: Reflecting on a collaborative project on post-partum health design, Catherine D'Ignazio (2019) asks,

> Could using anti-oppression frameworks in HCI actually be more harmful than traditional models because they lead to researchers relying on moral superiority ('trust us – we are some of the good guys') and inauthentic horizontal treatment ('we are the same as you') while failing to recognize the very real differences in identity, power and money that are at play?
>
> (D'Ignazio 2019, p. 3)

Of special concern is 'the tendency of academics to benefit from the marginality of others, without necessarily paying back to the collaborators' (Lea et al. 2021, p. 12). While not denying this danger – 'you go for a couple weeks, test something, get some data and publish' – Marisol Wong-Villacres emphasizes that this is not how most collaborations happen: 'They have long-term relationships with organizations there, and they're constantly engaging in conversations and trying to see how they can channel some of the resources. Though, it is a minefield, for sure' (Marisol Wong-Villacres, interview 09/13/2022). In their conversation, Débora de Castro Leal, Angelika Strohmayer and Max Krüger (2021) spoke about how to navigate this minefield – 'we build trust and engage in a dialogue where academic skills can be entangled with local knowledge' (p. 8). In their work on establishing a Community Network with the Mankosi community, South Africa, the researchers ensured that all decision-making was in the hands of the community and/or its elders. They also emphasize the importance of 'living locally' as well as local capacity-building when engaging in project activities within another culture (Rey-Moreno et al. 2013). While these are important conditions for ensuring local control and the integration of local knowledge, tensions created by the researchers' stance as expert and the ongoing colonial power relations in the production of knowledge are not easy to overcome.

Knowledge: How to Take a Feminist Perspective with Regard to Teaching

Already back in the 1990s researchers working on women in computing pointed to the ways computer science was taught as one of the sources of women's problems of relating to it as an interesting field. Clegg and Trayhurn (2000) presumed that the focus on mathematical formalisms, AI, and computer vision turned away women that may otherwise select computing; Frenkel (1990) suggested that working with software packages that allow students 'to do something functional quickly' (p. 41) would 'attract more women who prefer to use computers as tools rather than toys'. Ideas of feminist pedagogy influenced the following debates about how to teach computing. Yates and Plagnol (2022) define a feminist approach to teaching:

> ... in contrast to the traditional model which suggests a single reality and therefore silences and disempowers many learners, feminist pedagogy focuses on the idea of working together in a collaborative community, within a respectful and reflective culture, underpinned by the three central concepts of community, empowerment and leadership.
>
> (Yates and Pagnol 2022, p. 3084)

Ingrid Erickson practices a feminist pedagogy in her own teaching as a practice concerned with enabling learners to develop their own strategies of recognizing and valuing the complexities of real-life issues – to see that there can well be more than one 'right answer':

> If you engage in any of the things that we care about, there is no right answer, there's a process of trying to understand the complexities that might be involved, and you

know, weighing those things to be able to come up with the ... maybe the best answer, if you will, instead of the right answer. ... So, I think of ultimately my job for whatever gender experience you're coming from, is learn to speak from your voice. Have a voice, right?

(Ingrid Erickson, interview 03/30/2022)

Teaching from this perspective becomes visible as a practice that is very much concerned with a thoughtful balancing of power structures. This is also about learning to 'speak from your own voice'.

I'm nudging them a little bit in the beginning where it feels slightly uncomfortable, but then you can't shut them up in a certain sense. Like, if they want to have a voice, and then all of a sudden, it feels like the most magical superpower.

(Ingrid Erickson, interview 03/30/2022)

Such a learning atmosphere lets the teacher mindfully step back:

So, I consider that to be a very feminist, pedagogical manoeuvre. I don't orient it towards, like, I'm often also trying to get out of the way and trying to create a conversation amongst all of us. It's very hard to disabuse the role power that I have in the classroom, I do have power by that position. And I acknowledge that. But I also really like organized class around a lot of collective projects and a lot of open discussion. ... I think this idea of creating structures for equity, creating kind of, like structure, so everyone has a voice – it's maybe dated in the moment of intersectionality ... But to me, that's still a basic baseline that we need to have.

(Ingrid Erickson, interview 03/30/2022)

Also part of a feminist pedagogy is 'the exploration and thinking through of the use of digital tools in a hands-on manner' (Corneliussen et al. 2018, p. 6). There are numerous examples of this approach: for example; Buchholz et al. (2014) found that when children use e-textiles, 'materials like needles, fabric, and conductive thread rupture traditional gender scripts around electronics and implicitly gives girls hands-on access and leadership roles' (p. 1). Angelika Strohmayer et al. (e.g., 2020) engaged in various projects using digitally augmented participatory craft. Corneliussen et al. (2018) perceive in these and other exercises a chance for students to experience technologies 'in renewed and different ways from their assumed everyday leisure or work use'; with the result that through 'the process of building, co-creating and living in online spaces, it is possible for them to understand the production of selves as within gendered and raced hierarchies through technospatial praxis' (p. 6).

Sometimes it is the space and equipment itself that can foster supportive and welcoming ways of teaching and learning, as it enables new ways of exploration. Practitioners of a feminist pedagogy all emphasize the need for safe spaces, looking at this need from different angles. From an intersectionalist perspective, Ren (2022) highlights the need to focus 'on building a participatory, collaborative, inclusive, reflective, and experiential learning community where students' voices, experiences, identities, and contributions could be valued' (p. 459). In an online making and learning project with refugee, asylum seeking, and immigrant women (Sistercraft) Hedditch and Yvas (2023) formulate an ethos of care and safe spaces. The space was designed 'specifically for accessibility by an intersectional audience, situating the Sisters' experience, their level of comfort and discomfort, and care as central tenants to the design of the platform and its content' (p. 33). On the other hand, Smit and Fuchsberger (2020) argue, while it may be possible to design makerspaces in ways that are welcoming for women, in 'nerdy environments' women are often confronted with 'wicked ways(s) of closing a system' (p. 6).

Studying the role of humour at a computer science department, Valeria Borsotti and Pernille Bjørn identified 'ways in which traditions and rituals of humor risk iteratively re-producing negative stereotypes of underrepresented groups in computing' (Borsotti and Bjørn 2022, p. 777). Equity is the focus that helps 'zooming in on the unintentional or intentional barriers (often rooted in pervasive bias, or structural dynamics) that prevent certain groups of people from reaching their full potential' (p. 777). So, spaces for learning can be fundamentally unsafe and unwelcoming, exposing young women and other marginalized groups to harmful traditions and rituals. Borsotti and Bjørn add another valuable observation concerning the potential of learning spaces to strengthen students' political awareness:

> Students are aware of and critical of the socio-political aspects of global technology development, as it is clear from the social commentaries weaved into some of their songs, but a critical sensibility to the power differentials created along the axes of gender and race is missing. ... This could mean providing current students with the academic skills to better discuss, critically analyse and understand the impact of computing in shaping our future world.
>
> (Borsotti and Bjørn 2022, p. 795)

One of the baselines to these understandings of what a feminist pedagogy is, as Luigina Ciolfi puts it, is that it should not be just a specialized province of feminist women. Rather, feminist pedagogy should be broadly embedded in all learning about how to approach a technology design process:

> Ideally, it should be a concern for anyone who then goes into the world to design the things we use every day ... I would try and make it as explicit as I can in terms of requirements or scenarios: to try to include as many types of people and as many genders as possible.
>
> (Luigina Ciolfi, interview 03/31/2022)

Pernille Bjørn argues along similar lines:

> If we were to expand the idea of diversity and equity and inclusion in computing, we cannot just think about gender, we also need to think about other things and move from that. How do we make it relevant that this is not just about who participates? [It] is also about how it's relevant for data structures, how it's relevant for the entire design of user interface or how it's relevant for the algorithms we designed?
>
> (Pernille Bjørn, interview 04/20/2022)

Toni Robertson is quite clear about her pedagogy, emphasizing mutual learning and the need for students to understand that technologies are appropriated in use and how it is important to account for this in design. She also shared her insights about opening computer science for indigenous students. She and her colleagues did 'lots of interviews with indigenous academics, local indigenous people, admin people in organizations, to just to try and get a picture of where it was, we came out with a number of recommendations for setting up this particular program'. She is particularly proud of the way they set up this program. They

> deliberately referred to [it] as a non-heroic program, because the kids that were coming through that might be interested in studying computing, often came from Australia, were disadvantaged in their families to go to uni, and all sorts of things . . . were shy, came from a group of people who were treated very badly. So, they were losing self-confidence. That was all so that we said: These people do not want to be made into public figures, they want to be supported in their studies. And that's a different way of doing it.
>
> (Toni Robertson, interview 05/18/2022)

Resources: How to Get Funding and Get Published

There has been progress concerning the presence and visibility of women and other marginalized groups in design-related research fields. For example, the National Science Foundation (NSF), the main funder of computing and engineering research as well as social sciences and humanities research in the USA, regularly reports about the proportion of women graduating from STEM programs, as well as the proportion of women receiving funds from the NSF. However, there does not seem to be a formal requirement that applicants for funding address gender issues. In Canada, the Tri-Agency Equity, Diversity and Inclusion Action Plan for 2018–2025[2] highlights a number of

---

[2] www.nserc-crsng.gc.ca/InterAgency-Interorganismes/EDI-EDI/Action-Plan_Plan-dAction_ eng.asp, viewed 06/01/2023. One of the report's objectives (1.4) suggests that 'equity, diversity and inclusion considerations are integral to criteria used to assess research excellence, understood to include contributions of members of the research community, research design

changes to be implemented in an effort to more equitably distribute research funding to 'under-represented groups' (which include women). Canada's main health research funder – The Canadian Institutes of Health Research – is a signatory on the Government of Canada's Health Portfolio Sex- and Gender-Based Analysis Policy and Canada's Tri-Council Policy Statement on Ethical Conduct for Research Involving Humans, which both 'underscore the importance of integrating sex and gender into health research when appropriate'. CIHR has stated an expectation that 'all research applicants will integrate sex and gender into their research design and practices when appropriate' (CIHR, https://cihr-irsc.gc.ca/e/50833.html, viewed 06/01/2023).[3] However, many grant review committees are ill-equipped to evaluate the inclusion of sex and gender in research funding applications, and accountability is limited.

European funding bodies ask applicants to deal with gender in substantial ways. Researchers may add a statement about the need to attend to intersectionality beyond racialized and gendered stereotypes, Burtscher and Spiel (2020) propose:

> ... in detailing one's assumptions on gender and equity, clarifying specifically why and where this matters within the proposal creates a best practice. In that regard, being precise in language and acknowledging potential biases in data sets (whether pre-existing or created) guides reviewers' understanding of the subject matter.
>
> (Burtscher and Spiel 2020, p. 438)

However, a feminist/intersectional perspective is still at the margins of the 'mainstream' of research that gets funded and published. Revisiting the postpartum health design project, Catherine D'Ignazio (2019) asks,

> Why was it easier for a group of majority white women who had much less domain experience to secure funds? The fact that the money flows more freely to academia (and, likely, to any larger, whiter institution) is a power differential that we must contend with. What do anti-oppressive funding models (that still involve academics or academic institutions) look like? What might HCI research stand to gain if we prioritized (and rewarded) long-term thinking and long-term relationship building? Can people in HCI leverage racial and institutional privilege without reinscribing it?
>
> (D'Ignazio 2019, p. 4)

We want to emphasize the importance of 'long-term thinking and long-term relationship building'. This, however, is something most funding schemes do

---

and practices, and approaches to team-based research and training'. However, it remains to be seen how this will be addressed in practice.

[3] CIHR has, however, produced excellent resources to support researchers in developing a sex- and gender-based analysis in health research, which can easily be applied to other areas of research.

not support. Projects – the prevalent form of funding – usually are short-term, making it difficult to build relationships that would allow groups to tackle larger aims and/or consolidate results. There is a need for funding institutions to extend their time horizons and to also dedicate resources to the often-invisible work of building trust and developing practices of collaboration (Simone et al. 2022).[4]

The second of D'Ignazio's (2019) issues is anti-oppressive funding models. At its beginning, participatory designers strongly collaborated with trade unions; with the aim of increasing workplace democracy in terms of workers' rights to codetermine (technological and other) changes affecting their workplaces. Also, some of the early science shops in Europe, such as the so-called 'Berliner Wissenschaftsladen', launched in 1982, had as their goals support for a more 'humane' information technology. The 'Sassafras Tech Collective, a worker-cooperative tech consultancy', is continuing this tradition (Smith and Dimmond 2014). We think these traditions are worthwhile to think about in terms of funding.

Another strategy taken by researchers dedicated to a gender/intersectional and decolonizing perspective is to create spaces at the big and influential tech conferences for presenting and discussing local work. Bidwell (2016) has pointed to the growing number of local HCI conferences: 'AfriCHI '16 joins a list of HCI conferences (e.g., Latin America's CLIHC, Australia's OZCHI, and Asia-Pacific APCHI), which showcase local work, support regional attendance through accessibility, and contribute to international discourse' (p. 22). The US-based HCI conferences and CSCW conferences not only have been held in other parts of the world but are also brimming with events that provide space for voicing political agendas and presenting and discussing work from a feminist/intersectional perspective. Still researchers think that there is much more to do, as getting access to and having a paper accepted at one of these conferences is difficult. Rivera-Loaiza and Wong-Villacres (2022), for example, launched the Global Plaza event at CHI 2022 as members of the conference's Global Equity and Inclusion committee, 'with the intention of providing participation alternatives for as many people as possible. The result was the Global Plaza proposal; a space that, 'using the metaphor of a public square, offers a welcoming, highly informal, and collaborative environment as the entry point to the conference' (p. 2).

---

[4] Canadian funding agencies have a suite of funding programs that support early stages of partnership development as well as more mature partnerships. However, the more lucrative partnership grants require extensive in-kind and/or cash contributions from partners, which may limit the range of organizations able to participate.

The most critical issue is how to support researchers that write from a marginalized perspective in publishing their work. Achieving this requires addressing two issues: the peer-review process and the conference calls that propose specific publishing formats.[5] With respect to the first issue, groups of researchers have put forward some suggestions. From a Latin American perspective, Reynolds-Cuéllar et al. (2022) point to a

> political process of gatekeeping of marginalized voices ... [W]hen working within universalist, western knowledge structures, peer review serves as an instrument for perpetuating those structures' understanding of rigor and legitimacy of research, allowing for multiple biases to work against non-dominant views within academic communities.
>
> (Reynolds-Cuéllar et al. 2022, p. 3)

They propose an alternative approach to reviewing based on five principles: 'citational justice, epistemic justice, emancipation, relationality and position-ality'. They raise a number of critical questions that make it clear that changing the review process is an endeavour that has to be done with caution: 'We believe that further critical inquiry is required to re-imagine peer review, and scholarly knowledge-making more broadly, as a relational process. For once, during this exercise we weren't able to critically address the question: who is a peer and why?' (p. 9). Other issues of concern are language and the danger 'that selective incorporation of ideas from the South may depoliticize them and foreclose the sense of urgency with which intellectual pursuits are made in their context' (p. 9).

An important insight is the relational nature of doing research. This should be reflected in citational practices, the Citational Justice Collective (2022) contends. These practices 'could be transformed to underscore their relational nature, reconceptualizing them as acts of listening, as opposed to transactional or performative practices'. Among the questions to ask would be 'Who decides who is worthy of being listened to? Who disrupts, challenges, and enhances our thinking?' (p. 3). They also propose putting the collective effort upfront and having help organizing the research, collecting the data, discussing the findings, and motivation to write a paper count as part of its authorship.

Departing from the notion of situated knowledges, Chen et al. (2017) add a more general point to this debate:

---

[5] Of course, conference attendance itself has a gendered component, with mothers (particularly of young children) often having to either decline conference attendance in order to care for young children or juggle care and professional responsibilities at conferences at their own financial cost.

> But the promise of situated knowledges here often remains unfulfilled when
> transcribed into research papers, as we still require these practices to be
> communicated through the paper and are required to submit this writing so that it is
> subject to the same conferences and journals as non-situated practice.
>
> (Chen et al. 2017, p. 2080)

All these thoughts about citation practices, (collective) authorship, and publishing formats do apply to researchers from marginalized groups. What is not sufficiently honoured in academia is their special approach and way of presenting that seemingly do not fit the traditional publishing formats. Hence, Chen et al. (2017) propose to experiment with 'more curatorially-oriented decisions' in the design of calls in the hope to 'subvert the dominant "performative scripts" expected of us' (p. 2083). With respect to gender, there is an additional hurdle to take: that of having gender acknowledged as a research topic that fits into the agenda of a journal or conference.

Regulation of the Computer Industry

When we look at opportunities for gendered perspectives in IT design, we need to speak about the current trends in the computer industry. Over the last two decades, the software industry has developed business models based on the platform economy, big (personal) data, cloud computing, and ML, which are highly problematic, from a societal as well as a gender perspective. These business models destroy liberal democracies, but they also challenge and discriminate against the interests of women and minorities.

Zuboff (2019) has analyzed these developments in the computer industry and termed them 'surveillance capitalism' – the provision of ostensibly 'free' services while monitoring the users' behaviour in extraordinary detail. Users 'pay' for the services of the internet platforms with their data. Contextualizing these developments historically, Couldry and Mejias (2019) speak about 'data colonialism', the exploitation of human beings through big collections of their personal data that offer unprecedented opportunities for social discrimination and behavioural influence. Landwehr et al. (2019 and 2023) have pointed to the destructive influence of these business models on liberal democracies and sustainable economic development. Feminist scholars have discussed the relationship between data and power (e.g., D'Ignazio and Klein 2020) and contributed insights about the need to fight for 'data justice' (e.g., Dencik et al. 2019).

The issues at stake reach beyond data justice; they concern the IT industry and the ways that software is produced. We have argued in this book that designing for diversity requires attention towards context and participatory methods. Moreover, software infrastructures and applications should be flexible in a technical sense; hence, they should be adaptable to the specific needs in their fields of application, and these needs may evolve over time (Stiemerling et al. 1997). However, the current developments in the software industry undermine technical flexibility and make gender-sensitive design approaches difficult to implement on a larger scale.

Internet platforms tend to offer standardized functionalities for free and grab, in compensation, the personal data of their users. Cloud computing plays a key role in this process: by moving locally produced data towards anonymous data centres on the Internet, it supports storage and analysis of the extracted personal data under the control of the platform companies. Capitalizing on their cloud infrastructure, platform companies have built whole cloud eco-systems that aim at attracting additional parts of the software industry into their proprietary cloud. While the business model of these companies may vary, cloud computing here again comes at the cost that the functionality becomes more standardized – software in the cloud serves a big number of different users. Due to their proprietary nature, the platform companies' eco-systems lock-in and control increasing parts of the software industry.

Given the abundance of extracted data, ML and the training of neural networks have become crucially important and have reached new levels of performance. Trained networks enable the platforms to automatically adapt their functionality with regard to the individual users. However, this 'individualization' of an application's functionality follows the platforms' algorithms and embedded intentions; it does not offer any opportunity for tailoring by the individual. Such models foreclose opportunities to alter software, so it better meets the needs of women and minorities.

The obvious and somehow surprising success stories of ML in domains where platforms had extracted huge amounts of data (e.g., in image recognition, language processing, and translation) has reoriented big parts of the computer industry. The training of algorithms replaces traditional styles of programming, in which code explicitly and deterministically prescribes a program's functions. A modification of the algorithmic behaviour cannot be enacted manually in the code or during use while tailoring, but rather requires additional data that represent modified behaviours. In this way, options for socially just designs reflecting feminist and intersectional views of the world are narrowed.

All these developments lead to the creation of larger sets of mostly personal data that are not stored in the context of their emergence. They are typically stored on anonymous servers and can be used both for the training of neural networks as well as for surveillance and manipulation purposes. Decontextualized data are just as problematic as decontextualized design: both are prone to misinterpretation, and both leave ample room for reproduction of the status quo. The absence of context leaves feminist ideals and the goals of design justice blowing aimlessly about in the wind.

A feminist data ethics of care (e.g., Gray and Witt 2021), 'resistant data practices' (Milan and Treré 2021), as well as the meta-tagging of data (Schuurman and Balka 2009; Pot et al. 2019) have been proposed as strategies to challenge 'data colonialism' and halt the use of decontextualized data as the basis of algorithms that systematically reproduce bias and help maintain power structures. Moreover, Landwehr et al. (2019) have suggested that we abolish private ownership of platform eco-systems and regulate the platform economy in a strict sense, specifically to give users back control of their data. This would avoid technological lock-ins and reintroduce competition into monopolistic platform structures. The EU, China, and some other countries have started to build up first instances of significant regulatory frameworks in an effort to wrestle back control of our data. The different approaches to regulation represent the different societal values and political systems, and the opportunities for gender orientation in design. The support for diversity available to us will largely depend on the level of regulation and the ownership models of these internet monopolies.

Summary

With this chapter we have tried to reflect on some of the challenges surrounding the broader context of design. In the previous chapters (Chapters 10 and 11) we focussed on how to design for women and other marginalized groups by describing possible interventions in design processes, designing artifacts and work, and the outcomes of design processes. In contrast, here we have tried to reflect on the larger contexts in which these activities take place – the more 'macro' structures that present challenges, including the software industry. We have highlighted the need for data that describes not only women's experiences, but also the experiences of those who are gender-queer, belong to racialized groups, and for these and other reasons experience marginalization in life and exclusion in and through design. The need for sensitivity towards both language and identities will be essential to the creation of space that welcomes diverse populations often relegated to the margins. This, of course, needs to be accompanied by awareness of cultural differences and the need to make space for and honour cultural differences.

The foundations of all of this lie in the recognition that the ability to exercise citizenship – to walk through life with agency – is at the heart of all equality; for women, for gender queer individuals of all varieties and groups who have suffered through racism and colonialism. Agency is a key aspect of citizenship, and agency is a communal achievement, rather than an individual attribute. Arguably, that is what gender equality is about – having an equal ability to succeed and thrive whether you are cis-gendered, gender-queer, or trans; whether you are straight or gay or bi.; or of a dominant or minority ethnicity. We've tried to show throughout the book that achieving gender equality in relation to technology and work has many dimensions and will require many small and large interventions to produce work with technology that gives women agency and helps us restore citizenship.

Postscript

We have covered a considerable amount of ground. After beginning with some working definitions of gender and technology and providing an overview of the ethical-political approach to design, we went on to address historical and contemporary studies concerned with the interaction of gender and technology at work. The first step was to look back, collecting and presenting studies of women's paid employment in different areas of work. This was done with the aim to describe key insights about gender and technology that were gained in these early studies and analyze in what ways they influenced our approach to system design and design justice. A crucial role was, for example, played by findings about invisible work. We also demonstrated how the early studies of women and technology at work helped lay the foundation for related areas that are concerned with design justice in relation to technology at work – such as critical race studies, queer studies, and intersectionality.

We have paid particular attention to the importance of understanding context when it comes to creating IT systems, artifacts, and new forms of working that 'work' for women. Throughout each of the chapters we have also emphasized contributions that a focus on women's work offer for the practice of CSCW research, PD, and HCI. Many of the issues we identified can be captured through a focus on intersectionality.

We hope that our readers will close the book with a conviction that the approach we have outlined will be broadly applicable in addressing matters of design justice in relation to gender diversity and ethnicity (but of course will need to be appropriated and adopted in ways that reflect the nuances of different populations). We also hope that our readers are left with a passion to continue thinking about and working towards design justice for women and other disadvantaged people and communities.

Having said that, we are aware that there is much work to be done, and that many ambiguities and open issues remain that will require thoughtful dialogue. For example, as Rodriguez et al. (2016) point out in the editorial introduction to a special issue of *Gender, Work and Organizations* on intersectionality,

> Although scholarship on intersectionality has flourished, its impact has been uneven across disciplines. In the field of work and organizations, for example, despite the recognition of the workplace as a critical site for the (re)production of intersectional inequalities . . ., intersectionality has not been fully utilized to explore structures of discrimination and systems of power and inequality. Thus, despite its robust potential, intersectionality remains at the margins of dominant work and organization narratives of equality and inclusion even as global management and diversity initiatives abound.
>
> (p. 102)

Rodriguez et al. suggest that we, in the absence of a distinct intersectional methodology, develop methodological frameworks from within our disciplines, as this will increase the chances that the knowledge we produce will be accepted and legitimized within our disciplinary homes. They acknowledge that translating intersectional theory into methodologies will not be easy:

> The task is daunting and multifaceted: identify what data to collect and how to collect it; conduct analyses that address the mixture of the diversities and complex interactions of intersections; incorporate structural factors to account for the meaning and prioritization of categories in specific contexts, organizations and groups, all while capturing the fluidity and temporal nature of these simultaneous intersections.
>
> (p. 206)

They also argue that 'crafting methodologies' that are apt to capture all these complexities will be a formidable task. They suggest that we take up Mooney's (2016) call for a 'nimble' intersectionality that does not privilege one methodology over another but instead gives smart and agile attention to the alignment between intersectionality's theoretical assumptions and the methods selected to study them.

Change is uneven, complicated, and messy at the best of times, and arguably even more so when our goal is to challenge inequality with the aim of eliminating it. This can only be done by disrupting existing power relations and developing interventions on many levels aimed at challenging inequality across multiple settings, populations, and social locations. As we struggle to identify and disrupt the myriad ways that technologies are implicated in gendering processes (and how our engagements with technologies are implicated in the ways we understand ourselves as gendered beings), we need to care about and for one another, as the journey ahead will not be an easy one.

References

Abagi, Okwach, Sifuna, Olive, and Omamo, Salome Awuor (2009) Professional women empowered to succeed in Kenya's ICT sector. In Buskens, I. and Webb, A. (eds.), *African women & ICTs: Investigating technology, gender and empowerment*. London: Zed Books, 169–182.

Abbate, Janet (2012) *Recoding gender: Women's changing participation in computing*. Cambridge, MA: MIT Press.

Abrahamsson, Lena (2014) Gender and the modern organization, ten years after. *Nordic Journal of Working Life Studies* 4(4), 109–136.

Abrahamsson, Lena and Johansson, Jan (2020) Can new technology challenge macho-masculinities? The case of the mining industry. *Mineral Economics* 34, 263–275.

Abtan, Freida (2016) Where is she? Finding the women in electronic music culture. *Contemporary Music Review* 35(1), 53–60.

Acero, Liliana (1995) Conflicting demands of new technology and household work: Women's work in Brazilian and Argentinian textiles. In Mitter, S. and Rowbotham, S. (eds.), *Women encounter technology: Changing patterns of employment in the third world*. London: Routledge, 70–92.

Acker, Françoise (1995) Informatisation des unités de soins et travail de formalisation de l'activité infirmière. *Sciences Sociales et Santé* 13(3), 69–92.

Acker, Françoise (1997) Sortir de l'invisibilité: Le cas du travail infirmier. *Raisons pratiques* 8, 65–94.

Acker, Joan (1990) Hierarchies, jobs, bodies: A theory of gendered organizations. *Gender & Society* 4(2), 139–158.

Acker, Joan (1992) Gendering organizational analysis. In Mills, A.J. and Tancred, P. (eds.), *Classics of organizational theory*. Newbury Park, London, Delhi: Sage, 248–290.

Acker, Joan (1996) Review: Pleasure, power, & technology: Some tales of gender, engineering, and the cooperative workplace (Sally Hacker). *Contemporary Sociology* 25(4), 441.

Acker, Joan (2006) Inequality regimes: Gender, class, and race in organizations. *Gender & Society* 20(4), 441–464.

Adair, John G., Puhan, Biranci N., and Vohra, Neharika (1993) Indigenisation of psychology: Empirical assessment of progress in Indian research. *International Journal of Psychology* 28(2), 149–169.

Adam, Alison (1998) *Artificial knowing: Gender and the thinking machine*. London, New York: Taylor & Francis.

Adam, Alison (2001) Computer ethics in a different voice. *Information and Organization* 11(4), 235–261.

Addelson, Kathryn Pyne (1983) The man of professional wisdom. In Harding, S. and Hintikka, M.B. (eds.), *Discovering reality: Feminist perspectives on epistemology, metaphysics, methodology, and philosophy of science*. Dordrecht: Kluwer Academic Publisher, 165–186.

Agnew, John (2001) The new global economy: Time-space compression, geopolitics, and global uneven development. *Journal of World-Systems Research* 7(2), 133–154.

Ahmadi, Michael, Eilert, Rebecca, Weibert, Anne, Wulf, Volker, and Marsden, Nicola (2019) Hacking masculine cultures: Career ambitions of female young professionals in a video game company. In *Proceedings of the Annual Symposium on Computer–Human Interaction in Play CHI PLAY'19, October 22–25, 2019, Barcelona, Spain*. New York: ACM Press, 413–426.

Ahmadi, Michael, Eilert, Rebecca, Weibert, Anne, Wulf, Volker, and Marsden, Nicola (2020a) Feminist living labs as research infrastructures for HCI: The case of a video game company. In *Proceedings of the 2020 CHI Conference on Human Factors in Computing Systems CHI 2020, April 25–30, 2020, Honolulu, HI, USA*. New York: ACM Press, 1–15.

Ahmadi, Michael, Eilert, Rebecca, Weibert, Anne, Wulf, Volker and Marsden, Nicola (2020b) 'We want to push the industry via communication': Designing communication measures to foster gender diversity in a video game company. *Proceedings of the ACM on Human–Computer Interaction 4 (GROUP)*, 1–26.

Ahmed, Sara (2004) Affective economies. *Social Text* 22(2), 117–139.

Ainsworth, Susan, Batty, Alex, and Burchielli, Rosaria (2013) Women constructing masculinity in voluntary firefighting. *Gender, Work & Organization* 21(1), 37–56.

Akrich, Madeleine (1992) The de-scription of technical objects. In Bijker, W. and Law, J. (eds.), *Shaping technology/building society: Studies in sociotechnical change*. Cambridge, MA: MIT Press, 205–224.

Alegria, Sharla N. (2020) What do we mean by broadening participation? Race, inequality, and diversity in tech work. *Sociology Compass* 14(6), e12793.

Alemann, Anette von, Gruhlich, Julia, Horwath, Ilona, and Weber, Lena (2004) A plea to reflect on the entanglements of gendered work patterns and digital technologies. *Gender and Research* 21(2), 3–12.

Alfrey, Lauren and Twine, France Winddance (2017) Gender-fluid geek girls: Negotiating inequality regimes in the tech industry. *Gender & Society* 31(1), 28–50.

Ali, Mustafa (2014) Towards a decolonial computing. In Buchanan, E., de Laat, P., Tavani, H., and Klucarich, J. (eds.), *Ambiguous technologies: Philosophical issues, practical solutions*. Maidenhead: International Society of Ethics and Information Technology, The Open University, 28–35.

Almeida, Teresa, Balaam, Madeline, and Comber, Rob (2020) Woman-centered design through humanity, activism, and inclusion. *ACM Transactions on Computer–Human Interaction (TOCHI)* 27(4), 1–30.

Alper, Meryl (2017) *Giving voice: Mobile communication, disability, and inequality*. Cambridge, MA: MIT Press.

Amrute, Sareeta and Murillo, Luis Felipe R. (2020) Introduction: Computing in/from the South. *Catalyst: Feminism, Theory, Technoscience* 6(2), 1–23.

Andorno, Roberto (2014) Handbook of global bioethics. In Ten Have, H. and Gordijn, B. (eds.), *Human dignity and human rights*. Dordrecht: Springer, 45–57.

Andrew, Alison (2009) Challenging boundaries to 'employability': Women apprentices in a non-traditional occupation. *Social Policy and Society* 8(3), 347–359.

Arendt, Hannah (1958) *The human condition*. Chicago: Chicago University Press.

Arnstein, Sherry R. and Christakis, Alexander N. (1975) *Perspectives on technology assessment*. Jerusalem: Science and Technology Publishers.

Arora, Payal, Raman, Usha, and König, René (eds.) (2023) *Feminist futures of work: Reimagining labour in the digital economy*. Amsterdam: Amsterdam University Press.

Arun, Shoba and Arun, Thankom (2002) ICTs, gender and development: Women in software production in Kerala. *Journal of International Development: The Journal of the Development Studies Association* 14(1), 39–50.

Asad, Mariam (2019) Prefigurative design as a method for research justice. *Proceedings of the ACM on Human–Computer Interaction* 3, 1–18.

Ashcraft, Karen Lee (2022) *Wronged and dangerous: Viral masculinity and the populist pandemic*. Bristol: Bristol University Press.

Athreya, Bama (2021) *Bias in, bias out: Gender and work in the platform economy*. Ottawa: IDRC International Development Research Centre.

Baethge, Martin and Oberbeck, Herbert (1986) *Zukunft der Angestellten: neue Technologien und berufliche Perspektiven in Büro und Verwaltung*. Frankfurt: Campus Verlag.

Bagilhole, Barbara M., Dainty, Andrew R.J., and Neale, Richard H. (2002) A woman engineer's experiences of working on British construction sites. *International Journal of Engineering Education* 18(4), 422–429.

Baier, Annette (1986) Trust and antitrust. *Ethics* 29, 231–260.

Bainbridge, Lisanne (1983) Ironies of automation. *Automatica* 19(6), 775–779.

Balka, Ellen (1987) *Women and workplace technology: Educational strategies for change*. Vancouver: Simon Fraser University.

Balka, Ellen (1995) Technology as a factor in women's occupational stress: The case of telephone operators. In Messing, K., Dumais, L., and Neis, B. (eds.), *Invisible. La santé des travailleuses*. Charlottetown, PE: Gynergy, 75–103.

Balka, Ellen (1997) Sometimes texts speak louder than users: Locating invisible work through textual analysis. In Grundy, A.F., Kohler, D., Oechtering, V., and Petersen, U. (eds.), *Proceedings of the IFIP WG 9.1: Conference on Women, Work and Computerization: Spinning a Web from Past to Future*. New York: Springer, 163–176.

Balka, Ellen (2002) The invisibility of the everyday: New technology and women's work in telecommunications in Atlantic Canada. In Meehan, E. and Riordan, E. (eds.), *Sex and money: Feminism and political economy in the media*. Minneapolis: University of Minnesota Press, 60–74.

Balka, Ellen (2006) Inside the belly of the beast: The challenges and successes of a reformist participatory agenda. In *Proceedings of the Ninth Conference on Participatory Design: Expanding Boundaries in Design PDC 2006, Aug 1–5, 2006, Trento, Italy*, 134–143.

Balka, Ellen (2009) Gender, information technology and making health work: Unpacking complex relations at work. In Balka, E., Green, E., and Henwood, F. (eds.), *Gender, health and information in context*. Houndsmill and Basingstoke: Palgrave Macmillan, 104–121.

Balka, Ellen (2010) From categorization to public policy: The multiple roles of electronic triage. In Rudinow Sætnan, A., Lomell, H.M., and Hammer, S. (eds.), *By the very act of counting: The co-construction of statistics and society*. New York: Routledge, 172–190.

Balka, Ellen, Bøjrn, Pernille, and Wagner, Ina (2008) *Steps toward a typology for health informatics*. In Proceedings of the 2008 ACM conference on Computer supported cooperative work CSCW 2008, Nov 8–12, 2008, San Diego, 515–524.

Balka, Ellen and Butt, Arsalan (2008) Invisible logic: The role of software as an information intermediary in healthcare. In Wathen, N., Wyatt, S., and Harris, R. (eds.), *Mediating health information: The go-betweens in a changing socio-technical landscape*. Hampshire: Palgrave Press, 78–93.

Balka, Ellen, Doyle-Waters, Madeleine, Lecznarowicz, Dorota, and FitzGerald, J. Mark (2007) Technology, governance and patient safety: Systems issues in technology and patient safety. *International Journal of Medical Informatics* 76, S48–S57.

Balka, Ellen and Kahnamoui, Nickki (2004) Technology trouble? Talk to us! Findings from an ethnographic field study. In *Proceedings of the Eighth Conference on Participatory Design: Artful Integration: Interweaving Media, Materials and Practices PDC'04, July 27–31, 2004, Toronto, ON, Canada*. New York: ACM Press, 224–234.

Balka, Ellen, Reidl, Christine, and Wagner, Ina (2007) Using fieldwork in analyzing ethical issues related to IT in health care. In *Proceedings of the 12th World Congress on Health (Medical) Informatics MedInfo 2007 Brisbane*. AUS: IOS Press, 237–241.

Balka, Ellen and Star, Susan Leigh (2016) Mapping the body across diverse information systems: Shadow bodies and how they make us human. In Bowker, G.C., Timmermans, S., Clarke, A.E., and Balka, E. (eds.), *Boundary objects and beyond: Working with Leigh Star*. Cambridge, MA: MIT Press, 417–434.

Balka, Ellen and Wagner, Ina (2006) Making things work: Dimensions of configurability as appropriation work. In *Proceedings of the 20th Anniversary Conference on Computer Supported Cooperative Work, November 4–8, 2006, Banff, Alberta, Canada*. New York: ACM Press, 229–238.

Balka, Ellen and Wagner, Ina (2021) A historical view of studies of women's work. *Computer-Supported Cooperative Work (CSCW)* 30, 251–305.

Bannon, Liam, Schmidt, Kjeld, and Wagner, Ina (2011) Lest we forget: The European field study tradition and the issue of conditions of work in CSCW research. In *Proceedings of the 12th European Conference on Computer Supported Cooperative Work ECSCW 2011, 24–28 September 2011, Aarhus, Denmark*, 213–232.

Barber, Gerald, De Jong, Peter, and Hewitt, Carl (1983) *Semantic support for work in organizations*. Cambridge, MA: MIT Artificial Intelligence Laboratory.

Barbut, S. (2020) Meat industry 4.0: A distant future? *Animal Frontiers* 10(4), 38–47.

Bardzell, Shaowen (2010) Feminist HCI: Taking stock and outlining an agenda for design. In *Proceedings of the SIGCHI Conference on Human Factors in Computing Systems CHI 2010, April 10–15, 2010, Atlanta, GA*, 1301–1310.

Bardzell, Shaowen (2018) Utopias of participation: Feminism, design, and the futures. *ACM Transactions on Computer–Human Interaction (TOCHI)* 25(1), 1–24.

Barot, Rohit and Bird, John (2001) Racialization: The genealogy and critique of a concept. *Ethnic and Racial Studies* 24(4), 601–618.

Barua, Rukmini (2021) Feminine domesticity and emotions of gender: Work and women in 20th and early 21st century India. *L'Homme* 32(2), 59–78.

Bath, Corinna (2009) Searching for methodology: Feminist technology design in computer science. In Ernst, W. and Horwath, I. (eds.), *Gender in science and technology: Interdisciplinary approaches*. Bielefeld: Transcript Verlag, 57–76.

Beane, Matt and Orlikowski, Wanda J. (2015) What difference does a robot make? The material enactment of distributed coordination. *Organization Science* 26(6), 1553–1573.

Beauchamp, Tom L. and Childress, James F. (2001) *Principles of biomedical ethics*, 5th edn. New York: Oxford University Press.

Becker, Dana (2019) *Through the looking glass: Women and borderline personality disorder*. London and New York: Routledge.

Becker-Schmidt, Regina, Knapp, Gudrun-Axeli, and Schmidt, Beate (1984) *Eines ist zuwenig, beides ist zuviel: Erfahrungen von Arbeiterfrauen zwischen Familie und Fabrik*. Bonn: Neue Gesellschaft.

Beede, Emma, Baylor, Elizabeth, Hersch, Fred, Iurchenko, Anna, Wilcox, Lauren, Ruamviboonsuk, Paisan, and Vardoulakis, Laura M. (2020) A human-centered evaluation of a deep learning system deployed in clinics for the detection of diabetic retinopathy. In *Proceedings of the 2020 CHI Conference on Human Factors in Computing Systems CHI 2020, April 25–30, 2020, Honolulu, HI, USA*. New York: ACM Press, 1–12.

BEK (Austrian Bioethics Commission) (2020) *The work of physicians at the interface of big data, artificial intelligence and human experience*. Wien: Secretariat of the Bioethics Commission.

Belenky, Mary Field, Clinchy, Blythe McVicker, Goldberger, Nancy Rule, and Tarule, Jill Mattuck (1986) *Women's ways of knowing: The development of self, voice, and mind*. New York: Basic Books.

Bendl, Regine (2008) Gender subtexts – Reproduction of exclusion in organizational discourse. *British Journal of Management* 19, S50–S64.

Benner, Patricia (1954) *From novice to expert: Power and excellence in nursing practice*. Palo Alto, CA: Addison-Wellesley.

Bennett, Cynthia L. and Rosner, Daniela K. (2019) The promise of empathy: Design, disability, and knowing the 'other'. In *Proceedings of the 2019 CHI Conference on Human Factors in Computing Systems CHI 2019, May 4–9, 2019, Glasgow, Scotland, UK*. New York: ACM Press, 1–13.

Benschop, Yvonne and Doorewaard, Hans (1998a) Covered by equality: The gender subtext of organizations. *Organization Studies* 19(5), 787–805.

Benschop, Yvonne and Doorewaard, Hans (1998b) Six of one and half a dozen of the other: The gender subtext of Taylorism and team-based work. *Gender, Work & Organization* 5(1), 5–18.

Benston, Margaret Lowe (1988) Women's voices/men's voices: Technology as language. In Kramarae, C. (ed.), *Technology and women's voices: Keeping in touch*. London and New York: Routledge & Kegan Paul, 5–28.

Benston, Margaret Lowe (1989) Feminism and system design: Questions of control. In Benston, M. and Tomm, W. (eds.), *The effects of feminist approaches on research methodologies.* Waterloo, ON: Wilfrid Laurier University Press, 205–224.

Bentley, Richard and Dourish, Paul (1995) Medium versus mechanism: Supporting collaboration through customisation. In Marmolin, H., Sundblad, Y., and Schmidt, K. (eds.), *Proceedings of the Fourth European Conference on Computer-Supported Cooperative Work ECSCW'95: 10–14 September 1995, Stockholm, Sweden.* Dordrecht: Springer, 133–148.

Berg, Marc (1999) Accumulating and coordinating: Occasions for information technologies in medical work. *Computer Supported Cooperative Work (CSCW)* 8, 373–401.

Berger, Johannes and Offe, Claus (1982) Functionalism vs. rational choice? Some questions concerning the rationality of choosing one or the other. *Theory and Society* 11(4), 521–526.

Bernays, Marie (1910/2012) Auslese und Anpassung der Arbeiterschaft der geschlossenen Grossindustrie: dargestellt an den Verhältnissen der Gladbacher Spinnerei und Weberei AG zu München-Gladbach im Rheinland. [Edited new edition of the dissertation, printed in Leipzig, 1910 edn.] *Schriftenreihe des Fachbereiches Sozialwesen an der Hochschule Niederrhein.* Essen: Klartext Verlag.

Bidwell, Nicola J. (2016) Decolonising HCI and interaction design discourse: Some considerations in planning AfriCHI. *XRDS: Crossroads, The ACM Magazine for Students* 22(4), 22–27.

Biondi, Gianfranco and Rickards, Olga (2011) *L'errore della razza. Avventure e sventure di un mito pericoloso.* Roma: Carocci Editore.

Birbaumer, Andrea, Lebano, Adele, Ponzellini, Anna, Tolar, Marianne, and Wagner, Ina (2007) From the margins to a field of opportunities: Life story patterns of women in ICT. *Women's Studies International Forum* 30(6), 486–498.

Birbaumer, Andrea, Tolar, Marianne, and Wagner, Ina (2008) Biographical Stories of European Women Working in ICT. In Van Slyke, C. (ed.), *Information communication technologies: Concepts, methodologies, tools, and applications.* New York: IGI Global, 472–479.

Birhane, Abeba. (2021) Algorithmic injustice: A relational ethics approach. *Patterns* 2 (2), 100201.

Birke, Linda and Vines, Gail (1987) Beyond nature versus nurture: Process and biology in the development of gender. *Women's Studies International Forum* 10(6), 555–570.

Bjerknes, Gro and Bratteteig, Tone (1986) *Florence in wonderland: System development with nurses.* Oslo: Department of Informatics, University of Oslo.

Bjerknes, Gro and Bratteteig, Tone (1988) Computers – Utensils or epaulets? The application perspective revisited. *AI & Society* 2(3), 258–266.

Bjørn, Pernille and Balka, Ellen (2007) Health care categories have politics too: Unpacking the managerial agendas of electronic triage systems. In *Proceedings of the 10th European Conference on Computer-Supported Cooperative Work, 24–28 September 2007, Limerick, Ireland.* London: Springer, 371–390.

Bjørn, Pernille, Menendez-Blanco, Maria, and Borsotti, Valeria (2022) *Diversity in computer science: Design artefacts for equity and inclusion.* Cham: Springer Nature.

Bjørn, Pernille and Rosner, Daniela K. (2021) Intertextual design: The hidden stories of Atari women. *Human–Computer Interaction* 37(4), 370–395.

Blomberg, Jeanette, Giacomi, Jean, Mosher, Andrea and Swenton-Wall, Pat (1993) Ethnographic fieldwork methods and their relation to design. In Schuler, D. and Namioka, A. (eds.), *Participatory design: Principles and practices*. Boca Raton, FL: CRC Press, 123–155.

Blomberg, Jeanette and Karasti, Helena (2013) Reflections on 25 years of ethnography in CSCW. *Computer Supported Cooperative Work (CSCW)* 22(4–6), 1–51.

Blomberg, Jeanette, Megahed, Aly, and Strong, Ray (2018) Acting on analytics: Accuracy, precision, interpretation, and performativity. In *Proceedings of Ethnographic Praxis in Industry EPIC 2018, 10–12 September 2018, Honolulu, HI*, 281–300.

Blomberg, Jeanette, Suchman, Lucy, and Trigg, Randall (1996) Reflections on a work-oriented design project. *Human-Computer-Interaction* 11(3), 237–266.

Bluhm, Robyn (2013) New research, old problems: Methodological and ethical issues in fMRI research examining sex/gender differences in emotion processing. *Neuroethics* 6(2), 319–330.

Bock, Gisela (1991) Challenging dichotomies: Perspectives on women's history. In Offen, K.M., Pierson, R.R., and Rendall, J. (eds.), *Writing women's history*. London: Palgrave Macmillan, 1–23.

Bødker, Susanne, Dindler, Christian, and Iversen, Ole Sejer (2017) Tying knots: Participatory infrastructuring at work. *Computer Supported Cooperative Work (CSCW)* 26(1–2), 245–273.

Boivie, Inger (2010) Women, men and programming: Knowledge, metaphors and masculinity. In Booth, S., Goodman, S., and Kirkup, G. (eds.), *Gender issues in learning and working with information technology: Social constructs and cultural contexts*. Hershey, PA: IGI Global, 1–24.

Borau, Sylvie, Otterbring, Tobias, Laporte, Sandra, and Fosso Wamba, Samuel (2021) The most human bot: Female gendering increases humanness perceptions of bots and acceptance of AI. *Psychology & Marketing* 38(7), 1052–1068.

Borsotti, Valeria and Bjørn, Pernille (2022) Humor and stereotypes in computing: An equity-focused approach to institutional accountability. *Computer Supported Cooperative Work (JCSCW)* 31(4), 771–803.

Bossen, Claus, Jensen, Lotte Groth, and Witt, Flemming (2012) Medical secretaries' care of records: The cooperative work of a non-clinical group. In *Proceedings of the ACM 2012 Conference on Computer Supported Cooperative Work CSCW'12, February 11–15, 2012, Seattle, WA, USA*. New York: ACM Press, 921–930.

Bossen, Claus and Markussen, Randi (2010) Infrastructuring and ordering devices in health care: Medication plans and practices on a hospital ward. *Computer Supported Cooperative Work (CSCW)* 19, 615–637.

Bossen, Claus, Pine, Kathleen H., Cabitza, Federico, Ellingsen, Gunnar, and Piras, Enrico M. (2019) Data work in healthcare: An introduction. *Health Informatics Journal* 25 (3), 465–474.

Bourdage, Monique (2010) 'A young girl's dream': Examining the barriers facing female electric guitarists. *IASPM Journal* 1(1), 1–16.

Bowker, Geoffrey and Star, S. Leigh (1999) *Sorting things out: Classification and its consequences*. Cambridge, MA: MIT Press.

Boy, Guy A. (2013) From STEM to STEAM: Toward a human-centred education, creativity & learning thinking. In *Proceedings of the 31st European Conference on Cognitive Ergonomics, August 26–28, 2013, Toulouse, France*, Article 3, 1–7.

Boyer, Kate and England, Kim (2008) Gender, work and technology in the information workplace: From typewriters to ATMs. *Social & Cultural Geography* 9(3), 241–256.

Bracke, Maud Anne (2019) Labour, gender and deindustrialisation: Women workers at Fiat (Italy, 1970s–1980s). *Contemporary European History* 28(4), 484–499.

Branch, Ennobong Hannah (2016) Introduction. In Branch, E.H. (ed), *Pathways, potholes, and the persistence of women in science: Reconsidering the pipeline*. Lexington Books, viii–xx.

Bratteteig, Tone (2010) A matter of digital materiality. In Wagner, I., Bratteteig, T., and Stuedahl, D. (eds.), *Exploring digital design: Multi-disciplinary design practices*. London: Springer, 147–169.

Bratteteig, Tone and Wagner, Ina (2013) Moving healthcare to the home: The work to make homecare work. In *ECSCW 2013: Proceedings of the 13th European Conference on Computer Supported Cooperative Work*. Paphos: Springer, 141–160.

Bratteteig, Tone and Wagner, Ina (2014) *Disentangling participation: Power and decision-making in participatory design*. Cham: Springer International.

Bratteteig, Tone and Wagner, Ina (2016) Unpacking the notion of participation in Participatory Design. *Computer supported cooperative work (CSCW)* 25(6), 425–475.

Braverman, Harry (1974) *Labor and monopoly capital: The degradation of work in the twentieth century*. New York: Monthly Review.

Britton, Dana M. (2000) The epistemology of the gendered organization. *Gender & Society* 14(3), 418–434.

Bronfenbrenner, Kate and Warren, Dorian T. (2007) Race, gender, and the rebirth of trade unionism. *New Labor Forum* 16(3/4), 142–148.

Brown, Brad, Chui, Michael, and Manyika, James (2011) Are you ready for the era of 'big data'? *McKinsey Quarterly* 4(1), 24–35.

Brown, Jeffrey, Park, Tina, Chang, Jiyoo, Andrus, Mckane, Xiang, Alice, and Custis, Christine (2022) Attrition of workers with minoritized identities on AI teams. In Suresh, H. and Guttag, J.V. (eds.), *Equity and access in algorithms, mechanisms, and optimization EAAMO'22, October 6–9, 2022, Arlington, VA, USA*. New York: ACM Press, 1–9.

Brulé, Emeline and Spiel, Katta (2019) Negotiating gender and disability identities in participatory design. In *Proceedings of the 9th International Conference on Communities & Technologies-Transforming Communities C&T 2019, June 3–7, 2019, Vienna, Austria*. New York: ACM Press, 218–227.

Brumley, Krista M. (2018) 'It's more appropriate for men': Management and worker perceptions of the gendered ideal worker. *Sociological Spectrum* 6, 406–421.

Buchholz, Beth, Shively, Kate, Peppler, Kylie, and Wohlwend, Karen (2014) Hands on, hands off: Gendered access in crafting and electronics practices. *Mind, Culture, and Activity* 21(4), 278–297.

Buechley, Leah, Eisenberg, Mike, Catchen, Jaime, and Crockett, Ali (2008) The LilyPad Arduino: Using computational textiles to investigate engagement, aesthetics, and diversity in computer science education. In *Proceedings of the SIGCHI Conference on Human Factors in Computing Systems CHI2008, April 5–10, 2008, Florence, Italy*, 423–432.

Buolamwini, Joy and Gebru, Timnit (2018) Gender shades: Intersectional accuracy disparities in commercial gender classification. *Proceedings of Machine Learning Research 8*, 77–91.

Burtscher, Sabrina and Spiel, Katta (2020) 'But where would I even start?' Developing (gender) sensitivity in HCI research and practice. In *Proceedings of the Conference on Mensch und Computer MuC'20, September 6–9, 2020, Magdeburg, Germany*, 431–441.

Bush, Corlann Gee (1983) Women and the assessment of technology: To think, to be; to unthink, to free. In Rothschild, J. (ed.), *Machina ex Dea: Feminist perspectives on technology*. New York: Pergamon Press, 150–171.

Butler, Elizabeth Beardsley (1909) *Women and the trades: Pittsburgh, 1907–1908*. New York: Charities Publications Committee.

Butler, Judith (1990) *Gender trouble: Feminism and the subversion of identity*. New York: Routledge.

Cabitza, Federico, Ellingsen, Gunnar, Locoro, Angela, and Simone, Carla (2019) *Repetita iuvant*: Exploring and supporting redundancy in hospital practices. *Computer Supported Cooperative Work (CSCW) 28*, 61–94.

Cabitza, Federico and Simone, Carla (2017) Malleability in the hands of end-users. In Paternò, F. and Wulf, V. (eds.), *New perspectives in end-user development*. Cham: Springer, 137–163.

Cahill, Caitlin (2007) The personal is political: Developing new subjectivities through participatory action research. *Gender, Place and Culture 14*(3), 267–292.

Callon, Michel (1979) L'État face à l'innovation technique: le cas du véhicule électrique. *Revue française de science politique 29*(3), 426–447.

Campreguer França, N., Smit, Dorothé, Wuschitz, Stefanie, and Fuchsberger, Verena (2021) The women* who made it: Experiences from being a woman* at a maker festival. *Sustainability 13*(16), 9361.

Canedo, Edna Dias, Bonifácio, Rodrigo, Okimoto, Márcio Vinicius, Serebrenik, Alexander, Pinto, Gustavo, and Monteiro, Eduardo (2020) Work practices and perceptions from women core developers in OSS communities. In *Proceedings of the 14th ACM/IEEE International Symposium on Empirical Software Engineering and Measurement ESEM'20, October 8–9, 2020, Bari, Italy*. New York: ACM Press, 1–11.

Canedo, Edna Dias, Mendes, Fabiana Freitas, Cerqueira, Anderson Jefferson, Okimoto, Márcio Vinicius, Pinto, Gustavo and Bonifacio, Roberto (2021) Breaking one barrier at a time: How women developers cope in a men-dominated industry. In *Proceedings of the Brazilian Symposium on Software Engineering SBES'21, September 27-October 1, 2021, Joinville, Brazil*. New York: ACM Press, 378–387.

Capy, Marcelle and Valette, Aline (1984) *Femmes et travail au XIXe siècle: Enquêtes de la Fronde et la Bataille syndicaliste*. Paris: Syros.

Caraway, Teri L. (2007) *Assembling women: The feminization of global manufacturing*. New York: Cornell University Press.

Carros, F, Schwaninger, Preussner, Randall, Dave, Wieching, Rainer, Fitzpatrick, Geraldine, and Wulf, Volker (2022) Care workers making use of robots: Results of a three-month study on human–robot interaction within a care home. In *Proceedings of the 2022 CHI Conference on Human Factors in Computing Systems CHI'22, April 29–May 5, 2022, New Orleans, LA, USA.* New York: ACM Press, 1–15.

Cavarero, Adriana (1988) Eguaglianza e differenza sessuale: le amnesie del pensiero politico. In *Equality and difference: Gender dimensions in political thought, justice and morality. December 1988.* Firenze: European University.

Cedefop (2020) *Developing and matching skills in the online platform economy: Findings on new forms of digital work and learning from Cedefop's CrowdLearn study.* Luxembourg: European Center for the Development of Vocational Training.

Chen, Ko-Le, Clarke, Rachel, Almeida, Teresa, Wood, Matthew, and Kirk, David S. (2017) Situated dissemination through an HCI Workplace. In *Proceedings of the 2017 CHI Conference on Human Factors in Computing Systems CHI 2017, May 6–11, 2017, Denver, CO, USA.* New York: ACM Press, 2078–2090.

Chi, Do Quynh and van den Broek, Di (2020) Gendered labour activism in the Vietnamese manufacturing industry. *Gender, Work & Organization* 27(6), 1145–1164.

Chilisa, Bagele, Major, Thenjiwe Emily, Gaotlhobogwe, Michael, and Mokgolodi, Hildah (2016) Decolonizing and indigenizing evaluation practice in Africa: Toward African relational evaluation approaches. *Canadian Journal of Program Evaluation* 30(3), 313–328.

Chivukula, Sai Shruthi (2020) Feminisms through design: A practical guide to implement and extend feminism: Position. *Interactions* 27(6), 36–39.

Cipolla, Cyd (2019) Build it better: Tinkering in feminist maker pedagogy. *Women's Studies* 48(3), 261–282.

Citational Justice Collective: Ahmed, Syed, Amrute, Sareeta, Bardzell, Jeffrey, Bardzell, Shaowen, Bidwell, Nicola, Dillahunt, Tawanna, et al. (2022) Citational justice and the politics of knowledge production. *Interactions* Sep.–Oct., 79–82.

Clarke, Adele (1991) Social worlds/arena theory as organizational theory. In Maines, D.R. (ed.), *Social organization and social processes: Essays in honor of Anselm Strauss.* Edison, NJ: Aldine Transaction, 119–158.

Clarke, Adele E. (2021) From grounded theory to situational analysis: What's new? Why? How? In Morse, J.M., Bowers, B.J., Charmaz, K., Corbin, J., Stern, P.N., and Clarke, A.E. (eds.), *Developing grounded theory: The second generation.* London and New York: Routlege, 223–266.

Clarke, Michael F., Gonzales, Joseph, Harper, Richard, Randall, David, Ludwig, Thomas, and Ikeya, Nozomi (2019) Better supporting workers in ML workplaces. In *Conference Companion Publication of the 2019 on Computer Supported Cooperative Work and Social Computing CSCW'19, November 9–13, 2019, Austin, TX, USA.* New York: ACM Press, 443–448.

Clegg, Sue and Trayhurn, Deborah (2000) Gender and computing: Not the same old problem. *British Educational Research Journal* 26(1), 75–89.

Clement, Andrew (1990) Cooperative support for computer work: A social perspective on the empowering of end users. In *Proceedings of the 1990 ACM Conference on Computer-Supported Cooperative Work CSCW 90, 7–10 October 1990, Los Angeles, California.* New York: ACM Press, 223–236.

Clement, Andrew (1993) Looking for the designers: Transforming the 'invisible' infrastructure of computerised office work. *AI & Society* 7(4), 323–344.

Clement, Andrew and Van den Besselaar, Peter (1993) A retrospective look at PD projects. *Communications of the ACM* 36(6), 29–38.

Cockburn, Cynthia (1983a) *Brothers: Male dominance and technological change.* London: Pluto Press.

Cockburn, Cynthia (1983b) Caught in the wheels: The high cost of being a female cog in the male machinery of engineering. *Marxism Today* (November), 16–20.

Cockburn, Cynthia (1984) Trade unions and the radicalizing of socialist feminism. *Feminist Review* 16(1), 43–46.

Cockburn, Cynthia (1985a) *Machinery of dominance: Women, men and technical know-how.* London: Pluto Press.

Cockburn, Cynthia (1985b) The material of male power. In MacKenzie D. and Wajcman, J. (eds.), *The social shaping of technology: How the refrigerator got its hum.* Milton Keynes: Open University Press, 125–146.

Cockburn, Cynthia (1993) Technical competence, gender identity and women's autonomy. *Les Cahiers du Genre* 7(1), 111–122.

Cockburn, Cynthia and Ormrod, Susan (1993) *Gender and technology in the making.* London: Sage Publications.

Coeckelbergh, Mark (2010) Health care, capabilities, and AI assistive technologies. *Ethical Theory and Moral Practice* 13, 181–190.

Coeckelbergh, Mark (2015) The tragedy of the master: Automation, vulnerability, and distance. *Ethics and Information Technology* 17, 219–229.

Coeckelbergh, Mark (2021) Three responses to anthropomorphism in social robotics: Towards a critical, relational, and hermeneutic approach. *International Journal of Social Robotics* 14(10), 2049–2061.

Cohen, Marcy and White, Margaret (1987) *Taking control of our future: Clerical workers and new technology.* Vancouver: Women's Skill Development Society, printed by Press Gang Printers and Publishers.

Collett, Clementine and Dillon, Sarah (2019) *AI and gender: Four proposals for future research.* Cambridge: The Leverhulme Centre for the Future of Intelligence.

Collin, Françoise (2010) Le temps natal. *Les cahiers du GRIF* 30(1), 63–83.

Collins, Patricia Hill (1986) Learning from the outsider within: The sociological significance of Black feminist thought. *Social Problems* 33(6), s14–s32.

Collins, Patricia Hill (1990) *Black feminist thought: Knowledge, consciousness, and the politics of empowerment.* New York: Routledge.

Collins, Patricia Hill (2017) The difference that power makes: Intersectionality and participatory democracy. *Investigaciones Feministas* 8 (1), 19–39.

Connell, Raewyn (2009) *Gender.* Malden, MA: Polity Press.

Connell, Robert W. and Messerschmidt, James W. (2005) Hegemonic masculinity: Rethinking the concept. *Gender & Society* 19(6), 829–859.

Cooper, Brittney (2016) Intersectionality. In Disch, L. and Hawkesworth, M. (eds.), *The Oxford handbook of feminist theory.* Oxford: Oxford University Press.

Corneliussen, Hilde G. (2021) Unpacking the Nordic Gender Equality Paradox in ICT research and innovation. *Feminist Encounters: A Journal of Critical Studies in Culture and Politics* 5(2), 25.

Corneliussen, Hilde G., Herman, Clem, and Gajjala, Radhika (2018) ICT changes everything! But who changes ICT? In Kreps, D., Ess, C., Leenen, L., and Kimppa, K. (eds.), *This changes everything – ICT and climate change: What can we do?* Cham: Springer, 250–257.

Corneliussen, Hilde G. (2021) Women empowering themselves to fit into ICT. In Lechman, E. (ed.), *Technology and women's empowerment*. London and New York: Routledge, 46–62.

Coron, Clotilde (2020) What does 'gender equality' mean? Social representations of gender equality in the workplace among French workers. *Equality, Diversity and Inclusion: An International Journal* 39(8), 825–847.

Costanza-Chock, Sasha (2018) Design justice: Towards an intersectional feminist framework for design theory and practice. In *Proceedings of the Design Research Society DRS, 25–28 June 2018*. Limerick, Ireland.

Couldry, Nick and Mejías, Ulises A. (2019) *The costs of connection: How data is colonizing human life and appropriating it for capitalism*. Redwood City, CA: Stanford University Press.

Courtland, Rachel (2018) Bias detectives: The researchers striving to make algorithms fair. *Nature* 558(7710), 357–357.

Cox, Kevin R. (1997) Introduction. Globalization and its politics in question. In Cox, K.R. (ed.), *Spaces of globalization: Reasserting the power of the local*. New York and London: Guilford Press, 1–18.

Crenshaw, Kimberlé (1991) Mapping the margins: Identity politics, intersectionality, and violence against women. *Stanford Law Review* 43(6), 1241–1299.

Crompton, Rosemary and Reid, Stuart (1982) The deskilling of clerical work. In Wood, S. (ed.), *The degradation of work? Skill, deskilling, and the labour process*. London: Hutchinson and Co., Publishers.

Crompton, Rosemary and Jones, Gareth (1984) *White-collar proletariat: Deskilling and gender in clerical work*. London: MacMillan.

Cross, Simon and Bagilhole, Barbara M. (2002) Girls' jobs for the boys? Men, masculinity and non-traditional occupations. *Gender, Work & Organization* 9(2), 204–226.

Cukier, Wendy, Shortt, Denise, and Devine, Irene (2002) Gender and information technology: Implications of definitions. *ACM SIGCSE Bulletin* 34(4), 142–148.

Cummings, Thomas G. (1978) Self-regulating work groups: A socio-technical synthesis. *Academy of Management Review* 3(3), 625–634.

D'Ignazio, Catherine (2019) Four tensions between HCI research, social justice aspirations, and grassroots politics. In *CSCW'19 Workshop on Design and the Politics of Collaboration, November 9, 2019, Austin, TX, USA*. New York: ACM Press.

D'Ignazio, Catherine, Hope, Alexis, Michelson, Becky, Churchill, Robyn, and Zuckerman, Ethan (2016) A feminist HCI approach to designing postpartum technologies: 'When I first saw a breast pump I was wondering if it was a joke'. In *Proceedings of the 2016 CHI Conference on Human Factors in Computing Systems CHI'16, May 07–12, 2016, San Jose, CA, USA*. New York: ACM Press, 2612–2622.

D'Ignazio, Catherine and Klein, Lauren F. (2020) *Data feminism*. Cambridge, MA: MIT Press.

Dados, Nour and Connell, Raewyn (2012) The Global South. *Contexts* 11(1), 12–13.

Dalla Costa, Mariarosa and James, Selma (1973) *The power of women and the subversion of the community*. Bristol: Falling Wall Press.

Damodaran, Leela (1996) User involvement in the systems design process: A practical guide for users. *Behaviour & Information Technology* 15(6), 363–377.

Davies, Anne and Snaith, Pauline A. (1980) Mealtime problems in a continuing care hospital for the elderly. *Age and Ageing* 9(2), 100–105.

Davies, Sarah R. (2017) *Hackerspaces: Making the maker movement*. Hoboken, NJ: John Wiley & Sons.

De Laurentis, Teresa (1991) Queer theory: Lesbian and gay sexualities. An introduction. *differences* 3(2), iii–xviii.

De Oliveira Lobo, Mory Márcia, Da Silva Figueiredo Medeiros Ribeiro, Karen, and Maciel, Cristiano (2019) Black women in computing and technology: Identity affirmation and resistance. *CLEIEJ Electronic Journal* 22(2).

De Stefano, Valerio (2015) The rise of the just-in-time workforce: On-demand work, crowdwork, and labor protection in the gig-economy. *Comparative Labor Law & Policy Journal* 37, 471–504.

De Wilde, Mandy (2021) 'A heat pump needs a bit of care': On maintainability and repairing gender–technology relations. *Science, Technology, & Human Values* 46 (6), 1261–1285.

Dempsey, Sarah E., Zoller, Heather M., and Hunt, Kathleen P. (2022) The meatpacking industry's corporate exceptionalism: Racialized logics of food chain worker disposability during the COVID-19 crisis. *Food, Culture & Society* (February), 1–20.

Dencik, Lina, Hintz, Arne, Redden, Joanna, and Treré, Emiliano (2019) Exploring data justice: Conceptions, applications and directions. *Information, Communication & Society* 22(7), 873–881.

Denissen, Amy M. (2010) The right tools for the job: Constructing gender meanings and identities in the male-dominated building trades. *Human Relations* 63(7), 1051–1069.

Dessors, Dominique, Teiger, Catherine, Laville, Antoine, and Gadbois, Charles (1979) Conditions de travail des opératrices des renseignements téléphoniques et conséquences sur leur santé et leur vie personnelle et sociale. *Archives des maladies professionnelles, de médecine du travail et de Sécurité Sociale* 40(3–4), 469–500.

Deutsch, Francine M. (2007) Undoing gender. *Gender & Society* 21(1), 106–127.

Dhar-Bhattacharjee, Sunrita and Richardson, Helen (2018) A tour of India in one workplace: Investigating complex and gendered relations in IT. *Information Technology & People* 31(2), 578–594.

Díaz Andrade, Antonio, Techatassanasoontorn, Angsana A., Singh, Harminder, and Staniland, Nimbus (2021) Indigenous cultural re-presentation and re-affirmation: The case of Māori IT professionals. *Information Systems Journal* 31(6), 803–837.

Dobrosovestnova, Anna, Hannibal, Glenda, and Reinboth, Tim (2021) Service robots for affective labor: A sociology of labor perspective. *AI & Society* 37, 487–499.

Dombrowski, Lynn, Harmon, Ellie, and Fox, Sarah (2016) Social justice-oriented interaction design: Outlining key design strategies and commitments. In *Proceedings of the 2016 ACM Conference on Designing Interactive Systems DIS 2016, June 4–8, 2016, Brisbane, Australia*. New York: ACM Press, 656–671.

Donia, Joseph and Shaw, James A. (2021) Ethics and values in design: A structured review and theoretical critique. *Science and Engineering Ethics* 27(5), Article 57.

Donovan, Francis (1920) *The woman who waits*. Boston, MA: R.G. Badger.

Dotson, Kristie (2011) Tracking epistemic violence, tracking practices of silencing. *Hypatia* 26(2), 236–257.

Douglas, Susan J. (1999) *Listening In: Radio and the American imagination*. New York: New York Times Books.

Dourish, Paul (2016) Algorithms and their others: Algorithmic culture in context. *Big Data & Society* 3(2), Available at https://doi.org/10.1177/2053951716665128.

Draude, Claude, Klumbyte, Goda, Lücking, Phillip, and Treusch, Pat (2020) Situated algorithms: A sociotechnical systemic approach to bias. *Online Information Review* 44 (2), 325–342.

Draude, Claude and Maaß, Susanne (2018) Making IT work: Integrating gender research in computing through a process model. In *Proceedings of the 4th Conference on Gender & IT, 14–15 May 2018, Heilbronn, Germany*. New York: ACM Press, 43–50.

Dublin, Thomas (1979) *Women at work: The transformation of work and community in Lowell, Massachusetts, 1826–1860*. New York: Columbia University Press.

DuBois, L. Zachary and Shattuck-Heidorn, Heather (2021) Challenging the binary: Gender/sex and the bio-logics of normalcy. *American Journal of Human Biology* 33(5), e23623.

Dumais, Lucia, Messing, Karen, Seifert, Ana Maria, Courville, Julie, and Vezina, Nicole (1993) Make me a cake as fast as you can: Forces for and against change in the sexual division of labour at an industrial bakery. *Work, Employment and Society* 7(3), 363–382.

Dunbar-Hester, Christina (2008) Geeks, meta-geeks, and gender trouble: Activism, identity, and low-power FM radio. *Social Studies of Science* 38(2), 201–232.

Dunbar-Hester, Christina (2014) Radical inclusion? Locating accountability in technical DIY. In Ratto, M. and Boler, M. (eds.), *DIY citizenship: Critical making and social media*. Cambridge, MA: MIT Press, 75–88.

Duraffourg, Jacques, Guérin, Francois, Jankowsky, Frances, and Mascot, J.-C. (1976) *Analyse ergonomique du travail dans un atelier de presses en vue du transfert de certaines presses dans un nouvel atelier à construire*. Montrouge, Paris: Ministère du travail, Agence Nationale pour L'amélioration des Conditions de Travail (ANACT) & Laboratoire de Physiologie du Travail et d'Ergonomie du CNAM.

Durndell, A., Cameron, C., Knox, A., Stocks, R., and Haag, Z. (1997) Gender and computing: West and East Europe. *Computers in Human Behavior* 13(2), 269–280.

Dutt-Ballerstadt, Reshmi (2018) *Are you supporting white supremacy?* McMinnville, OR: Linfield.

Dutta, Madhumita (2019) Becoming factory workers: Understanding women's geographies of work through life stories in Tamil Nadu, India. *Gender, Place & Culture* 26(6), 888–904.

Ehn, Pelle (1988) Work-oriented design of computer artifacts. Doctoral dissertation, Department of Information Processing, Umeå University.

Ehn, Pelle and Kyng, Morten (1985) *A tool perspective on design of interactive computer support for skilled workers*. DAIMI Report Series (PB-190).

Elish, Madeleine Clare and Anne Watkins, Elizabeth (2020) *Repairing innovation: A study of integrating AI in clinical care*. New York: Data & Society.

Ellegård, Kajsa (1995) The creation of a new production system at the Volvo automobile assembly plant at Uddevalla, Sweden. In Sandberg, A. (ed.), *Enriching production: Perspectives on Volvo's Uddevalla plant as an alternative to lean production*. Aldershot: Avebury, 17–59.

Ely, Robin J. and Meyerson, Debra E. (2010) An organizational approach to undoing gender: The unlikely case of offshore oil platforms. *Research in Organizational Behavior* 30, 3–34.

Engeström, Yrjö (1999) Expansive visibilization of work: An activity-theoretical perspective. *Computer Supported Cooperative Work* 8, 63–93.

England, Paula and Dunn, Dana (1988) Evaluating work and comparable worth. *Annual Review of Sociology* 14(1), 227–248.

Ensmenger, Nathan (2010) Making programming masculine. In Misa, T.J. (ed.), *Gender codes: Why women are leaving computing*. Hoboken, NJ: John Wiley, 115–141.

Erdheim, Mario (1984) *Die gesellschaftliche Produktion von Unbewußtheit*. Frankfurt a. Main: Suhrkamp.

Erete, Sheena, Rankin, Yolanda A., and Thomas, Jakita O. (2021) I can't breathe: Reflections from Black women in CSCW and HCI. *Proceedings of the ACM on Human–Computer Interaction* 4(CSCW3), 1–23.

Eveline, Joan (1994) 'Normalization', 'leading ladies', and 'free men': Affirmative actions in Sweden and Australia. *Women's Studies International Forum* 17(2/3), 157–167.

Fanon, Frantz (1968/1963) *The wretched of the earth*. New York: Grove Press.

Faulkner, Wendy (2000) The power and the pleasure? A research agenda for 'making gender stick' to engineers. *Science, Technology, & Human Values* 25(1), 87–119.

Faulkner, Wendy. (2001) The technology question in feminism: A view from feminist technology studies. *Women's Studies International Forum* 24(1), 79–95.

Faulkner, Wendy (2007) 'Nuts and bolts and people'. Gender troubled engineering identities. *Social Studies of Science* 37(3), 331–356.

Fausto-Sterling, Anne (1985) The new research on women: How does it affect the natural sciences? *Women's Studies Quarterly* 13(2), 30–32.

Federici, Silvia (1975) *Wages against housework*. Bristol: Falling Wall Press.

Federici, Silvia (1975/2014) The reproduction of labour power in the global economy and the unfinished feminist revolution. In Atzeni, M. (ed.), *Workers and labour in a globalised capitalism: Contemporary themes and theoretical issues*. Basingstoke: Palgrave Macmillan, 85–110.

Feldberg, Roslyn L. (1984) Comparable worth: Toward theory and practice in the United States. *Signs: Journal of Women in Culture and Society* 10(2), 311–328.

Feldberg, Roslyn (1990) Computers in hospital care: A view of developments in the USA. In Dimitz E. (ed.), *Proceedings of the International Colloquium on Computers in Hospital Care*. Wien, Austria: Österreichische Akademie der Wissenschaften.

Feldberg, Roslyn L. (1992) Comparable worth and nurses in the USA. In Kahn, P. and Meehan E. (eds.), *Equal value/comparable worth in the UK and the USA*. London: Palgrave Macmillan, 181–214.

Feldberg, Roslyn L. and Glenn, Evelyn Nakano (1983) Incipient workplace democracy among United States clerical workers. *Economic and Industrial Democracy* 4(1), 47–67.

Feldfeber, Ivana, Quiroga, Yasmin B., Guevara Clarissa, and Ciolfi Felice, Marianela (2022) *Feminisms in Artificial Intelligence: Automation tools towards a feminist judiciary reform in Argentina and Mexico*. Available at: https://drive.google.com/file/d/1VKeeSdJz6-8DoEbetQ8f1wTH1ORqvIXV/view

Fenech, Angel Ellul, Kanji, Shireen, and Vargha, Zsuzsanna (2021) Gender-based exclusionary practices in performance appraisal. *Gender, Work & Organization* 29(2), 427–442.

Ferryman, Kadijaand and Pitcan, Mikaela (2018) *Fairness in precision medicine: What are the risks, benefits, and harms of precision medicine?* New York: Data and Society.

Fiesler, Casey, Morrison, Shannon, and Bruckman, Amy S. (2016) An archive of their own: A case study of feminist HCI and values in design. In *Proceedings of the 2016 CHI Conference on Human Factors in Computing Systems CHI'16, May 07–12, 2016, San Jose, CA, USA*. New York: ACM Press, 2574–2585.

Fine, Lisa M. (1993) 'Our big factory family': Masculinity and paternalism at the Reo Motor Car Company of Lansing, Michigan. *Labor History* 34(2–3), 274–291.

Firestone, Shulamith (1970) *The dialectic of sex: The case for feminist revolution*. New York: William Morrow and Company.

Fisher, Berenice and Tronto, Joan C. (1990) Toward a feminist theory of caring. In Abel, E.K. and Nelson, M.K. (eds.), *Circles of care: Work and identity in women's lives*. Albany, NY: State University of New York Press, 35–62.

Fiske, Amelia, Prainsack, Barbara, and Buyx, Alena (2019) Data work: Meaning-making in the era of data-rich medicine. *Journal of Medical Internet Research* 21(7), e11672.

Fitzpatrick, Geraldine (2004) Integrated care and the working record. *Health Informatics Journal* 10(4), 291–302.

Florman, S. (1976) *The existential pleasures of engineering*. New York: St. Martin's Press.

Foucault, Michel (1973) *The history of sexuality*. Harmondsworth: Penguin Books.

Foucault, Michel (1979) *Discipline and punish: The birth of prison*. New York: Vintage Books.

Freeman, Carla (1993) Designing women: Corporate discipline and Barbados's off-shore pink-collar sector. *Cultural Anthropology* 8(2), 169–186.

Freire, Paolo (1972) *Pedagogy of the oppressed*. New York: Penguin Books.

French, John D. and James, Daniel (1997) *The gendered worlds of Latin American women workers: From household and factory to the union hall and ballot box*. Durham, NC: Duke University Press.

Frenkel, Karen A. (1990) Women and computing. *Communications of the ACM* 33(11), 34–46.

Friedman, Batya and Nissenbaum, Helen (1996) Bias in computer systems. *ACM Transactions on Information Systems* 14(3), 330–347.

Gantt, M. and Nardi, B.A. (1992) Gardeners and gurus: Cooperation among CAD users. In *Proceedings of the ACM CHI 92 Human Factors in Computing Systems Conference June 3–7, 1992, Monterey, California*. New York: ACM Press, 107–117.

Garcia Johnson, Caroline Pia and Otto, Kathlees (2019) Better together: A model for women and LGBTQ equality in the workplace. *Frontiers in Psychology* 10, 272.

Gärtner, Johannes and Wagner, Ina (1996) Mapping actors and agenda: Political frameworks of design & participation. *Human–Computer Interaction* (11), 187–214.

Gender, Advisory Group for (2016) *For a better integration of the gender dimension in the Horizon 2020 Work Programme 2018–2020.*

Gherardi, Silvia (1996) Gendered organizational cultures: Narratives of women travellers in a male world. *Gender, Work & Organization* 3(4), 187–201.

Gilligan, Carol (1982) *In a different voice: Psychological theory and women's development.* Cambridge, MA: Harvard University Press.

Glenn, Evelyn Nakano and Feldberg, Roslyn L. (1977) Degraded and deskilled: The proletarianization of clerical work. *Social Problems* 25(1), 52–64.

Glenn, Evelyn Nakamo and Feldberg, Roslyn L. (1983) Technology and work degradation: Effects of office automation on women clerical workers. In Rothschild, J. (ed.), *Machina ex Dea: Feminist perspectives on technology.* New York: Pergamon Press, 52–64.

Gluck, Sherna Berger and Patai, Daphne (eds.) (1991) *Women's words: The feminist practice of oral history.* New York: Routledge.

Glucksmann, Miriam (aka Cavendish, Ruth) (1982) *Women on the line.* London: Routledge.

Goan, Melanie Beals (2001) Reviewed work(s): Devices and desires: Gender, technology, and American nursing by Margarete Sandelowski. *The Register of the Kentucky Historical Society* 99(2), 195–197.

Goldstein, Lisa S. (2003) Commitment, community; and passion: Dimensions of a care-centered approach to teacher education. *Teacher Education and Practice* 15(1/2), 36–56.

Goodman, Benny (2016) Lying to ourselves: Rationality, critical reflexivity, and the moral order as 'structured agency'. *Nursing Philosophy* 17, 211–221.

Goodrich, Kristopher, Luke, Melissa, and Smith, Aaron (2016) Queer humanism: Toward an epistemology of socially just, culturally responsive change. *Journal of Humanistic Psychology* 56(6), 612–623.

Govier, Trudy (1992) Trust, distrust, and feminist theory. *Hypatia* 7(1), 16–33.

Gray, Joanne and Witt, Alice (2021) A feminist data ethics of care framework for machine learning: The what, why, who and how. *First Monday* 26(12), Article 11833.

Gray, Mary L. and Suri, Siddharth (2017) The humans working behind the AI curtain. *Harvard Business Review* 9, 2–5.

Gray, Mary L., Suri, Siddharth, Ali, Syed Shoaib, and Kulkarni, Deepti (2016) The crowd is a collaborative network. In *Proceedings of the 19th ACM Conference on Computer-Supported Cooperative Work & Social Computing CSCW '16, February 27–March 02, 2016, San Francisco, CA, USA.* New York: ACM Press, 134–147.

Green, Eileen, Owen, Jenny, and Pain, Den (1993) *Gendered by Design? Information technology and office systems.* London: Taylor & Francis.

Greenbaum, Joan (1990) The head and the heart: Using gender analysis to study the social construction of computer systems. *ACM SIGCAS Computers and Society* 20 (2), 9–17.

Greenbaum, Joan (1995) *Windows on the workplace: Computers, jobs, and the organization of office work in the late 20th century.* New York: Monthly Review Press.

Gregg, Melissa (2015) Inside the data spectacle. *Television & New Media* 16(1), 37–51.

Gregory, Judith and Nussbaum, Karen (1982) Race against time: Automation of the office: An analysis of the trends in office automation and the impact on the office workforce. *Office: Technology and People* 1, 197–236.

Grønsund, Tor and Aanestad, Margunn (2020) Augmenting the algorithm: Emerging human-in-the-loop work configurations. *The Journal of Strategic Information Systems* 29(2), 101614.

Gunnarsson, Ewa (1994) Att våga väga jämnt: om kvalifikationer och kvinnliga förhållningssätt i ett tekniskt industriarbete [Daring to be equal: On qualifications and skills and women's ways of relating to work in a technical industrial field). Dissertation, Luleå Technical University.

Gupta, Namrata (2020) *Women in science and technology: Confronting inequalities.* New Delhi: Sage Publications India.

Gurumurthy, Anita, Zainab, Khawla, and Sanjay, Sadhana (2021) *The macro frames of microwork: A study of Indian women workers on AMT in the post-pandemic moment.* IT for Change. Available at https://papers.ssrn.com/sol3/papers.cfm?abstract_id=3872428

Gustafson, Diana L. and Brunger, Fern (2014) Ethics, 'vulnerability', and feminist participatory action research with a disability community. *Qualitative Health Research* 24(7), 997–1005.

Gutierrez, Miren (2021) Algorithmic gender bias and audiovisual data: A research agenda. *International Journal of Communication* 15, 439–461.

Guzman, Indira R. and Stanton, Jeffrey M. (2008) Women's adaptation to the IT culture. *Women's Studies* 37(3), 202–228.

Hacker, Sally (1981) The culture of engineering: Women, workplace and machine. *Women's Studies International Quarterly* 4(3), 341–354.

Hacker, Sally (1989) *Pleasure, power and technology: Some tales of gender, engineering, and the cooperative workplace.* London: Unwin Hyman.

Haigh, Thomas (2006) Remembering the office of the future: The origins of word processing and office automation. *IEEE Annals of the History of Computing* 28(4), 6–31.

Hales, Mike and O'Hara, Peter (1993) Strengths and weaknesses of participation: Learning by doing in local government. In Green, E., Owen, J., and Pain, D. (eds.), *Gendered by design? Information technology and office systems.* London: Taylor & Francis, 153–172.

Hall, Elizabeth Dorrance and Gettings, Patricia E. (2020) 'Who is this little girl they hired to work here?' Women's experiences of marginalizing communication in male-dominated workplaces. *Communication Monographs* 87(4), 484–505.

Hall, Lucy B. and Clapton, William (2021) Programming the machine: Gender, race, sexuality, AI, and the construction of credibility and deceit at the border. *Internet Policy Review* 10(4), 1–23.

Hampton, Lelia Marie (2021) Black feminist musings on algorithmic oppression. In *Proceedings of the Conference on Fairness, Accountability, and Transparency (FAccT'21), March 3–10, 2021, Virtual Event, Canada.* New York: ACM Press.

Handel, Michael J. (2004) *Implications of information technology for employment, skills, and wages: Findings from sectoral and case study research.* Arlington, VA: SRI International.

Hankivsky, Olena (2014) Rethinking care ethics: On the promise and potential of an intersectional analysis. *American Political Science Review* 108(2), 252–264.

Hanley, Caroline (2014) Putting the bias in skill-biased technological change? A relational perspective on white-collar automation at General Electric. *American Behavioral Scientist* 58(3), 400–415.

Haraway, Donna (1988) Situated knowledges: The science question in feminism and the privilege of partial perspective. *Feminist Studies* 14(3), 575–599.

Haraway, Donna (1990) A manifesto for cyborgs: Science, technology, and socialist feminism in the 1980's. In Nicholson, L.J. (ed.), *Feminism/postmodernism*. New York: Routledge, 191–233.

Harding, Sandra (1986a) *The science question in feminism*. Ithaca, NY: Cornell University Press.

Harding, Sandra (1986b) The instability of the analytical categories of feminist theory. *Signs* 11 (4), 645–664.

Harding, Sandra (1992) Rethinking standpoint epistemology: What is 'strong objectivity'? *The Centennial Review* 36(3), 437–470.

Harding, Sandra (2009) Postcolonial and feminist philosophies of science and technology: Convergences and dissonances. *Postcolonial Studies* 12(4), 401–421.

Harmon, Ellie and Silberman, M. Six (2019) Rating working conditions on digital labor platforms. *Computer Supported Cooperative Work (CSCW)* 28(5), 911–960.

Harrington, Christina, Erete, Sheena, and Piper, Anne Marie (2019) Deconstructing community-based collaborative design: Towards more equitable participatory design engagements. *Proceedings of the ACM on Human–Computer Interaction* 3(CSCW), Article 216.

Harrington, Christina N. (2020) The forgotten margins: What is community-based participatory health design telling us? *Interactions* 27(3), 24–29.

Hayes, Gillian R. (2011) The relationship of action research to human–computer interaction. *ACM Transactions on Computer-Human Interaction (TOCHI)* 18(3), 1–20.

Hedditch, Sonali and Vyas, Dhaval (2023) Design justice in practice: Community-led design of an online maker space for refugee and migrant women. In *Proceedings of the ACM on Human–Computer Interaction 7(GROUP)*, Article 4.

Heidenreich, Martin (1997) Arbeitsorganisation und Qualifikation. In Luczak, H. and Volpert, W. (eds.), *Handbuch Arbeitswissenschaft*. Stuttgart: Schäffer-Pöschl, 696–701.

Henson, Kevin D. and Rogers, Jackie Krasas (2001) 'Why Marcia you've changed!' Male clerical temporary workers doing masculinity in a feminized occupation. *Gender & Society* 15(2), 218–238.

Hester, Helen (2017) Technology becomes her. *New Vistas* 3(1), 46–50.

Hewamanne, Sandya (2018) Sewing their way up the social ladder? Paths to social mobility and empowerment among Sri Lanka's global factory workers. *Third World Quarterly* 39(11), 2173–2187.

Hicks, Marie (2010) Meritocracy and feminization in conflict: computerization in the British Government. In Misa, T. J. (ed.), *Gender codes: Why women are leaving computing*. Hoboken, NJ: John Wiley, 95–114.

Hinsley, Francis Harry and Strip, Alan (2001) *Codebreakers: The inside story of Bletchley Park*. Oxford: Oxford University Press.

Hirschauer, Stefan (2016) Judith, Niklas und das Dritte der Geschlechterdifferenz: undoing gender und die post gender studies. *GENDER–Zeitschrift für Geschlecht, Kultur und Gesellschaft* 8(3), 114–129.

Hirschmann, Nancy J. (2018) Care as a political concept: Now more than ever. *Politics and Gender* 14(4), 4–8.

Hirsh, Elizabeth, Olson, Gary A., and Harding, Sandra (1995) Starting from marginalized lives: A conversation with Sandra Harding. *JAC* 15(2), 193–225.

Hirshbein, Laura D. (2006) Science, gender, and the emergence of depression in American psychiatry, 1952–1980. *Journal of the History of Medicine and Allied Sciences* 61(2), 187–216.

Hochschild, Arlie Russel (1983) *The managed heart: Commercialization of human feeling.* Berkeley: University of California Press.

Holgersson, Charlotte and Romani, Laurence (2020) Tokenism revisited: When organizational culture challenges masculine norms, the experience of token is transformed. *European Management Review* 17(3), 649–661.

Holth, Line (2014) Passionate men and rational women: Gender contradictions in engineering. *NORMA: International Journal for Masculinity Studies* 9(2), 97–110.

Hoogeveen, Teresa (2021) Fracturing the private–public divide through action. Reading Les Cahier du Grif. *Ethics, Politics & Society* 4, 153–174.

Hornecker, Eva, Bischof, Andreas, Graf, Philipp, Franzkowiak, Lena, and Krüger, Norbert (2020) The interactive enactment of care technologies and its implications for human–robot–interaction in care. In *Proceedings of the 11th Nordic Conference on Human–Computer Interaction: Shaping Experiences, Shaping Society NordiCHI'20, October 25–29, 2020, Tallinn, Estonia.* New York: ACM Press, Article 78.

Horowitz, Roger (1997) 'Where men will not work': Gender, power, space, and the sexual division of labor in America's meatpacking industry, 1890–1990. *Technology and Culture* 38(1), 187–213.

Houben, Steven and Bardram, Jakob E. (2013) Activitydesk: Multi-device configuration work using an interactive desk. In *CHI'13 Extended Abstracts on Human Factors in Computing Systems, 27 April–2 May 2013, Paris, France.* New York: ACM Press, 721–726.

Howard, Dorothy and Irani, Lilly C. (2019) Ways of knowing when research subjects care. In *Proceedings of the 2019 CHI Conference on Human Factors in Computing Systems CHI 2019, May 4–9, 2019, Glasgow, Scotland, UK.* New York: ACM Press, Article 97.

Hughes, Karen D. (1989) Office automation: A review of the literature. *Relations Industrielles/Industrial Relations* 44(3), 654–679.

Hughes, John A., Sharrock, Wes W., Rodden, Tom A., O'Brien, Jo, Rouncefield, Mark, and Calvey, Dave (1994) Perspectives on the social organisation of work. In Hughes, J.A. et al. (eds.), *Field studies and CSCW.* Lancaster: Computing Department, Lancaster University, 129–160.

Hunter, Alison (2012) The professionalisation of computing work in New Zealand, 1960 to 2010: A feminist analysis. Doctoral thesis, University of Auckland.

Hunter, Rosemary (2006) Discrimination in IT organisations. *Labour & Industry: a Journal of the Social and Economic Relations of Work* 16(3), 91–108.

Huybrechts, Liesbeth, Benesch, Henric, and Geib, Jon (2017) Institutioning: Participatory design, co-design and the public realm. *CoDesign* 13(3), 148–159.

Ibáñez, Marta (2017) Women in the construction trades: Career types and associated barriers. *Women's Studies International Forum* 60, 39–48.

ILO (2000) *ABC of women workers' rights and gender equality.* Geneva: International Labour Office.

ILO (2021) *The role of digital labour platforms in transforming the world of work.* Geneva: International Labour Office.

Irani, Lilly C. and Silberman, M. Six (2013) Turkopticon: Interrupting worker invisibility in Amazon Mechanical Turk. In *Proceedings of the SIGCHI Conference on Human Factors in Computing Systems CHI 2013, April 27–May 2, 2013, Paris, France.* New York: ACM Press, 611–620.

Irani, Lilly C. and Silberman, M. Six (2016) Stories we tell about labor: Turkopticon and the trouble with design. In *Proceedings of the 2016 CHI Conference on Human Factors in Computing Systems CHI'16, May 07–12, 2016, San Jose, CA, USA.* New York: ACM Press, 4573–4586.

Isaksson, Anna, Börjesson, Emma, Gunn, Maja, Andersson, Camilla, and Ehrnberger, Karin (2017) Norm critical design and ethnography: Possibilities, objectives and stakeholders. *Sociological Research Online* 22(4), 232–252.

Isbister, Katherine (2004) Instrumental sociality: How machines reflect to us our own inhumanity. In *Workshop Dimensions of Sociality: Shaping Relationships with Machines.* Vienna: Institute of Philosophy of Science, University of Vienna and Austrian Institute for Artificial Intelligence.

Ismail, Azra and Kumar, Neha (2018) Engaging solidarity in data collection practices for community health. In *Proceedings of the ACM on Human–Computer Interaction 2(CSCW)*, Article 76.

Jackson, Gabriele (2019) The female problem: How male bias in medical trials ruined women's health. *The Guardian*, Nov. 13.

Jackson, Steven J., Pompe, Alex, and Krieshok, Gabriel (2012) Repair worlds: Maintenance, repair, and ICT for development in rural Namibia. In *Proceedings of the ACM 2012 Conference on Computer Supported Cooperative Work CSCW'12, Seattle, WA, USA – February 11–15, 2012.* New York: ACM Press, 107–116.

Jackson, Terence (2013) Reconstructing the indigenous in African management research: Implications for international management studies in a globalized world. *Management International Review* 53, 13–38.

Jacobi, Ursula and Weltz, Friedrich (1981) Zum Problem der Beanspruchung beim Maschinenschreiben. In Frese, M. (ed.), *Stress im Büro.* Bern: Huber, 80–198.

Jarrahi, Mohammad Hossein, Sutherland, Will, Nelson, Sarah Beth, and Sawyer, Steve (2020) Platformic management, boundary resources for gig work, and worker autonomy. *Computer Supported Cooperative Work (CSCW)* 29(1), 153–189.

Jenkins, Fiona and Smith, Julie (2021) Work-from-home during COVID-19: Accounting for the care economy to build back better. *The Economic and Labour Relations Review* 32(1), 22–38.

Jin, Zhouying (2005) *Global technological change: From hard technology to soft technology.* Bristol: Intellect Books.

Johansson, Janet, Morell, Ildikó Asztalos, and Lindell, Eva (2020) Gendering the digitalized metal industry. *Gender, Work & Organization* 27(6), 1321–1345.

Jonas, Hans (1979) Toward a philosophy of technology. *Hastings Center Report* 9(1), 34–43.

Jonas, Hans (1984) *The imperative of responsibility: In search of an ethics for the technological age.* Chicago: The University of Chicago Press.

Jussupow, Ekaterina, Spohrer, Kai, and Heinzl, Armin (2022) Radiologists' usage of diagnostic AI systems: The role of diagnostic self-efficacy for sensemaking from confirmation and disconfirmation. *Business & Information Systems Engineering* 64(3), 293–309.

Kafai, Yasmin B. and Burke, Quinn (2014) *Connected code: Why children need to learn programming.* Cambridge, MA: MIT Press.

Kafai, Yasmin B. and Peppler, Kylie A. (2014) Transparency reconsidered: Creative, critical, and connected making with e-textiles. In Ratto, M. and Boler, M. (eds.), *DIY citizenship: Critical making and social media.* Cambridge, MA: MIT Press, 179–188.

Kanter, Rosabeth Moss (1977) *Men and women of the corporation.* New York: Basic Books.

Katyal, Sonia K. and Jung, Jessica Y. (2021) The gender panopticon: AI, gender, and design Justice. *U.C.L.A. Law Review* 68, 692–785.

Keller, Evelyn F. (1982) Feminism and science. *Signs: Journal of Women in Culture and Society* 7(3), 589–602.

Keller, Evelyn F. (1985) *Reflections on gender and science.* New Haven, CT, and London: Yale University Press.

Keller, Evelyn F. (1987) The gender/science system: Or, is sex to gender as nature is to science? *Hypatia* 2(3), 37–49.

Keller, Evelyn Fox (1993) *A feeling for the organism. The life and work of Barbara McClintock.* New York: W.H. Freeman.

Kendall, Lori (1999) Nerd nation: Images of nerds in US popular culture. *International Journal of Cultural Studies* 2(2), 260–283.

Kennedy-Macfoy, Madeleine, Gausi, Tamara, and King, Chidi (2021) When a movement moves within a movement: Black women's feminist activism within trade unions. *Gender & Development* 29(2/3), 513–528.

Kenny, Etlyn J. and Donnelly, Rory (2020) Navigating the gender structure in information technology: How does this affect the experiences and behaviours of women? *Human Relations* 73(3), 326–350.

Kern, Horst and Schumann, Michael (1970) *Industriearbeit und Arbeiterbewußtsein: Eine empirische Untersuchung über den Einfluß der aktuellen technischen Entwicklung auf die industrielle Arbeit und das Arbeiterbewußtsein.* Frankfurt am Main: Europäische Verlagsanstalt.

Keyes, Os, May, Chandler, and Carrell, Annabelle (2021) You keep using that word: Ways of thinking about gender in computing research. *Proceedings of the ACM on Human–Computer Interaction* 5(CSCW1), Article 39.

Khenner, Evgeniy K. (2019) Women in computing. In Frieze, C. and Quesenberry, J.L. (eds.), *Cracking the digital ceiling: Women in computing around the world.* Cambridge: Cambridge University Press, 246–260.

Kim, Claire Jean (2004) Unyielding positions: A critique of the 'race' debate. *Ethnicities* 4(3), 337–355.

Kim, Pauline T. (2017) Data-driven discrimination at work. *William & Mary Law Review* 857(3), 857–936.

Kim, Seung-Kyung (1996) 'Big companies don't hire us, married women': Exploitation and empowerment among women workers in South Korea. *Feminist Studies* 22(3), 555–571.

Kissler, Leo and Sattel, Ulrike (1982) Humanization of work and social interests: Description and critical assessment of the state-sponsored program of humanization in the Federal Republic of Germany. *Economic and Industrial Democracy* 3(3), 221–261.

Kitchin, Rob (2014) *The data revolution: Big data, open data, data infrastructures and their consequences.* London: Sage.

Kitwood, Tom and Brooker, Dawn (2019) *Dementia reconsidered revisited: The person still comes first.* London: McGraw-Hill Education.

Klinge, Ineke (2010) Sex and gender in biomedicine: Promises for women and men. How incorporation of sex and gender in research will lead to a better health care. In Klinge, I. and Wiesemann, C. (eds.), *Sex and gender in biomedicine.* Göttingen: Universitätsverlag Göttingen, 15–32.

Klinge, Ineke and Bosch, Mineke (2005) Transforming research methodologies in EU life sciences and biomedicine: Gender-sensitive ways of doing research. *European Journal of Women's Studies* 12(3), 377–395.

Klumbytè, Goda, Draude, Claude, and Taylor, Alex S. (2022) Critical tools for machine learning: Working with intersectional critical concepts in machine learning systems design. In *Proceedings of the 2022 ACM Conference on Fairness, Accountability, and Transparency (FAccT'22), June 21–24, 2022, Seoul, Republic of Korea.* New York: ACM Press, 1528–1541.

Kohl, Karina and Prikladnicki, Rafael (2018) Perceptions on diversity in Brazilian agile software development teams: A survey. In *Proceedings of the 1st International Workshop on Gender Equality in Software Engineering GE '18, 28 May 2018, Gothenburg Sweden.* New York: ACM Press, 37–40.

Koller, Eva (2022) The impact of the fourth industrial revolution on potentially disadvantaged groups: An analysis of how industry 4.0 can promote decent work and equality for women and older employees. Masters thesis, Department of Economic History and International Relations, Stockholm University.

Kompast, Martin and Wagner, Ina (1997) Telework: Managing spatial, temporal and cultural boundaries. In Jackson, P. and Wielen, J.v.d. (eds.), *New international perspectives on telework: From telecommuting to the virtual organisation.* London: Routledge Kegan, 95–117.

Kramarae, Cheris (ed.) (1988) *Technology and women's voices: Keeping in touch.* London and New York: Routledge & Kegan Paul.

Krogh, Anders (2008) What are artificial neural networks? *Nature Biotechnology* 26(2), 195–197.

Krüger, Max, Weibert, Anne, Leal, Debora de Castro, Randall, Dave, and Wulf, Volker (2021) 'What is the topic of the group, please?' On migration, care and the challenges of participation in design. *Proceedings of the ACM on Human–Computer Interaction* 5(CSCW2), 1–29.

Krüger, Max, Weibert, Anne, Leal, Débora de Castro, Randall, Dave, and Wulf, Volker (2021) It takes more than one hand to clap: On the role of 'care' in maintaining design results. In *Proceedings of the 2021 CHI Conference on Human Factors in Computing Systems CHI'21, May 8–13, 2021, Yokohama, Japan.* New York: ACM Press, Article 302.

Kunda, Gideon (1992) *Engineering culture: Control and commitment in a high-tech corporation.* Philadelphia: Temple University Press.

Ladwig, Robin C. (2012) Silenced and invisible work experience of trans* and gender diverse individuals in intersectional identity relation. In Sojo, V., Wheeler, M. and Ryan, M. (eds.) *Proceedings of Gender and Sexuality at Work: A Multidisciplinary Research and Engagement Conference, Feb 18, 2020, Melbourne, Australia,* 71–77.

Lake, Danielle and Wendland, Joel (2018) Practical, epistemological, and ethical challenges of participatory action research: A cross-disciplinary review of the literature. *Journal of Higher Education Outreach and Engagement* 22(3), 11–42.

Lamoureux, Diane (2010) *Pensées rebelles: Autour de Rosa Luxembourg, Hannah Arendt et Françoise Collin.* Montreal: Éditions du Remue-ménage.

Landwehr, Marvin, Borning, Alan, and Wulf, Volker (2019) The high cost of free services: Problems with surveillance capitalism and possible alternatives for IT infrastructure. In *Proceedings of the Fifth Workshop on Computing within Limits (LIMITS 2019), June 10–11, 2019, Lappeenranta, Finland.* New York: ACM Press, Article 3.

Landwehr, Marvin, Borning, Alan, and Wulf, Volker (2023) Problems with surveillance capitalism and possible alternatives for IT infrastructure. *Information, Communication & Society* 26(1), 70–85.

Langer, Ellen (1989) Minding matters: The consequences of mindlessness-mindfulness. *Advances in Experimental Social Psychology* 22, 137–173.

Lappe, Lothar (1981) *Die Arbeitssituation erwerbstätiger Frauen. Geschlechtsspezifische Arbeitsmarktsegmentation und ihre Folgen.* Frankfurt and New York: Campus Verlag.

Larsen, Ann-Claire (2005) In the public interest: Autonomy and resistance to methods of standardising nurses' advice and practices from a health call centre in Perth, Western Australia. *Nursing Inquiry* 12(2), 135–143.

Latour, Bruno (2007) *Reassembling the Social: An introduction to actor-network-theory.* Oxford: Oxford University Press.

Lau, Francis (1997) A review on the use of action research in information systems studies. In Lee, A.S, Liebenau, J. and DeGross, J.I. (eds.) *Proceedings of the IFIP TC8 WG 8.2 International Conference on Information Systems and Qualitative Research, 31st May–3rd June 1997, Philadelphia, Pennsylvania, USA.* Boston: Springer, 31–68.

Laville, Antoine, Teiger, Catherine, and Duraffourg, Jacques (1972) *Conséquences du travail répétitif sous cadence sur la santé des travailleurs et les accidents.* Paris: Collection du Laboratoire de Physiologie du Travail et d'Ergonomie du Conservatoire National des Arts et Métiers.

Leach, Belinda. J. (2016) Jobs for women? Gender and class in Ontario's ruralized automotive manufacturing industry. In Pini, B. and Leach, B. (eds.), *Reshaping gender and class in rural spaces.* Franham: Ashgate, 129–144.

Leal, Debora de Castro, Strohmayer, Angelika, and Krüger, Max (2021) On activism and academia: Reflecting together and sharing experiences among critical friends. In *Proceedings of the 2021 CHI Conference on Human Factors in Computing Systems CHI'21, May 8–13, 2021, Yokohama, Japan*. New York: ACM Press, Article 303.

Lee, Una, Mutiti, Nontsikelelo, Garcia, Carlos, and Taylor, Wes (eds.) (2016) *Principles for design justice*. Design Justice. *Zine* 1. Detroit: Design Justice Network. http://designjusticenetwork.org/zine.

Leighton, Mary and Roberts, Elizabeth F. (2020) Trust/distrust in multi-disciplinary collaboration: Some feminist reflections. *Catalyst: Feminism, Theory, Technoscience* 6(2), 1–27.

Lerman, Nina E., Mohun, Arwen Palmer, and Oldenziel, Ruth (1997) Versatile tools: Gender analysis and the history of technology. *Technology and Culture* 38(1), 1–8.

Lesi, Onoja Barine (2020) Office automation and secretarial productivity in Rivers State University. *American International Journal of Nursing Education and Practice* 1(1), 22–34.

Lewis, Jen (2015) *Barriers to women's involvement in hackspaces and makerspaces*. Project report. The University of Sheffield (unpublished).

Lewis, Patricia, Benschop, Yvonne, and Simpson, Ruth (2017) Postfeminism, gender and organization. *Gender, Work and Organization* 24(3), 213–225.

Lewis, Patricia and Simpson, Ruth (eds.) (2010) *Revealing and concealing gender: Issues of visibility in organizations*. Houndsmill, Basingstoke: Palgrave Macmillan.

Lewis, Ruth, Sharp, Elizabeth, Remnant, Jennifer, and Redpath, Rhiannon (2015) 'Safe spaces': Experiences of feminist women-only space. *Sociological Research Online* 20(4).

Lie, Merete and Rasmussen, Bente (1985) Office work and skills. In Olerup, A., Schneider, L. and Monod, E. (eds.), *Proceedings of the IFIP WG 9.1 First Working Conference on Women, Work, and Computerization, 17–21 September 1984, Riva Del Sole, Italy*. Amsterdam: North-Holland, 43–52.

Lie, Merete and Sørensen, Knut H. (eds.) (1996) *Making technology our own? Domesticating technology into everyday life*. Olso: Scandinavian University Press.

Lieberman, Henry, Paternò, Fabio, Klann, Markus, and Wulf, Volker (2006) *End-user development: An emerging paradigm*. Cham: Springer International Publishing.

Liff, Sonia and Wajcman, Judy (1996) 'Sameness' and 'difference' revisited: Which way forward for equal opportunity initiatives? *Journal of Management Studies* 33(1), 79–94.

Light, Jennifer S. (1999) When computers were women. *Technology and Culture* 40(3), 455–483.

Lindemann, Hilde (2019) *An invitation to feminist ethics*, 2nd edn. Oxford: Oxford University Press.

Lips, Hilary M. (2017) *Sex and gender: An introduction*. Long Grove, IL: Waveland Press.

Lister, Ruth. (2005) Feminist citizenship theory: An alternative perspective on understanding women's social and political lives. In Franklin, J. (ed.), *Women and social capital*. London: Families & Social Capital ESRC Research Group London, South Bank University, 18–26.

Livingstone, Sonia (1992) The meaning of domestic technologies. In Silverstone, R. and Hirsch, E. (eds.), *Consuming technologies: Media and information in domestic spaces*. London and New York: Routledge, 113–130.

Lobato, Mirta Zaida (1997) Women workers in the 'cathedrals of corned beef': Structure and subjectivity in the Argentine meatpacking industry. In French, J.D. and James, D. (eds.), *The gendered worlds of Latin American women workers: From household and factory to the union hall and ballot box*. Durham, NC, and London: Duke University Press, 53–71.

Lobato, Mirta Zaida (2001) *La vida en las fábricas. Trabajo, protesta y política en una comunidad obrera, Berisso (1904–1970)*. Buenos Aires, Argentinia: Prometeo libros.

Loch-Drake, Cynthia (2007) 'A special breed': Packing men and the class and racial politics of manly discourses in post-1945 Edmonton, Alberta. *Atlantis: Critical Studies in Gender, Culture & Social Justice* 32(1), 136–147.

Lokatt, Erika, Holgersson, Charlotte, Lindgren, Monica, Packendorff, Johann, and Hagander, Louise (2019) An interprofessional perspective on healthcare work: Physicians and nurses co-constructing identities and spaces of action. *Journal of Management & Organization*, 1–17.

Lowe, Graham S. (1987) *Women in the administrative revolution: The feminization of clerical work*. Toronto: University of Toronto Press.

Lubar, Steven (1992) 'Do not fold, spindle or mutilate': A cultural history of the punch card. *Journal of American Culture* 15, 43–55.

Lucier, Brandi Lyn (2001) *From 'Chrysler girls' to 'Dodge boys': The emergence of women in Windsor's automotive industry, 1964–1976*. Windsor, ON: University of Windsor.

Luxton, Meg (2001) Feminism as a class act: Working-class feminism and the women's movement in Canada. *Labour/Le Travailleur* 48, 63–88.

Lynch, Casey R., Bissell, David, House-Peters, Lily A., and Del Casino Jr., Vincent J. (2022) Robotics, affective displacement, and the automation of care. *Annals of the American Association of Geographers* 112(3), 684–691.

Ma, Ning F., Rivera, Veronica A., Yao, Zheng, and Yoon, Dongwook (2022) 'Brush it off': How women workers manage and cope with bias and harassment in gender-agnostic gig platforms. In *Proceedings of the CHI Conference on Human Factors in Computing Systems (CHI'22), April 29–May 5, 2022, New Orleans, USA*. New York: ACM Press, Article 397.

Mackenzie, Catriona and Stoljar, Natalie (2000) *Relational autonomy: Feminist perspectives on autonomy, agency, and the social self*. New York: Oxford University Press.

MacKenzie, Donald and Wajcman, Judy (eds.) (1985) *The social shaping of technology*. Buckingham: Open University Press.

Maffía, Diana (2007) Epistemología feminista: la subversión semiótica de las mujeres en la ciencia. *Revista venezolana de estudios de la mujer* 12(28), 63–98.

Mahoney, Michael S. (1992) Computers and mathematics: The search for a discipline of computer science. In Echeverria, J., Ibarra, A., and Mormann, T. (eds.), *The space of mathematics. Philosophical, epistemological, and historical explorations.* Berlin and New York: Walter de Gruyter, 349–363.

Mahtani, Minelle (2001) Racial remappings: The potential of paradoxical space. *Gender, Place and Culture: A Journal of Feminist Geography* 8(3), 299–305.

Maji, Sucharita and Dixit, Shikha (2020) Gendered processes and women's stunted career growth: An exploratory study of female software engineers. *The Qualitative Report* 25(8), 3067–3084.

Mäkinen, Maarit (2006) Digital empowerment as a process for enhancing citizens' participation. *E-Learning and Digital Media* 3(3), 381–395.

Mansfield, Harvey C. Jr. (1981) Machiavelli's political science. *The American Political Science Review* 75(2), 293–305.

Marcus, Sharon (2005) Queer theory for everyone: A review essay. *Signs: Journal of Women in Culture and Society* 31(1), 191–218.

Margaret, Wright (1972) I want the right to be Black and me. In Lerner, G. (ed.), *Black women in white America.* New York: Random House, 608–609.

Margolis, Jane and Fisher, Allan (2002) *Unlocking the clubhouse: Women in computing.* Cambridge, MA: MIT Press.

Marschall, Daniel and Gregory, Judith (eds.) (1983) *Office Automation, Jekyll or Hyde? Highlights of the International Conference on Office Work & New Technology.* Cleveland, OH: 9to5 Working Women Education Fund.

Marsden, Nicola and Haag, Maren (2016) Stereotypes and politics: Reflections on personas. In *Proceedings of the 2016 CHI Conference on Human Factors in Computing Systems CHI'16, May 07–12, 2016, San Jose, CA, USA.* New York: ACM Press, 4017–4031.

Martin, Patrick and Bouchard, Louise (2020) Constraints, normative ideal, and actions to foster change in the practice of nursing: A qualitative study. *Advances in Nursing Science* 43(3), 306–321.

Marx, Leo (2010) Technology: The emergence of a hazardous concept. *Technology and Culture* 51(3), 561–577.

Matilal, Oindrila (2020) Time matters: Flexi-time and women's retention in the 24/7 workplace. In *Proceedings of the 18th European Conference on Computer-Supported Cooperative Work: The International Venue on Practice-centred Computing on the Design of Cooperation Technologies Siegen, Germany, 13–7 June 2020.* Exploratory paper. Reports of the European Society for Socially Embedded Technologies. Available at https://dl.eusset.eu/handle/20.500.12015/3413

Mbembe, Achille (2001) *On the postcolony.* Oakland: University of California Press.

McIntyre, Jonathan R.S., Burton, Candace, and Holmes, Dave (2020) From discipline to control in nursing practice: A poststructuralist reflection. *Nursing Philosophy* 21(4), e12317.

McLean, Jessica, Maalsen, Sophia, and Grech, Alana (2016) Learning about feminism in digital spaces: Online methodologies and participatory mapping. *Australian Geographer* 47(2), 157–177.

McNamarah, Chan Tov (2021) Misgendering. *California Law Review* 109, 2227–2322.

Meagher, Gabrielle and Parton, Nigel (2004) Modernising social work and the ethics of care. *Social Work & Society* 2(1), 10–27.

Mehta, Balwant Singh (2016) A decent work framework: Women in the ICT sector in India. *Information Development* 32(5), 1718–1729.

Mellström, Ulf (2009) The intersection of gender, race and cultural boundaries, or why is computer science in Malaysia dominated by women? *Social Studies of Science* 39(6), 885–907.

Menendez-Blanco, Maria, Bjørn, Pernille, Møller, Naja M. Holten, Bruun, Jens, Dybkjær, Hans, and Lorentzen, Kasper (2018) GRACE: Broadening narratives of computing through history, craft and technology. In *Proceedings of the 2018 ACM International Conference on Supporting Group Work GROUP '18, January 7–10, 2018, Sanibel Island, FL, USA*. New York: ACM Press, 397–400.

Menzies, Heather (1981) *Women and the chip: Case studies of the effects of informatics on employment in Canada*. Montréal: The Institute for Research on Public Policy (IRPP).

Messing, Karen (1992) Introduction. *Research Directed to Improving Women's Occupational Health* 18(3), 1–9.

Messing, Karen (2014) *Pain and prejudice: What science can learn about work from the people who do it*. Toronto: Between the Lines.

Messing, Karen, Chatigny, Céline, and Courville, Julie (1998) 'Light' and 'heavy' work in the housekeeping service of a hospital. *Applied Ergonomics* 29(6), 451–459.

Messing, Karen, Lefrançois, Mélanie, and Saint-Charles, Johanne (2021) Observing inequality: Can ergonomic observations help interventions transform the role of gender in work activity? *Computer Supported Cooperative Work (CSCW)* 30, 215–249.

Messing, Karen, Seifert, Ana Maria, Vézina, Nicole, Balka, Ellen, and Chatigny, Céline (2005) Qualitative research using numbers: An approach developed in France and used to transform work in North America. *New Solutions: A Journal of Environmental and Occupational Health Policy* 15(3), 245–260.

Messing, Karen and Stevenson, Joan (1996) Women in procrustean beds: Strength testing and the workplace. *Gender, Work, and Organization* 3(3), 156–167.

Miceli, Milagros and Posada, Julian (2022) The data-production dispositif. In *Proceedings of the ACM on Human–Computer Interaction*. New York: ACM Press, Article 460.

Miceli, Milagros, Yang, Tianling, Garcia, Adriana Alvarado, Posada, Julian, Wang, Sonj Mei, Pohl, Marc, and Hanna, Alex (2022) Documenting data production processes: A participatory approach for data work. In *Proceedings of the ACM Conference on Human–Computer Interaction CHI 2022 6 (CSCW2)*. New York: ACM Press, Article 510.

Mies, Maria (1986) *Patriarchy and accumulation on a world scale: Women in the international division of labour*. London: Zed Press.

Milan, Stefania and Treré, Emiliano (2021) Big data from the south(s): An analytical matrix to investigate data at the margins. In Rohlinger, D. and Sobieraj, S. (eds.), *The Oxford handbook of sociology and digital media*. Oxford: Oxford University Press, 76–96.

Milkman, Ruth (1983) Female factory labor and industrial structure: Control and conflict over 'woman's place' in auto and electrical manufacturing. *Politics & Society* 12(2), 159–203.

Miller, Ryan A., Vaccaro, Annemarie, Kimball, Ezekiel W., and Forester, Rachael (2021) 'It's dude culture': Students with minoritized identities of sexuality and/or gender navigating STEM majors. *Journal of Diversity in Higher Education* 14(3), 340–352.

Miltner, Kate M. (2019) Girls who coded: Gender in twentieth century UK and US computing. *Science, Technology, & Human Values* 44(1), 161–176.

Misa, Thomas J. (2021) Dynamics of gender bias in computing. *Communications of the ACM* 64(6), 76–83.

Mohanty, Chandra (1988) Under Western eyes: Feminist scholarship and colonial discourses. *Feminist Review* 30(1), 61–88.

Mohanty, Chandra (2003) 'Under Western eyes' revisited: Feminist solidarity through anticapitalist struggles. *Signs: Journal of Women in Culture and Society* 28(2), 499–535.

Mohla, Satyam, Bagh, Bishnupriya, and Guha, Anupam (2021) A material lens to investigate the gendered impact of the AI industry. In *IJCAI 2021 Workshop on AI for Social Good. August 19–26, 2021*. Virtual event.

Möhlmann, Marieke and Zalmanson, Lior (2017) Hands on the wheel: Navigating algorithmic management and Uber drivers' autonomy. In *Proceedings of the International Conference on Information Systems (ICIS 2017), December 10–13, Seoul, South Korea.*

Mol, Annemarie, Moser, Ingunn, and Pols, Jeannette (2010) Care: Putting practice into theory. In Mol, A., Moser, I., and Pols, J. (eds.), *Care in practice: On tinkering in clinics, homes and farms*. Bielefeld: Transcript Verlag, 7–27.

Møller, Naja L. Holten (2018) The future of clerical work is precarious. *InterActions: UCLA Journal of Education and Information Studies* 25(4), 75–77.

Møller, Naja L. Holten, Bossen, Claus, Pine, Kathleen H., Nielsen, Trine Rask, and Neff, Gina (2020) Who does the work of data? *Interactions* 27(3), 52–55.

Mooney, Shelagh (2016) 'Nimble' intersectionality in employment research: A way to resolve methodological dilemmas. *Work, Employment and Society* 30(4), 708–718.

Morgall, Janine (1981) Typing our way to freedom: Is it true that new office technology can liberate women? *Feminist Review* 9(1), 87–101.

Morley, Chantal and McDonnell, Martina (2015) The gendering of the computing field in Finland, France and the United Kingdom between 1960 and 1990. In Schafer, V. and Thierry, B.G. (eds.), *Connecting women: Women, gender and ICT in Europe in the nineteenth and twentieth century*. Cham: Springer International, 119–135.

Mosco, Vincent (1996) *The political economy of communication*. London: Sage.

Muller, Michael J. (1999) Invisible work of telephone operators: An ethnocritical analysis. *Computer Supported Cooperative Work (CSCW)* 8(1), 31–61.

Murphy, Kathleen, Strand, Lola, Theron, Linda, and Ungar, Michael (2021) 'I just gotta have tough skin': Women's experiences working in the oil and gas industry in Canada. *The Extractive Industries and Society* 8(2), 100882.

Murphy, Michelle (2015) Unsettling care: Troubling transnational itineraries of care in feminist health practices. *Social Studies of Science* 45(5), 717–737.

Mutlu, Bilge and Forlizzi, Jodi (2008) Robots in organizations: The role of workflow, social, and environmental factors in human–robot interaction. In *Proceedings of the*

3rd ACM/IEEE International Conference on Human–Robot Interaction, March 12–15, 2008, Amsterdam, The Netherlands. New York: ACM Press, 287–294.

Nafus, Dawn (2012) 'Patches don't have gender': What is not open in open source software. *New Media & Society* 14(4), 669–683.

Nair, Indira and Bulleit, William M. (2020) Pragmatism and care in engineering ethics. *Science and Engineering Ethics* 26(1), 65–87.

Nardi, Bonnie and Engeström, Yrjö (1999) A web on the wind: The structure of invisible work. *Computer Supported Cooperative Work* 8, 1–8.

Nedelsky, Jennifer (1987) Reconceiving autonomy: Sources, thoughts and possibilities. *Yale Journal of Law and Feminism* 1, 7–36.

Ngai, Pun (2005) *Made in China: Women factory workers in a global workplace.* Durham, NC, and London: Duke University Press.

Nielsen, Rasmus Kleis and Ganter, Sarah Anne (2022) *The power of platforms: Shaping media and society.* Oxford: Oxford University Press.

Nies, Sarah and Sauer, Dieter (2010) Was wird aus der Betriebsfallstudie? Forschungsstrategische Herausforderungen durch Entgrenzung von Arbeit und Betrieb. *AIS-Studien* 3(1), 14–23.

Nilsson, Åsa Wikberg and Jahnke, Marcus (2018) Tactics for norm-creative innovation. *She Ji: The Journal of Design, Economics, and Innovation* 4(4), 375–391.

Noble, David F. (1978) Social choice in machine design: The case of automatically controlled machine tools. *Politics & Society* 8(3–4), 313–347.

Noble, Safiya Umoja (2018) *Algorithms of oppression: How search engines reinforce racism.* New York: New York University Press.

Norlock, Kathryn (2019) Feminist ethics. In Zalta, E.N. et al. (ed.), *The Stanford encyclopedia of philosophy* (Summer 2019 Edition).

Nussbaum, Martha (1999) Women and equality: The capabilities approach. *International Labour Review* 138(3), 227–245.

Nussbaum, Martha (2003) Capabilities as fundamental entitlements: Sen and social justice. *Feminist Economics* 9(2–3), 33–59.

Nygaard, Kirsten and Bergo, O. Terje (1975) The Trade Unions: New Users of Research. *Personnel review*, 4(2), 5–10.

O'Brien, Mary (1981) *The politics of reproduction.* Boston, MA: Routledge & Kegan Paul.

O'Farrell, Rory, and Montagnier, Pierre (2019) *Measuring platform mediated workers.* Paris: OECD.

OECD (2019) *Measuring platform mediated workers.* Paris: OECD .

Oesterreich, Rainer and Volpert, Walter (1986) Task analysis for work design on the basis of action regulation theory. *Economic and Industrial Democracy* 7(4), 503–527.

Ogbonnaya-Ogburu, Ihudiya Finda, Smith, Angela, D.R., To, Alexandra, and Toyama, Kentaro (2020) Critical race theory for HCI. In *Proceedings of the 2020 CHI Conference on Human Factors in Computing Systems, April 25–30, 2020, Honolulu, HI, USA.* New York: ACM Press, 1–16.

Oldenziel, Ruth (1999) *Making technology masculine: Men, women and modern machines in America, 1870–1945.* Amsterdam: Amsterdam University Press.

Olson, Margrethe H. and Lucas, Henry C. Jr. (1982) The impact of office automation on the organization: Some implications for research and practice. *Communications of the ACM* 25(11), 838–847.

Onafuwa, Dimeji (2018) Allies and decoloniality: A review of the intersectional perspectives on design, politics, and power symposium. *Design and Culture* 10(1), 7–15.

Ong, Aihwa (1987) Disassembling gender in the electronics age. *Feminist Studies* 13(3), 609–626.

Orupabo, Julia (2022) Enacting efficient care within a context of rationalisation. *The Sociological Review* 70(1), 57–73.

Oyěwùmí, Oyèrónkẹ́ (1997) *The invention of women: Making an African sense of Western gender discourses.* Minneapolis and London: University of Minnesota Press.

Pacaud, Suzanne (1949) Recherches sur le travail des téléphonistes. Étude psychologique d'un métier. *Le Travail humain* 12, 46–65.

Paganini, Lavinia and Gama, Kiev (2021) A preliminary study about the low engagement of female participation in hackathons. In *Proceedings of the IEEE/ACM 42nd International Conference on Software Engineering Workshops ICSEW, 27 June–19 July 2020, Seoul, Republic of Korea.* New York: ACM Press, 193–194.

Pal, Joyojeet (2010) Of mouse and men: Computers and geeks as cinematic icons in the age of ICTD. In *Proceedings of the iConference, February 3–6, University of Illinois, Urbana-Champaign, USA.* 179–187.

Pantazidou, Marina and Nair, Indira (1999) Ethic of care: Guiding principles for engineering teaching and practice. *Journal of Engineering Education* 88(2), 205–212.

Panteli, Niki, Stack, Janet, and Ramsey, Harvie (2001) Gendered patterns in computing work in the late 1990s. *New Technology, Work and Employment* 16(1), 3–17.

Panteli, Niki and Urquhart, Cathy (2022) Job crafting for female contractors in a male-dominated profession. *New Technology, Work and Employment* 37(1), 102–123.

Parolini, Giuditta (2015) From computing girls to data processors: Women assistants in the Rothamsted Statistics Department. In Schafer, V. and Thierry, B.G. (eds.), *Connecting women.* Cham: Springer, 103–117.

Parsley, Samantha (2022) Feeling your way as an occupational minority: The gendered sensilisation of women electronic music artists. *Management Learning* 53(4), 697–717.

Pateman, Carol (1988) *The sexual contract.* Cambridge: Polity.

Pateman, Carol (1989) *The disorder of women.* Cambridge: Polity.

Paternò, Fabio and Wulf, Volker (eds.) (2017) *New perspectives in end-user development.* Cham: Springer International Publishing.

Paulson, Timothy Amund (2017) From 'knife men' to 'streamlining with curves': Structure, skill, and gender in British Columbia's meat-packing industry. *BC Studies: The British Columbian Quarterly* 193, 115–145.

Peter, Elizabeth and Morgan, Kathryn Pauly (2001) Explorations of a trust approach for nursing ethics. *Nursing Inquiry* 8(1), 3–10.

Phillips, Anne (2001) Feminism and liberalism revisited: Has Martha Nussbaum got it right? *Constellations* 8(2), 249–266.

Pierri, Paola (2016) Why people do not rebel. Issues of self-marginalization in design for mental health. In *Intersectional Perspectives on Design, Politics and Power, Nov 14–15, 2016, School of Arts and Communication, Malmö University, Sweden.*

Pine, Kathleen H. and Mazmanian, Melissa (2014) Institutional logics of the EMR and the problem of 'perfect but inaccurate accounts. In *Proceedings of the 17th ACM Conference on Computer Supported Cooperative Work & Social Computing, February 15–19, 2014, Baltimore, MD, USA*. New York: ACM Press, 283–294.

Pipek, Volkmar (2005) From tailoring to appropriation support: Negotiating groupware usage. PhD thesis, Faculty of Science, Department of Information Processing Science, University of Oulu.

Pipek, Volkmar and Wulf, Volker (2009) Infrastructuring: Toward an integrated perspective on the design and use of information technology. *Journal of the Association for Information Systems* 10(5), 447–473.

Plant, Zadie (1997) *Zeros + ones: Digital women + the new technoculture*. London: Fourth Estate.

Plantin, Jean-Christophe (2021) The data archive as factory: Alienation and resistance of data processors. *Big Data & Society* 8(1), 1–12.

Pollert, Anna (1981) *Girls, wives, factory lives*. London: Macmillan Press.

Pook, Zooey Sophia (2020) The challenge of implementing preferred gender pronouns: Queer autonomy in the age of information technologies. *InterAlia: A Journal of Queer Studies* 15, 6–16.

Posada, Julian (2022) Embedded reproduction in platform data work. *Information, Communication & Society* 25(6), 816–834.

Pot, Mirjam, Spahl, Wanda, and Prainsack, Barbara (2019) The gender of biomedical data: Challenges for personalised and precision medicine. *Somatechnics* 9(2–3), 170–187.

Probyn, Elspeth (1990) Travels in the postmodern: Making sense of the local. In Nicolson, L. (ed.), *Feminism/postmodernism*. New York: Routledge, 176–189.

Prosperi, Mattia, Min, Jae S., Bian, Jiang, and Modave, François (2018) Big data hurdles in precision medicine and precision public health. *BMC medical Informatics and Decision Making* 18, 1–15.

Prügl, Elisabeth (1996) Home-based workers: A comparative exploration of Mies's theory of housewifization. *Frontiers: A Journal of Women Studies* 17(1), 114–135.

Puig de la Bellacasa, Maria (2011) Matters of care in technoscience: Assembling neglected things. *Social Studies of Science* 41(1), 85–106.

Pullen, Alison, Thanem, Torkild, Tyler, Melissa, and Wallenberg, Louise (2016) Sexual politics, organizational practices: Interrogating queer theory, work and organization. *Gender, Work, and Organization* 23(1), 1–6.

Pullman, Cydney and Szymanski, Sharon (1986) *The impact of office technology on clerical worker skills in the banking, insurance and legal industries in New York City: Implications for training: A study for the Private Industry Council of New York City*. New York: The Labor Institute.

Qi, Jie, Buechley, Leah, Huang, Andrew 'bunnie', Ng, Patricia, Cross, Sean, and Paradiso, Joseph A. (2018) Chibitronics in the wild: Engaging new communities in creating technology with paper electronics. In *Proceedings of the 2018 CHI Conference on Human Factors in Computing Systems CHI 2018, April 21–26, 2018, Montréal, QC, Canada*. New York: ACM Press, Article 252.

Raghuram, Parvati, Herman, Clem, Ruiz Ben, Esther, and Sondhi, Gunjan (2017) *Women and IT scorecard – India, a survey of 55 firms*. Milton Keynes: The Open University.

Raji, Inioluwa Deborah (2020) Handle with care: Lessons for data science from Black female scholars. *Patterns* 1(8), 100150.

Randall, Dave (2022) Made to work: Mobilising contemporary worklives (book review). *Journal of Computer-Supported Cooperative Work* 31, 555–560.

Randall, David, Rouncefield, Mark, and Tolmie, Peter (2021) Ethnography, CSCW and ethnomethodology. *Computer Supported Cooperative Work (CSCW)* 30, 189–214.

Rankin, Yolanda A. and Thomas, Jakita O. (2020) The intersectional experiences of Black women in computing. In *Proceedings of the 51st ACM Technical Symposium on Computer Science Education SIGCSE'20, 11–14 March 2020, Portland, OR, USA*. New York: ACM Press, 199–205.

Rantalaiho, Liisa (1990) Office work as women's work. *The Polish Sociological Bulletin* 90, 63–74.

Rantalaiho, Liisa and Korvajärvi, Päivi (1985) *Women's office work and coping with technological change*. Tampere: Department of Sociology and Social Psychology, University of Tampere.

Raub, McKenzie (2018) Bots, bias and big data: Artificial intelligence, algorithmic bias and disparate impact liability in hiring practices. *Arkansas Law Review* 71(2), 529–570.

Raval, Noopur and Dourish, Paul (2016) Standing out from the crowd: Emotional labor, body labor, and temporal labor in ridesharing. In *Proceedings of the 19th ACM Conference on Computer-Supported Cooperative Work & Social Computing CSCW '16, February 27–March 2, 2016, San Francisco, California, USA*. New York: ACM Press, 97–107.

Reason, Peter and Bradbury, Hilary (eds.) (2001) *Handbook of action research: Participative inquiry and practice*. London: Sage.

Reisigl, Martin and Wodak, Ruth (2001) *Discourse and discrimination: Rhetorics of racism and antisemitism*. London and New York: Routledge.

Ren, Xinyue (2022) Adopting feminist pedagogy in computer science education to empower underrepresented populations: A critical review. *TechTrends* 66(3), 459–467.

Rentschler, Carrie (2019) Making culture and doing feminism. In Oren, T. and Press, A. (eds.), *The Routledge handbook of contemporary feminism*. London and New York: Routledge, 27–147.

Rey-Moreno, Carlos, Roro, Zukile, Tucker, William D., Siya, Masbulele Jay, Bidwell, Nicola J., and Simo-Reigadas, Javier (2013) Experiences, challenges and lessons from rolling out a rural WiFi mesh network. In *Proceedings of the 3rd ACM Symposium on Computing for Development ACM DEV '13, Bangalore, India – January 11–12, 2013*. New York: ACM Press, Article 11.

Reynolds-Cuéllar, Pedro, Serpa, Bibiana Oliveira, Grisales, Claudia, Goñi, Julián 'Iñaki', Wong-Villacres, Marisol, and Lemus, Oscar A. (2022) Reviews gone south: A subversive experiment on participatory design canons: Dedicated to the memory of Oscar A. Lemus. In *Proceedings of the Participatory Design Conference PDC 2022 August 19–September 1, 2022, Newcastle upon Tyne, UK*. New York: ACM Press, 206–217.

Richardson, Lizzie (2018) Feminist geographies of digital work. *Progress in Human Geography* 42(2), 244–263.

Riecken, Ted, Strong-Wilson, Teresa, Conibear, Frank, Michel, Corrine, and Riecken, Janet (2005) Connecting, speaking, listening: Toward an ethics of voice with/in participatory action research. *Forum Qualitative Sozialforschung/Forum: Qualitative Social Research* 6(1).

Riley, Donna (2013) Hidden in plain view: Feminists doing engineering ethics, engineers doing feminist ethics. *Science and Engineering Ethics* 19(1), 189–206.

Riley, Donna, Pawley, Alice L., Tucker, Jessica, and Catalano, George D. (2009) Feminisms in engineering education: Transformative possibilities. *NWSA Journal* 21(2), 21–40.

Rivera-Loaiza, Cuauhtemoc and Wong-Villacres, Marisol (2022) Global Plaza: Creating an inclusive and equitable space at high-level conferences. In *9th Mexican International Conference on Human–Computer Interaction (MexIHC'22), November 16–18, 2022, Virtual Event, Mexico. ACM, New York, NY, USA.* New York: ACM Press, Article 6.

Rizvi, Naba, Casanova-Perez, Reggie, Ramaswamy, Harshini, Dirks, Lisa G., Bascom, Emily, and Weibel, Nadir (2022) QTBIPOC PD: Exploring the intersections of race, gender, and sexual orientation. In *Conference on Human Factors in Computing Systems CHI'22, April 30–May 06, 2022, New Orleans, LA.* New York: ACM Press, Article 120.

Roan, Amanda and Whitehouse, Gillian (2007) Women, information technology and 'waves of optimism': Australian evidence on 'mixed-skill' jobs. *New Technology, Work and Employment* 22(1), 21–33.

Robertson, Toni (2000) Co-operative work, women and the working environments of technology design. *Australian Feminist Studies* 15(32), 205–219.

Robertson, Toni and Wagner, Ina (2012) Ethics: Engagement, representation and politics-in-action. In Simonsen, J. and Robertson, T. (eds.), *Routledge international handbook of participatory design.* London and New York: Routledge, 64–85.

Roby, Pamela (1992) Women and the ASA: Degendering organizational structures and processes, 1964–1974. *The American Sociologist* 23(1), 18–48.

Rode, Jennifer A., Weibert, Anne, Marshall, Andrea, Aal, Konstantin, Von Rekowski, Thomas, Elmimouni, Houda, and Booker, Jennifer (2015) From computational thinking to computational making. In *Proceedings of the 2015 ACM International Joint Conference on Pervasive and Ubiquitous Computing UbiComp '15, September 7–11, 2015, Osaka, Japan.* New York: ACM Press, 239–250.

Rodriguez, Clemencia (2017) Studying media at the margins: Learning from the field. In Pickard, V. and Yang, G. (eds.), *Media activism in the digital age.* London and New York: Routledge, 49–60.

Rodriguez, Jenny K., Holvino, Evangelina, Fletcher, Joyce K., and Nkomo, Stella M. (2016) The theory and praxis of intersectionality in work and organisations: Where do we go from here? *Gender, Work and Organization* 23(3), 201–222.

Rose, Gillian (1993) *Feminism & geography: The limits of geographical knowledge.* Minneapolis: University of Minnesota Press.

Rothschild, Joan (ed.) (1983) *Machina ex Dea: Feminist perspectives on technology.* New York: Pergamon Press.

Roussel, Natacha and Stolfi, Ariane (2020) Taking back the future: A short history of singular technologies in Brazil. *Catalyst: Feminism, Theory, Technoscience* 6(2), 1–27.

Ruiz Ben, Esther (2007) Defining expertise in software development while doing gender. *Gender, Work & Organization* 14(4), 312–332.

Rycroft-Malone, Jo, Fontenla, Marina, Seers, Kate, and Bick, Debra (2009) Protocol-based care: The standardisation of decision-making? *Journal of Clinical Nursing* 18(10), 1490–1500.

Ryle, Gilbert (1949) *The concept of mind*. London: Hutchinson.

Saifuddin, Samina, Dyke, Lorraine, and Hossain, Md Sajjad (2022) Doing and undoing gender: Women professionals' persistence in technology occupations. *Equality, Diversity and Inclusion: An International Journal* 41(4), 673–690.

Salehi, Nihoumar, Irani, Lily C., Bernstein, Michael S., Alkhatib, Ali, Ogbe, Eva, and Milland, Kristy (2015) We are dynamo: Overcoming stalling and friction in collective action for crowd workers. In *Proceedings of the 33rd Annual ACM Conference on Human Factors in Computing Systems CHI 2015, April 18 – 23, 2015, Seoul, Republic of Korea*. New York: ACM Press, 1621–1630.

Salembier, Pascal and Wagner, Ina (2021) Studies of work 'in the wild': The field study tradition in work practice research. *Computer Supported Cooperative Work (CSCW)* 30, 169–188.

Salminen-Karlsson, Minna and Golay, Diane (2022) Information systems in nurses' work: Technical rationality versus an ethic of care. *New Technology, Work and Employment* 37(2), 270–287.

Saloma-Akpdeonu, Czarina, Ng, Cecilia, and Mitter, Swasti (2005) Female spaces in the Philippines' ICT industry. In Ng, C. and Mitter, S. (eds.), *Gender and the digital economy: Perspectives from the developing world*. Thousand Oaks, CA: Sage, 61–84.

Salzinger, Leslie (2001) Making fantasies real. Producing women and men on the maquila shop floor. *NACLA Report on the Americas* 34(5), 13–19.

Samulowitz, Anke, Gremyr, Ida, Eriksson, Erik, and Hensing, Gunnel (2018) 'Brave men' and 'emotional women': A theory-guided literature review on gender bias in health care and gendered norms towards patients with chronic pain. *Pain Research and Management*. Article 6358624. https://doi.org/10.1155/2018/6358624.

Sandberg, Åke (ed.) (1995) *Enriching production: Perspectives on Volvo's Uddevalla plant as an alternative to lean production*. Stockholm: Swedish Institute for Work Life Research.

Sandelowski, Margarete (1997) Exploring the gender–technology relation in nursing. *Nursing Inquiry* 4(4), 219–228.

Sangster, Joan (1994) Telling our stories: Feminist debates and the use of oral history. *Women's History Review* 3(1), 5–28.

Santoni de Sio, Filippo and van Wynsberghe, Aimee (2016) When should we use care robots? The nature-of-activities approach. *Science and Engineering Ethics* 22, 1745–1760.

Sappleton, Natalie and Takruri-Rizk, Haifa (2008) The gender subtext of science, engineering, and technology (SET) organizations: A review and critique. *Women's Studies* 37(3), 284–316.

Sarkar, Sreela (2016) Beyond the 'digital divide': The 'computer girls' of Seelampur. *Feminist Media Studies* 16(6), 968–983.

Scacchi, Anna (2016) Nodi e questioni intorno al 'parlare di razza'. *The European South* 1, 63–73.

Schaffer, Simon (1996) Babbage's dancer and the impresarios of mechanism. In Spufford, F. and Uglow, J. (eds.), *Cultural babbage: Technology, time and invention*. London: Faber & Faber, 53–80.

Scheuerman, Morgan Klaus, Branham, Stacy M., and Hamidi, Foad (2018) Safe spaces and safe places: Unpacking technology-mediated experiences of safety and harm with transgender people. *Proceedings of the ACM on Human–Computer Interaction 2(CSCW)*, 1–27.

Schiebinger, Londa (2012) Gendered innovations in biomedicine and public health research. In Oertelt-Prigione, S. and Regitz-Zagrosek, V. (eds.), *Sex and gender aspects in clinical medicine*. London: Springer, 5–8.

Schild, Verónica (2000) 'Gender equity' without social justice. Women's rights in the neoliberal age. *NACLA Report on the Americas* 34(1), 25–28.

Schinzel, Britta (2004) Epistemische Veränderungen an der Schnittstelle Informatik und Naturwissenschaften. In Schmitz, S. and Schinzel, B. (eds.), *Grenzgänge. Genderforschung in Informatik und Naturwissenschaften*. Sulzbach: Ulrike Helmer Verlag, 30–49.

Schinzel, Britta (2017) Women in computing and the contingency of informatics cultures. In Werthner, H. and Harmelen, F.v. (eds.) *Informatics in the Future: Proceedings of the 11th European Computer Science Summit (ECSS 2015), Vienna, October 2015*. Cham: Springer International Publishing, 87–98.

Schlesinger, Ari, Edwards, W. Keith, and Grinter, Rebecca E. (2017) Intersectional HCI: Engaging identity through gender, race, and class. In *Proceedings of the 2017 CHI Conference on Human Factors in Computing Systems CHI 2017, May 6–11, 2017, Denver, CO, USA*. New York: ACM Press, 5412–5427.

Schmidt, Kjeld (2000) The critical role of workplace studies. In Luff, P., Hindmarsh, J. and Heath, C. (eds.), *Workplace studies: Recovering work practice and informing systems design*. Cambridge: Cambridge University Press, 141–149.

Schmidt, Kjeld (2011) *Cooperative work and coordinative practices*. New York: Springer.

Schmidt, Kjeld (2018) Practice and technology: On the conceptual foundations of practice-centered computing. In Wulf, V., Pipek, V., Randall, D., Rohde, M., Schmidt, K., and Stevens, G. (eds.), *Socio-informatics: A practice-based perspective*. Oxford: Oxford University Press, 47–104.

Schmidt, Kjeld and Bannon, Liam (2013) Constructing CSCW: The first quarter century. *Computer Supported Cooperative Work (CSCW)* 22(4), 345–372.

Schön, Donald A. (1983) *The reflective practitioner: How professionals think in action*. New York: Basic Books.

Schorch, Marén, Wan, Lin, Randall, Dave, and Wulf, Volker (2016) Designing for those who are overlooked: Insider perspectives on care practices and cooperative work of elderly informal caregivers. In *Proceedings of the 19th ACM Conference on Computer-Supported Cooperative Work & Social Computing CSCW'16, February 27–March 2, 2016, San Francisco, CA, USA*. New York: ACM Press, 787–799.

Schultz, T., Abdulla, D., Ansari, A., Canlı, E., Keshavarz, M., Kiem, M., and JS Vieira de Oliveira, P. (2018) What is at stake with decolonizing design? A roundtable. *Design and Culture* 10(1), 81–101.

Schuurman, Nadine and Balka, Ellen (2009) alt.metadata.health: Ontological context for data use and integration. *Computer Supported Cooperative Work (CSCW)* 18, 83–108.

Schwennesen, Nete (2019) Algorithmic assemblages of care: Imaginaries, epistemologies and repair work. *Sociology of Health & Illness* 41(S1), 176–192.

Scott, Joan W. and Tilly, Louise A. (1975) Women's work and the family in nineteenth-century Europe. *Comparative Studies in Society and History* 17(1), 36–64.

Segal, Lynne (2017) Gender, power and Feminist resistance. In Bolsø, A., Svendsen, B.S.H., and Sørensen, Ø.S. (eds.), *Bodies, symbols and organizational practice: The gendered dynamics of power*. London: Routledge, 227–244.

Sen, Amartya (1993) Capability and well-being. In Nussbaum, M. and Sen, A. (eds.), *The quality of life*. Oxford: Clarendon Press, 30–53.

Sendak, Mark, Elish, Madeleine Clare, Gao, Michael, Futoma, Joseph, et al. (2020) 'The human body is a black box': Supporting clinical decision-making with deep learning. In *Proceedings of the 2020 Conference on Fairness, Accountability, and Transparency FAT* '20, January 27–30, 2020, Barcelona, Spain*. New York: ACM Press, 99–109.

Shadowen, Ashley Nicole (2017) *Ethics and bias in machine learning: A technical study of what makes us 'good'*. New York: Academic Works, City University of New York.

Sharkey, Noel and Sharkey, Amanda (2012) The eldercare factory. *Gerontology* 58(3), 282–288.

Shestakofsky, Benjamin (2017) Working algorithms: Software automation and the future of work. *Work and Occupations* 44(4), 376–423.

Shetterly, Margot Lee (2016) *Hidden figures: The American dream and the untold story of the Black women mathematicians who helped win the space race*. New York: HarperCollins.

Shields, Stephanie A. (2002) *Speaking from the heart: Gender and the social meaning of emotion*. Cambridge: Cambridge University Press.

Silverstone, Roger and Haddon, Leslie (1996) Design and the domestication of ICTs: Technical change and everyday life. In Silverstone, R. (ed.), *Communicating by design: The politics of information and communication technologies*. Oxford: Oxford University Press, 44–74.

Silverstone, Rosalie and Towler, Rosemary (1984) Secretaries at work. *Ergonomics* 27(5), 557–564.

Simone, Carla (2018) Everything is permitted unless stated otherwise: Models and representations in socio-technical (re) design. In Rossignoli, C., Virili, F., and Za, S. (eds.), *Digital technology and organizational change: Reshaping technology, people, and organizations towards a global society*. Cham: Springer, 49–59.

Simone, Carla, Wagner, Ina, Müller, Claudia, Weibert, Anne, and Wulf, Volker (2022) *Future-proofing: Making practice-based IT design sustainable*. Oxford: Oxford University Press.

Simonsen, Jesper and Robertson, Toni (eds.) (2012) *Routledge international handbook of participatory design*. London and New York: Routledge.

Sinders, Caroline (2020) Feminist data set. Clinic for Open Source Arts. Available at https://carolinesinders.

Small, Stephen A. and Uttal, Lynet (2005) Action-oriented research: Strategies for engaged scholarship. *Journal of Marriage and Family* 67(4), 936–948.

Smit, Dorothé and Fuchsberger, Verena (2020) Sprinkling diversity: Hurdles on the way to inclusiveness in makerspaces. In *Proceedings of the 11th Nordic Conference on Human–Computer Interaction: Shaping Experiences, Shaping Society NordiCHI'20, October 25–29, 2020, Tallinn, Estonia*. New York: ACM Press, Article 96.

Smith, Anita (2013) Using a theory to understand triage decision making. *International Emergency Nursing* 21(2), 113–117.

Smith, Dorothy E. (1987) *The everyday world as problematic: A feminist sociology.* Boston: Northeastern University Press.

Smith, Dorothy E. (1990) *The conceptual practices of power: A feminist sociology of knowledge.* Boston: Northeastern University Press.

Smolevitskaya, Marina (2021) Women in computer world of the USSR and Russia. In *Proceedings of International Conference Engineering Technologies and Computer Science EnT, 18–19 August 2021, Moscow, Russian Federation,* 11–19.

Smyth, Thomas and Dimond, Jill (2014) Anti-oppressive design. *Interactions* 21(6), 68–71.

Somerville, Margaret (2005) 'Working' culture: Exploring notions of workplace culture and learning at work. *Pedagogy, Culture and Society* 13(1), 5–26.

Soper, Kate (1993) Productive contradictions. In Ramazanoglu, C. (ed.), *Up against Foucault: Explorations of some tensions between Foucault and feminism.* London and New York: Routledge, 29–50.

Sørensen, Björg Aase (1982) Ansvarsrasjonalitet [Responsible rationality]. In Holter, H. (ed.), *Kvinner i fellesskap [Women in collectives].* Oslo: Oslo University Press.

Sørensen, Knut H. (1992) Towards a feminized technology? Gendered values in the construction of technology. *Social Studies of Science* 22(1), 5–31.

Sparrow, Robert (2015) Robots in aged care: A dystopian future? *AI & Society* 31(4), 445–454.

Sparrow, Robert and Sparrow, Linda (2006) In the hands of machines? The future of aged care. *Minds and Machines* 16(2), 141–161.

Star, S. Leigh and Strauss, Anselm (1999) Layers of silence, arenas of voice: The ecology of visible and invisible work. *Computer Supported Cooperative Work* 8(1/2), 9–30.

Stefancic, Jean and Delgado, Richard (2023) *Critical race theory: An introduction.* New York: New York University Press.

Stevens, Gunnar, Rohde, Markus, Korn, Matthias, and Wulf, Volker (2018) Grounded design: A research paradigm in practice-based computing. In Wulf, V., Pipek, V., Randall, D., Rohde, M., Schmidt, K., and Stevens, G. (eds.), *Socio informatics – A practice-based perspective on the design and use of IT artefacts.* Oxford: Oxford University Press, 23–46.

Stiemerling, Oliver, Kahler, Helge, and Wulf, Volker (1997) How to make software softer – Designing tailorable applications. In *Proceedings of the ACM Symposium on Designing Interactive Systems, Aug 18–20, 1997, Amsterdam, NL.* New York: ACM Press, 365–376.

Stoljar, Natalie (2022) Feminist perspectives on autonomy. In Zalta, E.N. and Nodelman, U. (eds.), *The Stanford Encyclopedia of Philosophy* (Winter 2022 edition). https://plato.stanford.edu/archives/win2022/entries/feminism-autonomy/.

Strauss, Anselm (1982) Interorganizational negotiation. *Urban Life* 11(3), 350–367.

Strauss, Anselm (1988) The articulation of project work: An organizational process. *Sociological Quarterly* 29(2), 163–178.

Strauss, Anselm, Fagerhaugh, Shizuko, Suczek, Barabara, and Wiener, Carolyn (1985) *Social Organization of Medical Work*. Chicago: The University of Chicago Press.

Strauss, A.L., Fagerhaugh, S., Suczek, B., and Wiener, C. (1982) The work of hospitalized patients. *Social Science & Medicine* 16(9), 977–986.

Strohmayer, Angelika (2021) *Digitally augmenting traditional craft practices for social justice: The partnership quilt*. London: Palgrave Macmillan.

Strohmayer, Angelika, Laing, Mary, and Comber, Rob (2017) Technologies and social justice outcomes in sex work charities: Fighting stigma, saving lives. In *Proceedings of the 2017 CHI Conference on Human Factors in Computing Systems CHI 2017, May 6–11, 2017, Denver, CO, USA*. New York: ACM Press, 3352–3364.

Strohmayer, Angelika, Meissner, Janis Lena, Wilson, Alexander, Charlton, Sarah, and McIntyre, Laura (2020) 'We come together as one . . . and hope for solidarity to live on'. On designing technologies for activism and the commemoration of lost lives. In *Proceedings of the 2020 ACM Designing Interactive Systems Conference DIS'20, July 6–10, 2020, Eindhoven, Netherlands*. New York: ACM Press, 87–100.

Stumpf, Simone, Peters, Anicia, Bardzell, Shaowen, Burnett, Margaret, Busse, Daniela, Cauchard, Jessica, and Churchill, Elizabeth (2020) Gender-inclusive HCI research and design: A conceptual review. *Foundations and Trends in Human–Computer Interaction* 13(1), 1–69.

Styhre, Alexander, Backman, Maria, and Börjesson, Sofia (2005) YCC: A gendered carnival? Project work at Volvo cars. *Women in Management Review* 20(2), 96–106.

Suárez, Marcela (2016) Colectivos sociales y ciborgs: hacia una lectura feminista de los drones. *Teknokultura* 13(1), 271–288.

Suchman, Lucy (1994) Do categories have politics? The language/action perspective reconsidered. *Computer Supported Cooperative Work (CSCW)* 2, 177–190.

Suchman, Lucy (1995) Making work visible. *Communications of the ACM* 38(9), 56–64.

Suchman, Lucy (2000) Embodied practices of engineering work. *Mind, Culture, and Activity* 7(1–2), 4–18.

Suchman, Lucy (2002) Located accountabilities in technology production. *Scandinavian Journal of Information Systems* 14(2), 91–105.

Suchman, Lucy (2007) Feminist STS and the sciences of the artificial. In Hackett, E., Amsterdamska, O., Lynch, M., and Wajcman, J. (eds.), *The handbook of science and technology studies*, 3rd edn. Cambridge, MA: MIT Press, 139–163.

Suchman, Lucy (2007) *Human–machine reconfigurations: Plans and situated actions*. Cambridge: Cambridge University Press.

Suchman, Lucy (2011) Subject objects. *Feminist Theory* 12(2), 119–145.

Suchman, Lucy (2019) Agencies in technology design: Feminist reconfigurations. In Wallach, W. and Asaro, P. (eds.), *Machine ethics and robot ethics*. London: Routledge, 361–375.

Suchman, Lucy and Jordan, Brigitte (1988) Computerization and women's knowledge. In Tijdens, K., Jennings, M., Wagner, I., and Weggelaar, M. (eds.), *Proceedings of IFIP WG 9.1. Conference on Women. Work and Computerization: Forming New Alliances*. Amsterdam: North-Holland.

Suchman, Lucy and Wynn, Eleanor (1984) Procedures and problems in the office. *Office Technology and People* 2(2), 133–154.

Sued, Gabriela Elisa (2018) The cyborg metaphor in Ibero-American science, technology and gender literature. *Tapuya: Latin American Science, Technology and Society* 1(1), 95–108.

Tassabehji, Rana, Harding, Nancy, Lee, Hugh, and Dominguez-Pery, Carine (2021) From female computers to male comput♂rs: Or why there are so few women writing algorithms and developing software. *Human Relations* 74(8), 1296–1326.

Teiger, Catherine (2006) 'Les femmes aussi ont un cerveau!' Le travail des femmes en ergonomie: réflexions sur quelques paradoxes. *Travailler* 1(15), 71–130.

Terrin, Jean-Jacques and Wagner, Ina (2023) *L'urbanism informel. Au-delà du droit à la ville*. Paris: Presses des Ponts.

Theureau, Jacques, Wisner, Alain, Estryn-Béhar, Madeleine, and Vaichère, A. (1979) *L'analyse des activités des infirmiers (es) des unités de soins hospitalières*. Paris: Laboratoire de physiologie du travail et d'ergonomie du CNAM.

Thil, Laurène et al. (2022) *Artificial intelligence, platform work and gender equality*. Luxembourg: European Institute for Gender Equality, EIGE.

Thompson, Lucy, Rickett, Bridgette, and Day, Katy (2018) Feminist relational discourse analysis: Putting the personal in the political in feminist research. *Qualitative Research in Psychology* 15(1), 93–115.

Tietze, Mari and McBride, Susan (2020) *Robotics and the impact on nursing practice: Case study and pilot site analyses*. Silver Spring, MD: American Nurses Association.

Tinsman, Heidi (2004) More than victims: Women agricultural workers and social change in rural Chile. In Winn, P. (ed.), *Victims of the Chilean miracle: Workers and neoliberalism in the Pinochet era, 1973–2002*. Durham, NC: Duke University Press, 261–297.

Tolson, Andrew (1977) *The limits of masculinity*. London: Tavistock Publications.

Toombs, Austin, Gross, Shad, Bardzell, Shaowen, and Bardzell, Jeffrey (2017) From empathy to care: A feminist care ethics perspective on long-term researcher–participant relations. *Interacting with Computers* 29(1), 45–57.

Tornbjerg, Kristina, Kanstrup, Anne Marie, Skov, Mikael B., and Rehm, Matthias (2021) Investigating human–robot cooperation in a hospital environment: Scrutinising visions and actual realisation of mobile robots in service work. In *Proceedings of the Designing Interactive Systems Conference, June 28–July 2, 2021, Virtual Event*. New York: ACM Press, 381–391.

Toupin, Sophie (2023) *Shaping feminist artificial intelligence*. New Media & Society.

Toxtli, Carlos, Suri, Siddharth, and Savage, Saiph (2021) Quantifying the invisible labor in crowd work. In *Proceedings of the ACM Conference on Human–Computer Interaction. 5 (CSCW2)*, Article 319.

Trauth, Eileen M. (2002) Odd girl out: An individual differences perspective on women in the IT profession. *Information Technology & People* 15(2), 98–118.

Trigg, Randall H. and Bødker, Susanne (1994) From implementation to design: tailoring and the emergence of systematization in CSCW. In *Proceedings of the 1994 ACM Conference on Computer Supported Cooperative Work, 22–26 October 1994, Chapel Hill, North Carolina, USA.* New York: ACM Press, 45–54.

Tronto, Joan C. (1987) Beyond gender difference to a theory of care. *Signs: Journal of Women in Culture and Society* 12(4), 644–663.

Tronto, Joan C. (1993) *Moral boundaries: A political argument for an ethic of care.* New York: Routledge.

Tronto, Joan C. (2013) *Caring democracy: Markets, equality, and justice.* New York: New York University Press.

Truss, Catherine, Alfes, Kerstin, Shantz, Amanda, and Rosewarne, Amanda (2013) Still in the ghetto? Experiences of secretarial work in the 21st century. *Gender, Work & Organization* 20(4), 349–363.

Tubaro, Paola and Casilli, Antonio A. (2020) Portraits of micro-workers: The real people behind AI in France. In *2nd Crowdworking Symposium Research program 'Digital Future', Universities of Paderborn and Bielefeld, Oct 2020, Paderborn, Germany.* Hal-02960775.

Tubaro, Paola, Le Ludec, Clément, and Casilli, Antonio A. (2020) Counting 'micro-workers': Societal and methodological challenges around new forms of labour. *Work Organisation, Labour & Globalisation* 14(1), 67–82.

Tunstall, Elizabeth Dori (2023) *Decolonizing design: A cultural justice guidebook.* Cambridge, MA: MIT Press.

Turkle, Sherry and Papert, Seymour (1990) Epistemological pluralism: Styles and voices within the computer culture. *Signs: Journal of Women in Culture and Society* 16(1), 128–157.

Turner, Michelle, Holdsworth, Sarah, Scott-Young, Christina M., and Sandri, Kara (2021) Resilience in a hostile workplace: The experience of women onsite in construction. *Construction Management and Economics* 39(10), 839–852.

Twagira, Laura Ann (2020) Machines that cook or women who cook? Lessons from Mali on technology, labor, and women's things. *Technology and Culture* 61(2), S77–S103.

Utzeri, Mounia (2019) The dark side of gender equality schemes in management – A deep dive into a German auto manufacturer. *Vezetéstudomány – Budapest Management Review* 50(5), 38–47.

Van den Ende, Jan and van Oost, Ellen CJ (2001) Making women count: Gender-typing, technology and path dependencies in Dutch statistical data processing, 1900–1970. *European Journal of Women's Studies* 8(4), 491–510.

Van der Velden, Maja (2019) Women's health, decent work and the electronics industry. In Blogging for Sustainability. Sustainable Market Actors for Responsible Trade (March 8, SMART).

Van der Velden, Maja and Mörtberg, Christina (2012) Between need and desire: Exploring strategies for gendering design. *Science, Technology, & Human Values* 37(6), 663–683.

Van Doorn, Niels (2017) Platform labor: On the gendered and racialized exploitation of low-income service work in the 'on-demand' economy. *Information, Communication & Society* 20(6), 898–914.

Van Doorn, Niels and Badger, Adam (2020) Platform capitalism's hidden abode: Producing data assets in the gig economy. *Antipode* 52(5), 1475–1495.

Van Wynsberghe, Aimee (2013) Designing robots for care: Care centered value-sensitive design. *Science and Engineering Ethics* 19(2), 407–433.

Van Wynsberghe, Aimee (2022) Social robots and the risks to reciprocity. *AI & Society* 37(2), 479–485.

Varanasi, Rama Adithya, Siddarth, Divya, Seshadri, Vivek, Bali, Kalika, and Vashistha, Aditya (2022) Feeling proud, feeling embarrassed: Experiences of low-income women with crowd work. In *CHI Conference on Human Factors in Computing Systems CHI'22, April 29–May 5, 2022, New Orleans, LA, USA*. New York: ACM Press, Article 298.

Ve, Hildur (1998) Rationality and identity in Norwegian feminism. In von der Fehr, D., Jonasdottir, A., and Rosenbeck, B. (eds.), *Is there a Nordic feminism? Nordic feminist thought on culture and society*. London: Routledge, 343–361.

Vehviläinen, Marja (1999) Gender and computing in retrospect: The case of Finland. *IEEE Annals of the History of Computing* 21(2), 44–51.

Vehviläinen, Marja (1991) Gender in information system development – A women office workers' standpoint. In Eriksson, I., Kitchenham, B., and Tijdens, K. (eds.), *Proceedings of the IFIP TC9/WG9.1 Conference Women, Work and Computerization: Understanding and Overcoming Bias in Work and Education*. Amsterdam: North-Holland, 247–262.

Vehviläinen, Marja and Brunila, Kristiina (2007) Cartography of gender equality projects in ICT: Liberal equality from the perspective of situated equality. *Information, Community and Society* 10(3), 384–403.

Verbeek, Peter-Paul (2006) Materializing morality: Design ethics and technological mediation. *Science, Technology, & Human Values* 31(3), 361–380.

Vitores, Anna and Gil-Juárez, Adriana (2016) The trouble with 'women in computing': A critical examination of the deployment of research on the gender gap in computer science. *Journal of Gender Studies* 25(6), 666–680.

Volpert, Walter (1985) Psychologische Aspekte industrieller Arbeit. In Georg, W., Kißler, L. and Sattel, U. (eds.), *Arbeit und Wissenschaft: Arbeitswissenschaft?*. Bonn: Verlag Neue Gesellschaft, 9–36.

Volst, Angelika and Wagner, Ina (1988) Inequality in the automated office: The impact of computers on the division of labour. *International Sociology* 3(2), 129–154.

Waerness, Kari (1996) The rationality of caring. In Noddings, N., Benner, P.E., and Gordon, S. (eds.), *Caregiving: Readings in knowledge, practice, ethics, and politics*. Philadelphia: University of Pennsylvania Press, 231–255.

Wagner, Ina (1986) Equal talents – Unequal measures. Skilled women workers in Austria's metal industry. *European Journal for Engieering Education* 11(3), 321–329.

Wagner, Ina (1987) The office between humanization and control. In Doherty, P., Fuchs-Kittowski, K., and Kolm, P. (eds.) *The IFIP TC 9/WG 9.1 Working Conference on System Design for Human Development and Productivity: Participation and Beyond, January 1987, Berlin, Germany*. Amsterdam: North-Holland, 141–154.

Wagner, Ina (1993) Women's voice: The case of nursing information systems. *AI & Society* 7(4), 295–310.

Wagner, Ina (1994) Connecting communities of practice: Feminism, science, and technology. *Women's Studies International Forum* 17(2–3), 257–265.

Wagner, Ina (1995) Hard times: The politics of women's work in computerized environments. *The European Journal of Women's Studies* 2, 295–324.

Wagner, Ina, Birbaumer, Andrea, and Tolar, Marianne (2003) Widening women's work in information and communication technology. Professional Trajectories and Biographies. Brussels: European Commission.

Wajcman, Judy (1991) Patriarchy, technology, and conceptions of skill. *Work and Occupations* 18(1), 29–45.

Wajcman, Judy (2006) Technocapitalism meets technofeminism: Women and technology in a wireless world. *Labour & Industry: A Journal of the Social and Economic Relations of Work* 16(3), 7–20.

Wajcman, Judy (2007) From women and technology to gendered technoscience. *Information, Community and Society* 10(3), 287–298.

Walker, Maggie, Kukutai, Tahu, Russo Carroll, Stephanie, and Rodriguez-Lonebear, Desi (eds.) (2021) *Indigenous data sovereignty and policy.* London and New York: Routledge.

Wallace, Terry (1999) 'It's a man's world!' Restructuring gender imbalance in the Volvo truck company? *Gender, Work & Organization* 6(1), 20–31.

Wang, Cynthia Changxin, Mussi, Eveline, and Sunindijo, Riza Yosia (2021) Analysing gender issues in the Australian construction industry through the lens of empowerment. *Buildings* 11(11), 23p.

Warouw, Nicolaas (2008) Industrial workers in transition: Women's experiences of factory work in Tangerang. In Ford, M. and Parker, L. (eds.), *Women and work in Indonesia.* New York: Routledge, 104–119.

Washington, Nicki, Payton, Fay Cobb, McAlear, Frieda, Chapman, Gail, and Diaz, Lien (2012) Panel: Dismantling the master's house: effective allyship, advocacy, and activism for women in computing. In *Proceedings of the 52nd ACM Technical Symposium on Computer Science Education SIGCSE '21, March 13–20, 2021, Virtual Event, USA.* New York: ACM Press, 604–605.

Watson, Katherine (2005) Queer theory. *Group Analysis* 38(1), 67–81.

Waycott, Jenny, Davis, Hilary, Warr, Deborah, Edmonds, Fran, and Taylor, Gretel (2017) Co-constructing meaning and negotiating participation: Ethical tensions when 'giving voice' through digital storytelling. *Interacting with Computers* 29(2), 237–247.

Webb, Beatrice Potter (1902) The diary of an investigator. In Webb, S. and Webb, B.P. (eds.), *Problems of modern industry.* London, New York, and Bombay: Longmans, Greens, and Co., 1–19.

Weber, Jutta (2005) Helpless machines and true loving care givers: A feminist critique of recent trends in human–robot interaction. *Journal of Information, Communication and Ethics in Society* 3(4), 209–218.

Weber, Jutta (2014) Opacity versus computational reflection: Modelling human–robot interaction in personal service robotics. *Science, Technology & Innovation* 10(1), 187–199.

Webster, Juliet (1986) The effects of word processing on secretarial and typing work: Changes in work processes and responses to change with special reference to dedicated word processing in selected offices in Bradford. PhD dissertation, University of Bradford.

Webster, Juliet (1993) Gender issues in the development of information technology in the office. In Green, E., Owen, J., and Pain, D. (eds.), *Gendered design? Information technology and office systems.* London: Taylor & Francis, 111–126.

Webster, Juliet (1996) *Shaping women's work: Gender, employment and information technology.* London: Routledge.

Weibert, Anne, Krüger, Max, Aal, Konstantin, Salehee, Setareh Sadat, Khatib, Renad, Randall, Dave, and Wulf, Volker (2019) Finding language classes: Designing a digital language Wizard with refugees and migrants. *Proceedings of the ACM on Human–Computer Interaction 3(CSCW),* 111–116.

Weibert, Anne, Marshall, Andrea, Aal, Konstantin, Schubert, Kai, and Rode, Jennifer A. (2014) Sewing interest in e-textiles: Analyzing making from a gendered perspective. In *Proceedings of the 2014 Conference on Designing Interactive Systems DIS 2014, June 21–25, 2014, Vancouver, BC, Canada.* New York: ACM Press, 15–24.

Weick, Karl E. and Roberts, Karlene H. (1993) Collective mind in organizations: Heedful interrelating on flight decks. *Administrative Science Quarterly* 38, 357–381.

Welfare, Katherine S., Hallowell, Matthew R., Shah, Julie A., and Riek, Laurel D. (2019) Consider the human work experience when integrating robotics in the workplace. In *Proceedings of the 14th ACM/IEEE International Conference on Human–Robot Interaction HRI, 11–14 March 2019, Daegu, South Korea.* New York: ACM Press, 75–84.

West, Candace and Zimmerman, Don H. (1987) Doing gender. *Gender & Society* 1(2), 125–151.

Westwood, Sally (1984) *All day, every day: Factory and family in the making of women's lives.* London: Pluto Press.

Wharton, Amy and Burris, Val (1983) Office automation and its impact on women workers. *Humboldt Journal of Social Relations* 10(2), 112–126.

Whiting, Rebecca and Symon, Gillian (2020) Digi-housekeeping: The invisible work of flexibility. *Work, Employment and Society* 34(6), 1079–1096.

Wichroski, Mary (1994) The secretary: Invisible labor in the workworld of women. *Human Organization* 53(1), 33–41.

Wickson, Fern, Preston, Christopher, Binimelis, Rosa, Herrero, Amaranta, Hartley, Sarah, Wynberg, Rachel, and Wynne, Brian (2017) Addressing socio-economic and ethical considerations in biotechnology governance: The potential of a new politics of care. *Food Ethics* 1(2), 193–199.

Willcocks, Leslie (2020) Robo-apocalypse cancelled? Reframing the automation and future of work debate. *Journal of Information Technology* 35(4), 286–302.

Wilson, Cara, McNaney, Roisin, Roper, Abi, et al. (2020) Rethinking notions of 'giving voice' in design. In *Extended Abstracts of the 2020 CHI Conference on Human Factors in Computing Systems CHI'20, April 25–30, 2020, Honolulu, HI, USA.* New York: ACM Press, 1–8.

Wing, Jeannette M. (2006) Computational thinking. *Communications of the ACM* 49(3), 33–35.

Wing, Jeannette M. (2008) Computational thinking and thinking about computing. *Philosophical Transactions of the Royal Society A: Mathematical, Physical and Engineering Sciences* 366(1881), 3717–3725.

Winner, Langdon (1981) *Autonomous technology: Technics-out-of-control as a theme in political thought.* Cambridge, MA: MIT Press.

Winschiers-Theophilus, Heike, Zaman, Tariq, and Stanley, Colin (2019) A classification of cultural engagements in community technology design: Introducing a transcultural approach. *AI & Society* 34, 419–435.

Winter, Peter and Carusi, Annamaria (2022) Professional expectations and patient expectations concerning the development of Artificial Intelligence (AI) for the early diagnosis of Pulmonary Hypertension (PH). *Journal of Responsible Technology* 12, 100052.

Wirtz, Veronika, Cribb, Alan, and Barber, Nick (2006) Patient–doctor decision-making about treatment within the consultation – A critical analysis of models. *Social Science & Medicine* 62(1), 116–124.

Wise, Sarah, Duffield, Christine, Fry, Margaret, and Roche, Michael (2017) Workforce flexibility – In defence of professional healthcare work. *Journal of Health Organization and Management* 31(4), 503–516.

Wisner, Kirsten, Lyndon, Audrey, and Chesla, Catherine A. (2019) The electronic health record's impact on nurses' cognitive work: An integrative review. *International Journal of Nursing Studies* 94, 74–84.

Wolf, Christine (2019) Conceptualizing care in the everyday work practices of machine learning developers. In *Designing Interactive Systems Conference DIS'19 Companion, June 23–28, 2019, San Diego, CA, USA.* New York: ACM Press, 331–335.

Wolf, Christine and Blomberg, Jeanette (2019a) Explainability in context: Lessons from an intelligent system in the IT services domain. In *Joint Proceedings of the ACM IUI 2019 Workshops, 20 March, 2019, Los Angeles, USA.*

Wolf, Christine and Blomberg, Jeanette (2019b) Evaluating the promise of human–algorithm collaborations in everyday work practices. *Proceedings of the ACM on Human–Computer Interaction* 3(CSCW), 1–23.

Woodhall, Julia R. and Leach, Belinda (20109) Who will fight for us? Union designated women's advocates in auto manufacturing workplaces. *Just Labour: A Canadian Journal of Work and Society* 16, 44–58.

World Bank (2020) *Pivoting to inclusion: Leveraging lessons from the COVID-19 crisis for learners with disabilities.* Washington, DC: The World Bank Group.

Wulf, Volker, Müller, Claudia, Pipek, Volkmar, Randall, David, Rohde, Markus, and Stevens, Gunnar (2015) Practice-based computing: Empirically-grounded conceptualizations derived from design case studies. In Wulf, V., Schmidt, K., and Randall, D. (eds.), *Designing socially embedded technologies in the real-world.* London: Springer, 111–150.

Wulf, Volker, Rohde, Markus, Pipek, Volkmar, and Stevens, Gunnar (2011) Engaging with practices: Design case studies as a research framework in CSCW. In *Proceedings of the ACM 2011 Conference on Computer Supported Cooperative Work CSCW 2011, 19–23 March 2011, Hangzhou, China.* New York: ACM Press, 505–512.

Wulff, Elizabeth, Bridges, Donna, Bamberry, Larissa, and Krivokapic-Skoko, Branka (2022) Women who 'talk the tools' and 'walk the work': Using capital to do gender differently and re-gender the skilled trades. *Journal of Sociology*, 58(1), 26–44.

Wyche, Susan, Dillahunt, Tawanna R., Simiyu, Nightingale, and Alaka, Sharon (2015) 'If god gives me the chance i will design my own phone': Exploring mobile phone repair and postcolonial approaches to design in rural Kenya. In *Proceedings of the 2015 ACM International Joint Conference on Pervasive and Ubiquitous Computing, 07–11 September 2015, Osaka, Japan*. New York: ACM Press, 463–473.

Wynn, Eleanor (1979) Office communication as an information medium. Doctoral dissertation, University of California, Berkeley.

Yao, Zheng, Weden, Silas, Emerlyn, Lea, Zhu, Haiyi, and Kraut, Robert E. (2021) Together but alone: Atomization and peer support among gig workers. *Proceedings of the ACM on Human–Computer Interaction 5 (CSCW)*, Article 391.

Yates, Julia and Plagnol, Anke C. (2022) Female computer science students: A qualitative exploration of women's experiences studying computer science at university in the UK. *Education and Information Technologies* 27(3), 3079–3105.

Yuval-Davis, Nira (2006) Human/women's rights and feminist transversal politics. In Ferree, M.M. and Tripp, A.M. (eds.), *Global feminism: Transnational women's activism, organizing, and human rights*. New York: New York University Press, 275–295.

Zheng, Yingqin and Walsham, Geoff (2021) Inequality of what? An intersectional approach to digital inequality under Covid-19. *Information and Organization* 31(1), 100341.

Zimmerman, Jan (ed.) (1983) *The technological woman: Interfacing with tomorrow*. New York: Praeger Publishers.

Zhang, Ming and Yin, Yichun (2019) More Chinese women needed to hold up half the computing sky. In *Proceedings of the ACM Turing Celebration Conference – China, May 17–19, 2019, Chengdu, China*. New York: ACM Press, Article 69.

Zhou, Xiaomu, Ackerman, Mark S., and Zheng, Kai (2009) I just don't know why it's gone: Maintaining informal information use in inpatient care. In *Proceedings of the SIGCHI Conference on Human Factors in Computing Systems, April 4–9, 2009, Boston, Massachusetts, USA*. New York: ACM Press, 2061–2070.

Zou, James and Schiebinger, Londa (2018) AI can be sexist and racist – It's time to make it fair. *Nature* 559, 324–326.

Zuboff, Shoshana (2019) *The age of surveillance capitalism: The fight for a human future at the new frontier of power*. New York: Public Affairs Books.

Zuin, Débora Carneiro (2013) Revisiting the study of occupations: A holistic view of contemporary secretarial work. Doctoral dissertation, The University of Edinburgh.

Index

385

Printed in the United States
by Baker & Taylor Publisher Services